Specialty Cut Flowers

The production of annuals, perennials, bulbs and woody plants for fresh and dried cut flowers

Allan M. Armitage

Illustrations by Rachel Theis

VARSITY PRESS/TIMBER PRESS
Portland, Oregon

Illustrations by
Rachel Theis
1346 Village Lane
Chester Springs, PA 19425
(215) 827-9322

Photograph of *Carthamus tinctorius* 'Lasting Orange' courtesy Park Seed Co.;
photograph of *Zinnia elegans* Ruffles mix courtesy Bodger Seed Co. All other
photographs are either by Dr. Michael Dirr or the author.

Reprinted 1995

ISBN 0-88192-225-0
Printed in Hong Kong

Varsity Press, Inc./Timber Press, Inc.
The Haseltine Building
133 S.W. Second Ave., Suite 450
Portland, Oregon 97204, U.S.A.

Library of Congress Cataloging-in-Publication Data

Armitage, A. M. (Allan M.)
    Specialty cut flowers : the production of annuals, perennials,
bulbs, and woody plants for fresh and dried cut flowers / Allan
M. Armitage ; illustrations by Rachel Theis.
        p.   cm.
    Includes bibliographical references and indexes.
    ISBN 0-88192-225-0
    1. Floriculture. 2. Cut flower industry. 3. Cut flowers. 4. Cut
flowers--Postharvest technology. 5. Floriculture--United States.
6. Cut flower industry--United States. I. Title.
SB405.A68   1993
635.9'66--dc20   92-34463
                                                                CIP

Table of Contents

Color photographs follow page 272.

Dedication

This book is dedicated to my wife, Susan, who constantly strives for perfection in everything she attempts. She is my role model.

Preface

This book is an attempt to put the business of specialty cut flower production in perspective and to provide growers with updated information on the production and handling of specialty cut flowers. Of all aspects of floriculture, the marketing of cut flowers is the most global; flowers routinely cross borders. The most common and rarest flowers may share the same cooler in Bangkok or Baltimore. The demand for specialty cut flowers—essentially all flowers but roses, carnations and chrysanthemums—continues to increase and with it, there will be a parallel increase in production. The American cut flower grower must compete for the leisure dollar not only with other growers, but with movie theaters, wine merchants and restaurants. The ability to compete often revolves around the accessibility of pertinent information and the ability to use that information to make decisions. Little information has been available in the past, and this book brings together details about the production and handling of specialty cut flowers and tries to distill them into useful knowledge.

Potential cut flower species have been grouped together as annuals, perennials, bulbs or woody plants. Each plant entry provides a common name, height and spread in feet, flower color, country or region of origin, family and hardiness adaptation, if applicable. Also included are means of propagation and growing-on techniques. An in-depth section on how the environment affects growth and flowering is also included to provide readers with more detail and background information than normally found in catalogs. When data are available on field culture, they are included. Greenhouse production techniques have also been outlined for most species and pertinent postharvest information is included. Cultivars and additional species suitable for cutting and further reading, if available, may be found with each species. Reference to a particular article in the species entry or chapter is shown by a numeral in parentheses: (1), (2), and so on. The numbers correspond to the additional reading suggestions at the close of each entry or chapter.

A great deal of the new information presented in this book is the result of experiments at the New Crop Program at the University of Georgia. However, I have tried to make the book national in scope by securing data from other areas of the country, referring to published literature and asking numerous growers, academicians and allied tradespeople for help in reviewing many of the sections. They did so willingly, professionally and with great skill.

I have tried my best to present what is happening today in the production and handling of specialty cut flowers, but, without doubt, significant gaps in our knowledge of these plants still exist. I look forward to your assistance in filling them.

Best success to everyone.

Allan M. Armitage
May 1993

Acknowledgments

Sincere thanks to the following people, who reviewed sections of the book. Their expertise was invaluable and their time is greatly appreciated.

Dr. Robert Anderson, Dept. of Horticulture, University of Kentucky, Lexington, Kentucky.

Ms. Jo Brownold, California Everlastings, Dunnigan, California.

Mr. and Mrs. Ken and Suzy Cook, Ken Cook Flowers, Atlanta, Georgia.

Dr. Douglas Cox, Dept. of Horticulture, Auburn University, Auburn, Alabama.

Mr. Ralph Cramer, Cramer's Posie Patch, Columbia, Pennsylvania.

Ms. Mindy De Vita, Blairsville, Georgia.

Dr. Michael Dirr, Dept. of Horticulture, University of Georgia, Athens, Georgia.

Ms. Fran Foley, Consultant, Aptos, California.

Mr. Keith Funnell, Dept. of Horticulture, Massey University, Palmerston North, New Zealand.

Mr. Jim Garner, Dept. of Horticulture, University of Georgia, Athens, Georgia.

Dr. Ken Goldsberry, Dept. of Horticulture, Colorado State University, Fort Collins, Colorado. (Retired)

Mr. Jack Graham, Dramm and Echkter, Watsonville, California.

Dr. Will Healy, Ball Seed Company, West Chicago, Illinois.

Mr. Brent Heath, The Daffodil Mart, Gloucester, Virginia.

Dr. Peter Hicklenton, Floriculture and Ornamental Physiology, Agriculture Canada, Kentville, Nova Scotia, Canada.

Ms. Christy Holstead-Klink, Floral Communication and Technical Services, Nazareth, Pennsylvania.

Dr. John Kelley, Dept. of Horticulture, Clemson University, Clemson, South Carolina.

Mr. Roy Klehm, Klehm Nursery, South Barrington, Illinois.

Mr. Mark Koch, Robert Koch Industies Inc., Bennett, Colorado.

Ms. Judy Laushman, Executive Director, Association of Specialty Cut Flower Growers, Oberlin, Ohio.

Mr. Tom Lukens, Golden State Bulb Growers, Watsonville, California.

Dr. Robert Lyons, Dept. of Horticulture, Virginia Polytechnic Institute and State University, Blacksburg, Virginia.

Mr. Jeff McGrew, Summersun Greenhouse Co., Mt. Vernon, Washington.

Mr. Don Mitchell, Flora Pacifica, Brookings, Oregon.

Ms. Sally Nakasawa, Nakasawa Everlastings, Yuma, Arizona.

Mr. Jim Nau, Ball Seed Company, West Chicago, Illinois.

Mr. Knud Nielsen III, Knud Nielson Company Inc., Evergreen, Alabama.

Mr. Peter Nissen, Sunshine State Carnations, Hobe Sound, Florida.

Dr. Leonard Perry, Dept. of Horticulture, University of Vermont, Burlington, Vermont.

Mr. Robert Pollioni, Consultant, Ventura, California.

Mr. Whiting Preston, Manatee Fruit Company, Palmetto, Florida.

Mr. Paul Sansone, Here and Now Garden, Gales Creek, Oregon.

Dr. George Staby, Perishables Research Organization, Grafton, California.

Dr. Dennis Stimart, Dept. of Horticulture, University of Wisconsin, Madison, Wisconsin.

Mr. Mike Wallace, Wood Creek Farm, Cygnet, Ohio.

Dr. Ian Warrington, Dept. of Scientific and Industrial Research, Plant Physiology Division, Palmerston North, New Zealand.

Mr. Eddie Welsh, Dept. of Horticulture, Massey University, Palmerston North, New Zealand.

Ms. Linda White-Mays, Sundance Nursery and Flowers, Irvine, Kentucky.

Mr. Jack Zonnveld, M. van Waveren Co., Mt. Airy, North Carolina.

I extend very special thanks to Judy Laushman, who, as my former technician (1985–87), initiated, directed and cared for so much of the cut flower program at the University of Georgia, and to Meg Green, my present technician, who continues to plant, weed, harvest and evaluate without complaint.

Introduction

Specialty cut flowers are crops other than roses, carnations and chrysanthemums. Those 3 traditional crops have historically comprised the largest portion of cut flower production and sales in the world market and, in all likelihood, will continue to do so. Significant research funds have been spent to provide growers of traditional cut flowers the cultural and marketing information necessary to help them succeed. The unwieldy number of specialty species, the difficulty in controlling field conditions and the popularity of greenhouse-grown flowers made traditional crops easier to fund and information flowed readily. The business of growing specialty cut flower crops has been practiced nonetheless for hundreds of years. European and Asian growers produced a vast variety of cut flowers in fields and conservatories. The American grower joined in with large acreages of peonies, tuberose, larkspur, baby's breath and gladioli, reaching a zenith in the 1940s and 1950s.

While growers came and went, the world market remained consistently strong. The consumption of cut flowers has been high in European countries, but their use in all developed countries continues to increase. In the United States, per capita consumption of cut flowers is approximately $21. This contrasts with much higher Japanese ($50), Dutch, Swiss ($45) and western German demand ($38). We are not as flower ignorant as many believe, however. Per capita consumption throughout the United States may be only $21 now but has been continuously increasing. Demand for cut flowers in areas such as Boston, New York, Philadelphia, San Francisco and Chicago is significantly higher. If one compares per capita consumption for all Europe to the United States, differences are far less noteworthy. The American grower should not see the relatively low per capita consumption as indifference but as an indicator of untapped market potential. Every

11

flower-producing country in the world believes that the American markets will continue to rise faster than any other. Shouldn't the American grower believe the same? Isn't it satisfying to know that, far from markets being saturated, there is significant room for expansion?

People buy flowers for 3 main reasons. The type of floral product purchased and the amount of money spent are often more dependent on intended use than on the product itself. In America, the most important reason is to celebrate special occasions. These include anniversaries, birthdays, Valentine's Day, Secretary's Day, funerals and weddings. People spend considerably more money for such flowers than they do for flowers meant for personal use. A recent study by Dr. Bridget Behe and Dennis Wolnick (2,3) provided some interesting insights into marketing floral crops. The consumer spent $20 on anniversary flowers, followed by $18 for Valentine's Day, $17 for Mother's Day and $15 for birthday flowers or as a gift to cheer someone who is ill. Cut flowers, either as arrangements or loose bouquets, were popular for all occasions (1), although Easter and Christmas were most closely associated with the potted easter lily and poinsettia, respectively. However, competition for the special-occasion dollar remains fierce. Flowers must go neck and neck against restaurants, movies, theaters, chocolates and gifts.

A second reason for purchasing flowers is to communicate fleeting emotions such as thanks, forgiveness, apologies and congratulations. In these very individual cases, flowers perfectly express the unexpressable but may be quickly forgotten once the purpose is served. The third and relatively untapped reason for purchasing cut flowers is to create a pleasant atmosphere at home and work. Bringing flowers into the home or workplace is not something the average American often does and is a huge potential source of sales. Promoting the use of flowers for everyday occasions must increase if they are to become a "mainstream" item. Enhancing sales, for whatever reasons, can only be accomplished through production of high-quality flowers, aggressive promotion and an increase in the number of outlets.

The Role of Imports

According to various wholesale houses, approximately 75% of the flowers Americans purchase arrive from offshore sources, mainly Latin American countries. This includes roses, carnations and chrysanthemums as well as other standards like baby's breath and gladioli. Recent scientific developments in horticulture, advances in refrigeration, and breakthroughs in breeding have made many obscure crops available to the market. Cut flowers have also been politically expedient in some countries and their development has been aggressively supported. Flowers arrive every day from offshore suppliers and, although many may disagree, their presence has had a positive influence on the American grower. The marketing skills of the Dutch, the inexpensive stems from Colombia and the acceptance of these crops by the American florist have resulted in more crops and a significantly higher volume of cut flower sales in this country.

Before one complains about foreign supply, one need only study the evolution of *Liatris*, an American native flower. Less than a decade ago, liatris was relatively unknown and a minor item in the cut flower market. That it is now a standard cut flower is because of the improved cultivars and the aggressive marketing of the crop by the Dutch, not because America suddenly became enamored of this spiky plant. Today, the American market for liatris is well established and plants produced by American growers supply a significant part of that market. Other crops have followed similar routes to acceptance. For growers to complain about the role of the Dutch in cut flower marketing is tantamount to beer manufacturers complaining about the proliferation of football games.

Undoubtedly, inequalities in tariff structures and trade rules between the United States and other countries exist. It also seems unfair that we must compete with the minuscule wages paid to workers in developing countries. However, there is little growers can do about such things. Regional or national organizations which fight against such discrepancies can be supported, but unfortunately, many rose, carnation and chrysanthemum growers have already left the business. Many specialty flowers are not as persistent or as tough as the carnation and mum, however, and while production of specialty cut flowers will continue to increase in flower-producing countries, American growers can compete more effectively than carnation and mum growers a decade ago. Competition from abroad will no doubt increase for all species of cut flowers and some buyers will always base their purchases solely on price; anyone who does not believe this has their head in the sand.

The question, then, begs to be asked: how can American growers compete? They can best compete by growing the highest quality product possible, by providing the best service available and by ensuring that proper handling and harvesting methods have resulted in a reasonable price. Local growers can supply local outlets with specific products that can be produced efficiently in their area but ship poorly. In fact, growers must always look for local niches for flowers which are poor shippers and otherwise difficult to find. Quality, freshness and consistency are the keys to competiveness, whether one is competing with Colombia, the Netherlands, California or Georgia. Domestic growers must provide fresh-dated flowers and guarantee on-time delivery of all the flowers on the contract. If flowers are going to be supplied by overseas growers, make them earn every dollar. American growers can waste time looking over their shoulders or spend it doing a better job of what they know must be done: provide a consistently high-quality, fresh-dated crop on time and for a realistic price.

Product Mix

Hundreds of species are useful as cut flowers but the decision of what to grow must be based on climatic conditions, availability of seed and plants and, most important, what will sell in a given area. Diversity of product is important; however, it is easy to be overextended and suddenly find oneself producing 100 different species and/or cultivars. Growers should always be on the lookout for something new, and the importance of constantly staying up to date cannot be overstated, but it is impossible to grow everything. More than ever before, the consumer reacts to and is willing to pay for the unusual. Although there are few "new" species, the public is blissfully unaware of many lesser-grown plants. With the emergence of better cultivars and aggressive marketing, obscure species may turn out to be major winners. The public may be tired of a steady diet of carnations, mums and even roses, but there is no limit to their interest once aroused by the fresh and unusual. Growers of specialty flowers should not believe their products will replace popular species; to believe so is unrealistic and self-defeating. Growers, wholesalers and retailers should rather strive to complement the rose, enhance the carnation, show off the chrysanthemum and liven up the gladiolus.

Dried Flowers

Dried flowers have become a major segment of the specialty market. A recent survey by the Association of Specialty Cut Flower Growers found that over 65% of the members grew flowers for processing. Methods for rapid drying which maintain the color, shape and size of the flowers or foliage have made significant gains in recent years. Growers of dried flowers must be efficient because their products may be shipped from anywhere at any time. Freshness, however, is still a significant marketing advantage. Producers who provide dried material should do so as a primary focus and not as means of using up unsold fresh production. Cultural methods, harvest stage and postharvest techniques differ for fresh and dried production. "Fresh" dried material—harvested at the optimum stage, treated correctly and smartly displayed—can compete with flowers anywhere and is far more appealing than "leftovers" dried as an afterthought.

Plant Diversity

The diversity of available plants and seeds includes annual, perennials, bulbs and woody species. Each class of cut flowers (or the berries, foliage and stems of woody species) includes a wealth of species and cultivars which may be used throughout the growing season. Still, many flowers are seldom seen in florist outlets or garden shops. Some do not hold up to the rigors of dry shipping in boxes which may be neglected for 24 hours. Such species can be routed through auctions, local flower or farmers' markets, or sold directly to florists. Contacts between growers and salespersons can be made if there is a will to do so. Nowhere is it written that all produce must go through a distributor, ending up as generic product in a generic market for faceless people.

More cut flowers should be grown more often with the local market in mind. Something is not quite right when the majority of flowers have to be shipped long distances before being sold. Growing areas near large cities should be established to provide material for distribution to those areas. There is no reason why growers near New York or Chicago or Denver should not be be efficient enough to supply their own areas with product first, supplemented with materials from distant fields and lands.

Volume and Price

The volume of material in the market directly affects its price. Many growers fall into the trap that results. For example, a new grower may find the demand for a crop is higher than expected, and immediately doubles production. More than likely, such a decision will prove unprofitable. Simply because 2000 bunches of flowers sold for $3 a bunch does not mean that 4000 bunches will sell for the same price. Not only does the unit price for the product fall, so do prices for other growers of the same product. The classic thinking that more is better must be changed. Similarly, the price a grower demands for a crop should not automatically fall in times of market glut. If the quality is consistent throughout the year, the grower need not acquiesce to claims of cheaper sources by the wholesaler. If trust and consistency of quality have been cultivated with the buyer, discounting the product to the point where profit has disappeared is poor business. Sometimes it is better not to harvest the excess than to sell it as a lost leader. No one wants to throw out potential earnings, but once prices are lowered, it is difficult to raise them again.

Grading

No grades exist for most specialty cut flowers in America. The lack of obligatory standards reflects the difficulty of adequately enforcing standards in a country with such diverse market outlets. In western Europe, most of the flowers are distributed through flower auctions where standards can be demanded, but more importantly, can be enforced. Standards set by the United Nations Economic Commission for Europe (ECE) include 3 grade categories: Extra, Class I, and Class II. In the Netherlands, the Regulations for Supply of Cut Flowers in Dutch Auctions (1990) has standards for maturity of flowers, bunch size and minimum criteria for Class I and Class II flowers. Standards for stems of all major crops are outlined as well as those for most "summer flowers" (i.e., specialty flowers). In America, the Society of American Florists (SAF) has developed voluntary grading standards for major cut flowers such as carnations, chrysanthemums, gladioli, roses and snapdragons. They are graded as U.S. Blue, Red, Green and Yellow, somewhat equivalent to the European Extra, First and Second Class.

While specific crops call for specific standards, minimum baseline standards for appearance and quality of American crops seem to make sense. The standards for specialty cut flower crops presented here reflect the bare-bones quality one should be able to expect when one opens a box of cut flowers or foliage. I have borrowed ideas from the ECE, the SAF, Dr. Charles Conover (4), the Standards Committee of the Association of Specialty Cut Flower Growers (ASCFG) and many grower and wholesaler friends and acquaintances.

In **Class I,** all flowers, stems and foliage must be fresh (harvested within the last 12 hours; no indication of senescence or fading) and free from damage caused mechanically or from insects, mites and diseases. Stems must be straight and sufficiently strong to carry the flower(s) without bending. There should be no evidence of chemical residues or growth disorders and distortions.

Similar to Class I, plant material in **Class II** is nearly fresh (harvested within the last 12–24 hours; minor senescence; no fading). No more than 10% of the flowers, stems or foliage may show slight mechanical or pest damage. All plant material must be reasonably free of residues and of sufficient ornamental value. One should be able to expect stems to maintain that value for a reasonable length of time.

Class III includes products that are of sufficient quality but do not meet Class I or II criteria. For example, a product may be of excellent flower quality, but stems may be too short to be acceptable as higher grades. Class III is not meant as a dumping ground for inferior product.

Bunches of stems for all 3 classes must be uniform in length and flower maturity. The difference in stem length should not be greater than 10% of the shortest stem. Deviations in uniformity should be written on the box or bunch.

Particulars—relating to weight, length of stems and specific disorders— for individual species must be worked out, but adherence to the simple standards just outlined must occur first.

Time alone will determine if American growers can discipline themselves to voluntarily adhere to published standards, whether those of the European community, the SAF, or the preceding hybrid. Until that time, grading will continue to be the domain of the producer. However, that is not all bad. Good businesses will become known not only for the quality of their product but for the consistency of their grading. Strict grading enhances trust because the buyer will soon realize that bunch after bunch, box after box, week after week, the product is consistent and true to grade. Grading should be based on a combination of flower quality, stem strength and stem length and, once grower standards are established, must be adhered to throughout the growing season. The number of flowers in a bunch should be established and maintained. For most flowers, a minimum of 10 stems/bunch should be the standard. People know how to count by 10s, while 8, 12 or 15 stems/bunch simply confuses the issue. Obviously, some flowers, such as *Anthurium* or orchids, will not be bunched in 10s and *Gypsophila* is often sold in 5-stem bunches or weight because of the physical size of the inflorescences. However, they are the exception rather than the rule for specialty cut flowers.

Simply because stems are fatter or flowers a little larger does not excuse bunches with fewer stems. Similarly, if stems are thin, adding more flowers to the bunch does not raise the quality of the flowers; they still have thin stems! Placing poor quality stems in the middle of a bunch or at the bottom of the box fools no one. Such tactics eventually fail and someone gets hurt. Flowers must be graded as if the grower were the buyer, not the seller.

Consignment

Let the system of consignment die; it is a wasteful unproductive method of marketing that benefits no one in the long run. The product should be bought, not rented from the grower, and the responsibility for final sale and distribution of the fresh product must rest with the distributor or wholesaler, not the producer. Consignment systems inevitably result in ill-will between producer and distributor and tend to weigh down a distribution system already burdened with lingering mistrust.

Trust

Trust between wholesaler and producer is a necessity when large amounts of flowers must be moved. In a good working relationship, problems on either the producer's or the wholesaler's part can be discussed and corrected in professional terms. An open and frank communication makes the business of specialty cut flowers far more enjoyable for all concerned. Similarly, discussion among growers is essential if the specialty cut flower industry is to blossom and succeed in this country. Few secrets exist and those people who refuse to share experiences and methods with others do themselves a great disservice in the end. There are enough problems—seasonality, imports, hail, rain, freezing temperatures, drought, heat and rodents—without tripping over each other to keep "secrets" secure. A free-flowing exchange of ideas is essential in any business and this one is no exception. To that end, membership in the Association of Specialty Cut

Flower Growers is highly recommended for anyone in the business. A national network for communication, it serves as a conduit for information on culture, sources of plant material and names of members with similar problems who are willing to share their experiences. The address is

Association of Specialty Cut Flower Growers
MPO Box 268, Oberlin, OH
44074

Reading

1. Behe, B. H. 1991. 1992 holiday marketing ideas. *Society of American Florists Mag.* (December) 8(9):38–40.

2. Behe, B. H., and D. J. Wolnick. 1991. Type of floral product purchased and demographic characteristics and floral knowledge of consumers. *HortScience* 26(4):414–416.

3. _____ . Market segmentation of Pennsylvania floral consumers by purchase volume and primary retail outlet. *HortScience* 26(10):1328–1331.

4. Conover, C. A. 1986. Quality. In Third International Symposium on Post-harvest Physiology of Ornamentals. *Acta Hortic.* 181:201–205.

Postharvest Care

It may be argued that no one step in the chain of marketing flowers to the consumer is more important than any other. That is, if even one step is poorly accomplished, the whole chain is weakened. If water quality is poor, the fertility program is out of balance or the incorrect cultivar or species is grown, quality and potential sales of the crop suffer. Once the plant is grown, proper harvesting, handling and postharvest treatments are essential for maintaining the quality of the flowers. Without a suitable postharvest program, the wholesaler, florist or consumer is being sold a defective item. The grower is responsible for the first stage of postharvest treatment, but others who handle the flowers (wholesaler, trucker, florist) have equal responsibility. The most important part of any program is the recognition of its importance. The lack of a consistent postharvest program is one important reason sales of fresh flowers are not higher. Consumers feel they are being cheated when the flowers they purchase decline prematurely. The perception of "not getting one's money's worth" is extremely dangerous to this industry and must be eliminated.

Carnations and chrysanthemums are so popular because, in addition to shipping well, florists and the public perceive that they are a good value for the money. *That perception is the key to success in the fresh cut flower industry*. The flowers sold by the American grower must be fresher, of better quality and longer lasting than those from overseas. Only if the industry accomplishes these characteristics will consumers demand American-grown flowers. An additional benefit of better postharvest care is that more flowers will be sold, regardless of origin. More flowers translate to additional sales for everyone and higher visibility and perceived necessity of the product. Purchasing flowers should be as commonplace as buying a theater ticket or a meal at a restaurant. The value for the money spent must be perceived to be at least equal to that play or meal. The industry must not only believe in the importance of correct postharvest treatments but practice them as well, for if flowers are not better handled, the future of the American grower of specialty cut flowers is questionable.

Considerations of the Crop in the Field

Numerous practices to enhance postharvest longevity of the flower may be practiced before any flowers are cut. The practices begin with the selection of the cultivar and extend to maintaining the health of the plant in the field.

Species and cultivar selection: The environments under which plants are grown dictate the species and cultivars selected. If a crop is grown in an unsuitable area, plants will never be as vigorous and active as they could be under more hospitable conditions. In general, plants are stunted, flower less prolifically, produce off-colored foliage and have shorter vase life when grown in marginal environments. Attempting to grow a crop unsuitable to the area invariably results in low quality and a decline in postharvest life.

Health of the plants in the field: Research has shown that anything which results in prolonged stress (water, cold, heat, improper fertility) reduces postharvest life. Healthy plants produce long-lasting flowers. However, it does not necessarily follow that the lushest, most vigorous plants have the best postharvest life. In fact, plants which have been heavily fertilized or grown under warm temperatures often exhibit shorter shelf life than those which are grown a little "leaner" and cooler. Integrating good postharvest methods with a growing regime to produce reasonable yields and high-quality stems is a goal to which all growers should aspire. In the greenhouse, plants are often hardened off by reducing temperature, fertilizer or water prior to harvest to increase the life of the flower.

Harvesting: The best time to harvest flowers is a compromise reached by weighing various factors. Flowers harvested in the heat of the day can be stressed by high temperatures. Dark-colored flowers can be as much as 10F warmer than white flowers on a bright, hot day. Harvesting in the morning is beneficial because plants are turgid, but they also may be wet with dew and more susceptible to postharvest diseases. Cutting in the late afternoon or evening provides stems with high carbohydrate levels, but temperatures may be too warm at the time the cutting crew is on the job. To avoid the high temperatures in some parts of the country, flowers should ideally be cut at 8:00 PM, but this is not always possible. High natural sugars in the stem are less important if stems are properly treated after cutting. Morning is recommended for most flowers, particularly those that lose water rapidly after harvesting. Harvesting, however, should be delayed until plants are dry of dew, rain or other moisture. Cutting at high temperatures (above 80F) and high light intensity should be avoided whenever possible.

If flowers are not ethylene-sensitive (see the list beginning on p. 23), transfer them immediately to a floral preservative and then to a cool storage facility to prevent water loss. Ethylene-sensitive flowers should be placed in water in the field until treated with silver compounds in the grading area.

Stage of development of the flower: In general, harvesting in the bud stage or as flowers begin to show color results in better postharvest life for many crops. The main reason for cutting flowers in a tight stage is to reduce space during shipping. Tight flowers are not as susceptible to mechanical damage or ethylene and more stems may be shipped in the box than stems with open flowers. However, the tight flower stage is not the optimum stage for all flowers. Spikelike flowers such as *Aconitum, Delphinium* and *Physostegia* should have 1 or 2 basal flowers open while some members of the daisy family require that flowers be fully open prior to harvest (*Achillea*). If one is not shipping long distances, harvesting during the tight stage is not necessary. In general, if flowers are cut tight, placing stems in a bud-opening solution (see "Sources of Postharvest Treatment Solutions" later in this chapter) is useful for the secondary user (wholesaler, florist or consumer). Research has not been conducted for every specialty cut flower, but the optimum harvest stage is provided for all crops discussed in the book at each species entry. The optimum stage has been determined by research, observation or discussion with growers and wholesalers. Appendix 1 is a brief summation of the recommendations.

Considerations of the Cut Stem

Air temperature: No one factor affects the life of cut flowers as much as temperature. Growing cut flowers without a cooler is like having a restaurant without a kitchen. Warm temperatures cause increased water loss, loss of stored food and rapid reduction of vase life. Most cut stems should be cooled to 33–36F. It is imperative to rapidly reduce field heat and to maintain cool temperatures throughout the marketing chain of the flowers. If possible, stems should be graded and packed in a 36–40F cooler; though not particularly popular with employees, the quality of the flowers is greatly enhanced. If field heat is not removed, or if loose flowers or flower boxes are simply stacked in a refrigerated room, rapid deterioration takes place. It can take 2–4 days to cool a stack of packed boxes of warm flowers, and this same stack will never reach recommended temperatures, even after 3 days in a refrigerated truck (2). Forced-air cooling of boxes to quickly remove heat and proper box design significantly enhances the cooling of flowers and, in turn, their postharvest life.

Forced-air cooling: Boxes with holes or closeable flaps are necessary and air is sucked out of (or blown into) the boxes with an inexpensive fan. In general, cooling times are calculated as the time to reach ⅞ of the recommended cool temperature for a particular species. Usually, the time to reach

40F is calculated. Cooling times for some flowers have been calculated based on the airflow passing through the box (cfm/min), fan static pressure and the type of flower being cooled (2). For example, a box of baby's breath measuring $42 \times 21 \times 12''$ with 3" wide vent holes in each of the 2 ends requires approximately 8 minutes to reach ⅞ cooling at 260 cfm/min and 1.0" of static pressure (2). A similar box of sinuata statice requires 18 minutes at 210 cfm/min (2). The ⅞ cooling times vary from 4 to 20 minutes depending on the flowers, box design and packing method (1). Dr. Roger Rij and coworkers (2) provide an excellent synopsis of precooling, methods of setting up small forced-air systems and necessary information for calculating cooling times.

Initial and final box temperature should be measured and entered on data sheets. Although actual temperatures should be appraised with a long-probed thermometer, the final temperature of the flowers can be estimated by using a temperature probe to measure the air being exhausted from the box. The air coming out of the box will always be cooler than the flowers and an experienced operator knows the relation between exhaust temperature and flower temperature.

The heat extracted from the boxes must be exhausted from the cooler. This can be a problem in small coolers and compressor capacity should be upgraded if forced-air cooling of boxes is done. For example, if 200 pounds of flowers (5–10 boxes) are cooled from 80F to a cooler temperature, a compressor of at least 1 ton (1–1.5 hp) is needed (1).

Water temperature: Although water uptake is more rapid at warm temperatures than cool, flower stems should not be placed in warm water unless needed. Warm water is useful if flowers are particularly dehydrated coming out of the field, or for bud opening. In such cases, water heated to 100–110F is most effective for rehydration. Some growers actually immerse stems up to the flowers in a deep bucket of cold water, creating a mini hydro-cooling system. While the use of warm water seldom causes problems, it is not particularly beneficial on a routine basis.

Water quality: The water used for holding cut flowers affects the quality of the flower. Tap water is most commonly used and, depending on the source, may be high in salinity, vary in pH or be contaminated with microorganisms. Sensitivity to saline conditions varies with species but measurements of salinity must be treated with caution. A more important measure is the measurement of the buffering capacity of the water, or its alkalinity. A salinity reading of 190 appears dangerously high at first glance; however, the reading may consist of 40 ppm alkalinity and 150 ppm saline components. Such water is fine. The higher the alkalinity, the more difficult it is to adjust the pH of the water. This can be important when using preservatives because most preservatives are effective at low pH (3.0–5.5). If the pH cannot be adjusted due to high alkalinity, then the preservative may be useless. Some preservative solutions work well in high alkaline waters, others do not. Knowing the alkalinity value of the water used to treat cut flowers allows one to choose the most efficient preservative. Water may be tested through state universities or private laboratories for a reasonable price. It is money well spent. Simple test kits are also available through the Hach Company, P.O. Box 389, Loveland, CO 80537 (303-669-3050).

Tap water often contains fluoride, which is injurious to many cut flowers. The presence of as little as 1 ppm may injure flowers such as gerberas and freesias although other crops such as snapdragons are less sensitive. Daffodils, lilacs and some orchids are insensitive.

Flowers persist in acidic water longer than basic pH water. Water that is acidic (pH 3.0–5.5) is taken up more rapidly and deters the growth of numerous microorganisms. The pH of the solution also affects the efficacy of the germicide in the preservative. Matching the proper preservative with the available water should result .in good water quality and enhanced post-harvest life of the flowers.

Depth of water: Relatively little water is absorbed through the walls of the stem (the majority is absorbed through the base), therefore the water or solution in which the stems are held need not be deep. The only advantage of plunging stems into 6" of water rather than 1" is that the water flows 6" up the water-conducting tissues of the stem, reducing the height the water must be moved by capillary action. Plunging stems in water more than 6" deep reduces air circulation around the leaves and crowds the stems and flowers together.

Ethylene: Ethylene is a gas released by all flowers, although ripening fruit and damaged flowers result in a significant rise of the gas. It is also produced during the combustion of gasoline or propane and during welding. Low levels (less than 1 ppm) for short periods can result in premature senescing, shattering or other damage to ethylene-sensitive flowers. To avoid the effects of ethylene, hold flowers in cool areas, away from senescing flowers or ripening fruit and keep in a well-ventilated area. The metal silver reduces the effects of ethylene and is provided by silver thiosulfate (STS). Only those genera shown in the following list, adapted from Holstead-Klink (2) and Staby (4), should be treated with STS. Not all species are equally responsive; for example, *Rudbeckia* is very much less sensitive to ethylene and therefore less responsive to STS than *Delphinium*. The following genera have been shown to be sensitive to ethylene.

Achillea	*Astilbe*	*Dianthus*
Aconitum	*Bouvardia*	*Eremurus*
Agapanthus	*Campanula*	*Eustoma*
Alstroemeria	*Celosia*	*Freesia*
Anemone	*Centaurea*	*Godetia*
Antirrhinum	*Chamaelaucium*	*Gypsophila*
Aquilegia	*Consolida*	*Kniphofia*
Asclepias	*Delphinium*	*Lathyrus*

Lilium	*Rosa*	*Solidago*
Lysimachia	*Rudbeckia*	*Trachelium*
Matthiola	*Saponaria*	*Triteleia*
Phlox	*Scabiosa*	*Veronica*
Physostegia	*Silene*	*Veronicastrum*

Pulsing: Placing freshly harvested flowers for a short time (a few seconds to a few hours) in a solution to extend vase life is referred to as pulsing. Sugar and STS are common pulsing ingredients but short pulses (10 sec) of silver nitrate (100–200 ppm) have also been reported with a few species. Silver nitrate, however, is seldom used commercially.

STS pulsing: Pretreatment with STS is critical if flowers are ethylene-sensitive (sweet pea, carnation, alstroemeria, delphinium, lily and snapdragon). A short pulse or long pulse can be used. Solutions containing STS are available through a number of manufacturers and have been extensively field tested (see "Sources of Postharvest Treatment Solutions" later in this chapter). The effectiveness of STS is dependent on the concentration of silver, the time the stems are in the solution and the temperature at which they are treated. A long pulse time (e.g., 48 hours) at a high concentration will be taken up more rapidly at warm temperatures than at cool temperatures. In general, a 1- to 2-hour pulse of STS at room temperature or an overnight pulse in the cooler is sufficient for most flowers.

Test kits are available to determine if silver is present in the preservative. If the silver concentration is greater than 100 ppm, the test is positive. Not all products test positive with the kits and sufficient silver may be present at lower concentrations even if the test is negative.

Disposal of STS is a problem which must be addressed by the floriculture industry. Disposal of solutions with more than 5 ppm silver is against federal law. State laws may be more or less stringent. Some companies offer silver filters to the grower for disposal of silver and silver products (see "Sources of Postharvest Treatment Solutions" later in this chapter). Used solutions of STS are poured through the filter and the silver is trapped in a can. After a period of time, the can, with the silver inside, is exchanged for a new one. Costs of a silver filtration system is around $200. The filter should last for 6 months to 1 year, depending on usage.

Removal of leaves: As a rule, approximately ⅓ of the leaves are removed from the base of the stem and in some cases all leaves are removed, especially if flowers will be dried. Foliage immersed in water results in bacterial growth and toxin buildup, reducing the postharvest life of the flower.

Availability of food: Since few or no leaves are cut with many flowers, little food for respiration is available to the stem and flower. It may be argued that harvesting should be accomplished in late afternoon because the buildup of food from photosynthesis is greater than in the morning. However, in the morning, water content of the stem is high and temperatures are low. These beneficial factors, combined with the practical considerations of packing, grading and shipping of the same stems, means that stems are generally cut early in the day.

The quality and longevity of cut flowers are improved when stems are pulsed in a solution containing sucrose or table sugar. In general, concentrations of 1.5–2% sugar are used, although higher concentrations are effective for certain species. Snapdragons respond well to a 1–2% solution; carnations take 2–3% for bud opening or 4% for open flowers. Gladiolus spikes are provided with 3–4% sugar solution, but may be treated with up to 20% sugar. In general, most commercial preservatives contain approximately 1% sugar. This is sufficient for most flowers. Sugar solutions can be made up if necessary by the grower. Add 13 oz of sucrose to 10 gallons of water per percentage required. That is, for a 1% solution, dissolve 13 oz of sucrose in 10 gallons of water; for a 4% solution, add 52 oz (3.25 pounds) to 10 gallons of water.

Stem plugging: Air bubbles, which restrict the upward flow of water, occur after harvesting with many types of flower stems. Recutting stems (approx. 1") under water reduces the blockages. Warm water (approx. 110F) and acidic (pH 3.0–4.0) conditions reduce the effects of air bubbles. This is a particularly effective and simple means of treating limp and droopy flowers.

Bacteria can also block the ends of stems. Clean containers and acidified water greatly reduce the problem of bacterial blockage. Floral preservatives contain antibacterial agents and are effective in reducing bacterial and fungal growth.

The most common antibacterial and antifungal agents in floral preservatives used to be 8-hydroxyquinoline citrate or sulfate (8-HQC, 8-HQS). However, they are very difficult to locate and seldom used today. Making 8-HQC solutions is best left to the chemist and not recommended for the grower. Commercial floral preservatives are effective for reducing bacterial and fungal growth and additional agents should not be necessary.

Conditioning: Conditioning or hardening of cut stems restores the turgor of wilted flowers and should be done by florists, wholesalers and/or growers. In general, demineralized water should be used when conditioning solutions are prepared. When stems are placed in solutions, they should be held at room temperature initially (a few hours to overnight) then placed in cold storage for several hours. Warm water (approx. 110F) is highly recommended for restoring turgor in wilted stems. Badly wilted stems, especially those with woody stems, may benefit from being placed in hot water (180–200F) prior to placing them in room-temperature solutions.

Sources of Postharvest Treatment Solutions

A word about "in house" mixing of chemicals: Flower preservatives, silver solutions, bacteriocides, bud openers, conditioners and sugar solutions are all part of the postharvest jargon. While all of these can be mixed up in the back room, what is the point? It is doubtful that the solutions will be significantly different from those commercially available, and often mistakes are made in the mixing, resulting in solutions which are either ineffective or phytotoxic. A grower is a busy individual, already functioning as grower, market analyst and information gatherer combined. Why add chemist, waste disposal technician and preservative manufacturer to the list? Preservative companies provide information, effective chemicals and good service. Growers don't manufacture insecticides; why should they concoct preservatives? Last but not least, it is illegal to manufacture "in house" preservatives without necessary Materials Safety Data Sheets. More paperwork!

The following companies have full-time research and service staffs and cater to the flower grower.

Floralife

Floralife provides numerous flower products, including dispensing systems for large-volume operations and technical assistance. They also publish an excellent guide to postharvest care of cut flowers, *Dew-y's Floracare Manual*.

Address: Floralife, Inc., 120 Tower Drive, Burr Ridge, IL 60521. Phone 800-323-3689, Fax 708-325-4924.

Grower pretreatments.

Use	Product
Hydration	Hydraflor 100™
	Hydraflor Quick Dip™
Ethylene inhibitor	Silflor/50™
	Silflor/RTU™
	Silflor™, 2.5 gal pump set
Bucket cleaner	Formula DCD™

Plant food for growers, wholesalers and retailers.

Use	Product
Flower preservative	Floralife™, powder and liquid
	Special blend pure (for high-quality water)
	Special blend hard (for hard water)
	Crystal Clear™ (all-around liquid preservative)
Silver filter	

Gard Environmental Group

Gard Environmental Group first introduced floral preservative products in 1974 under the name Gard/Rogard and now market a liquid formulation of flower preservative, an ethylene inhibitor and a combination preservative plus inhibiting agent. They have developed a system for mixing flower preservative with ethylene-inhibitor chemicals for enhanced postharvest life. An automatic proportioning system to eliminate mixing of chemicals is popular. The company provides written assessments of their products and has an excellent support staff.

Address: Gard Environmental Group, Inc., 903 Armstrong Road, Algonquin, IL 60102. Phone 800-GEE-GARD, Fax 708-658-7075.

Grower pretreatments.

Use	Product
Flower preservative	Rogard RS™ (also available in crystal packets for retailers and consumers)
Ethylene inhibitor	Silgard RS™ (may be mixed with Rogard RS™)

Plant food for growers, wholesalers and retailers.

Use	Product
Flower preservative	Rogard RS™ crystal packs

Pokon & Chrysal USA

Pokon & Chrysal USA manufactures numerous analyses of floral preservatives, pretreatments, and conditioners. Some products have been designed for specific species. For example, Chrysal GVB™ is recommended for *Gypsophila* and other summer flowers; Chrysal LVB™ is an STS product for lilies. The firm also has some excellent research material available. Contact a distributor to sort out the various products.

Address: Pokon & Chrysal USA, 7977 N.W. 21st Street, Miami, FL 33122. Phone 800-247-9725, Fax 305-477-1284.

Grower pretreatments.

Use	Product
Conditioner	Chrysal CVB™ Chrysal OVB™* Chrysal RVB™* Chrysal HVB™
Ethylene inhibitor	Chrysal AVB™* Chrysal LVB™ Chrysal SVB™*
Improved bud opening	Chrysal GVB™ Chrysal AKC™
Bucket cleaner	Chrysal™ cleaners

*Most widely used.

Plant food for growers, wholesalers and retailers.

Use	Product
Flower preservative	Chrysal Universal™ Chrysal Select™

Robert Koch Industries

Robert Koch Industries supplies dyes, preservatives and fragrances. Some products are manufactured for use in preserved and dried flowers or foliage while others are recommended for fresh floral preservatives or dyes. The company developed Prairie View Farms as a research arm for testing and developing dyes and preservatives. Excellent service people are on staff and helpful information sheets are available.

Address: Robert Koch Industries, Rte. 1, Box 4HH, Bennett, CO 80102. Phone 303-644-3763, Fax 303-644-3045.

Dyes, preservatives and fragrances.

Use	Product application
Glycerine	Used to preserve flowers and avoid the brittleness associated with air-dried products.
Absorption dye	Used for coloring fresh and dried flowers such as baby's breath, carnations, iris, gladioli and wax flower; can be directly added to glycerine-based preservatives for coloring preserved material such as

	eucalyptus, sinuata stems, baby's breath and foliage of palms, cedars and junipers.
Dip dye	Used to dye dried products by immersion; generally limited to daisies and chrysanthemums.
Fragrance	Consist of compounded fragrances and essential oils, mainly used in potpourri.
Flower preservative	Include a silver thiosulfate solution, a general-purpose preservative (Prolong™) and a hydrating solution (Rose Life™).

Wetting agents and glycerine may also be purchased by companies wishing to make their own solutions.

Smithers Oasis

Smithers Oasis has been serving the floriculture industry for many years. Although primarily known for their greenhouse and floral products, they also manufacture commodities for the cut flower grower.

Address: Smithers Oasis, 919 Marvin Avenue, P.O. Box 118, Kent, OH 44240. Phone 216-673-5831, Fax 216-678-5279.

Grower pretreatments.

Use	Product
Flower conditioner	Oasis™ flower conditioner
Ethylene inhibitor	CT 2000™

Plant food for growers, wholesalers and retailers.

Use	Product
Flower preservative	Oasis™ flower preservative
Silver filter	

Reading

1. Evans, R. Y., and M. S. Reid. 1990. Postharvest care of specialty cut flowers. In *Proceedings of 3rd National Conference on Specialty Cut Flowers*. Ventura, CA. 26–44.

2. Holstead-Klink, C. 1992. Postharvest handling of fresh flowers. In *Proceedings of 4th National Conference on Specialty Cut Flowers*. Cleveland, OH. 120–135.

3. Rij, R. E., J. F. Thompson and D. Farnham. 1979. Handling, precooling,

and temperature management of cut flowers for truck transportation. In *Advances in Agricultural Technology,* AAT-W-5/June. USDA, Science and Education Admin.

4. Staby, G. L. 1991. Personal communication.

Many thanks to Dr. George Staby and Ms. Christy Holstead-Klink for reviewing this section.

Drying and Preserving

In a recent survey of the membership of the Association of Specialty Cut Flower Growers, nearly 65% of the growers stated that drying and preserving flowers are important parts of their business. Dried materials are not "dead sticks and twigs," but include colorful flowers, preserved fruits and soft, supple stems whose postharvest life is indefinite. Much of the following counsel is based on information provided by Mr. Mark Koch of Robert Koch Industries, Bennett, CO.

Air-drying

Plants for drying: In general, plants with a high water content (e.g., peonies) do not dry as well as those with a moderate or low moisture volume. Delicate flowers (iris, carnations) are more difficult to air-dry than tougher flowers like sinuata statice. Tropical flowers do not air-dry well. Unfortunately, flowers which do not dry well are equally difficult to preserve with glycerine treatments. Some flowers with high water content are more easily dried using freeze-dry techniques. Roses, calla lilies and peonies can all be freeze-dried and preserved for many years.

Facilities for air-drying: Drying sheds range from basements to elaborate greenhouses or storage areas with sophisticated equipment. Whether flowers are dried in the attic or in converted warehouse space, all sheds must have a few characteristics in common.

Protection: Protection from excessive sunlight, wind, water and dust is important. Concrete floors are expensive but highly recommended. Not only do they act as excellent heat sinks, warming up during the day and slowly releasing heat at night, they also reduce dust. Dust particles become permanently attached to stems that have been treated with sealers or flame retardants.

Ventilation: During the drying process, materials release moisture to the air. Without adequate means of air exchange, drying rates are considerably prolonged. Sheds should be constructed to take advantage of natural ventilation (e.g., prevailing winds), but fans are often incorporated to aid air circulation. Poor air movement also encourages the buildup of molds and disease organisms. If fumigation is necessary to kill insects, the shed must also be airtight. Some drying sheds are constructed so that all or a portion of space may be sealed for fumigant application and then properly vented in keeping with regulatory statutes.

Temperature and humidity: The rate of drying increases with increasing temperature and decreasing humidity. Plant materials with waxy cuticles, large stem diameters and high moisture content require longer times for drying than those with low water content. Temperatures in the drying shed vary widely but range from 50F to 120F. Humidity levels are seldom controlled by smaller producers, and generally reflect the outside humidity. Air-drying equipment is available with humidity and temperature control and is popular with larger processors and those whose natural environment is humid. Optimum humidity levels range from 20 to 60% and should be monitored by all processors.

Exposure to light: Some materials are best dried in darkness while others are dried in the sunlight. Drying sheds with the ability to adjust the amount of light provide additional flexibility for drying different materials. Most plant materials, when exposed to sunlight, fade to pale yellow. This sun bleaching is used by many processors in preparation for drying. Grasses, for example, must be bleached if light color shades are to be produced. Sun bleaching also provides an autumnal look for grasses, grains and thin-stemmed flowers. If the natural plant color is to be retained, drying in the absence of light is recommended.

Bunch size and handling: Stems are generally grouped in bunches for resale. Bunches with too many stems may reduce air circulation and should not be placed so close together as to reduce air movement. They are normally hung on strings or wires from the roof and it is common to date each line as stems are hung to ensure proper drying times.

Required drying times: Drying times vary considerably depending on species, location, drying shed design and season of year. In general, times range from 3 days to 3 weeks. Failure to adequately dry a plant can lead to serious mold problems if sleeved and boxed too early.

Preserving with Glycerine

Many flowers may be preserved with glycerine. Flowers to be preserved should be treated as soon after harvest as possible. In general, 1 part of glycerine is mixed with 2–3 parts very hot water (by volume) and a 0.5–1% surfactant such as a mild detergent. A surfactant is designed to reduce the surface tension of water and differences among surfactants are considerable. Tween 20™ and Tween 80™ are excellent surfactants and seem to be less phytotoxic than other wetting agents. Using tall buckets reduces air circulation around the leaves and should be avoided. Stems should be placed in approximately 3″ of solution in a well-ventilated area indoors at 70–85F. After treatment, the portion of the stems immersed in glycerine/dye should be removed; the solution bleeds from the treated area otherwise. In general, the smaller the diameter of the stem, the less glycerine is used. Normal preserving time is 3–4 days. Water-soluble dyes may be added at the same time.

If stems are allowed to remain in glycerine too long, the glycerine will move through the plants and be pumped out through the flowers and foliage resulting in stems which may be wet, oily and essentially unuseable. After treating, the stems should be rinsed with clear water and hung to dry. Approximately 1–2 weeks drying time is necessary. If stems are still not sufficiently soft 4–5 days after removal from the glycerine, a misting of the glycerine solution over the foliage helps to make them more supple. Most plants are preserved in the dark; however, eucalyptus is light-treated, and baby's breath is also preserved in the light to give an amber glow to the stems and flowers. The glycerine solution may be reused up to 3 times by pouring through a fine screen to remove leaves and other debris.

Plant material for drying: A survey of members of the Association of Specialty Cut Flower Growers resulted in the following list of the most popular flowers, branches and grasses for drying (prepared by the ASCFG, 1991).

Achillea (yarrow)—many species
Ammobium (winged everlasting)
Artemisia (silver king, silver queen and annual sweet annie [*A. annua*])
Branches—palm, myrtle, cedar, willow, eucalyptus
Carthamus tinctorius (safflower)
Celosia cristata (cockscomb)
Chrysanthemum parthenium (feverfew)
Consolida (larkspur)
Daucus carota (queen anne's lace)

Echinops (globe thistle)
Eryngium (sea holly)
Gomphrena globosa (globe amaranth)
Grasses—wheat, rye, buffalo, quaking
Gypsophila paniculata (baby's breath)
Helichrysum bracteatum (strawflower)
Helipterum manglesii (rhodanthe)
Helipterum roseum (sunray everlasting)

Hydrangea—many forms
Iberis sempervirens (candytuft)
Lavandula (lavender)
Lepidium (peppergrass)
Limonium (latifolia, sinuata, caspia
    and german)
Lunaria annua (money plant)

Nigella damascena (love-in-a-mist)
Papaver somniferum (opium
    poppy)—pods
Rosa (rose)
Xeranthemum annuum (immortelle)
Zea mays (ornamental corn)

Freeze-drying

Advances in freeze-drying equipment and polymer chemistry have resulted in more and more flowers being freeze-dried, particularly stems and flowers with high water content. Small equipment is available for the florist industry as well as high volume dryers for the wholesaler and wholesale/grower. Freeze-drying provides flowers with a natural shape and color and extended longevity; as technology increases and prices for equipment decrease, many more flowers will be dried in this way.

Thanks to Mr. Mark Koch for reviewing this section.

Annuals for Cut Flowers

Botanically, an annual is a plant which completes its life cycle in a single season. In a practical sense, plants which do not survive the winter and must be replanted each year are referred to as annuals. Commercially, however, many crops which are perennial in nature are replanted each year because yield or quality significantly declines in subsequent years. Annuals may be grown from seed in the greenhouse and transplanted to the field or direct-sown. Growers who use annuals are closest to classical farmers; they utilize similar equipment for sowing, transplanting, tilling and bed preparation. In this sense, little difference exists between the soybean farmer and the grower of annual statice. However, the harvesting, grading, bunching, transport and sale of the 2 crops are significantly different, to say nothing of the difference in potential profit.

The advantages of growing annuals over other types of cut flower species are that seed is usually less expensive and more generally available than perennials or bulbs crops. Direct sowing, when appropriate, is more cost-effective than transplanting crowns or bulbs to the field. For difficult field-germinators, single cell transplants (plugs) are offered for many cultivars of annuals. Annuals may be sown at intervals throughout the season, allowing for selective harvesting of only the highest-quality flowers. Relatively unknown species and numerous new cultivars of annuals, including flowers for drying, become available rapidly and should be tried by those who wish to evaluate new products. Getting annual flowers to the market only requires 1 year and a relatively small investment compared with perennials and bulbous species.

Disadvantages include the necessity of annual soil preparation, bed maintenance and planting. Germination may be erratic from year to year and seed is not always available. Harvesting is highly labor-intensive and common species may flood the market and deflate market prices.

More species and cultivars of annuals are used as cut flowers than any other type of plant. Many are discussed in this chapter, and although significant new information is included, numerous gaps in our understanding of many crops still exist.

AGERATUM TO ZINNIA

In the following listings, the first line for each annual provides the name of the genus and species, followed by the common name and then the normal height/spread of the mature plant. The second line provides the flower color of the species, the country or region of origin and finally the botanical family to which the species belongs.

Ageratum houstonianum	Blue Flossflower	2–3'/2'
Blue	Mexico	Asteraceae

Flossflower provides summer-blooming, blue flowers which provide excellent material for local markets. Though most cultivars have been bred for the bedding plant trade, 1 or 2 are used for cut flowers.

Propagation

Seed: Seed germinates in 8–10 days if sown at 80–85F under intermittent mist or in a sweat tent (2). Seed of cut flower cultivars is sown in plugs for planting out to the field; seed is not direct-sown. Cover seed lightly or not at all, as seed germinates better under light. Approximately 1/64 oz of seed yields 1000 plants (1).

Growing-on

Grow plugs at 60–65F for 4–6 weeks. If sown in open flats, transplant to 3" containers 3–4 weeks after sowing. Fertilize with 100 ppm N, using a complete fertilizer, until plants are ready to transplant to the field. Approximately 7 weeks are needed between sowing and transplanting to the field (2).

Environmental Factors

Plants have no photoperiodic requirement and flowering occurs as temperatures increase. Flowering occurs throughout the summer. Temperatures below 50F and above 90F inhibit flowering.

Field Performance

Few data are available, but the goal of 10–20 stems/plant is easily attainable at a 9–12" spacing. Place in full sun in the field after the danger of frost has passed (3). Make at least 3 separate plantings in southern locations.

Ageratum houstonianum

Greenhouse Performance

Flowers may be forced any time in the greenhouse without artificial photoperiod control. Under 62–65F nights and 70F days, 12–13 weeks are required between sowing and flowering. Flowering occurs 10–14 days earlier in the South. Additional time is needed if temperatures are maintained below 62F. Plant in final containers or in ground beds at 6–9" spacing, and fertilize with 200 ppm N and K with potassium nitrate/calcium nitrate in the winter. A complete fertilizer, such as 20–20–20, may be used when light levels and temperatures increase in the spring. A single tier of netting is useful. Reduce fertilization when flowers begin to show color.

Stage of Harvest

Harvest when flowers are just opening.

Postharvest

Fresh: Flowers persist for 7–10 days in floral preservative. Flowers do not store well and are best for local markets.

Dried: Flowers may be air-dried, but flower color often fades.

Cultivars

'Blue Horizon' is an F_1 cultivar which grows 2–3' tall and bears mid-blue flowers.

Pests and Diseases

No diseases particular to *Ageratum* occur. The worst pests are whiteflies which seem to be able to detect the presence of *Ageratum* from miles away. Once they've detected it, they tell all their friends and the banquet begins. Plants tend to "melt out" in areas of hot humid summers (e.g., southern United States). If staggered plantings are practiced, this problem is of little concern.

Reading

1. Kieft, C. 1989. *Kieft's Growing Manual* .... Kieft Bloemzaden, Venhuizen, The Netherlands.

2. Nau, J. 1989. *Ball Culture Guide: The Encyclopedia of Seed Germination.* Ball Seed Co., West Chicago, IL.

3. Utami, L., R. G. Anderson, R. L. Geneve and S. Kester. 1990. Quality and yield of *Ageratum, Aster, Celosia* and *Godetia* grown as field grown cut flowers. *HortScience* 25:851. (Abstr.)

Agrostemma githago

Agrostemma githago	Corn Cockle	3–4'/2'
Purple	Western Europe	Caryophyllaceae

Corn cockle is native to the meadows and fields of western Europe and is considered little more than a weed in its native habitat. The 1–2" wide, purple-mauve flowers have dark veins and are borne singly or in groups of 3–5 on thin, branched stems. Plants perform best in cool summers and cannot be recommended as a summer crop in the South. However, if planted in mid-March to mid-April, southern growers can succeed with this crop. Although not a spectacular species, it provides handsome flowers for bouquets.

Propagation

Seed: Seed may be direct-sown (0.5 oz/100 linear ft or 5.2 oz/1000 ft^2) in early spring. Seed may also be germinated at 68–72F under mist or a sweat tent. Germination under controlled temperatures occurs in 10–14 days. Approximately ⅓ oz of seed yields 1000 plants (3). The seed of *Agrostemma* is poisonous; it contains saponin, which can account for 5–7% of the dry weight of the seed (2). Seed may be stored dry at 32F for up to 20 years (4).

Cuttings: Take 1–3" long vegetative cuttings. Rooting hormone is not necessary. Cuttings root in 10–12 days if placed in 70F propagation beds.

Growing-on

Although most plants are direct-sown to the field, they may be grown in the greenhouse at 65/55F day/night temperatures. Fertilize with 50–75 ppm N in the form of potassium or calcium nitrate at each irrigation. Plants are ready to transplant to the field in 4–5 weeks. Warmer temperatures and high nitrogen nutrition result in internode elongation and soft transplants which are prone to injury in the field.

Environmental Factors

Photoperiod: Agrostemma is a long day rosette plant (4). That is, plants remain vegetative (in a rosette) and stems do not elongate under short days. Transfer of plants to LD results in rapid stem elongation and subsequent flowering. Flowering occurs approximately 40 days after transfer to LD. The critical photoperiod (i.e., the length of the long day) is not known, but probably 12- to 14-hour days are necessary. Long days are needed for initiation and subsequent flower development (1).

Temperature: Plants are cool-season crops. Yield and stem length decline as temperatures rise. Plants planted in April in north Georgia (zone 7b) died by late July. In warm climates, harvesting is completed within 4–6 weeks.

Field Performance

Spacing: Plants are normally spaced 9" apart but may be planted as close as 6" × 6" or as wide as 18" centers. Field-sown plants may be spaced on 6–9" centers.

Yield: Plants were trialed in north Georgia at different spacings to evaluate the yield and stem quality. Stems harvested June–July.

The effect of spacing on yield and stem quality of *Agrostemma* **'Purple Queen' (Athens, GA).**

Spacing (in)	Stems/ plant	Stems/ft^2	Stem length (in)
12	2.3	2.3	24.0
15	2.5	1.1	22.6
24	2.9	0.7	22.9

Each stem carries 4–6 flowers. Although yield/plant and stem length slightly increase with greater spacing, the differences are not dramatic. The yield/ft^2 declines rapidly as spacing increases, therefore close spacing is recommended.

Direct sowing: Seed broadcast over 150 ft^2 on February 15 in Athens, GA, resulted in 806 stems (5.4 stems/ft^2) with an average stem length of 26.1". This is a significantly higher yield than from plants spaced on 12" centers (see previous table), but flowering time and stem length were not different. Direct sowing is useful in climates where seed may be sown early. Two to three successive sowings, 2 weeks apart, early in the season are most useful.

Greenhouse Performance

Plants can be produced in the greenhouse although stem prices are seldom high enough to justify greenhouse production. To force flowers, space transplants 6–12" apart and maintain under short days (<12 hours) until plants are well rosetted. Temperatures of 55–60F result in optimum growth. Incandescent lamps to provide 10–20 fc of light may then be used to provide LD. Lights should then be used to extend the daylength to 16 hours and continued until flowers appear. Flowers occur 6–7 weeks after the beginning of LD. Fertilize with 100–200 ppm N until flowers show color.

Stage of Harvest
Stems should be harvested when 1–2 flowers are open on the inflorescence.

Postharvest
Place cut stems immediately in a postharvest solution in the field prior to grading. Place in fresh solution and store upright in 40F cooler after grading. Stems may be shipped dry.

Cultivars
'Milos' has lilac-pink flowers with dark veins.
'Purple Queen' produces purple-rose flowers.

Additional Species
No other species of *Agrostemma* are used.

Pests and Diseases
Leaf spots and aphids are the most serious diseases of corn cockle.

Related Genera
Various species of *Lychnis*, a short-lived perennial, are similar. *Lychnis coronaria* (rose campion) and *L. coeli-rosa* (rose of heaven) have potential as cut flowers.

Reading
1. Jones, M. G., and J. A. D. Zeevaart. 1980. Gibberellins and the photoperiodic control of stem elongation in the long day plant *Agrostemma githago* L. *Planta* 149:274–279.
2. Kingsbury, J. A. 1964. *Poisonous Plants of the United States and Canada.* Prentice Hall, Englewood Cliffs, NJ. 245–246.
3. Seals, J. 1991. Some uncommon and common (but choice) cut flowers from seed for field growing. *The Cut Flower Quarterly* 3(2):13–14.
4. Zeevaart, J. A. D. 1989. *Agrostemma githago.* In A. H. Halevy (ed.), *The Handbook of Flowering,* vol. 6. CRC Press, Boca Raton, FL. 15–21.

Amaranthus caudatus

	Love-lies-bleeding	4–6'/2'
Red, green	Tropics	Amaranthaceae

Plants bear drooping, deep red flowers on 12–15" long racemes. Although I find plants of this genus rather gaudy, my friend Jo Brownold set me straight. As she says, "Not every cut or dried flower needs the grace of lilies or the charm of larkspur. Amaranths have long histories as food, religious and ceremonial plants; their use as ornamentals is just the latest chapter." They may be used fresh or dried, and their ease of cultivation makes them attractive to small growers looking for colorful additions to their crop palette.

Propagation

Seed: In the greenhouse, lightly cover seed in a peat/perlite medium and place under mist at 70–74F. Germination occurs in 7–10 days. Approximately 1/16 oz (2 grams) of seed yields 1000 plants (4). Most amaranth seed is direct-sown.

Seed may be directly sown in the field after potential for frost has passed. Sow at the rate of 0.17 oz/100 linear ft or 2 oz/1000 ft^2.

Growing-on

If transplants are used, plants may be transplanted to final containers about 3 weeks from sowing. Grow at 62–65F until ready to transplant to the field. Fertilize sparingly with 50–75 ppm N once a week. Green plants (plants not in flower) are generally ready for field planting 6–7 weeks from sowing.

Environmental Factors

Photoperiod: *Amaranthus* is a short day plant, although critical daylengths may be as high as 16 hours (2,5). Plants provided with 8-hour photoperiods flower 1.5–2 times faster than those provided with 16-hour photoperiods (1,3). Generally plants become sensitive to short days after a 4-week juvenile period (5).

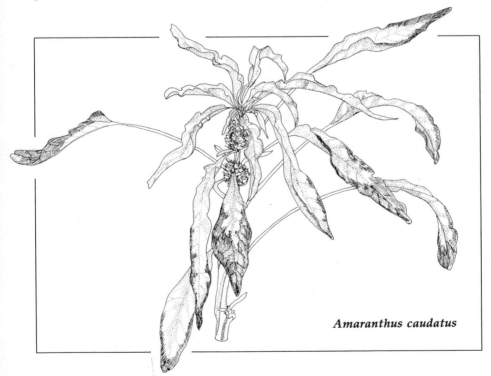

Amaranthus caudatus

Light intensity: Full sun is best; flowering time is delayed and plants become significantly taller under shade regardless of daylengths (3).

Temperature: No cold treatment (vernalization) is necessary for *Amaranthus*. Warm temperatures (above 70F) result in faster flowering than cool temperatures (below 65F), particularly under long days (3).

Field Performance

Spacing: If plants are transplanted, spacing of 12" × 12" to 12" × 15" are common. Closer spacing (<9" centers) results in spindly stems.

Irrigation: Infrequent, deep irrigation is best. Overwatering can cause plants to fall over, especially if overhead irrigation is used.

Fertilization: Lightly or not at all in the field.

Support: Although stems are relatively sturdy, 1–2 layers of support netting are useful to prevent stems from falling over in areas of frequent summer rainfall.

Shading: Not necessary except where longer stems are required. Shading will delay flowering and increase stem length and leaf number. Too much shade (>30%) results in tall but weak stems.

Greenhouse Performance

Transplant to ground beds or 8–10" pots, and place in full sun under long days of at least 17 hours. Place under natural short days or SD of 8–10 hours when plants are approximately 2' tall. Fertilize with 75–100 ppm N using a complete nitrogen fertilizer (e.g., 20–20–20, 15–16–17). Maintain temperatures of 68–70F during long days, and reduce to 60–65F during short days. Reduce further to 55F 5–7 days prior to harvesting to enhance color.

Support is necessary.

Stage of Harvest

For fresh flowers, cut when at least ¾ of the flowers on the inflorescence are open. If producing dried flowers, allow the flowers of all species to grow until seed has begun to set and the flowers feel firm to the touch. If picked too early, they shrivel to thin strings. Harvest the main flowers and allow side flowers to develop.

Postharvest

Fresh: Flowers persist approximately 7–10 days in water. Store at 36–41F but no longer than 7 days.

Dried: Flowers may be air-dried. Hang upside down to dry for approximately 10 days.

Cultivars

var. *atropurpureus* has blood-red leaves and is usually more dwarf than the species.

var. *roseus* bears rose-pink tassels on 4–5' tall plants. One of the more handsome choices in the species.

var. *viridis* has hanging, yellow-green spikes which are not overly appealing.

Additional Species

Amaranthus bicolor is grown for the yellow-on-green, two-tone foliage. This species is also known as *A. gangeticus* var. *melancholicus* 'Bicolor'. 'Illumination' has orange-scarlet flowers. 'Early Splendor' is taller and shows color about 2 weeks earlier than 'Molten Fire' (*A. tricolor*).

A. cruentus (red cathedral) has erect, blood-red panicles and grows 3–4' tall.

A. hypochondriacus (prince's feather) grows 4–5' tall and has purple or purplish green foliage with deep crimson, densely packed, erect panicles. This is sometimes listed as *A. cruentus* 'Oeschberg'. 'Green Thumb' bears yellow-green flowers and grows 1–2' tall. It is useful for designers who seek green tones. 'Pygmy Torch' has brilliant crimson flowers but the height of 1–1.5' may be a little short for cut flowers.

A. splendens (joseph's coat) has multicolored foliage of brown, dark green, red and golden yellow. Flowers are bright red. This is also referred to as *A. gangeticus* var. *melancholicus* 'Splendens'. 'Perfecta' has red, yellow and green foliage.

A. tricolor has three-colored foliage, usually in hues of yellow, green and red. This species is also known as *A. gangeticus* var. *melancholicus* 'Tricolor'. 'Molten Fire' has crimson foliage. It is particularly useful for shock value.

Pests and Diseases

Few serious pests or diseases affect ornamental amaranths. I think they are scared of them.

Reading

1. Kigel, J., and B. Rubin. 1985. *Amaranthus*. In A. H. Halevy (ed.), *The Handbook of Flowering*, vol. 1. CRC Press, Boca Raton, FL. 427–433.

2. Kohdi, R. K., and S. Sawhney. 1979. Promotory effect of GA on flowering of *Amaranthus*, a short day plant. *Biol. Plant.* 21:206–213.

3. Koller, D., J. Kigel, I. Nir and M. Ofir. 1975. Environmental control of weed physiology. Final report. Project A10-CR27. USDA Washington, DC.

4. Seals, J. 1991. Some uncommon and common (but choice) cut flowers from seed for field growing. *The Cut Flower Quarterly* 3(2):13–14.

5. Zabda, J. J. 1961. Photoperiodism in *Amaranthus caudatus*. *Amer. J. Bot.* 48:21–28.

Many thanks to Ms. Jo Brownold for reviewing this section.

Ammi majus	False Queen Anne's Lace	2–3'/2'
White	Europe, Asia, N. Africa	Apiaceae

Relatively new to the cut flower market, *Ammi* is now produced throughout the United States, Europe and South America. Approximately 6 species occur, but only *A. majus* is grown commercially. The white flowers are similar to the common roadside weed, queen anne's lace, thus its common name.

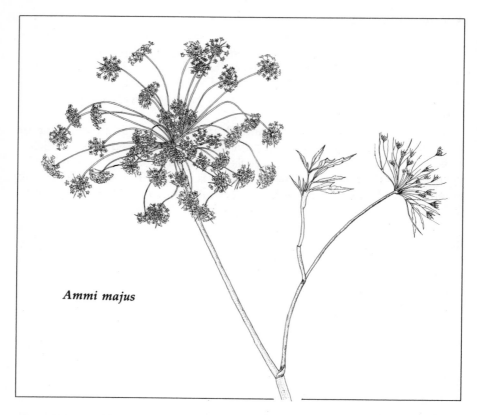

Ammi majus

Although native to the Old World, the species appears to be as adaptable to Alabama as it is to Arizona.

Harvesting of *A. majus* requires the use of gloves and protective clothing. The sap of the cut stems may result in severe contact dermatitis in sensitive individuals. Serious cases may cause permanent scars.

Propagation

Seed: In the greenhouse, chill seed at 40–45F for 1–2 weeks prior to sowing. Sow in 200-cell plugs or directly to the field. In controlled environments, cover seed lightly and place at alternating day/night temperatures of 68/86F (2). Germination of prechilled seed placed at alternating temperatures is approximately 75–80%, otherwise germination may be well below 50%. Germination occurs in 7–14 days. Approximately 1/16 oz of seed yields 1000 plants.

Seed may be sown directly in the field in the fall (this is a must in southern areas) or early spring. Temperatures may fall to as low as 18F during the winter. Night temperatures should be consistently below 50F for best germination. Sow 0.35 oz/100 linear ft or 3.5 oz/1000 ft^2. The seed is small (54,000 seeds/oz) and spacing is often dictated by available equipment. Germination is often better in the field than in the greenhouse because of natural alternating temperatures. If sown in the field in the summer, chill the seed prior to planting. Two to three successive sowings, 2 weeks apart are often used.

Growing-on

If not direct-sown, transplant seedlings to 2–3" containers approximately 3 weeks after sowing or maintain in 200-cell plugs for 4–5 weeks. Fertilize with 50–75 ppm N after transplanting. Temperatures of 58–62F are recommended to establish the seedlings. Place in the field when plants are large enough to handle (approx. 3 weeks after transplanting).

Environmental Factors

No photoperiod response is known. Plants do not perform well at temperatures above 85F and are best handled as a winter crop in zones 8–10. In areas where summer temperatures are not excessive (zones 3–7), it is a useful summer crop. Total crop time from greenhouse sowing to flowering in the field is approximately 15 weeks (3).

Field Performance

Yield: Plants transplanted to 12" centers yielded 4–6 stems/plant at Maryland (1). Spring planting is important because plants should be 3–4' tall prior to budding up. If they flower before 3', they have probably been planted too late. Plants which were transplanted on April 2 in Kentucky flowered in late May. Eight to twelve stems/plant with stem lengths of 18–24" occurred over a 4- to 5-week harvest period (3).

Spacing: Direct sow in fall (South), after danger of heavy frost in the North (see "Propagation" for rates) or transplant 9–12" apart. If spring planting, transplant no later than April 20 in the South, May 15 in the Midwest, May 21 in the North. Late frosts, after warm spring temperatures, may result in significant losses.

Support: Plants can grow 5–6' tall and should be supported with at least 1 tier of mesh, 2 layers if spring rains are common. Without fail, torrential rain storms will occur the day before harvest. Each small, perfect blossom collects water, and without support, plants will no doubt end up in the mud. The lateral stems do not always grow straight, and although the twists and curves cause problems with bunching, they are handsome and should still be marketable.

Greenhouse Performance

Transplant to ground beds in January and February for flowering plants in May and June. Start plants under night temperatures of 60–63F to establish the crop. After 2–4 weeks, reduce night temperatures to 55–60F until flowering.

Stage of Harvest

Harvest when approximately 80% of the flowers in the umbel are open. Flowers cut too early (½ open) do not take up water and tend to wilt. The flowers should be a crisp white with only the slightest green tint and no hint of pollen shed. Once pollen sheds, flowers decline rapidly. This is an excellent local item because it is difficult to cut at the proper stage if plants are to be shipped long distances. Some growers cut the initial center flower with only a 6–12" stem length allowing the secondary flowers to bloom on 20–24" long stems.

Postharvest

Fresh: Flowers persist for 5–8 days in preservative. They may be stored at 37–40F for approximately 1 week.

Dried: Flowers may be air-dried for 2–3 weeks in a dark, dry place. Darkness is necessary to maintain green stems and keep the white flowers from browning.

Cultivars

'Snowflake' has 2–3" wide flower heads and grows 3' tall.

'White Dill' has been selected from the species and bears flowers which are slightly whiter; otherwise, plants are the same.

Related Genera

Daucus carota (queen anne's lace) is a popular filler for eastern and southern growers. The species is biennial; two years are necessary for efficient flowering. Many growers simply cut from roadside populations which, if done too aggressively, may result in significant decline in plant numbers. Plants may be easily grown from seed and planted in the field. Populations can be continued through self-seeding.

Reading

1. Healy, W., and S. Aker. 1989. Cut flower field studies, 1989. HE 141-89. Univ. of Maryland Hort. Production, Co-op Ext. Serv.

2. Nau, J. 1989. *Ball Culture Guide: The Encyclopedia of Seed Germination*. Ball Seed Co., West Chicago, IL.

3. White-Mays, L. 1992. *Ammi majus*, false queen anne's lace. In *Proceedings of the 4th National Conference on Specialty Cut Flowers*. Cleveland, OH. 38–40.

Many thanks to Mr. Knud Nielsen III and Ms. Linda White-Mays for reviewing this section.

Antirrhinum majus   Snapdragon   3–4'/2'

Various colors   Mediterranean   Scrophulariaceae

The market for snapdragons fluctuates a great deal, primarily due to over- and underproduction. When prices are poor, production is decreased and, in time, prices become sufficiently strong to warrant additional production volume, resulting in another cycle. The length of time the highs persist is directly related to the number of growers producing snapdragons. While this is true of all crops, snaps seem to be buffeted around more than most. In the

Antirrhinum majus

1990s, the market for snapdragons appears to be strong and getting stronger. Snapdragons and anemones have become the carnations of the '90s.

There is always a market for spike flowers, and few species can provide the range of colors and strength of stem commonplace in today's cultivars. Crops are often greenhouse-produced, but may also be produced in the field in the spring in the far west and south, and in the summer further north. They have similar cultural requirements as other cool-loving plants such as larkspur, lupines and delphiniums. In areas where winters are sufficiently cold for flower production but not so cold as to damage or destroy the plants, early spring production in the field is feasible.

Propagation

All plants are raised from seed, generally in a "200" or "400" plug tray. For optimum germination, seed should be sown, watered in and cooled at 40F for 2 weeks (6). After cooling, germinate at 72F under mist or sweat tent. Although cooling is beneficial, it is not a requirement; if it is not possible to provide cooling, commence germination temperatures immediately. Seedlings should emerge in 7–14 days. Approximately 1/64 to 1/32 oz (0.7 grams) of seed yields 1000 seedlings, depending on cultivar (6).

Growing-on

After plants have 3–5 true leaves, grow at 50–55F night temperature. Maintain day temperatures as close to 60F as possible. Warm temperatures cause stem elongation, resulting in lanky transplants. Fertilize at approximately 200 ppm N when grown in warm temperatures, reduce by half when growing at 50–55F. Transplant to field or greenhouse as soon as plants can be handled without damage (usually 5–6 weeks). In spring (late March through early May, depending on frost dates), transplant to the field. In areas where fall transplanting may be accomplished, transplant in mid-September through early November. In the greenhouse, transplanting may take place year-round.

Environmental Factors

Photoperiod: The snapdragon is essentially a quantitative long day plant, meaning that it is capable of flowering under short days but flowers earlier and at a lower leaf number in LD (3,5). Although this is a typical response, some cultivars are virtually unaffected by daylength, particularly the late-flowering ones. Plants grown under SD produce more vegetative growth, while LD mainly affects the initiation of flowers. Once initiated, the subsequent development is relatively unaffected by daylength (5). Photoperiod also affects the juvenile stage, that is, the number of leaves which must form before flowers occur. The minimum number of leaves is higher under SD than LD (1). Greenhouse (forcing) cultivars have been bred to flower virtually at any time of year under natural daylenths; photoperiod is less important today than it was for older cultivars.

Light intensity: Snapdragons flower with stronger stems, more rapidly and with higher yields under high light. Low light results in more blind shoots and reduces in yield and stem quality. Light intensity is more of a concern for winter greenhouse production than field production. Some winter cultivars have been bred for low light response and may be used for winter production.

Temperature: Snapdragons have no vernalization requirement and those grown cool (50F or below) initiate and open flowers later than those grown warmer (4,5). Although warm temperatures hasten flowering, it reduces spike length and stem strength (8). During summer temperatures, stem strength is poor in the field in the Southeast.

Field Performance

Planting time: In the Midwest and North, plant as soon as ground can be worked in the spring. Harden transplants by putting greenhouse plantlets outside during the day or placing them in cold frames day and night for about 2 weeks prior to planting out. If properly hardened off, plants can survive 25–28F frosts; if not hardened, they will produce snapper soup. In the South, plant in September through early November. In north Georgia, 5F temperatures were recorded in late December and plants flowered well the next spring. Plants had, however, gone through a cool fall. The major cultivars for field production are the Rockets and Potomacs (see "Cultivars").

Spacing: Plant on approximately 9–12" centers. Two to three rows in a 3' wide bed are often used. If plants are to be pinched, place on 12–15" centers.

Yield: In Maryland, yields of crops planted out on April 15 produced averages of 7 and 10 stems/plant for Potomac and Rocket strains, respectively (2).

Fertilization: Side dress with a complete fertilizer as soon as temperatures warm up.

Shade: Shade is not necessary, but growing under cloth tents (such as cheesecloth) results in longer stems and better quality flowers. In snapdragons, pollination results in petal shatter. The absence of bees under the tent will assure more persistent flowers.

Greenhouse Performance

Cultivar selection is very important in greenhouse production. Winter cultivars should be selected for winter forcing, summer varieties for summer (see "Cultivars"). Talk with a seed supplier for the best cultivars for a particular area and season. Transplant to ground beds as close as 9" apart or as wide as 15" apart. After transplanting, provide as much light as possible. If cultivars are properly selected, manipulation of photoperiod is not particularly important nor generally practiced. However, providing LD (12–16 hours) ensures flowering. Set temperatures to 50–55F throughout the crop cycle. Higher temperatures during the day are unavoidable in most areas, and occasional 70F temperatures are not detrimental, if not too persistent. Fertilize with a complete liquid fertilizer (150–200 ppm N and K) which is low in ammonium at each irrigation or double the concentration if feeding only once a week. Fertilize only until flower buds begin to swell. At least 2 tiers of support are needed, the bottom one about 12" from the soil. The use of a cheesecloth cover inhibits pollination by bees.

Stage of Harvest

For local production, harvest flowers when ½ to ⅔ of the flowers are open. This would consist of 10 or more open flowers on the stem. For long distance shipping, stems may be harvested when ⅓ of the flowers are open (5–7 open flowers) (9). For long-term storage or if preservatives are to be used, flowers can be cut as early as 2–3 buds showing color (7).

Postharvest

Fresh: Fresh flowers persist up to 5–8 days in water; they will persist a little longer if treated with STS. Treatment with STS pulse (1 hour) is common, although it does not always provide additional vase life. Differences in STS efficacy may be due to cultivar differences or treatment variability.

Storage: Stems may be stored at 40F for 3–4 days either dry or wet. If wrapped in plastic film to reduce desiccation, they may be stored up to 10 days. Preservatives and temperature have been shown to affect wet storage. At 32–35F, storage can occur for 1–2 weeks in water, 4–8 weeks in a preservative (7). Use a fungicide to inhibit *Botrytis* spp. if storing for more than 4 days. A bud-opening solution should be used after long-term storage. Place stems in solution at 70F, 75–85% RH, 16-hour daylengths and high light intensity (approx. 200 fc) (7). Long-term storage can result in poor flower development and faded color (8). Always store and ship stems upright. Ship stems in refrigerated trucks, even if travelling a short distance. Warm temperatures such as those found in airport loading docks are disastrous. Maintaining cool temperatures is essential.

Dried: Flowers may be dried in warm air but the use of silica gel will improve color retention (10).

Grading

The Society of American Florists (SAF) has developed grading standards for snapdragons.

| Grade | Weight/stem (oz) | | Min. open flowers/stem | Min. stem length (in) |
	Min.	Max.		
Blue (special)	2.5	4.0	15	36
Red (fancy)	1.5	2.4	12	30
Green (extra)	1.0	1.4	9	24
Yellow (first)	0.5	0.9	6	18

Cultivars

Outdoor: Rocket, Maryland and Potomac strains are the 3 main forms used for outdoor production. Potomac appears to be more resistant to rust than Rocket (2). In north Georgia, the Liberty strain, a greenhouse (forcing) variety, was also successful. For additional forcing types, contact seed suppliers in your area.

Greenhouse: Four main groups for forcing snaps are offered based on the environment under which they are grown. Growers in the North may use all cultivars from all groups, while those in the South should use groups III and IV only. A few are listed but many more are available from a reputable seed supplier. Some cultivars perform equally well in more than one group.

Group	Environment	Cultivars (examples only)
I	Short days, low light, low temperature	'Bismarck' (pink), 'Cheyenne' (yellow), 'Oakland' (white)
II	Short days, moderate light, low temperature	'Bismarck', 'Cheyenne', 'Maryland Pink', 'Oakland'
III	Moderate day length, medium to high light, low to medium temperature	'Pan American Summer Pink', 'Potomac Ivory', 'Potomac Yellow', 'Potomac White'
IV	Long days, high light, warm temperature	'Potomac Ivory', 'Potomac Yellow', 'Winchester' (pink)

Pests and Diseases

High humidity, overhead watering and debris around the plants increases the incidence of botrytis. Spray with proper fungicide and keep area clear of plant trash.

Rust is one of the most serious diseases of snapdragons. Brown pustules break out in large numbers surrounded by yellowish areas of leaf tissue. Selecting rust-resistant cultivars is important and increasing spacing density is helpful. Avoid overhead watering. The use of a preventative application of fungicide should be practiced. Once rust begins, it is most difficult to eradicate.

Aphids, spider mites and caterpillars are the most troublesome pests on snapdragon.

Reading

1. Cockshull, K. E. 1985. *Antirrhinum majus*. In A. H. Halevy (ed.), *The Handbook of Flowering*, vol. 1. CRC Press, Boca Raton, FL. 476–481.

2. Healy, W., and S. Aker. 1989. Production techniques for fresh cut annuals. In *Proceedings of Commercial Field Production of Cut and Dried Flowers*. Univ. of Minnesota, The Center for Alternative Crops and Products, St. Paul, MN. 139–146.

3. Laurie, A., and G. H. Poesch. 1932. Photoperiodism—the value of supplementary illumination and reduction of light on flowering plants in the greenhouse. Ohio Agr. Exp. Sta. Bul. 512:1–42.

4. Maginnes, E. A., and R. W. Langhans. 1960. Daylength and temperature affect flower initiation and flowering of snapdragons. NY State Flower Growers Bul. 171(1).

5. _____ . 1961. The effect of photoperiod and temperature on initiation and flowering of snapdragon (*Antirrhinum majus*-variety Jackpot). *Proc. Amer. Soc. Hort. Sci.* 77:600–607.

6. Nau, J. 1989. *Ball Culture Guide: The Encyclopedia of Seed Germination.* Ball Seed Co., West Chicago, IL.

7. Nowak, J., and R. M. Rudnicki. 1990. *Postharvest Handling and Storage of Cut Flowers, Florist Greens, and Potted Plants.* Timber Press, Portland, OR.

8. Post, K. 1955. *Florist Crop Production and Marketing.* Orange Judd, New York, NY.

9. Sacalis, J. N. 1989. *Fresh (Cut) Flowers for Designs: Postproduction Guide* I, D. C. Kiplinger Chair in Floriculture, The Ohio State Univ., Columbus, OH.

10. Vaughan, M. J. 1988. *The Complete Book of Cut Flower Care.* Timber Press, Portland, OR.

Many thanks to Mr. Peter Nissen for reviewing this section.

Cacalia spp. see *Emilia javanica*

Callistephus chinensis	China Aster	1–3'/2'
Various colors	China	Asteraceae

China asters have undergone significant breeding to develop cultivars for bedding plants and cut flowers. Numerous flower colors, including pastels, bright blues and electric reds, are presently available. Although popular in many circles, the main drawbacks of china asters are the relatively low yields and susceptibility to disease. China aster, an annual, should not be confused with perennial asters which are included in the section on perennials.

Propagation

Seed germinates in approximately 14 days if placed under intermittent mist at 70–72F. Approximately 1/5 oz of seed yields 1000 plants (9). Seed may also be direct-sown in the field in early spring at the rate of 0.35 oz/100 linear ft for summer production.

Growing-on

Seedlings should be transplanted to cell packs or 3–4" pots at the first true leaf stage, then grown at 70/60–62F day/night until roots are well established. Do not allow plants to become root bound. Maintain plants under long days of approximately 15 hours with incandescent lights when natural short days occur. Fertilize with 50–75 ppm N with potassium or calcium nitrate.

Environmental Factors

Photoperiod: Flowers develop most rapidly when a period of long days (LD) is followed by short days (SD) (2). That is, plants are "primed" or induced to flower under LD and then develop more rapidly under SD after induction. If plants are provided with continuous LD, they flower more slowly but on longer stems than those which are exposed only to SD, a useful characteristic for cut flower production. Flowering of laterals is also delayed when plants do not receive SD treatment (6) . Approximately 4–5 weeks of LD are necessary to "prime" the plant for SD treatment. Less than 4 weeks of LD followed by SD do not accelerate flowering compared with plants which receive only SD. The critical LD photoperiod is approximately 14 hours and satisfactory LD effects can be obtained by a 16-hour day extension with incandescent lights or with continuous light (3). In summary, research indicates that for pot plant use, 3–4 weeks of LD should be followed by SD for compact, rapidly flowering specimens. However, for cut flower production, LD should be continued until harvest.

Recent work at Colorado State University (5,6) with modern cultivars verified much of the older research. The following table summarizes the effects of photoperiod on numerous growth and flowering characteristics.

The effect of photoperiod on growth and flowering of *Callistephus chinensis.*[a]

Photoperiod	Time to flower (days)	Stem length (in)	Breaks
Continuous SD	49	17.5	5
1 wk LD, then SD	51	17.4	5
2 wk LD, then SD	53	19.5	4
3 wk LD, then SD	56	23.5	4
4 wk LD, then SD	57	25.0	4
5 wk LD, then SD	62	25.2	4

[a]Adapted from (5,6).

In this work, the highest-quality flowers occurred with 3 or 4 weeks of LD, followed by SD.

Long days also promote leaf expansion, stem extension and dry matter accumulation but slightly inhibited the formation of lateral breaks (see previous table) (5). The promotion of flower development due to SD inhibits stem elongation.

Temperature: A pronounced interaction between temperature and photoperiod occurs in china asters. Plants grown at 55F or below flower only if LD are provided but remain as basal rosettes if grown under SD. Raising the temperature from 55F to 68F resulted in 16 days earlier flowering when plants were grown under LD, but the effect was considerably greater when plants were grown under SD (1).

Field Performance

Field production has been difficult because of the plant's susceptibility to aster yellows virus. The virus is carried by leafhoppers which must be controlled. Asters historically have been grown under cloth in the field to reduce the incidence of these hopping bugs.

Flowers of spray asters are generally harvested approximately 8 weeks after transplanting to the field. Early flowering in the field may be stimulated by placing seedlings under LD immediately after they come out of the propagation area. For example, seedlings resulting from February and March sowings should receive 4-hour nightbreak lighting and temperatures above 62F until planted in the field. Since natural photoperiod outside is less than 14 hours when transplanted to the field, flowering will occur on significantly longer stems than on seedlings grown under natural SD in the greenhouse.

Spacing: Space plants as close as 4" × 4" or up to 1' apart depending on the cultivar grown and weed control practices. A spacing of 6" × 6" (approx. 4 plants/ft^2) is typical.

Shading: China asters stretch appreciably if grown under shade cloth (8). This may be useful in the South where shading is used to reduce heat in the field. Use of shade cloth also inhibits the entry of leafhoppers. Cloth for exclusion of hoppers should have approximately 22 threads/inch.

Yield: Work at the University of Maryland (7) showed yields of approximately 3 flowers/plant when only the main stems were harvested (all lateral shoots included with the main stem) and relatively short stem length (<20" long) with many cultivars of china asters. At the University of Kentucky, yields of approximately 3 stems/ft^2 were recorded with a spacing of 4 plants/ft^2. Stems averaged approximately 18" in length (10). Although yields are significantly better in coastal California, stems of 'Matsumoto' only averaged 12–18" in length. When all flowers were harvested separately (laterals and main stem) at Georgia, 22 stems/plant with an average stem length of 15" occurred during a 3-week period in the summer. Lateral stems should be disbudded and some of the lower branches removed for best quality flowers.

Greenhouse Performance

Asters may be grown year-round but prices are traditionally higher in fall and winter. Seed sown August 1 and grown under LD (incandescent lights) until flowering results in flowers in late November at 42° latitude. Plant on 4" (high light) to 8" (low light) centers. On a year-round program, Dr. Ken Goldsberry from Colorado State University found that at least 5 crops (unpinched) per square foot of bench could be realized under Colorado conditions. He grew single-stem plants in cell packs under long days, then moved them to 6" pots (3 plants/pot) containing pea gravel when the foliage covered the entire cell pack. Continuous feed and carbon dioxide were applied. Asters are highly sensitive to nightbreak lighting or light drift and less than 1 fc is effective in stimulating stem elongation. Therefore, spotlights or floodlights are effective means of lighting large areas of the greenhouse. Daylength control is particularly important in southern Florida, where temperatures are always sufficiently warm for growth but winter daylengths are usually too short to promote stem elongation.

Scheduling: Other excellent work in Colorado demonstrated that with night temperatures of 60–62F and 70F days, asters flowered approximately 4 months from sowing. There was a progressive increase in flowering lateral stems as planting date was delayed from December to March (5). At night temperatures of 50F, approximately 5 months are necessary in the fall and winter from seed to flower; 4 months are required in spring and summer. At warmer temperatures, crop time may be slightly reduced, although in Kentucky, 14 weeks appears to be as fast as plants can develop (10). Temperatures above 70F should be avoided in the greenhouse.

Stage of Harvest

Harvest terminal when outside ray florets begin to open.

Postharvest

Fresh: The vase life is 5–7 days and generally the foliage wilts before the flower declines. Neck droop may also occur, resulting in shortened vase life. A 10-second pulse in 1000 ppm solution of silver nitrate significantly extended the vase life (4). Asters treated with silver nitrate may be stored up to 1 week at 33–35F. Use caution when working with silver nitrate.

Dried: Harvest when flowers are fully open. Allow leaves to remain on stems and hang in small bunches upside down to dry. Flowers may also be dried in a desiccant such as silica gel.

Cultivars

Many cultivars are available from American and European seed companies. One Dutch catalogue alone offers more than 120 different cultivars suitable for cut flowers.

American Beauty mix produces 3" wide, double flowers on 2–3' tall stems in many colors.

Ball Florist mix is an old favorite consisting of 3" wide flowers of white, pink, blue, rose and purple.

'Bouquet Powderpuffs' has 2–2.5" wide, fully double flowers with no yellow centers. Plants grow 2–2.5' tall. Separate colors are available. Because of uniform flowering, the entire plant can be harvested at one time. Other Bouquet types are available in separate colors such as azure, blue, rose, purple, scarlet and white.

'Crego' bears a many-colored mixture of feathery, 3" wide flowers on 2' tall plants.

Emperor series bears 2.5" wide flowers on 2–3' tall stems. 'Emperor Carmine' and 'Emperor Red' have carmine and deep red flowers, respectively.

Florett strain is available in separate colors, including deep and pale pink, crimson, blue and a pastel "champagne" color. The 2–3" wide flowers consist of fully double quill forms and are produced on 3' tall stems.

Matador series is similar to Matsumoto but flowers are slightly smaller. Separate colors and a mix are available.

Matsumoto series produces sprays of 2–2.5" wide flowers with distinct yellow centers and has become one of the leading series of asters for cut flower production. Mixtures and separate colors are available. Plants have good fusarium disease resistance.

Perfection mixture produces 2–3' tall, 3–4" wide, fully double flowers with incurved petals.

Princess and Super Princess series are 3–3.5' tall with quilled petals. The "Super" designation refers to the larger flowers and stronger stems on this selection. Numerous cultivars in separate colors may be found under the Super Princess logo such as 'Alice' (light blue), 'Hilda' (light yellow), 'Scarletto' (copper-scarlet) and 'Victoria' (scarlet).

Prinette series has long, thin, curved outer petals and small, tubular center flowers. Flowers are available in pink and red. Plants were Fleuroselect winners.

Rainbow mixes may be ordered as single- or double-flowered forms. Flowers generally have a prominent yellow eye and are borne on 2–3' tall stems.

Serene series bears pompon spray flowers on 2' tall stems. Plants flower approximately 14 weeks after sowing. Light blue, red and rose colors are available.

'Sparkler' has double incurved flowers on 2–3' tall stems. Flowers are mainly available as a mixture.

Pests and Diseases

Aster yellows: Yellowing of all or part of the plant, distorted, malformed flowers (flowers partly or entirely greenish and yellow) and spindly stems are indications of infection by aster yellows virus. Affected plants may also exhibit considerably increased branching. The best means of control is to reduce or eliminate the population of leafhoppers which carry the virus. Once plants have been infected, they must be discarded. The use of soil sterilants reduces the incidence of the virus in the soil but crop rotation should be routinely practiced.

Aster wilt: Plants suddenly wilt, usually near maturity, when attacked by the aster wilt fungus (*Fusarium conglutinans* var. *callistephi*). The stem completely rots at the soil line and often a streak of blackened tissue extends up one side. The wilt fungus may be carried on the seed, which should be surface sterilized. The advent of wilt-resistant cultivars has greatly reduced the severity of this problem.

Aster spotted wilt: This disease causes streaks on the stems or circular patches on the foliage. Infected plants may exhibit increased branching and should be discarded. The wilt organism is spread by thrips, the presence of which must be controlled.

Root rot and rust: *Phytophthora cryptogea* and *Coleosporium solidaginis*, respectively, result in loss of yield and flower quality.

Leafhoppers, thrips, aphids and Japanese beetles cause significant damage or are responsible for the spread of disease. Thrips can wipe out greenhouse crops in the blink of an eye.

Caution: Asters are highly susceptible to some pesticides. Test spray a few plants to determine phytotoxicity.

Related Genera

Perennial asters such as *Aster ericoides* (september aster), *A. novae-angliae* (new england aster) and *A. novi-belgii* (new york aster) are becoming more popular as cut flowers. Their culture is covered in the section on perennials.

Reading

1. Biebel, J. 1936. Temperature, photoperiod, flowering and morphology in Cosmos and China aster. *Proc. Amer. Soc. Hort. Sci.* 34:635–643.

2. Cockshull, K. E. 1985. *Callistephus chinensis*. In A. H. Halevy (ed.), *The Handbook of Flowering*, vol. 2. CRC Press, Boca Raton, FL. 112–114.

3. Cockshull, K. E., and A. P. Hughes. 1969. Growth and dry-weight distribution in *Callistephus chinensis* as influenced by lighting treatment. *Ann. Bot.* 33:367–379.

4. Evans, R. Y., and M. S. Reid. 1990. Postharvest care of specialty cut flowers. In *Proceedings of 3rd National Conference on Specialty Cut Flowers*. Ventura, CA. 26–44.

5. Goldsberry, K. L., L. Kell-Gunderson and R. Silver. 1988. Scheduling single stem Japanese cut asters. Part 1. Winter and spring responses of Japanese cut asters. CSU Research Bul. 462.

6. _____. 1989. Scheduling single stem Japanese cut asters. Part 2. Winter and spring responses of Japanese cut asters. CSU Research Bul. 463.

7. Healy, W., and S. Aker. 1989. Cut flower field studies, 1989. HE 141–89. Univ. of Maryland Hort. Production, Co-op Ext. Serv.

8. Post, K. 1955. *Florist Crop Production and Marketing*. Orange Judd, New York, NY.

9. Seals, J. 1991. Some uncommon and common (but choice) cut flowers from seed for field growing. *The Cut Flower Quarterly* 3(2):13–14.

10. Utami, L., R. G. Anderson, R. L. Geneve and S. Kester. 1990. Quality and yield of *Ageratum*, *Aster*, *Celosia* and *Godetia* grown as field grown cut flowers. *HortScience* 25:851. (Abstr.)

Many thanks to Drs. Bob Anderson, Ken Goldsberry and Will Healy for reviewing this section.

Carthamus tinctorius	Safflower	2–3'/2'
Orange-red	Europe, Asia	Asteraceae

As hard as I try to like this flower, its beauty still eludes me. Flowers always seem to appear ragged and bedraggled and in need of tidying up. However, safflower has been harvested for many years and its popularity has withstood the test of time and Armitage. Fortunately for safflower growers, I am not a flower buyer. Flowers may be dried which means we can be assailed with safflower all year long.

Propagation

Sow seed and cover lightly to permit exposure to light. If placed under mist at 68–72F, seed germinates in 10–14 days. Approximately 3 oz of seed yield 1000 plants (1). Seed may be directly sown into the field or bench at the rate of 1.6 oz/100 linear ft.

Growing-on

Plants should be grown at 65F night temperature to establish seedlings. Little nutrition is needed at this stage but fertilization with 50–75 ppm N is beneficial. Plants are ready to transplant to final location in 8–10 weeks.

Environmental Factors

No studies on safflower responses to the environment could be located. The plants do not appear to have significant photoperiodic responses.

Field Performance

Spacing: If transplanting, space on 9–12" centers.

Shading: Grow in full sun in northern areas but the addition of 30–40% shade is beneficial in the South.

Greenhouse Performance

Plants resulting from seed sown in January can be harvested in early spring (12–16 weeks later). Space transplants as close as 6" × 6" or as far as 10" × 10". Plants should be fertilized with 100–150 ppm N once or twice a week with a nitrate source of fertilizer. Support may be necessary, particularly if a high-density planting is used.

Stage of Harvest

Cut stems when the majority of buds have begun to open and color is clearly visible. If harvested before onset of color, most buds do not open.

Postharvest

Fresh: The flowers persist for about 1 week in water but the foliage declines more rapidly. The foliage is often removed at harvest or grading due to its short vase life and somewhat thorny feel. Plants do not store well, but if storage is necessary, they may be placed in water or preservative at 35–40F.

Dried: Flowers may be air-dried.

Cultivars

'Early Round Leaved' has rounded leaves and bears 1" wide orange or white flowers on 3–4' tall stems.

'Goldtuft' bears fuzzy balls of golden orange on 2–3' tall stems. One of the most popular cultivars for cutting.

'Lasting Orange', 'Lasting Tangerine' and 'Lasting White' are spineless (a definite advantage) and grow 2–3' tall.

'Shiro' has cream-white flowers that deepen to light yellow as the flowers age.

'Tall Splendid Orange' bears orange-yellow flowers on 3' tall stems.

Pests and Diseases
Root rots can be a problem in warm climates and poorly drained soils. Aphids are a serious pest.

Reading
1. Nau, J. 1989. *Ball Culture Guide: The Encyclopedia of Seed Germination.* Ball Seed Co., West Chicago, IL.

Caryopteris incana	Blue Spirea	2–4′/3′
Blue	China, Japan	Verbenaceae

Caryopteris incana produces many stems of whorled, lavender-blue flowers and dark green foliage. Some authorities believe that the species is a hybrid and it may be listed as *C.* × *bungei.* Flowers are produced in late summer and fall and have outstanding potential as a cut flower both in the field and the greenhouse.

Caryopteris incana

Propagation

Seed: Seed sown at 70–75F under high humidity or intermittent mist germinates in approximately 12 days. Transplanting seedlings is most common but seed may also be direct-sown. Approximately ¼ oz of seed yields 5000 plants.

Cuttings: Terminal cuttings (2–3″ long) of vegetative shoots may be taken during the summer. Application of low strength rooting hormones (IBA, NAA) is beneficial. Hormodin #1™ (1000 ppm IBA in talc) is beneficial. Roots appear in 7–10 days if bottom heat is applied.

Growing-on

Grow seedlings in low-density plugs, cell packs or 3″ pots. Fertilize with 50–75 ppm N using calcium nitrate for the first 2–3 weeks followed by 100–150 ppm N of a complete fertilizer. If produced in plugs, allow 5–7 weeks before planting out.

Environmental Factors

Photoperiod: Work at the University of Georgia showed that *Caryopteris* flowers faster under short days (8 hours) than long days (16 hours). Plants were intermediate in their flowering response when grown in 12-hour photoperiods. The following table summarizes some of the responses to photoperiod.

The effect of photoperiod on flowering and stem quality of *Caryopteris incana* (experiment terminated 100 days after start of photoperiod treatment).

Photoperiod (hr)	Time to flower (days)[a]	Stem length (in)
8	72	12.9
12	92	16.6
16	—[b]	15.3

[a] Time calculated from beginning of photoperiod treatment.
[b] Plants did not flower by end of experiment.

Although the above experiment was terminated after 100 days, plants eventually flowered even under long days.

Light intensity: In areas of hot summers and high light intensities, flower stems are longer and less brittle when grown under approximately 55% shade compared to full sun. Flowers also have a longer vase life when provided with some shade (see table at "Stage of Harvest").

Temperature: Plants grow rapidly under temperatures of 70–85F. Temperatures below 55F and above 85F reduce growth and flowering.

Field Performance

Yield: Crops grown at the University of Georgia trials produced approximately 48 marketable stems/plant with an average stem length of 25.8″. Plants were grown at 12″ × 12″ spacing and in both shade and sun.

Shading: In warm, bright summer climates, such as zones 7–10, the addition of 50–60% shade results in longer, less brittle flower stems, although as the next table shows, no differences in yield occurred regardless of shade or sun.

The effect of shade on yield and stem quality of *Caryopteris incana* **(experiment conducted summer, 1989; Athens, GA).**

Shade level (%)	Stems/plant	Stem length (in)
0	52	19.4
55	51	23.0

Shade is not necessary in areas of cooler summer temperatures. For example, growers in coastal California grow the crop in full sun and growers in the Northeast, Northwest and northern Plain states would likely not require shade.

Lateral breaks: Like many other crops, the main stem produces many lateral stems, all of which produce a flower. The dilemma for the cutter is whether to cut the long main stem and sacrifice the laterals, or cut a shorter main stem to allow some of the laterals to flower for subsequent harvest. The former method yields longer but fewer stems, while the latter results in many more stems, but shorter. The decision must be based on acceptability of certain standards for stem length and is determined by the market. The following table provides an example of the differences between harvesting techniques.

The effect of harvesting methods on yield and stem quality of *Caryopteris incana* **(40 plants used for each treatment).**

Harvesting method	Stems	Stem length (in)
1. Whole stem cut from base	40	30.8
2. Short terminal cut only,	40	16.5
then 1 harvest of subsequent laterals	261[a]	22.5

[a] From 1 harvest only. Over 1000 lateral stems were harvested from test plants over the season.

More labor and time is necessary to harvest by method 2 and market price must dictate its feasibility.

Greenhouse Performance

Little work has been attempted with this crop in the greenhouse, but preliminary results indicate that plantlets, plugs or cuttings should be spaced 9–12" apart in well-drained soils. Plants should be grown under long days (>16 hours) until they are 2–2.5' tall, then transferred to short days (<12 hours). Fertilize with 150–200 ppm N every other irrigation and support plants with greenhouse netting as needed. Preliminary studies in Georgia yielded 40 stems/plant over 3 harvests.

Guideline for Foliar Analyses

At field trials in Athens, GA, foliage was sampled from vigorously growing healthy plants when flower buds were visible, but prior to flower opening. These are guidelines only and should not be considered absolute standards. Numbers are the average of sun- and shade-grown plants and are based on dry weight analysis.

(%)						(ppm)				
N	P	K	Ca	Mg		Fe	Mn	B	Al	Zn
3.0	0.21	1.47	1.00	0.16		125	80	15	42	57

Stage of Harvest

Stems should be harvested when buds show color or when the first whorl (lowermost) of flowers is open. Later harvesting reduces vase life by approximately 3 days. The following table provides some additional information. Once cut, the stem continues to grow and flowers continue to develop.

The effect of stage of harvest and exposure on vase life of *Caryopteris incana*.

Flower development at harvest	Vase life (days)	
	Grown in sun	Grown in shade
Buds showing color	7	9
First and second whorls open	6	8
First and second whorls spent	6	7

Postharvest

Fresh: Stems persist for 7–10 days in water and an additional 2–3 days in preservative.

Storage: Stems may be stored at 34–40F for 3–5 days. Stems must be rehydrated immediately after shipping.

Dried: Stems may be air-dried by hanging upside down in a warm well-ventilated area for 7–10 days.

Cultivars

None are presently available, but I expect some bright plant breeder to develop cultivars in the near future.

Additional Species

Caryopteris × *clandonensis* (hybrid blue-beard) is more winter hardy than *C. incana*, overwintering to zone 5 where it is treated as a herbaceous perennial. The flowers range from lavender to dark blue, and numerous cultivars are available. The flowers are not as full or whorled as those of *C. incana* and not as ornamental. However, terrific potential also exists for this hybrid. 'Blue Mist' (light blue), 'Dark Knight' (dark blue), 'Heavenly Blue' (deep blue) and 'Longwood Blue' (sky blue) are available.

Pests and Diseases

Root rot fungi (*Pythium*, etc.) can be a problem, but no diseases or pests are unique to *Caryopteris*.

Many thanks to Ms. Mindy De Vita for her help in preparing the material for this crop.

Celosia argentea	Cockscomb	2–3'/2'
Various colors	Hybrid origin	Amaranthaceae

Three forms of *Celosia* are used as cut flowers. Variety *cristata*, known as cockscomb, has convoluted flowers which remind me of colored brains. Variety *plumosa* consists of feathery, vertical flowers that are sometimes called prince of wales feather. Variety *spicata*, known as wheat celosia, has recently appeared on the market. Its silvery rose flowers are borne in slender spires, and the plants are taller and particularly useful for cut stems. Sometimes marketed as flamingo flower, it is excellent as a fresh or dried cut flower (4). Several excellent cultivars have been bred for cut flowers and significant numbers of *Celosia* stems are now sold in the wholesale flower markets.

Propagation

Seed count varies with the strain, from 34,000 to 56,000 seeds/oz. Approximately 1/16 oz of seed yields 1000 seedlings (5). Sow seed and place

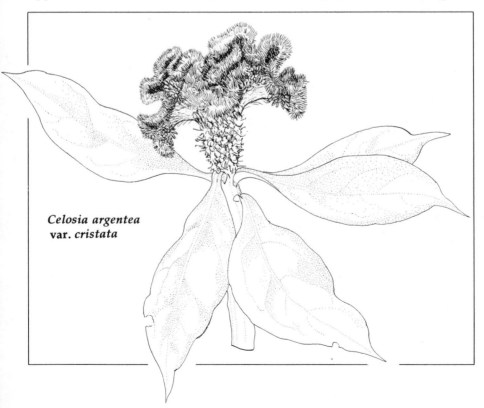

Celosia argentea
var. *cristata*

at 70–75F under mist. Germination occurs in 10–14 days. Direct seeding in the field is not recommended.

Growing-on

Grow seedlings at 63–68F night temperatures and long days (>12 hours). Low temperatures and short days result in premature flowering. Fertilize with 100–150 ppm N once or twice a week. Plants may be transplanted to the bench or field 4–6 weeks after sowing.

Environmental Factors

Photoperiod: *Celosia* is a quantitative short day plant, meaning that although it will flower at any photoperiod, it flowers faster under photoperiods of 14 hours or less (1). Four to five weeks of short days are necessary for most rapid flowering. After 4 weeks, plants may be placed in long days with no detrimental effects of rate or quality of flowering.

Long days also increase the amount of deformity or fasciation in *Celosia*, particularly the var. *cristata* forms. Fasciation is the broadening and flattening of the flower stem at the base of the flower. In one study, 69% of the plants subjected to 16-hour or longer photoperiods produced fasciated stems whereas only 3% of plants grown at 8-hour photoperiods developed fasciated stems. Those grown under 12-hour conditions were intermediate in their response (2,3).

Temperature: Temperature plays a significant role in flowering. Once plants are established, warm temperatures result in faster flowering than cool temperatures. Temperatures below 50F result in a significant delay of flowering compared with 80F.

Field Performance

Spacing: Plants may be transplanted 6″ × 6″ if grown as a single-harvest, single-stem crop. This results in the longest stem lengths but plants must be planted sequentially for full season harvesting. Plants may also be grown on 12″ centers, 8″ × 12″ or as far as 18″ apart if plants are to be harvested continuously.

Harvesting: Flowers are harvested from early July through late September in north Georgia, similar to most other parts of the United States. The highest percentage of long stems are harvested early in the season.

Yield: Yield is cultivar-dependent. The yield and average stem length for a number of cultivars follow. Plant on 14″ centers.

Yield and stem quality of various cultivars of *Celosia* Chief series.

Cultivar	Stems/plant	Stems/ft^2	Stem length (in)
'Carmine Chief'	20	14	18.9
'Fire Chief'	14	11	16.7
'Gold Chief'	17	12	22.6
'Tall Rose Chief'	5	3	14.4

Only 'Tall Rose Chief' was unsatisfactory in trials conducted in Georgia.

At the University of Kentucky (6), an average of 4.5 stems/ft^2 were harvested 8–9 weeks after transplanting when 'Red Chief', 'Gold Chief' and 'Fire Chief' were grown as a single-cut, single-stem crop. Production for the whole season averaged 12 stems/ft^2 from crops planted 6" apart (4 plants/ft^2). Over 60% of the stems were 18" or longer.

Greenhouse Performance

Space plants 8" × 8" or on 12" centers. Use of support netting is desirable. Initially, place plants under 2–3 weeks of long days (>16 hours) and then grow under short days (<14 hours) at 60–62F night temperatures. For best-quality stems, replant every 2–4 weeks. Fertilize with calcium nitrate or potassium nitrate at the rate of 150–200 ppm N with every irrigation. Leach thoroughly every fourth to fifth irrigation.

Guideline for Foliar Analyses

At field trials in Athens, GA, foliage was sampled from vigorously growing healthy plants when flower buds were visible, but prior to flower opening. These are guidelines only and should not be considered absolute standards. Based on dry weight analysis.

(%)						(ppm)				
N	P	K	Ca	Mg		Fe	Mn	B	Al	Zn
				'Fire Chief'						
3.9	0.43	5.06	2.86	1.36		189	261	23	96	182

Stage of Harvest

Flowers should be fully developed on crested forms and 90–100% developed in the plumose form.

Postharvest

Fresh: Flowers of the crested form persist significantly longer than the plumose form. The foliage on both declines rapidly and should be removed as it wilts. A minimum of 7 days may be expected for flowers of *Celosia*. If necessary, flowers may be stored for a few days at 36–41F.

Dried: Flowers may be air-dried. Strip foliage and hang upside down in small bunches. The crested form is more popular for dried use than the plumose form. Wheat celosia tends to shatter when dried.

Cultivars

Crested forms (var. *cristata*):

Chief series is exceptional for cut flowers. Flowers are available in red, scarlet, cherry, yellow, gold and a mix. The red and scarlet strains are more vigorous than other colors. Plants grow 2–3' tall. Netting is beneficial but not necessary.

Kurume strain is about 3' tall and available in separate colors and a mix. Plants with scarlet flowers are available with either bronzed or green foliage.

'Red Velvet' bears some of the largest flower heads I have seen. The deep crimson heads are at least 10" across on 2–3' tall stems. This could be a lethal weapon in the wrong hands. Flowers are excellent for drying.

Plumose forms (var. *plumosa*):

'Apricot Brandy' has large plumes of apricot flowers and performs well in most areas of the country. Plants were developed for use as bedding plants and stem length (1.5–2' long) is a little short for most cut flower operations.

'Forest Fire' bears dense, scarlet plumes atop 2.5' tall stems. 'Forest Fire Improved' has a longer flowering time and larger plumes than 'Forest Fire'.

Pampas Plume mix contains yellow and red shades approximately 3' tall. Also available in gold.

'Red Fox' has 2' tall stems with brilliant carmine plumes.

Sparkler series bears strong flower stems in many colors. Space closely together for single-stem cut flowers. Carmine, cream, orange, red, yellow and mixtures are available.

'Toreador' bears bright red flowers on 2' tall plants.

Spired forms (var. *spicata*):

'Flamingo Feather' is the only cultivar presently available. It grows 3–3.5' tall and received some of the highest ratings in trials held across the United States in 1992. As additional colors become available, this form of *Celosia* could become a major flower in the dried or fresh market.

Pests and Diseases

Botrytis occurs on the flower head in the field during warm, humid conditions or after considerable rainfall. This is particularly true with the crested forms whose flowers are so tightly produced that water is trapped within the inflorescence.

Leaf spots (*Cercospora, Phyllosticta, Alternaria*) on the foliage occur more readily during wet seasons. General-purpose fungicides are useful in their control.

Reading

1. Armitage, A. M. 1985. *Celosia*. In A. H. Halevy (ed.), *The Handbook of Flowering*, vol. 5. CRC Press, Boca Raton, FL. 56–60.

2. Driss-Ecole, D. 1977. Influence de la photoperiode sur de comporte-ment du meristeme caulinaire du *Celosia cristata. Can. J. Bot.* 55:1488–1500.

3. _____ . 1978. Influence de la photoperiode sur la fasciation et la phase reproductrice du *Celosia cristata* (Amarantaceae). *Can. J. Bot.* 56:166–169.

4. Seals, J. 1990. *Celosia. The Cut Flower Quarterly* 2(3):5–6.

5. _____ . 1991. Some uncommon and common (but choice) cut flowers from seed for field growing. *The Cut Flower Quarterly* 3(2):13–14.

6. Utami, L., R. G. Anderson, R. L. Geneve and S. Kester. 1990. Quality and yield of *Ageratum, Aster, Celosia* and *Godetia* grown as field grown cut flowers. *HortScience* 25:851. (Abstr.).

Many thanks to Dr. Robert Anderson for reviewing this section.

Centaurea **spp.**   Basket Flower, Cornflower, Sweet Sultan   2–4'/2–3'
Various colors   Europe   Asteraceae

Centaurea, also known as cornflower, consists of numerous species with excellent cut flower characteristics. *Centaurea macrocephala* (golden basket flower) and *C. montana* (mountain bluet) are discussed in the perennial section. *Centaurea americana* (american basket flower), *C. cyanus* (cornflower or bachelor's buttons), and *C. moschata* (sweet sultan) are annuals and suitable for use as cut flowers. In the eastern half of the country, *C. cyanus* has escaped to clothe the roadsides in a mantle of blue and grows more aggressively than other annuals in the genus. In the Northwest, northern California and Northeast, few problems with any species should be encountered.

All species have small, brown-to-black bracts at the base of the flower bud, a handsome characteristic which further enhances the cut flower possibilities.

Propagation

Greenhouse: Sow in seed flats or directly to the cutting bench (for greenhouse production). Optimum germination occurs at 60–65F and when seed is covered by ¼ to ½" of medium. Seedlings emerge in 7–14 days under proper germination conditions.

Direct sowing: Seed may be sown directly in early spring but germination is delayed until temperatures rise. Seed should be covered lightly. Germination occurs in approximately 10 days at 65–75F. The various species should be sown at the rates given in the following table (4,7).

Species	oz/1000 plants	oz/1000 ft^2
C. americana	0.75–1	4–4.5
C. cyanus	0.25–0.5	3–3.5
C. moschata	0.33–0.75	3–4

In Florida and California, seed sown in the open field in fall flowers from February to June. Seed direct-sown in early spring in the Midwest and Southeast results in flowering from June to September.

Growing-on

Although most seed is direct-sown, numerous growers transplant seedlings to the field. Transplant seedlings to small containers or place plugs in field when danger of frost has passed.

Plants respond best to short days followed by long days. Planting in early spring generally provides such conditions, but if plants are started in July or August, the lack of natural short days results in short plants, rapid flowering and low yield. Apply SD for 4–6 weeks prior to putting them in the field.

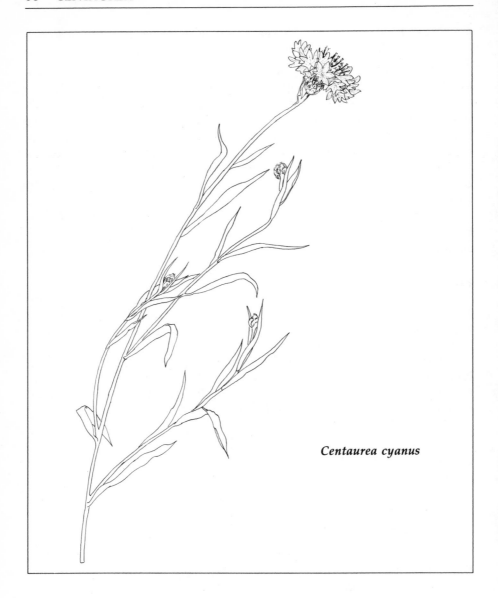

Centaurea cyanus

Environmental Factors

Most of the research on *Centaurea* has been with *C. cyanus*, common corn-flower. It is likely, however, that similar results occur with *C. americana* and *C. moschata* (1).

Photoperiod: *Centaurea* is a long day plant (2). Long days are needed for flower induction, but, once induced, flowering continues even under short day conditions, although the rate of flower development is delayed. Approximately 3 weeks of LD are necessary (1). Plants flower equally well if provided with nightbreak lighting (30 minutes of light in the middle of the night) or if the daylength is extended to provide a 15-hour day. Since plants are sensitive to LD even in the seedling stage, it is important that they should be provided with SD at the start of production to permit basal branching and a larger plant. Plants grown entirely in LD elongate rapidly, produce a few flowers and die (6).

Temperature: Vernalization does not appear to be necessary for flowering; however, the literature is somewhat contradictory on this point. One study showed that exposing the seedlings to 10 days of temperatures at 38–50F resulted in a slight acceleration of flowering under LD but not SD conditions (3). However, from the commercial point of view, vernalization does not appear to have a significant effect on flowering.

Gibberellic acid: GA sprays greatly increase stem elongation but have no effect on flowering, regardless of daylength (1).

Field Performance

Flowers of *C. cyanus* are harvested from June to September in the northern tier of states, as early as mid-May in the Southeast and in the winter and spring in California and Florida. The summers are too hot and winters too cold for successful production of *C. americana* and *C. moschata* in zones 7 and 8. *Centaurea cyanus*, however, may be produced throughout the country.

Spacing: Space seedlings on 6–9" centers.

Yield: *Centaurea americana* (american basket flower), grown in field trials at the University of Georgia in full sun, produced 11–15 stems/plant with an average stem length of 37.8". Stem diameter was approximately ¼".

C. cyanus (cornflower) produces about 5–12 flowers with an average stem length of 15". Stems are strong and make excellent cut flowers.

C. moschata (sweet sultan), also grown at the University of Georgia in full sun, produced 5–8 stems/plant with an average stem length of 18". The cultivar tested was 'The Bride'. Stem length was unsatisfactory under Georgia conditions and the data showed that field production in areas of hot, humid summers is likely uneconomical.

Shading: Cornflowers do best in full sun, even in hot areas of the country. With *C. cyanus*, experiments showed that plants with the greatest southern exposure produced significantly more flowers than plants in rows with a more northerly exposure. Mutual shading results in reduced flowering (8).

Work at the University of Georgia with *C. americana* also showed reduced flowering and little difference in stem length when plants were shaded.

The effect of shade on yield and stem quality of *Centaurea americana* (Athens, GA).

Shade level (%)	Stems/plant	Stem length (in)
0	13.1	38.3
55	7.3	54.0
68	3.0	47.1

Greenhouse Performance

Plants should be grown for 8–12 weeks under SD conditions or until plants are large enough to support flower development. Maintain temperatures of 50–55F. Plants should be fertilized with 100–150 ppm N; do not overfertilize as plants may become too leafy and lax.

After SD, provide 15- to 16-hour LD either by extending the daylength or by giving a night break for at least 30 minutes. Many growers use 4 hours of night break (11:00 PM–2:00 AM) with 10–15 fc of incandescent lighting. The following table shows the effect of temperature and LD provided from October to March. Plants were started in August.

The effect of temperature and night lighting on
Centaurea cyanus.[a]

Temperature (F)	Photoperiod	Flowers/stem
50	LD[b]	36.2
50	SD	10.4
55	LD	67.8
55	SD	9.6
60	LD	77.8
60	SD	34.0

[a]Adapted from (5).
[b]All LD provided after 8–10 weeks of SD.

The lowest temperature for best flowering is 55F and the use of long days is essential.

Scheduling: For mid-March flowering of *C. cyanus*, sow seed in mid-September. For May flowering, sow in early January. Other species may require more time in the greenhouse.

Stage of Harvest

All cornflowers should be harvested when flowers are ¼ to ½ open. In the case of multiple flowered stems (i.e., sprays), the uppermost flower may be ¾ open.

Postharvest

Fresh: Flowers persist for 6–10 days. They may be stored at 35–41F for 2–3 days but long-term storage is not recommended.

Dried: Flowers may be air-dried. The fully double forms are best for drying. Retain foliage and hang upside down in a warm, dark area.

Cultivars

Centaurea americana (american basket flower):
   'Aloha' has 3" wide, lilac-rose flowers on 3–4' tall stems.
   'Jolly Joker' bears 3" wide, lavender flowers on 4' tall stems.

C. cyanus (bachelor's buttons, cornflower):
   Single-flowered

'Emperor William' is 2–3' tall with marine-blue flowers.

Double-flowered

Boy series is approximately 3' tall and most popular for cut flowers. 'Blue Boy' bears light blue flowers, 'Black Boy' has blackish maroon blossoms and 'Red Boy' produces carmine-red flowers.

Frostie mix ('Frosted Queen') bears flowers of various colors with petals fringed with white.

'Jubilee Gem' has sky-blue flowers but is only about 2' tall.

'Pinkie' has bright pink flowers.

'Snowman' has creamy white flowers.

C. moschata (sweet sultan):

'Antique Lace' grows approximately 2' tall and bears flowers in pastel shades of pink, lilac and lavender.

Imperialis mix consists of lavender, lilac, pink, purple, rose, yellow and white on 2–2.5' tall stems.

'Lucida' has dark red flowers.

var. *suaveolens*, whose correct name is var. *flava*, is often listed as a separate species (*C. suaveolens*). The flowers are canary yellow and stems are approximately 2' tall.

'The Bride' bears clean white flowers.

Additional Species

Centaurea imperialis is sometimes listed as a separate species but is a synonym of *C. moschata*, sweet sultan.

Pests and Diseases

Aster yellows, spread by leafhoppers, causes one side of the plant to become yellow and flowers to become greenish. Plants should be eradicated and crop rotation practiced.

Botrytis results in desiccation of the tips of some stems and flower buds. Additional air circulation is necessary.

Downy mildew (*Bremia lactucae*) results in pale green to red, irregular spots on the upper side of the foliage and soft, moldy growth beneath. Infected plant parts generally collapse and die. Young plants are particularly susceptible. Remove and destroy infected leaves. Control with wider spacing, better aeration and appropriate spray solutions.

Stem rots caused by *Phytophthora*, *Sclerotinia* and *Pellicularia* result in significant losses, particularly in cold, waterlogged soils. Use clean soils and sterilized containers.

Aphids and leafhoppers are the worst insect pests of most species of cornflower.

Reading

1. Kadman-Zahavi, A., and H. Yavel. 1985. *Centaurea cyanus*. In A. H. Halevy (ed.), *The Handbook of Flowering*, vol. 2. CRC Press, Boca Raton, FL. 169–175.

2. Laurie, A., and G. H. Poesch. 1932. Photoperiodism—the value of supplementary illumination and reduction of light on flowering plants in the greenhouse. Ohio Agr. Exp. Sta. Bul. 512:1–42.

3. Listowski, A., and A. Jasmanowicz. 1973. In P. L. Altman and D. S. Ditmer (eds.), *Biological Data Book.* Federation of Amer. Soc. for Exp. Biol. Bethesda, MD. 898.

4. Nau, J. 1989. *Ball Culture Guide: The Encyclopedia of Seed Germination.* Ball Seed Co., West Chicago, IL.

5. Post, K. 1942. Effects of daylength and temperature on growth and flowering of some florist crops. Cornell Univ. Agr. Exp. Sta. Bul. 787:1–70.

6. _____ . 1955. *Florist Crop Production and Marketing.* Orange Judd, New York, NY.

7. Seals, J. 1991. Some uncommon and common (but choice) cut flowers from seed for field growing. *The Cut Flower Quarterly* 3(2):13–14.

8. Yahel, H., A. Kadman-Zahavi and E. Erhrat. 1972. On winter flowering of *Centaurea cyanus* for export (in Hebrew). *Hassadeh* 52:1514–1516.

Clarkia spp. see *Godetia* spp.

Consolida spp.	Larkspur	2–4'/1'
Various colors	Mediterranean	Ranunculaceae

Larkspur has been a mainstay for cut flower growers for many years. The market for larkspur continues to be strong even while other species come and go. Numerous cultivars offer a wide range of colors and germination is relatively high even when direct sown to the field. The nomenclature of larkspur was recently changed from *Delphinium* to *Consolida*. The two species used in the cut flower trade are *C. ambigua* and *C. orientalis* (both formally *D. ajacis*). The differences between them are slight but plants of *C. orientalis* are more upright than *C. ambigua*, and the flowers are often in shades of bright pink and purple. Plants of *C. ambigua* are more branched initially, and flowers are usually light pink or blue (7).

Flowers are generally dried but may also be used in fresh bouquets and arrangements.

Propagation

Approximately 10,000 seeds/oz is typical and 1/5 oz of seed yields 1000 seedlings in the field (7).

Most cultivars are direct-sown in the field but plugs may be transplanted in early spring for late summer harvest. Seed does not germinate well above 55F soil temperature (6) and should be sown in the fall in most parts of the country. Many growers, particularly those in the warmer areas of the country, chill the seed for 7–14 days at 35–40F prior to planting to enhance germination. In areas south of zone 5, seed may be sown in the fall without appreciable loss due to winter conditions. Fresh seed germinates better than old seed.

Consolida **hybrid**

In cooler areas, seed may be sown in plugs or other containers and germinated in a cool greenhouse or cold frame (50–55F) or seed may be chilled at 35F for 2–3 weeks prior to sowing in the spring. Sow as soon as the ground can be worked. Approximately 3 oz of seed/1000 ft^2 is needed (5).

Growing-on

If plants are started in the greenhouse, grow at 55F until ready to plant to the field. Use large plugs (no smaller than a 208-plug tray) or transplant seedlings to final plug container after 3–4 weeks. Fertilize lightly (50–100 ppm N using a nitrate-based fertilizer once a week) while growing at temperatures below 60F.

Environmental Factors

Temperature: Plants of larkspur require a vernalization (cold) period for shoot elongation and flower initiation and development (1,6). Vernalization is not effective on the seed. If plants remain below 55F for 6 weeks, then further development is enhanced. Below 55F, plants will rosette and shoot elongation will occur, but little rosetting or flowering occurs above 60F. The elongation of the stem and subsequent flowering occur at higher temperatures only if the cool treatment has been satisfied. In the experiment summarized in the upcoming table, seeds were greenhouse-sown in October, and seedlings were grown in the greenhouse at 50F until January 1. After January 1, various treatments were applied. If seedlings are exposed to high temperatures for several days, flower initiation, development and shoot elongation occur rapidly with very poor stem and flower quality.

Photoperiod: Development of the plant is best under long days, which can be satisfied by nightbreak lighting or day extension. Long days (>16 hours) result in longer stems and higher yield than short days. The effect of photoperiod and temperature on larkspur is shown in the following table.

The effect of daylength extension and growing temperature on yield of *Consolida* (seed sown in October; treatments applied after January 1).[a]

Treatment	50% of flowers harvested before . . .	Stems/plant
50F + LD	Apr 17	16.2
50F + ND[b]	May 3	7.0
55F + LD	Apr 8	17.0
55F + ND	Apr 16	12.0
60F + LD	Mar 21	20.7
60F + ND	Mar 12	12.6

[a]From (6).
[b]ND = natural days, as opposed to long days (LD).

Gibberellic acid: GA accelerates flowering of larkspur (2,3); however, few growers employ the chemical.

Field Performance

Planting time: Seed may be sown every 2 weeks from September to November in the Midwest. In New York and similar latitudes, initial sowing may be done from September 1 to 15 for spring production. Further south and in California, early to mid-October through early November allows for sufficient exposure to the cold. In Florida and the Southwest (Arizona, Texas), planting occurs from mid-October to mid-November. Sowing in more northerly environments may be accomplished in early spring as soon as the ground can be worked (8). In general, allow a minimum of 6 weeks before temperatures rise above 55F.

Spacing: Space seed 4–6" apart or 0.3 oz/100 linear ft. If sown more thickly, thin to a 4–6" spacing. Some growers use 42" wide rows and direct sow 2 lines of plants in the bed (4). For 1000 ft^2, 2–3.5 oz are recommended (5). The more dense the spacing, the higher the incidence of disease that may occur.

Scheduling: Flowers occur as spring temperatures rise, but approximately 4–6 months are required after sowing.

Shading: Larkspur does not require shading. However, yield and stem quality are not adversely affected under 30–50% shade.

Yield: Under wide spacing (10–12" apart), expect 6 stems/ft^2 or 500 bunches (10–12 stems) per 1000 ft^2. At closer spacings, higher yield per square foot but lower yield per plant occurs.

Support: One to two tiers of support (6" × 8" wire or string) may be used, particularly if the site is windy. The first tier should be 12–14" off the ground and the second 18" above the first (4).

Irrigation: Use drip irrigation if possible.

Greenhouse Performance

Sow or transplant approximately 10" apart. Maintain 50F temperatures for 8–10 weeks. After plants are well established, raise temperatures to 55–60F and apply long days by extending the days (>16 hours) or with 2-hour nightbreak lighting using incandescent lamps. Sowing in September results in flowering in early to mid-March in the Midwest, for a December sowing, mid-April. Sowing after January is not recommended because high greenhouse temperatures usually occur during extension of the flower stem and development of flowers. Quality subsequently declines. Support is necessary for all sowing dates.

Stage of Harvest

For fresh flowers, allow 2–5 basal flowers to open or up to ⅓ of the stem. Fresh stems are generally bunched in 10–12 stems (heavy) or 20 stems (light). For dried flowers, harvest when the majority of flowers are open but before petals drop. Some growers harvest the terminal flower stem for fresh flowers and the laterals for dry flowers.

Postharvest

Fresh: The vase life of larkspur is approximately 6–8 days. Flowers are highly sensitive to ethylene; silver thiosulfate (STS) is effective in reducing flower drop in larkspur and delphinium (9). Commercial flower preservatives with silver in their makeup are effective treatments for cut stems. Store fresh flowers away from fruit, vegetables or other drying flowers. If flowers are stored overnight, keep upright in water at 36–41F. Keep constantly hydrated; dry storage for fresh flowers is not recommended.

Dried: Larkspurs are excellent for drying and may be air-dried at 70–80F for 2–4 weeks. Foliage need not be removed. Stems may also be dehydrated with a desiccant such as silica gel.

Cultivars

The following are cultivars of *Consolida orientalis.*

'Blue Cloud' has a more airy, open flower habit than other cultivars and is often used as a filler. The single flowers are violet-blue.

'Blue Picotee' is an interesting (and expensive) bicolor with white flowers surrounded by a blue picotee edge.

Early Bird series is earlier flowering than the Imperials and is available in blue, lilac, rose, white and mixed. Stems are 3–4' tall.

Giant Imperial series is the standard of the industry. Plants stand approximately 4' tall and are available in numerous colors including carmine, deep blue ('Blue Spire'), deep rose, light blue, lilac, pink, salmon, white and a mix.

Messenger series is approximately the same height as the Imperial Giant series but flowers about 2 weeks earlier. Blue, lilac, rose, white and a mix of colors are available.

QIS series (formerly Sunburst series) has been selected for uniformity and stem quality. Colors available include carmine, dark blue, light pink, lilac, rose, white and a mix.

Pests and Diseases

Botrytis basal rot causes a soft brown basal rot which results in plants wilting and falling over. Fungicides and aeration are useful preventatives.

Black leaf spot results from *Pseudomonas delphinii*, a bacterium, and causes irregular, shining, tarlike spots, especially on the upper surface of the foliage. The lower leaves show symptoms first, but petioles, stems and flowers may also be attacked. Remove infected foliage and destroy. Other leaf spots may be carried on the seed and seed may be treated in 125–130F water for 10 minutes.

Crown rot and root rot caused by *Sclerotinia delphinii* result in sudden wilting, stunting and death of plants. The saying "here today, gone tomorrow" is particularly appropriate for plants afflicted with this disease. It seems to occur in the weaker-growing colors and sometimes may be most destructive on that one color. The fungi live through the winter and are distributed by tools or rain. Crop rotation, use of soil sterilants and clean tools relieve the problem.

Cyclamen mites cause blackened buds and downward-cupped, deformed leaves. The "blacks" are distinguished from pseudomonas leaf spot because of the deformities caused by the mites. Use of a miticide is useful but not always effective. Aphids and leaf miners can also be problems.

Powdery mildew (*Erysiphe* and *Sphaerotheca*) is particularly prevalent during cool, moist seasons. Larkspur, however, is much less susceptible than delphinium. Avoid dense spacing and wet soils when planting.

Stem canker (*Fusarium oxysporum* f. *delphinii*) first appears as light brown, water-soaked areas on the stems. Eventually the fungus reaches the crown and invades the vascular tissues. Plants show yellowing of the basal leaves that progresses upward. Use of *Fusarium*-resistant strains and soil sterilization is useful.

Reading

1. Bajpal, P. N., and V. N. Nerikar. 1959. Effect of sowing at different dates on the growth and flowering of *Cosmos, Caryopsis,* and larkspur. *Sci. Cul.* 25:140–142.

2. Bose, T. K. 1965. Effect of growth substances on growth and flowering of ornamental annuals. *Sci. Cul.* 31:34–36.

3. Lindstrom, R. S., S. W. Wittwer and M. J. Bukovac. 1957. Gibberellin and higher plants. IV. Flowering responses of some flower crops. Q. Bul. Mich. Agr. Exp. Sta. 39:673–681.

4. Nakasawa, S. 1990. How we field grow larkspur. In *Proceedings of 3rd National Conference on Specialty Cut Flowers*. Ventura, CA. 115–118.

5. Nau, J. 1989. *Ball Culture Guide: The Encyclopedia of Seed Germination*. Ball Seed Co., West Chicago, IL.

6. Post, K. 1955. *Florist Crop Production and Marketing*. Orange Judd, New York, NY.

7. *Royal Horticultural Society Dictionary of Gardening*. 1974. Supplement.

8. Seals, J. 1989. Culture profile, field larkspur. *The Cut Flower Quarterly* 1(3):5–6.

9. Shillo, R., Y. Mor and A. H. Halevy. 1980. Prevention of flower drop in cut sweet peas and delphinium (in Hebrew). *Hassadeh* 61:274–276.

Many thanks to Ms. Sally Nakasawa for reviewing this section.

Cosmos bipinnatus	Lace Cosmos	3–5'/2'
Various colors	Mexico	Asteraceae

Cosmos is a common bedding plant and most of the favor in the United States rests upon the dwarf sulphur cosmos, *C. sulphureus*. The best species for cut flowers, however, is lace cosmos, *C. bipinnatus*, whose stems grow 3–5' tall. It is available in numerous colors.

Propagation

Seed emerges in 7–10 days if germinated at 70–72F under intermittent mist. Seed should be lightly covered for best germination. Approximately ⅓ oz of seed yields 1000 seedlings (2). Seed may be direct-sown at the rate of 0.5 oz/100 linear ft but field temperatures must be warm (above 60F) before direct sowing.

Growing-on

Plants should be grown at 60–65F. Low nitrogen fertilization is recommended. Apply 50–100 ppm N during the growing-on stage; higher nutrition results in tall, spindly growth. Green plants may be planted out 4–6 weeks after sowing.

Environmental Factors

Photoperiod: *Cosmos bipinnatus* is a quantitative short day plant. This means that plants flower more rapidly under short days than under long days but eventually flower under all photoperiods. The optimum photoperiod for flowering is less than 14 hours. At daylengths greater than 14 hours, flower development is delayed and flower buds appear sporadically. The following table illustrates the effect of photoperiod on 'Sensation'.

The effect of photoperiod on *Cosmos bipinnatus* 'Sensation'.[a]

Photoperiod (hr)	Plants in flower (%)	Germination to visible bud (days)	Nodes	Height (in)
9	100	47	12	37.0
18	75	56	12	39.8

[a] From (3).

Temperature: *Cosmos* is a heat-loving plant and grows and flowers well at temperatures above 60F. Temperatures below 55F inhibit growth and flowering.

Plant age: As plants mature, the need for short days decreases. Therefore, older plants are more likely to flower under long day conditions than young plants. Plants with 6–8 pairs of leaves are sufficiently mature to flower regardless of photoperiod (1).

Gibberellic acid: GA_3 substitutes for short day treatments (1). Approximately 100 ppm as a foliar spray may be used but GA is not as efficient as SD treatment nor are GA-induced flowers as large as those induced under SD (1). Plants treated with GA are elongated with greater internode and generally are of inferior quality. Seldom used by commercial growers.

Field Performance

Space plants 9–12" apart; support mesh is necessary especially if wind is a problem. Sequential planting (planting every 2–4 weeks) results in better quality stems than harvesting from the same plants throughout the season.

Fertilize with a granular 10–10–10 fertilizer or an application of 200 ppm

Cosmos bipinnatus

N using a complete soluble fertilizer in early spring when plants are placed in the field. Repeat in midsummer but do not overfertilize or lanky, leafy plants will result.

Greenhouse Performance

Space plants 6–9″ apart. Apply LD (>14 hours) until plants have approximately 6 pairs of leaves. Apply SD for most rapid flowering at that time. If stems are too short, continue LD for a longer period of time. Maintain temperatures at 60–65F.

Fertilize newly transplanted plants in the bench with 50–75 ppm N using potassium nitrate and continue with weekly applications of 150–200 ppm N from a complete soluble fertilizer. Do not overapply nutrients.

Stage of Harvest

Harvest when petals on first flower are just opening, but have not yet flattened out. If flowers are to be dried, allow the outer row of petals to fully open.

Postharvest

Fresh: Vase life is only about 4–6 days in water but may be somewhat extended with floral preservatives.

Storage: Store stems at 36–40F for 3–4 days only if necessary. Storage is not recommended.

Dried: *Cosmos* can be dried in silica gel (2–3 days) or borax (4–6 days).

Cultivars

'Candystripe' has white, rose or red flowers with crimson markings on the petals. Plants are 2.5–3' tall.

'Collarette' is a mixture of different colors of semi-double flowers, although single flowers are also present. Plants are 2–3' tall.

'Daydream' produces handsome, pale pink flowers with a deep rose center on 3' tall stems.

'Klondyke' occurs in mixed colors and grows 3–5' tall.

'Picotee' is a mix of flowers ranging from white with red edges to red with faint white markings. Plants grow 3–4' tall.

'Pink Fairytales' bears sprays of pink and white, daisylike flowers on 2–3' tall stems.

'Sea Shells' comes in a color mix and consists of interesting flowers with tubular petals. Most decorative.

'Sensation' bears 3" wide flowers in numerous colors. Plants generally grow 3–5' tall. Single colors are available and sold under different names. 'Dazzler' has fiery red flowers on 3' tall stems, 'Gloria' produces rose flowers with a carmine zone and 'Purity' bears large, white flowers.

'Versailles' has large, single, lilac-rose flowers with crimson rings. A particularly good cut flower selection.

'Yellow Garden' bears pastel yellow flowers on 3' tall stems.

Additional Species

Cosmos sulphureus may be used as a cut flower, but generally plants are too short for commercial cut flower use. 'Diablo' and the Sunny series have been bred as bedding plants and are not as useful for cut flowers as *C. bipinnatus*.

Pests and Diseases

Bacterial wilt (*Pseudomonas solanacearum*) results in sudden wilting and collapse of the plants. Plants shrivel and dry up within 2–3 days. Infected plants should be destroyed immediately. Because bacteria can overwinter, crop rotation should also be practiced.

Canker (*Diaporthe stewartii*) usually affects stems and branches at blooming time. The lesions are first dark brown and later ash gray. Remove and destroy infected plants.

Root and stem rots are particularly damaging in southern states and in areas where plants are overwatered. Soil drenches with appropriate fungicides are useful.

Aphids, Japanese beetles and leafhoppers are the most common pests on *Cosmos*.

Reading

1. Molder, M., and J. N. Owens. 1974. The effects of gibberellin A_3, photoperiod and age on vegetative growth and flowering of *Cosmos bipinnatus* var. 'Sensation'. *Can. J. Bot.* 52:1249–1258.

2. Seals, J. 1991. Some uncommon and common (but choice) cut flowers from seed for field growing. *The Cut Flower Quarterly* 3(2):13–14.

3. Wittwer, S. J., and M. J. Bukovac. 1959. Effects of gibberellin on the photoperiodic response of some higher plants. In R. B. Withrow (ed.), *Photoperiodism and Related Phenomena in Plants and Animals.* American Assoc. Advancement of Science, Washington, DC. 373–380.

Emilia javanica	Tassel Flower	1.5–2'/2'
Scarlet, orange	Tropics	Asteraceae

This species, sometimes sold as *Cacalia javanica*, is useful as a colorful filler. Plants bear numerous small (½" wide), fuzzy, scarlet and orange flowers on 12–15" long stems. Many lateral flower stems are produced per main stem and each lateral may be used as a short-stemmed (6–8") filler. Although plants are annuals, they self-sow prolifically.

Propagation

Seed may be direct-sown at the rate of 1 oz/1000 linear ft (1) in fall in the South or in early spring in the North. If not direct-sown, 1/32 oz yields approximately 1000 plants. Seed sown under mist at 68–72F germinates in 7–10 days.

Growing-on

Plantlets produced in the greenhouse should be grown at 55–60F night temperatures and fertilized with no more than 100 ppm N prior to setting out in the field or greenhouse. Plants are large enough to transplant in approximately 8 weeks. Direct sowing is also possible.

Environmental Factors

Little research work has been done with *Emilia* but based on trials at the University of Georgia, it appears to have little photoperiodic sensitivity. Plants continue to flower even under hot, humid conditions showing that such conditions do not inhibit flower initiation or development.

Field Performance

Spacing: Space plants 6" × 6" or as far apart as 10" × 12". They fill in readily.

Yield: In trials at the University of Georgia, we were overwhelmed by the number of flower stems produced in a single season. My students revolted at the sight of yet another 5000 stems awaiting their gentle harvest. Only *Cirsium* and *Eryngium* were viewed with more dislike. Plants lend themselves well to mechanical harvesting as flowers are continuously produced. Cutting one stem at a time is a never-ending process. In our trials, plants produced over 100 stems/plant with an average length of 17.7". Each stem carried approximately 7 flowers.

In the above work, stems were harvested by hand; if mechanical harvesting is employed, yield would be significantly reduced. Labor costs, however, would also plunge. To be honest, how much *Emilia* can one use?

Greenhouse Performance

Plants are seldom produced commercially as cut flowers in the greenhouse. However, if one is determined to produce these in the greenhouse, high light conditions, warm temperatures and moderate fertility practices (100 ppm N) should be maintained.

Stage of Harvest

Harvest stems when the first flower is fully open. Not all flowers on the individual stem may open in water.

Postharvest

Fresh: Flowers persist for 3–6 days in plain water. Short stems persist longer than long stems. Water does not move well through the longer stems. Store in water in 35F rooms only if necessary.

Dried: Flowers may be air-dried, but some of the color is lost.

Cultivars

None available, but seed-grown plants result in scarlet and orange flowers.

Additional Species

Two similar species are available resulting in some confusion as to the identity of the seed strains on the market. *Emilia coccinea, E. flammea* and *E. sagittata* are synonyms of *E. javanica*, but *E. sonchifolia* differs slightly. *Emilia sonchifolia* has toothed or wavy margins, and the flowers are usually rose or purple. Both species are naturalized in southern Florida.

Pests and Diseases

The only problem in field trials in Georgia was the incidence of botrytis (*Botrytis cinerea*) during times of heavy rains.

Reading

1. Kieft, C. 1989. *Kieft's Growing Manual* .... Kieft Bloemzaden, Venhuizen, The Netherlands.

2. Nau, J. 1989. *Ball Culture Guide: The Encyclopedia of Seed Germination.* Ball Seed Co., West Chicago, IL.

Euphorbia marginata

Euphorbia marginata	Snow-on-the-mountain	2–4'/3'
White bracts around flowers	North America	Euphorbiaceae

Well-branched plants have variegated or entirely white upper foliage. The flowers are inconsequential but are surrounded by large, white bracts. The long-lasting cut stems are most useful in bouquets. Gloves and long-sleeved shirts should be worn when harvesting because the sap results in severe dermatitis in sensitive individuals.

Propagation

Sow seed at the rate of approximately 1 oz/1000 plants (2) at 60–68F under intermittent mist. Although seed may emerge in 10–14 days, germination is erratic and may require a 1- to 2-month period. For field germination, seed in the amount of approximately 0.7 oz/100 linear ft or 7 oz/100 ft² is necessary for a good stand (2). Three to four successive sowings, 2 weeks apart, are recommended.

Growing-on

Seed germinated in the greenhouse or frame should be grown at 60F and fertilized with 75–100 ppm N. Plants may be transplanted to the field in 4–6 weeks.

Environmental Factors

Photoperiod: Snow-on-the-mountain is a short day species. Flowers are initiated under short days and vegetative growth occurs under long days.

Temperature: Stems are thicker and flowers larger when average temperatures remain below 75F. High temperatures result in poor initiation and spindly stems.

Field Performance

Yield: Little information is available on yield in field production but the goal of 3–5 stems/plant is not unrealistic.

Spacing: Space plants 6" × 6", 6" × 9" or 9" × 9". No shade is necessary.

Plants are of a better quality when night temperatures remain below 75F. If plants are produced in the South (zones 7–10), they should be scheduled to flower in late summer and fall.

Greenhouse Performance

Plant in ground beds or raised beds at 6" × 6" or 6" × 9" spacing. Fertilize with approximately 100 ppm N and grow plants under long days (14- to 16-hour photoperiod) for 6–8 weeks. Provide short days (<14- to 16-hour photoperiod) when stems are 1–2' long.

Stage of Harvest

Cut stems when bracts are fully colored but before the flowers are fully open.

Postharvest

Fresh: Bracts and flowers persist for 7–10 days. The foliage does not remain fresh as long as the bracts and flowers do. Many florists remove the foliage prior to making an arrangement. The milky sap can be troublesome but if stems are cut under water, the latex coagulates. Searing the latex with flame or immersing the cut ends in alcohol or boiling water also rids the stems of latex.

Storage: Storage is not recommended but temperatures of 42–55F can be used.

Additional Species

Euphorbia fulgens (scarlet plume) is a common greenhouse-produced cut flower with scarlet blooms. Plants require SD for flowering and initiate with 12-hour photoperiods at 68F. They are excellent cut flowers and are mainly imported from Europe. Short days provided on August 1, September 1 and October 1 resulted in plants which flowered on September 20, October 30 and December 15, respectively (1).

Pests and Diseases

Few problems occur with *E. marginata* although warm temperatures result in stress-related infections of root rots and botrytis. Plants grown north of zone 7 have few problems.

Reading

1. Post, K. 1955. *Florist Crop Production and Marketing.* Orange Judd, New York, NY.

2. Seals, J. 1991. Some uncommon and common (but choice) cut flowers from seed for field growing. *The Cut Flower Quarterly* 3(2):13–14.

Eustoma grandiflorum   Lisianthus, Prairie Gentian   2–3'/2'
Various colors   Nebraska, Colorado, Texas   Gentianaceae

This native species has returned home after being bred and selected by Japanese breeders and is becoming more popular every year. The blue flower color of the species has been complemented by cultivars with white, pink and purple flowers. Though plants are technically perennials in their native habitat, they should be treated as annuals in the field. Postharvest life is excellent; *Eustoma* is definitely a winner for the future.

Propagation

Seed: Plants are raised almost exclusively from seed by specialist propagators; terminal cuttings are only occasionally used. For the small- to medium-sized operation, mature plugs should be purchased. However, if seed propagation is attempted, sow seed on top of medium (do not cover) at 70–80F. Germination usually occurs in 10–15 days. Seed is small (1/256 oz yields 1000 seedlings) and pelleted seed is available in most cultivars.

Cuttings: Terminal cuttings root under mist in approximately 2 weeks at 75F. Stock plants should be maintained under LD (>12 hours) for maximum cutting production. Some plants, once established from cuttings, are shorter, weaker and have fewer flowers than those propagated from seed (3).

Growing-on

Two distinct growing phases occur with *Eustoma*. The first phase is the seedling (growing-on) stage. Growth occurs very slowly, forming only 3–5 leaf pairs in 3 months without forming an elongated flower shoot. Temperatures of 40–65F result in stronger, taller flower stems and increased flower number (3). Temperatures above 70F should be avoided. Research has shown that cooling the seedlings for 5 weeks at 54F prior to greenhouse planting accelerated flowering by 10 days (4). During the growing-on phase, short days (<12 hours) should be maintained. High intensity lighting during the growing-on phase to accelerate the growth of seedlings has been unsuccessful.

Environmental Factors

Photoperiod: *Eustoma* is a quantitative long day plant (that is, plants will flower faster under LD, but will eventually flower regardless of photoperiod) (3,5). However, the effects of LD are relatively small. When 30–45 long days

Eustoma grandiflorum

were applied when seedlings were 90 days old, flowering was not accelerated. In order to significantly accelerate growth, LD had to be given continuously until flowering (5). Even under 8-hour days, plants form flowers (2). The difference between growth and flowering under natural fall and winter conditions compared to LD conditions (nightbreak lighting or day extension) is minimal.

Light intensity: Although light intensity does not accelerate flowering, an increase in flower number occurs when high intensity sodium lights are used to supplement winter light (1). Plants are more vigorous and produce more flowers in areas of high natural light intensity.

Temperature: Temperatures above 70F in the greenhouse should be avoided, particularly in the seedling stage.

Field Performance

Good drainage is essential for *Eustoma*. Plant in raised beds if drainage is suspect or in areas where summer rains are plentiful. Irrigation is necessary after transplanting to the field because plants are growing rapidly. Drying out at this stage reduces yield and quality. Two tiers of support are recommended.

Some of the following information comes from field production in Kentucky (6). Plugs, moved up to cell packs (48 cells/tray), are planted to the field as soon as threat of frost has passed. Approximately 4 weeks are necessary from transplant to the field until the first flowers are harvested. Three to four stems/plant are harvested over a 3- to 4-week period. Stem length in Kentucky ranged from 15 to 30" long (6).

After the harvest, cut the plants back to 1 or 2 pairs of leaves to stimulate a second harvest. The second harvest occurs 6–8 weeks after the first and flowers are cut for an additional 6 weeks.

Greenhouse Performance

Winter greenhouse production provides flowers at excellent prices for which there is a remarkable demand. However, the long time needed between sowing and flowering (5–7 months) limits the usefulness of sowing the crop for greenhouse operators. Unless one has an overwhelming desire for masochism, mature plugs should be purchased.

Place plugs in ground beds on 4–9" centers; alternatively, place 1–2 plants per 4" pot or 3–5 per 6" pot, placed pot to pot. One tier of support is usually needed. Natural daylength is appropriate but LD (>12 hours) slightly accelerate flowering. If HID sodium or metal halide lamps are available, additional flowers may be formed but it is questionable whether their use is cost-effective. Warm day temperatures (78–86F) and 65F nights result in faster flowering than 68–75F days and 55F nights (2). One to two months are required between visible flower bud and open flower.

Stage of Harvest

Best results occur when the central bud is removed. Harvest when 1 flower is fully colored—when the white flower is totally white, not partially green. The flower need not be fully open.

Postharvest

Fresh: Postharvest life is generally good (10–15 days). However, small buds often fail to develop after harvesting, and flowers, particularly blue and pink flowers, fade badly in low light conditions. If placed in high light, these conditions become less severe (2).

Preservatives are effective in lengthening postharvest life and should be used. Continuous use of 4% sucrose solutions plus antimicrobial agents resulted in stems persisting for 30 days, each flower lasting approximately 13 days (1). Another recipe, consisting of 10% sugar, citric acid and antimicrobial agents, pulsed for 24 hours, resulted in 13-day postharvest life and opening of all flower buds on the cut stem (2).

Cultivars

Though research has been conducted on many cultivars, only a few cut flower forms are easily obtainable.

Double Eagle series is tall (3–4') and produces mainly double flowers in various shades and bicolors.

Echo series is nearly 100% double and flowers a little earlier than some of the single forms. Flowers in chiffon blue ('Misty Blue'), light blue, mid-blue, picotee blue, picotee pink, pink, white and a mix are available. Cut stems are approximately 2' long.

Heidi series bears sprays of single flowers atop 2–2.5' tall stems. Nine separate colors plus a mix are offered.

Royal series is earlier than some others and is available in pink, light purple, purple, violet and white.

Yodel series is popular with field and greenhouse growers and bears large, single flowers on 2–3' tall stems. Blue, deep blue, lilac, mid-blue, pink, rose, white and mix of colors have been selected.

Pests and Diseases

The major problem in the greenhouse occurs during the long seedling stage. Seedlings develop so slowly that employees often overwater plants, allowing water molds such as *Pythium* and *Rhizoctonia* to strike. Attention to watering is very important during the seedling stage. In the field, poor drainage is a serious problem. Plants are native to the American prairie, and heavy summer rains where drainage has not been improved often result in root rots. This can be particularly devastating in areas of hot, humid summers. Raised beds or well-drained fields are recommended in such areas.

Aphids and whiteflies can be a problem.

Reading

1. Grueuber, K. L., B. E. Corr and H. F. Wilkins. 1984. *Eustoma grandiflorum, Lisianthus russellianius*. Minn. State Flor. Bul. 33(6):10–14.

2. Halevy, A. H., and A. M. Kofranek. 1984. Evaluation of *Lisianthus* as a

new flower crop. *HortScience* 19:845–847.

3. Roh, M. S., A. H. Halevy and H. F. Wilkins. 1989. *Eustoma grandiflorum*. In A. H. Halevy (ed.), *The Handbook of Flowering*, vol. 6. CRC Press, Boca Raton, FL. 322–327.

4. Sclomo, E., and A. H. Halevy. 1987. Studies on the growth and flowering of *Lisianthus* (in Hebrew). *Hassadeh* 67:1628–1631.

5. Tsukada, T., T. Kobayashi and Y. Nagase. 1982. Studies on the physiological characters and cultivation of prairie gentian. II. Effect of temperature and photoperiod on growth and flowering. Bul. Nagano Veg. Ornam. Crops Exp. Sta. 2:77–88.

6. White-Mays, L. 1992. *Eustoma grandiflorum*, Lisianthus. In *Proceedings of 4th National Conference on Specialty Cut Flowers*. Cleveland, OH. 41–43.

Godetia spp.	Satin Flower	16–30"/15"
Various colors	Western North America	Onagraceae

This genus consists of about 20 species and is closely related to *Oenothera* and *Clarkia*. The flowers are showy and arranged in racemes or spikes. All species are native to the West Coast, mainly California and Oregon, and are not particularly suitable for field production in the Midwest, East or South. They may, however, be greenhouse-produced in the winter and spring in most areas of the country. The tall cut flower species are mainly derived from *G. amoena*, while the dwarf garden plants originate from *G. grandiflora*.

Propagation

Germination occurs within 10 days at 70F in a sweat tent or under intermittent mist. Approximately 1/10 oz of seed yields 1000 plants. If direct-sown, 0.7–0.9 oz/1000 ft^2 is necessary (4).

Growing-on

Seedlings should be grown at 50–60F. Warmer temperatures result in more spindly growth. Fertilize sparingly (50–75 ppm N) with a complete fertilizer or potassium nitrate. Supplemental high intensity discharge lighting accelerates growth of seedlings considerably.

Environmental Factors

Photoperiod: Early observations showed that *Godetia* did not respond to daylength or temperature for flower bud formation (3). However, more recent work revealed that cultivars of the F_1 Grace series are clearly long day plants, even though plants also flower in short days. As shown in the following table, plants require less time to flower when grown under long days and supplemental light.

In this work, the highest quality stems were produced with long days and

The effect of photoperiod and supplemental lighting on flowering of Godetia.[a]

Photoperiod (hr)	Supplemental (HPS) light	Time to flower (wk)	Nodes before flowering
8	no	21	75
8	yes	17	70
20	no	13	37
20	yes	10	32

[a]From (1).

supplemental light. The supplemental light level was approximately 800 fc from high pressure sodium lamps (HPS). Not only do LD influence the flowering time but work from Israel also showed that stem lengths are significantly longer when LD were applied. Plants grown under natural short days were about 33" long while those under LD were over 4' tall (2). Stems growing with LD have more erect growth than plants under SD.

Temperature: *Godetia* is a cool-season plant and does not tolerate high temperatures. The best temperature for growth is 50–55F nights and day temperatures below 75F. Greenhouse production at 60–62F nights has been successful in the winter. Overall quality of flowers and stems deteriorates rapidly at temperatures above 75F (2) and is the main reason most outdoor production in this country is limited to the West Coast. However, plants may be grown in the East or Midwest if planted in early spring. Cold-acclimated plants transplanted on April 5 in Lexington, KY, tolerated temperatures of 26F a few days later and produced flowers in mid-June (1). Protective row covers could be used to foster earlier plant growth and development.

Field Performance

Yield: Little information is available but 30 stems/plant are common. Work at the University of Kentucky (5) in 1989 and 1990 resulted in 25–75 stems per pinched plant spaced on 2' centers, depending on cultivar. Production was highest when planted no later than April 10; later plantings were much less successful. Stems were 10–15" long.

Spacing: Spacing is dependent on whether plants will be pinched or grown single-stemmed. Unpinched plants should be closely spaced on 4–5" centers (5–9 plants/ft^2). Pinched plants should be spaced at 20–24" in rows 3' apart. Although stems attain only about 18" in height, field support is necessary in the East, particularly in areas with heavy spring rains, even with pinched plants. Bamboo stakes (1 per plant) or at least 1 tier of netting should be used.

Fertilization: Fertilize in field with 200 ppm N from calcium nitrate and 25 ppm magnesium sulfate approximately once every 2–3 weeks to maintain and increase stem strength. Higher frequency of fertilization should be practiced in coastal California areas, lower frequency in eastern sites. Too much fertility results in weak stems and lanky growth while lack of fertilization causes bronzing of the lower foliage and stunting. If nutrition continues

Godetia amoena

to be withheld, plants turn brown and die.

Pinching: Although plants do not require pinching, it results in more flowers and more uniform flowering of axillary shoots. Dr. Bob Andersen of the University of Kentucky suggests 2 kinds of pinches. An early pinch is accomplished 3–5 weeks after germination to leave 4–6 lateral (secondary) breaks. In the field, these secondary branches fall over and the tertiary stems which arise may be harvested with 12–16" long stems. A late pinch (actually a disbud), removing the first visible flower buds, allows the upper laterals to develop a spray of short stems, much like a spray mum. According to Dr. Andersen, pinching is not necessary under dense spacing (4–6 plants/ft^2). At such a spacing, a yield of 35 stems/ft^2 was recorded; 75% of the stems were 22–34" long.

Protection: If rain during the harvest period is common, some overhead protection, such as shade cloth or single poly, is recommended to reduce the damage. Overhead irrigation or excess rain can result in significant decline in quality.

Greenhouse Performance

Successful greenhouse production must occur under long day conditions, high light intensity and cool temperatures. These conditions may be found in most greenhouses in late winter and early spring. In Kentucky, a late January sowing resulted in mid-May flowering (1). Midwinter production is not possible without high intensity discharge supplemental lighting (approx. 800 fc for 18 hours/day). Additional research is being conducted to reduce the expense of HID lighting.

Single-stem plants may be grown at 8–10 plants/ft^2 for the first 7 weeks if grown under supplemental light. Plants may be finished at 5–6 plants/ft^2 (5" × 6") or up to 8" × 8".

Flowering begins approximately 10–12 weeks from sowing and continues for about 2 weeks. Yields of 15–30 flowers/plant are not uncommon under such conditions. Plants need support throughout the duration of the crop. Sub-irrigation is essential, particularly as flower buds form.

If plants are to be pinched, pinch once upon transplanting to the greenhouse bench. Use the same fertility program as for field production.

Guideline for Foliar Analyses

At field trials in Watsonville, CA, foliage was sampled from vigorously growing healthy plants when flower buds were visible, but prior to flower opening. These are guidelines only and should not be considered absolute standards. Based on dry weight analysis.

(%)						(ppm)				
N	P	K	Ca	Mg		Fe	Mn	B	Al	Zn
Grace mix										
3.2	0.26	4.18	1.03	0.34		189	239	23	96	36

Stage of Harvest

Harvest when the first flowers on the stem are open. For dried flowers, allow as many flowers to open as possible. Flowers harvested in the tight bud stage (to reduce shipping weight and damage) often do not open. This is an excellent flower for local sales due to its relatively poor shipability.

Postharvest

Fresh: In water, vase life is approximately 5–10 days, although the fresher the flowers, the better the vase life. Individual flowers may last only 5–6 days but flower buds continue to open without fading. Therefore, the more flowers present on the stem, the longer the vase life. A vase life of 2 weeks is not uncommon. Silver thiosulfate does not significantly improve vase life. Preservatives enhance the vase life by an additional 1–2 days.

Storage: Storage is not recommended but plants may be kept in water at 36–41F if necessary. This is an excellent plant for local growers as stems do not ship well dry.

Dried: Strip foliage and hang upside down in a warm, dark, well-ventilated area.

Cultivars

The following are cultivars of *Godetia amoena.*

Single-flowered

'Aurora' has salmon-orange flowers.

'Furora' bears crimson-scarlet flowers on 2.5' tall stems.

'Gloria' produces clear pink flowers.

Grace series is an F_1 hybrid, and although seed is more expensive than open pollinated forms, the uniformity and color selection are excellent. The upright habit, 2–3' height and the availability of individual cultivars with light pink, rose-pink, salmon, red and lavender flowers and a formula mix make the series particularly attractive.

'Memoria' bears clean white flowers on 2' tall stems.

Double-flowered

Azaleaflora mixture is available as a mix or in numerous single colors. The many colors of the series include 'Maidenblush' with bright rose flowers, 'Ruddigore' with flowers of crimson-red and 'White Bouquet' with white flowers. Carmine ('Brilliant'), pink ('Sweetheart') and orange ('Orange Glory') flowering cultivars are also included in the series. Plants generally flower on 1–2' tall stems.

'Grandiflora' is taller (2.5') than 'Azaleaflora' but only available as a mix-ture of colors.

Pests and Diseases

Root rots (*Pythium, Phytophthora, Rhizoctonia*, etc.) infect seedlings in the propagation area or at transplant. *Rhizoctonia* is very pathogenic and can be lethal 3–7 days after symptoms appear. In the field, the foliage turns pink, then red and finally the whole plant declines. The pathogen may be seed-borne. Use clean soil and tools and apply a fungicide as needed.

Rusts have been reported in field plants. Infected plants should be removed and destroyed.

Aster yellows may also occur in field plantings. Rotate crops every 1–2 years.

Aphids and Western flower thrips are the most serious pests in the field. Aphids, whiteflies, mites and thrips are significant problems in the greenhouse.

Related Genera

Clarkia and *Godetia* are used interchangeably and one genus is often sold as the other. Most taxonomists treat them as synonyms; however, some authorities have split one from the other. According to the "splitters," the petals of *Clarkia* are distinctly clawed (bottom half of the petal much more narrow than upper half) while those of *Godetia* are scarcely clawed. Plants of *Clarkia* will not flower well below 60F. Plants should be started when temperatures are below 55F and grown for 4–6 weeks to develop a sizeable plant prior to raising the temperature to 60F. Cultivars of *Clarkia grandiflora* include 'Appleblossom' (pale pink), 'Enchantress' (salmon-pink) and 'Vesuvius' (scarlet).

Reading

1. Anderson, R. G., and R. L. Geneve. 1992. Field production of satin flower or *Godetia*. In *Proceedings of the 4th National Conference of Specialty Cut Flowers*. Cleveland, OH. 28–32.

2. Halevy, A. H., and D. Weiss. 1990. Flowering control of recently introduced hybrid cultivars of *Godetia*. *Scientia Hortic*. 46:295–299.

3. Post, K. 1955. *Florist Crop Production and Marketing*. Orange Judd, New York, NY.

4. Seals, J. 1991. Some uncommon and common (but choice) cut flowers from seed for field growing. *The Cut Flower Quarterly* 3(2):13–14.

5. Utami, L. S. 1991. *Environmental factors influencing the cut flower production of satin flower* (Clarkia amoena *ssp.* whitneyi). M.S. Thesis, Univ. of Kentucky.

Many thanks to Dr. Robert Anderson and Mr. Jeff McGrew for reviewing this section.

Gomphrena globosa   Globe Amaranth   2–3'/2'
Various colors   Mediterranean   Amaranthaceae

Globe amaranth is widely used as a dried flower and is available in numerous colors and sizes. Excellent selections of *G. globosa*, *G. haageana* and hybrids between the 2 species have been identified. Plants are heat and drought tolerant, easy to grow and may be harvested mechanically.

Propagation

Few things are as messy as uncleaned *Gomphrena* seed. If purchasing seed, buy cleaned seed. Seed is often sold by weight. *Gomphrena globosa* has approximately 19,000 clean seeds/oz but there are only about 8000 uncleaned seeds for the same weight. *Gomphrena haageana* has 11,000 clean seeds/oz. Although more expensive, greater percentages and more uniform germination can be expected from properly cleaned seed. In fact, it is ludicrous not to purchase clean seed. Germination can be erratic but a number of producers have improved seed emergence with various treatments. Germination is approximately doubled by scarification and scarified seed should be purchased if available. Seed may also be separated by size for higher germination. Larger seed results in greater germination and "high-tech" seed is recommended.

Germination occurs in as little as 4–5 days in a sweat chamber at 78–80F or may take as long as 10 days when sown in the greenhouse at 70–72F under

Gomphrena globosa **(dried)**

mist. One grower has had successful and very rapid germination at temperatures as high as 100F. No difference in germination between light and dark conditions has been shown. Due to erratic germination of untreated seed, direct sowing is not recommended. However, if direct sowing is to be accomplished, use clean, scarified and preferably sized seed. With direct sowing of clean seed, a rate of 1.5–2 oz/1000 ft^2 is recommended (1).

Growing-on

Grow seedlings at 65F nights, 70F days for most rapid growth. Capillary mats are useful for growing-on seedlings after the first flush of germination. Temperatures of 70–72F are useful when capillary mats are used. Seedlings from open packs may be transplanted to cell packs or small containers in about 3 weeks from sowing and planted to the field 4–5 weeks later. Transplant prior to flowering. If grown in plugs, allow 6–8 weeks before transplanting to container or field, depending on size of plug.

Fertilize seedlings initially with 50–100 ppm N; over 50% of the nitrogen should be in the nitrate form. As seedlings grow more actively, fertility may be increased to 100–150 ppm N and K. Overfertilizing results in tall, soft growth which transplants poorly.

Environmental Factors

Photoperiod: Flowering of *Gomphrena* occurs as plants mature, regardless of photoperiod. Flowers initiate as the plant produces additional nodes and is likely most affected by light intensity and temperature.

Temperature: Plants are heat tolerant and grow and flower more rapidly as temperatures rise above 70F. Temperatures below 65F result in slow growth and reduced flowering. *Gomphrena* is an excellent plant for the Midwest and Southeast because of its tolerance of warm, humid weather.

Field Performance

Spacing: Plants should be grown on 6–9" centers. Some growers plant a double row on ridges 16" apart. Two rows are planted 8" apart on top of each ridge. This computes to approximately 16,000 plants/acre. No pinching or support is necessary.

Harvesting: *Gomphrena* may be sequentially planted and each planting machine-harvested at one time. Although fewer stems/plant are harvested compared with hand harvesting, the labor savings far outweigh the value of the lost stems. Yield is often measured in dry weight per acre or plant. An average of $\frac{1}{2}$ to $\frac{3}{4}$ pound of dried stems per plant occurs at Woodcreek Farm in Ohio; red cultivars yield up to 1 lb/plant, purple under $\frac{1}{2}$ pound. Flowers may be picked all summer long from single spring plantings.

Work at the University of Georgia in which stems of *Gomphrena* 'Strawberry Fields' were hand-harvested resulted in approximately 58 stems/plant with an average stem length over the entire season of 15". The distribution of yield is shown in Figure 1. The numbers above each bar represent the percentage of total yield for the time period.

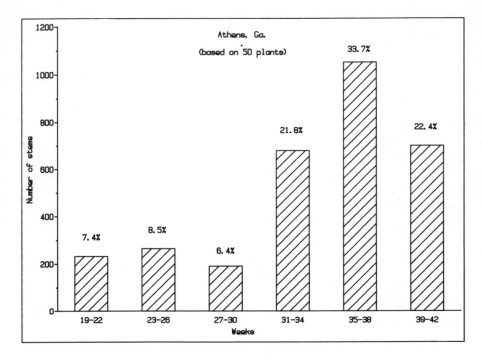

Figure 1. Yield and percentage of total stems on *Gomphrena* 'Strawberry Fields' over time (data from University of Georgia, 1987).

Stem quality: The length of stems is not as critical a quality in *Gomphrena* as it is with other cut flower species because fresh flowers are normally used as bouquets and fillers. However, stem length cannot be ignored and breeding efforts have concentrated on flower color and shape as well as longer, stronger stems. Short stems, however, are still useful. The distribution of stem length from field trials at the University of Georgia is provided in Figure 2.

Shading: *Gomphrena* is a full-sun plant and shading is not recommended.

Greenhouse Performance

Gomphrena is seldom grown in the greenhouse for cut flower production. However, if grown in the greenhouse, use 63–65F nights and 70F days. Allow as much light penetration as possible and fertilize at 200 ppm N with nitrate nitrogen. Space on 6–9" centers.

Stage of Harvest

Harvest when flowers are in color but before fully open. If stems are mechanically harvested, select only those flowers which are swollen and nearly fully colored. If harvested for drying, allow flowers to open completely.

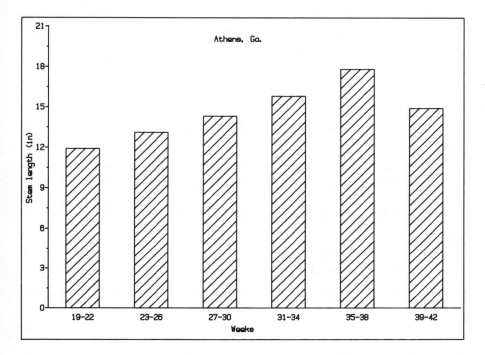

Figure 2. Stem length on *Gomphrena* 'Strawberry Fields' over time (data from University of Georgia, 1987).

Postharvest

Fresh: Fresh flowers persist for approximately 1 week.

Dried: Most of the flowers grown in the United States are used for drying. Flowers may be air-dried and held indefinitely. Strip leaves prior to drying and hang upside down in small bunches. Reduce field moisture as much as possible, use good air circulation and reduce humidity. Treating with glycerine is also practiced but is more costly than air-drying.

Storage: Storage of fresh flowers is not recommended, but if necessary, store at 36–41F.

Cultivars

Gomphrena globosa comes in red ('Rubra'), white, rose, lavender ('Lavender Queen') and purple-violet. Stems are 12–15" tall. Bedding plant cultivars are also available (e.g., Buddy series) but are not recommended for cut flower production.

Additional Species

Gomphrena haageana (golden amaranth), native to India, has a longer, less rounded flower and is an attractive yellow-orange color. Cultivation is similar to *G. globosa*.

'Strawberry Fields' ('Woodcreek Red') is the standard for cut *Gomphrena* today. The stems are longer than on other cultivars, the flowers are a deep red and hold their color exceptionally well when dried. It appears to be a selection of *G. haageana* but may be a hybrid with some *G. globosa* characteristics. 'Cramer's Raspberry' is similar to 'Strawberry Fields', but the flower is a marvelous soft rose color rather than red. It has been selected by Ralph Cramer of Cramer's Posie Patch.

Other exciting colors, including bicolors, are being actively developed.

Pests and Diseases

Several leaf-spotting fungi, the worst being *Cercospora gomphrenae*, occur on globe amaranth in the southern United States. It is also host to several viral diseases.

Pests include aphids, thrips and two-spotted spider mite.

Reading

1. Nau, J. 1989. *Ball Culture Guide: The Encyclopedia of Seed Germination.* Ball Seed Co., West Chicago, IL.

Sincere thanks to Mr. Ralph Cramer and Mr. Mike Wallace for reviewing this section.

Helianthus annuus	Annual Sunflower	4–7'/3'
Gold, yellow	Western United States, Midwest	Asteraceae

The annual sunflower is native from Minnesota to Washington and California and has become one of the most important crops in the world due to the importance of its oil and forage properties. The flower, the subject of painters and the passion of birds, has found renewed life as a cut flower in Japan, Europe and the United States. Plants are relatively easy to grow and flowers are prolifically produced.

Propagation

All plants are produced from seed; there are approximately 700 seeds/oz depending on species and cultivar. Approximately 3.5 oz of seed yield 1000 plants and are usually direct-sown (1).

Greenhouse: Although most sunflower seed is direct-sown, seed may be greenhouse-sown at 70–75F in final containers 3–4 weeks prior to placing in the field. Do not sow too early or plants will not transplant well.

Field: Most seed is direct-sown 9–12" apart in the field after all threat of frost has passed; some growers direct seed as close as 6" apart. Soil should be well drained for best germination and growth.

Growing-on

Plants should be held in the greenhouse for no more than 4 weeks prior to planting in the field. Provide full light, high fertility levels (150–200 ppm N) and good air movement.

Helianthus annuus

Environmental Factors

Photoperiod: Plants show a remarkable cultivar-dependent response to photoperiod (2) but most appear to be day-neutral or flower somewhat faster under short days.

Temperature: Warm temperatures result in faster flower development than cool temperatures. Temperatures below 50F slow development significantly; temperatures of 65–75F appear optimal for growth and development of cut flower cultivars.

Gibberellic acid: The use of gibberellic acid shortens the vegetative stage and slightly accelerates flowering (2).

Field Performance

Spacing: Space seed or transplants 9–12" apart.

Fertilization: Sunflowers are heavy feeders and plants should be fed at least 3 times a season. Side dress with granular 10–10–10 or liquid feed at 200 ppm N with a complete soluble fertilizer.

Support: Some cultivars can grow 8' tall and may fall over from the weight of the heavy foliage and flowers. Stems of newer cultivars are sufficiently strong to carry the flowers under calm conditions but support may be necessary in windy areas.

Planting: Sequential planting every 2–4 weeks is useful to take advantage of long terminal flower stems. Laterals are shorter and flowers are smaller after the terminal has been cut.

Greenhouse Performance

Sunflowers may be produced during the winter in the greenhouse if market price and demand so warrant. Supplemental light may be necessary in northern greenhouses.

Sow seed directly in the bench at 6–9" spacing or in a 6–8" container and fertilize lightly (100 ppm N) when seedlings have emerged. Maintain 50–55F night temperatures and 65–70F day temperatures. For tallest plants, grow under long days for 4–6 weeks, then change to short days (12 hours or less) for tallest stems, but photoperiod manipulation is not necessary for flowering, especially if plants are grown at a dense spacing. Plants may be grown under natural photoperiod throughout. Fertilize with a constant liquid feed program of 100–150 ppm N or once a week with 300 ppm N. Plants must be supported with stakes or strong netting. With newer cultivars, a crop time of 60–70 days from sowing is not uncommon.

Stage of Harvest

Harvest stems when the flowers are almost completely open.

Postharvest

Fresh: Flowers remain fresh in water or preservative for 7–10 days. The foliage declines more rapidly than the flower.

Storage: Flowers may be stored at 36–41F for up to 1 week.

Dried: Flowers air dry well.

Cultivars

'Abendsonne' is 7–8' tall with yellow flowers around a bronze center.

'Full Sun' is 3–4' tall and bears gold-yellow flowers. It is day-neutral and does not produce pollen.

'Goldburst' is an excellent new cultivar with 3–4" wide, golden, double flowers on 4–6' tall stems. In nationwide trials in 1992, it scored higher than any other tested.

'Sunbright' is a uniform F_1 hybrid which produces high-quality 4–5" wide flowers. Flowers are without pollen, thereby enhancing vase life.

'Sunrich Lemon' is a pollenless, day-neutral F_1 hybrid. Flowers are more yellow than lemon, but they contrast well with the black center. Plants flower earlier than 'Sunbright'.

The last 2 cultivars flower well under cool, short day environments.

Additional Species

Helianthus decapetalus (thinleaf sunflower) has smaller flowers than annual sunflower and may bear multiple flowers per stem. 'Italian White' has creamy white flowers with a contrasting black center. Variety *multiflorus* is excellent for cut flower production and bears numerous, light yellow, single flowers on 4–6' tall plants. It is a perennial in most areas of the country. 'Soleil d'Or' is a good cut flower and has semi-double, primrose-yellow flowers.

Pests and Diseases

Aphids are the most common pest of sunflowers. Control with aphicides if necessary.

Leaf spots are caused by several fungal species, resulting in brown-to-black spotting of the foliage. Alternating fungicides provides some control.

Powdery mildew (*Erysiphe cichoracearum*) causes white, powdery growth, particularly on the undersides of leaves. Use of appropriate fungicides or sulfur is recommended.

Stem rot (*Sclerotinia sclerotiorum*) normally affects plants when they are several feet tall. The thick, white, feltlike growth occurs on the stems, and the tissue beneath becomes discolored. The disease is worse in hot, wet summers. Destroy infected plants, pasteurize the soil and rotate crops every other year. Avoid close spacings and moist conditions.

Rust, in the form of red-brown pustules, affects the undersides of leaves and causes the foliage to dry up and fall. Several organisms cause rust, but the main one is *Puccinia helianthi*. Destroy infected tissue.

Wilt symptoms are caused by various organisms (*Plasmopara, Verticillium*) and cause young plants to wilt and die. Older plants may survive, but the leaves may be mottled with mosaic patterns of light yellow. Pasteurize soil and rotate crops. Do not put sunflowers in the same area more than 2 years in a row.

Reading

1. Seals, J. 1991. Some uncommon and common (but choice) cut flowers

from seed for field growing. *The Cut Flower Quarterly* 3(2):13–14.

2. Shuster, W. H. 1985. *Helianthus annuus.* In A. H. Halevy (ed.), *The Handbook of Flowering,* vol. 3, CRC Press, Boca Raton, FL. 98–121.

Many thanks to Mr. Jim Garner for reviewing this section.

Helichrysum bracteatum	Strawflower	15–30"/2'
Various colors	Australia	Asteraceae

The genus consists of about 300 species of annuals, perennials, subshrubs and shrubs. Most are native to Australia and South Africa. The flowers are surrounded by dry, papery ornamental bracts and are easily dried. Common names for flowers of the genus include strawflowers, everlastings and immortelles. *Helichrysum bracteatum* has 1–2" wide flowers on stems up to 2' tall.

Propagation

Although usually direct-sown, seed may be started at 70–75F in a sweat tent and lightly covered. Germination occurs in 7–10 days, and seedlings may be transplanted in 3–4 weeks. Approximately 1/10 oz of seed yields 1000 plants. If direct-sown in the field, use a rate of 3–3.5 oz/1000 ft^2 and thin to 10–12" apart within rows (2,3).

Growing-on

Provide 60F night temperatures, 65–70F day temperatures to seedlings. If sown in open flats, transplant to cells or small pots 3–4 weeks from sowing.

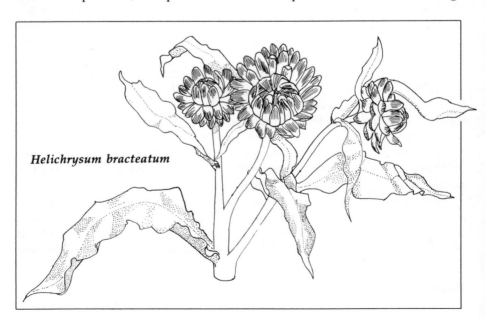

Helichrysum bracteatum

If germinated in plugs, maintain the plug for 5–6 weeks before transplanting to the field. Fertilize with 75–100 ppm N with a complete fertilizer. Overfertilization results in tall, lanky seedlings. Maintain low moisture levels; plants are susceptible to overwatering and should be allowed to dry out. Transplant to the field or final greenhouse spacing when plants are still vegetative or in small flower bud; do not transplant with flowers.

Environmental Factors

Photoperiod: Long days result in faster flowering, but flowering occurs regardless of photoperiod. Flowering is mainly a result of light intensity and temperature. Growth is more rapid—therefore flowering occurs faster—under full sun and warm temperatures.

Temperature: Temperatures below 55F result in slow growth and additional problems with root rot fungi. Temperatures of 70–75F are optimum for growth and flowering.

Field Performance

Spacing: Space on 10–12" centers.

Support: Plants, particularly the tetraploid types, require at least 1 tier of support.

Planting: Sequentially direct-sow or transplant every 2–4 weeks. The main flower head may be removed to harvest the resul ng initial laterals. With sequential planting, only the first 2–4 lateral flowers are harvested and subsequent flower stems are disregarded. If only a single planting occurs, lateral stems eventually become too short for high-c·iality stems.

Location: Plants are not tolerant of poorly drained soils or areas of heavy rainfall. Warm temperatures, combined with wet w· ather, result in root rots and foliar spotting. Plants do better in areas of dry summers (California, Arizona) than in areas of high moisture (Southeast).

Greenhouse Performance

Place on 6–9" centers, maintain 65–75F temperatures and high light intensity.

Stage of Harvest

Cut flowers when bracts are unfolding and centers are visible. Always harvest before flowers are fully open. If picked open, petals turn backward as they dry, resulting in a rather ugly blossom (1).

Postharvest

Fresh: Fresh flowers persist for 7–10 days.

Dried: When dried, flowers persist indefinitely. Strip leaves and hang in tight bunches upside down in a warm, well-ventilated area. Flower heads themselves may be wired singly and dried straight up. Leave ½ to 1" of stem and stand them in a shallow container to dry.

Storage: Storage of fresh flowers is not recommended; store at 36–41F if necessary.

Cultivars

Numerous cultivars are available ranging from 18–24" dwarf to 3' tetraploid cultivars.

Ball Florists series is a tetraploid series growing 2–3' tall with little basal branching. Bronze, gold, purple, red, white and a mix are available.

Bikini series is shorter than most cultivars (18–24") and available in gold, red and a mix.

King Size series bears double flowers on 2.5–3' tall stems. Sulfur yellow, orange, red, rose and white flowers are available.

var. *monstrosum*, the most common variety in the trade, has double flowers and has been selected in numerous colors and heights.

'Paper Daisy' produces many 1" wide, yellow flowers on 15–18" tall stems.

Standard series grows approximately 3' tall and has double flowers in single colors or as a mix. Pink, red, purple, yellow, orange, salmon and white flowers are available. Seed is less expensive than King Size series but has not been as aggressively selected.

Tetraploid selections are offered under various names, such as Swiss Giant series. Plants grow 3–4' tall and are available in numerous flower colors as well as a mix.

Additional Species

A few "minor" species of *Helichrysum* are available through specialty sources. In general, they are native to Australia, New Zealand or South Africa and are best suited to the Pacific Northwest, northern California or the Northeast. High temperatures, high humidity and prolonged rain are not to their liking.

Helichrysum cassianum has single to semi-double pink flowers and grows approximately 1.5–2' tall. 'Rose Beauty' has rose-pink flowers. Germination is erratic and slow, and seed order should be double that of *H. bracteatum*.

H. subulifolium, although relatively difficult to find, grows 1.5–2' tall and bears many clear yellow flowers. Often sold as 'Golden Sun'. They should be harvested when flowers are fully open (1), unlike *H. bracteatum*.

H. thianshanicum Golden Baby has silvery gray foliage and yellow-to-orange double flowers on 12" tall stems. Plants require excellent drainage and relatively high fertility levels. This species is perennial in warmer areas of the country.

Pests and Diseases

Aster leafhoppers suck the juice from the plant and also transmit aster yellows disease.

Root and stem rot fungi result in loss of plants in areas of poor drainage and high rainfall.

Wilt caused by *Verticillium albo-atrum* may cause severe damage, particularly in California.

Reading
1. Bullivant, E. 1989. *Dried Fresh Flowers From Your Garden.* Pelham Books/Stephen Greene Press, London, U.K.

2. Nau, J. 1989. *Ball Culture Guide: The Encyclopedia of Seed Germination.* Ball Seed Co., West Chicago, IL.

3. Seals, J. 1991. Some uncommon and common (but choice) cut flowers from seed for field growing. *The Cut Flower Quarterly* 3(2):13–14.

Lavatera trimestris	Mallow Flower	2–2.5'/2'
White, pink	Mediterranean	Malvaceae

Mallow bears some of the most handsome cut flowers I have seen. The 3–4" wide flowers are normally rose-pink but some separate colors are available. The West Coast of the United States is more suitable for production than the East Coast because of the number of diseases which affect mallow in wet, hot summers.

Propagation
Seed sown under mist or sweat tent at 70–72F germinates in 7–14 days. Approximately 0.7 oz of seed yields 1000 plants (2). Seed is also direct-sown after threat of frost. Sow at the rate of 0.6 oz/100 linear ft (1) or 6 oz/1000 ft^2. Thin to 12" apart or more in the rows (see "Field Performance" for spacing recommendations).

Growing-on
Grow at 60F night temperature, 65–70F during the day. Fertilize sparingly (50–75 ppm N) with a nitrate-type fertilizer. Overwatering results in proliferation of root rot organisms, therefore, the plants should be maintained on the "dry side of moist".

Environmental Factors
Photoperiod: Flower initiation and development are not dependent on photoperiod.

Temperature: Warm temperatures result in more rapid growth and flowering. However, cool night temperatures (55–60F) produce higher quality plants and flowers than warm nights (above 70F).

Humidity: *Lavatera* is susceptible to numerous foliar diseases. Plants should not be grown in areas of high humidity (e.g., Southeast) without an aggressive spray program for pests and diseases. *Lavatera* has been trialed at the University of Georgia on 3 separate occasions and each time has ended in a dismal, disease-ridden and pest-infested failure.

Field Performance
Spacing: Space plants 18–24" apart. Although plants can be spaced as closely as 12" centers, wider spacing helps reduce disease and insect pressure.

Yield: An average of 10 stems/plant is not uncommon.

Greenhouse Performance

Lavatera for cut flower production is seldom grown in the greenhouse. However, if produced under cover, grow 12" apart at 58–60F night temperatures, 70–75F during the day. Fertilize with 100–150 ppm N constant liquid feed or with 300 ppm N once a week.

Stage of Harvest

Cut when the flowers are uncurling or when they have just begun to open. Harvest before flowers lie flat.

Postharvest

Fresh flowers persist for approximately 1 week; storage is not recommended. Flowers do not dry well.

Cultivars

'Loveliness' produces bright flowers of carmine-rose.

'Mont Blanc' has white flowers and grows 2–3' tall.

'Mont Rose' bears pink flowers.

'Silver Cup' has salmon-rose flowers with dark veins.

'Tanagra', a tetraploid cultivar, has 4–5" wide, deep rose flowers on plants 2–3' tall.

Additional Species

Lavatera thuringiaca is a half-hardy perennial which bears rose flowers on 4' tall plants.

Pests and Diseases

Leaf spots resulting from at least 5 fungi, leaf and stem blight (from 3 fungi) and rust are common on *Lavatera*, particularly in warm climates.

Aphids, spider mites and Western flower thrips also enjoy dining on *Lavatera*. In fact, *Lavatera* seems to be a preferred appetizer for most beasties in the field and greenhouse.

Reading

1. Kieft, C. 1989. *Kieft's Growing Manual* .... Kieft Bloemzaden, Venhuizen, The Netherlands.

2. Seals, J. 1991. Some uncommon and common (but choice) cut flowers from seed for field growing. *The Cut Flower Quarterly* 3(2):13–14.

Limonium sinuatum	Annual Statice	18–24"/2'
Various colors	Mediterranean	Plumbaginaceae

One of the most popular cut flowers in the world, annual or sinuata statice continues to be produced in vast quantities. Breeding of annual statice has provided numerous hybrids of various strains and colors suitable for both drying and fresh use. Flowers may be grown everywhere in the country although California and Florida are the leading producers in the United States.

Limonium sinuatum

Propagation

Approximately 10,000 clean seeds/oz occur. At "normal" germination percentages, 0.2 oz produces approximately 1000 seedlings (2). Clean seed is more expensive than unprocessed seed but is easier to handle and germinates more rapidly. Seed should be sown and covered lightly or left exposed to ensure that light reaches the seed. Seed provided with 70F germinates in 5–14 days, depending on cultivar, and may be transplanted in 3 weeks. Large plugs or transplants may be placed in the field 6–8 weeks after sowing.

Growing-on

Provide 60F temperatures for 1–2 weeks after cotyledons emerge to encourage rooting. Plants flower more rapidly and are of better quality if subjected to a cold treatment (vernalized) when young and should initially be grown at cool temperatures (50–55F). The seedling is most responsive to vernalization but cold treatment of seeds is ineffective. Plants should be cooled from the cotyledon to the 5-leaf stage, which requires 5–8 weeks. Some growers germinate seed in the greenhouse and then place seedling or plug flats in cold frames for cool temperature treatment. As daylength increases, the length of the cold treatment can be decreased. If seedlings are vernalized under LD, however, flowering is also enhanced. Fertilize seedlings with 50–100 ppm N and K.

Environmental Factors

Photoperiod: Long days promote flowering in 2 ways. The optimum photoperiod is greater than 13 hours (6). If LD are provided during the seedling stage, the length of the vernalization may be reduced. Long days without vernalization are relatively ineffective. Long days applied to actively growing plants induce a greater percentage of flowering plants regardless of temperature compared with short days. LD applied to seedlings have little effect if not accompanied by cool temperatures. The following table shows the effectiveness of LD on percentage of flowering plants.

The effect of photoperiod on flowering of *Limonium sinuatum* (LD of 16 hours; SD of 8 hours; plants treated 8 weeks from sowing; temperatures not reported).[a]

Cultivar	Flowering (%)	
	LD	SD
'American Beauty'	100	48
'Iceberg'	100	83
'Midnight Beauty'	100	55
'Twilight Lavender'	100	52

[a] Adapted from (3).

LD are most effective after plants have been cooled and are actively growing and promote earlier flowering, greater percentage of flowering plants and higher yields.

Temperature: As mentioned above, a cold treatment hastens flower initiation. High temperatures promote leaf initiation, leaf growth and stem elongation but inhibit flowering. This helps to explain why nonvernalized plants placed under warm field conditions grow well but have poor yield. Researchers at Beltsville, MD, placed seedlings in controlled temperature chambers for 6 weeks (1). They showed that plants grown at 80/75F day/night temperature formed a vegetative rosette which persisted for approximately 4 months. Day/night temperatures of 70/64F resulted in only 20% flowering plants but temperatures below 65F caused flower initiation in all plants. The optimum temperatures were 60/55F day/night. In general, blue-flowered cultivars have the greatest cold requirement (lower temperature and longer duration) followed by lavender, pink, white and yellow (4).

In summary, high temperature during the seedling stage is the most important constraint to flowering. Temperatures of 50–55F should be applied at the seedling stage for 3–8 weeks depending on season and cultivar. This treatment may occur naturally in the field with spring-planted crops or may be applied artificially in coolers for summer-planted crops.

The length of precooling varies with the season. This was shown in Israel where plants are cropped throughout the winter; in fall plantings, a maximum flowering response was obtained with 8 weeks of precooling but in early spring plantings, only 3 weeks precooling was necessary (5). The reduction in precooling time in the spring plantings was likely due to cooler night temperatures when the plants were young and longer photoperiods as the plants matured.

After vernalization is completed, high temperatures speed up the flower development process, but should not be applied immediately after planting. In practical terms, this means that precooled plants should not immediately be transplanted to 80–90F fields; transplanting in the spring is recommended. An optimum temperature regime for early and profuse flowering is 73/60F day/night temperatures (4).

Gibberellic acid: Gibberellic acid (GA_3) has been used to reduce the need for precooling in annual statice. Work in Florida and Israel has shown that application of GA_3 partially overcomes the precooling requirement. The following table shows the influence of GA on 'Midnight Blue' statice; notice that it is relatively ineffective if the precooling requirements have been satisfied.

The effect of GA on flowering of *Limonium sinuatum* 'Midnight Blue'.[a]

Precooling (days)	GA applied	Flowering (%)
0	No	40
	Yes	83
6	No	42
	Yes	94
12	No	72
	Yes	100
28	No	95
	Yes	100

[a]From (5,7).

The table shows that as more precooling was applied, GA became less effective, but with 0–12 days of precooling, the application of GA was effective in promoting flowering.

The optimum application time and concentration appear to be approximately 12 weeks after seeding and 500 ppm, respectively. GA should not be applied when plants are budded. An application in the amount of 10 ml/plant is effective. Work by Wilfret and Raulston (7) showed that 'Iceberg' and 'Midnight Blue' flowered in 134 and 160 days from seed, respectively, with a GA application but required 238 and 229 days without GA.

Field Performance

Soil: Statice prefers soil high in lime: pH 6.5–7.5.

Spacing: Space either on 1' centers or 10" × 12". Plants may be grown in rows which are 12–14" wide, allowing for 2–3 staggered rows/bed. Space plants 14–16" apart down the length of the bed (2). Neither support nor pinching is necessary.

Scheduling: The first harvest occurs in the South approximately 3–5 months after sowing; in the North 4–6 months are necessary. Place in the field after danger of frost has passed but before night temperatures rise above 55–60F. In northern California, plant from October to January for April to October production. Harvest is heavy for the first 4–6 weeks and levels off as plants mature.

Plants may be planted at 2-week or monthly intervals if provided with precooling (see "Environmental Factors") or if gibberellic acid is applied. Plants will begin to flower 6–10 weeks after transplanting. In warm-winter areas, continuous cropping may be accomplished by sowing at 2- to 4-week intervals. However, in areas where temperatures seldom go below 55F, the use of GA may be warranted.

Yield: In northern California, approximately 20 stems/plant are produced from April to October. This translates to approximately 25,000 bunches (12 stems/bunch) per acre from 15,000 plants. Research at the University of Georgia resulted in 21.7 stems/plant between mid-June and August with the Fortress series. Figure 1 shows the distribution of yield over time for a typical series during a single harvesting period.

Distribution percentages of total yield from California and Georgia (Fig. 2) show similar trends although harvesting persists for many more weeks in California than in Georgia.

Some growers sell statice by the pound and yields of 10,000–40,000 lbs/acre depending on cultivar and environment may be expected.

Stem quality: At Georgia, stem lengths ranged from less than 12" to greater than 30" for Fortress mix. Longer and thicker stems occurred during initial harvest dates compared with later harvests. In general, blue-flowered stems were thicker than average, yellow-flowered stems thinner than average. Figure 3 shows the change in stem length over time.

Greenhouse Performance

Space seedlings 10" × 10" and grow in a cool greenhouse (50–55F) in order to initiate flowers. Cool temperatures must be maintained for at least 6 weeks. After the cool treatment, temperatures may be raised to 60/70F night/day. In the absence of cool temperatures, a spray of 500 ppm gibberellic acid may be applied when plants are 6–8" across. Maintain plants under photoperiods of approximately 16 hours. Fertilize with a nitrate-N fertilizer at 100 ppm each irrigation when plants are grown cool and raise fertility levels when temperatures are raised.

Plants sown in November and January will flower in March and May, respectively, depending on cultivar and location.

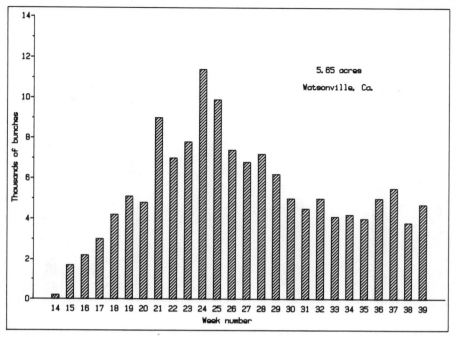

Figure 1. Yield of *Limonium sinuatum* (from 5.65 acres; Watsonville, CA).

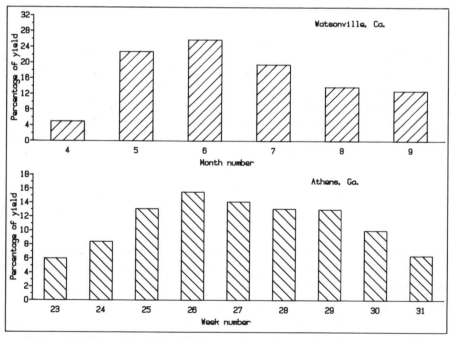

Figure 2. Flowering of *Limonium sinuatum* as percentage of total yield (Watsonville, CA, and Athens, GA).

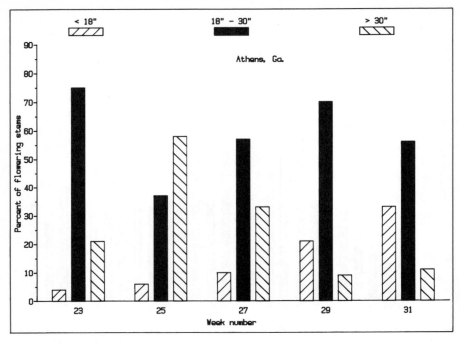

Figure 3. Stem length of *Limonium sinuatum* (Fortress mix; Athens, GA).

Guideline for Foliar Analyses

At field trials in Athens, GA, and Watsonville, CA, foliage was sampled from vigorously growing healthy plants when flower buds were visible, but prior to flower opening. These are guidelines only and should not be considered absolute standards. Based on dry weight analysis. Numbers shown are the average of 'Heavenly Blue' (Athens, GA), 'Fortress Blue' and 'Fortress Yellow' (Watsonville, CA).

(%)						(ppm)				
N	P	K	Ca	Mg		Fe	Mn	B	Al	Zn
3.5	0.66	3.11	0.57	0.92		159	117	20	105	70

Stage of Harvest

Harvest when the individual flowers are mostly open and showing color. The white of the flowers (petals) should be visible and the rest of the flower color (sepals) well developed.

Postharvest

Flowers persist for approximately 2 weeks in water without any particular care. Stems must be dry prior to shipping or botrytis will take hold.

Storage: Stems may be stored dry at 36–41F for 2–3 weeks (2).

Dried: Strip the large, fleshy leaves and hang upside down in a warm, well-ventilated area. The drying barn must be dark, or the color of stems and flowers will rapidly decline. Stems remain green if dried rapidly.

Cultivars

Many cultivars are available and more are being developed every year.

'Blue River' has intense blue flowers with somewhat shorter stems than Fortress.

Excellent series has numerous colors and comes into production more rapidly than others. Uniformity of colors is excellent. Colors include deep yellow, light blue, purple, shades of rose, pink and salmon, and sky blue.

Fortress series is one of the most popular series for cut flower production. Individual colors are apricot, dark blue, heavenly blue, purple, rose, white, yellow and a mix.

'Kampf's Blue Improved' has rich, dark blue flowers.

'Lavandin' bears clear lavender flowers and appears to resist sunburn better than other cultivars.

'Market Grower Blue' produces tall, uniformly blue flowers.

'Midnight Blue' has uniform, rich, dark blue flowers.

'Oriental Blue' has been one of the standard cultivars for cut flower production for many years. The rich, deep blue color is consistent and uniform.

Pacific strain is available as a mix or in individual colors. Colors include 'American Beauty' (deep rose), 'Apricot Beauty', 'Gold Coast' (deep yellow), 'Heavenly Blue', 'Iceberg' (white), 'Roselight' (rose-pink) and 'Twilight' (lavender-pink). Some growers, particularly in the Northwest, claim that yield of the Pacific strain is significantly higher than Fortress.

'Pastel Shades' is a mixture of lavender and purple shades on 2–3' tall stems. 'Sophia' consists of rose and pale pink flowers and is part of the series.

QIS series (formerly Sunburst series) has proven to be excellent for greenhouse and field production. The series has uniform colors, is fast-flowering and grows 2.5' tall. Colors include dark blue, pale blue, lilac, purple, red, rose (earlier than other cultivars), white and yellow.

'Rose Strike' has rose-pink shades with a loose flower habit.

Soiree series is relatively new and includes apricot, rose, purple, light blue, white, deep blue and a mixture of colors.

Sunset series bears flowers in fall colors. Shades of yellow, orange, salmon, rose and apricot are available.

Turbo series is known for its pastel shades, early flowering habit and long stems. Plants grow 2.5' tall. Colors are blue, carmine, peach, purple, white and yellow.

Additional Species

Limonium bonduellii is a half-hardy annual or perennial. Flowers are yellow, borne on 1–2' tall flower stems and known by their spiny bracts. Plants are marginally tall enough to be included in a cut flower program.

Sometimes yellow-flowering plants listed under annual statice are actually this species.

L. sinense bears flowers with white sepals and yellow petals. Plants are approximately 2' tall. See the section on perennial *Limonium* for more details.

L. suworowii (sometimes called *Psylliostachys suworowii*; rat tail or russian statice) has a terminal spike of lavender flowers up to 1' long and is an excellent flower for drying. The flower stems are 2–2.5' long. Harvest in full flower (no less than 80% open) and hang upside down with leaves remaining. Plants are best grown in a cool greenhouse in the Southeast but may be produced in the field in winter in Florida and California. They are not tolerant of warm summer conditions and should be avoided as an outdoor summer cut flower in the Midwest and Southeast.

Pests and Diseases

Root rots, caused by water molds, are a common problem particularly in warm, wet weather. A fungicidal drench is useful when transplants are placed in the field. Yellow-colored cultivars are more sensitive to root rots than other colors are.

Leaf spots are caused by at least 5 fungal species. Spray with a wide-spectrum fungicide.

Reading

1. Krizek, D. T., and P. Semeniuk. 1972. Influence of day/night temperature under controlled environments on the growth and flowering of *Limonium* 'Midnight Blue'. *J. Amer. Soc. Hort. Sci.* 97:597–599.

2. Seals, J. 1989. Culture profile: *Limonium sinuatum.* Gatherings. *The Cut Flower Quarterly.* 1(1):6,11.

3. Semeniuk, P., and D. T. Krizek. 1972. Long days and cool night temperature increase flowering of greenhouse grown *Limonium* cultivars. *HortScience* 7:293.

4. _____ . 1973. Influence of germination and growing temperature on flowering of six cultivars of annual statice (*Limonium* cv.). *J: Amer. Soc. Hort. Sci.* 98:140–142.

5. Shillo, R. 1977. Influence of GA and the number of cold days on flowering of statice 'Midnight Blue' (in Hebrew). Annual Report Dept. Ornamental Hortic., Hebrew Univ., Rehovot, Israel. 26–40.

6. Shillo R., and E. Zamski. 1985. *Limonium sinuatum.* In A. H. Halevy (ed.). *The Handbook of Flowering,* vol. 3. CRC Press, Boca Raton, FL. 292–301.

7. Wilfret, G. J., and J. C. Raulston. 1975. Acceleration of flowering of statice. *HortScience* 10:37–38.

Sincere thanks to Ms. Fran Foley for reviewing this section.

Lunaria annua   Honesty   2–3′/2′
  Violet, white   Europe   Brassicaceae

Although technically a biennial, 1-year-old plantlets should be planted every year. The flowers, although handsome, are of little value as cut flowers because of their tendency to shatter. The transparent, round, slim fruits form rapidly after flowering and are excellent dried material. Although honesty is normally treated as a biennial, an annual genotype which doesn't require cold was recently discovered (3).

Propagation

Although usually direct-sown, seed may be sown in the greenhouse at 65–70F under intermittent mist and will germinate in 10–14 days. Approximately 1.8 oz of seed yield 1000 seedlings (2). Plantlets, grown in open pack, may be transplanted in 3–4 weeks. If grown in plugs, transplant to the field or 4″ containers after 6–8 weeks.

Seed should be direct-sown at the rate of 0.8 oz/100 linear ft (1) or 8.9 g/1000 ft^2 (2). Germination occurs in the field in 2–3 weeks.

Growing-on

Grow at 60F night temperatures. Fertilize with 100 ppm N, using a complete fertilizer.

Environmental Factors

Photoperiod: *Lunaria* is a biennial and requires a cold treatment (vernalization) for proper flowering. Although the main trigger to flowering is cold temperature, LD (16 hours) after vernalization result in faster flowering than SD (8 hours) (3). Once vernalized, however, plants will flower regardless of photoperiod.

Light intensity: High light intensity results in faster flowering after vernalization.

Temperature: Cold temperatures (40F) are necessary for flowering. Seedlings should be at least 6 weeks old before vernalization is applied. Approximately 10 weeks of cold treatment are successful. If vernalization is not sufficiently long or cold, less than 100% of the plants flower and lateral flowers predominate. Under optimal vernalization conditions, lateral and terminal flowers occur side by side. Seed vernalization has a partial effect on flower induction (3).

Field Performance

Spacing: Space transplants or thin seedlings to 10″ × 18″ or 12″ × 12″ spacing. One-year-old transplants may be purchased and planted at the proper spacing. Partial shade is useful in hot climates; full sun in more temperate areas.

Fertilization: Apply side dressings of granular fertilizer such as 8–8–8 in the spring and summer, or apply 500–700 ppm N once a week with a water-soluble fertilizer.

Lunaria annua

Greenhouse Performance

Using 1-year-old precooled plants only, grow in 6–8" containers or space 9" apart in a greenhouse bench. After approximately 3 weeks in the greenhouse, use incandescent lights to provide 16-hour days until flower buds are visible. Fertilize with a water-soluble fertilizer (100–150 ppm N) with each irrigation. Support may be necessary.

Stage of Harvest

Harvest the pods when they are fully developed. Pods may be purple (var. *purpurea*) or silvery white as they dry naturally on the plant. Strip the main leaves but allow the finer ones to remain. Bunch and hang upside down in a warm, dark place for 4–5 weeks. The pods are ready when the papery covering is easily removed.

Postharvest

The flowers, which are generally harvested in May and June, may be cut for fresh arrangements and persist for 3–5 days. The seed pods, once air-dried, should persist indefinitely.

Cultivars

With regard to fruit, a purple-fruited form (var. *purpurea*) occurs. If the color could be retained, the purple fruits would be a welcome addition to this species. Seeds of white-, red- and purple-flowered cultivars are available but they all produce the same color and shape of fruit. A cultivar with variegated foliage (var. *folio-variegata*) may also be found.

Additional Species

Lunaria rediviva (perennial honesty) bears elliptical seed pods. The plants, once established, are perennial and persist for 3–5 years. The fruit is not considered to be as ornamental as the biennial form, an unfortunate misconception.

Pests and Diseases

Numerous fungal species (*Alternaria oleracea, Helminthosporium lunariae*) attack the foliage or pods and result in brown-to-black spotting of the infected areas. Application of a general fungicide can reduce the damage. Root rots from *Phytophthora* and *Rhizoctonia* spp. also occur. Waterlogged soils result in *Phytophthora* infections. Club root, in which the feeder roots are destroyed and the main roots develop abnormally, is a result of *Plasmodiophora brassicae*. Use of fungicidal drenches has been effective.

Leaf rollers, thrips and aphids are the major insect pests.

Reading

1. Kieft, C. 1989. *Kieft's Growing Manual* . . . . Kieft Bloemzaden, Venhuizen, The Netherlands.

2. Seals, J. 1991. Some uncommon and common (but choice) cut flowers from seed for field growing. *The Cut Flower Quarterly* 3(2):13–14.

3. Wellensiek, S. J. 1985. *Lunaria annua*. In A. H. Halevy (ed.), *The Handbook of Flowering*, vol. 3. CRC Press, Boca Raton, FL. 324–329.

Matthiola incana	Stock	2–3'/2'
Various colors	Mediterranean	Brassicaceae

Stocks have long been a favorite as a cut flower and are grown throughout the northern flower-producing areas. They require cool temperatures for optimum flowering and quality. Most cultivars bear 50–60% double flowers. However, the greater the percentage of double flowers, the better the crop will be. Doubleness has been genetically linked with light green leaves when grown at 50F and it is theoretically possible to select for 100% double flowers in some seed strains if started in the greenhouse. Numerous cultivars are available but additional work to stabilize doubleness and fragrance in flowers is necessary.

Propagation

Seed sown at 65–70F germinates in 7–14 days. If sown in open packs, transplant to 3–4" containers 14–21 days from sowing. If grown in plugs, grow for 4–6 weeks. Single forms are gray-green and generally less vigorous than double forms and may be pricked out. In fact, many cultivars have been bred for ease of selection in the greenhouse. This is a difficult job at best, and almost impossible if seeds are direct-sown in the field, but one which can result in a greater percentage of double flowers. The cost and availability of labor may force direct sowing in the field instead of transplanting, but the percent of doubles will be lower if direct-sown. Approximately ¼ oz of seed yields 1000 double-flowered plants.

Growing-on

If produced in plugs, apply 75–100 ppm N fertilizer at each irrigation. Temperatures of 50–55F should be applied as soon as plants are removed from the propagation area. Plants may be placed in the field in fall or early spring after 8–10 weeks in the greenhouse.

Environmental Factors

Temperature is the main environmental factor affecting flowering in stock, although photoperiod and juvenility also influence flowering time.

Photoperiod: Long days provided before or during the cold treatment usually result in faster flowering at a lower leaf number compared to SD (1,3,7). LD can partially substitute for cold in some cultivars and result in earlier flowering where temperature treatments are not fully satisfied (1,3,9). Long day treatments may be provided by daylength extension or nightbreak lighting.

Temperature: Although great diversity exists in the response of different cultivars, high temperature generally delays flowering while low temperature promotes it (3,4,9). Most cultivars ('Column', 'Bismarck' and 'Avalanche') fail to initiate flowers at temperatures above 65F and those that do ('Brilliant') are usually later and produce more leaves than when grown below 60F.

Matthiola incana

Late-flowering types require lower temperatures for a longer period of time than those classified as early-flowering types. In general, early-flowering types require fewer than 10 days at 50–55F whereas about 3 weeks are necessary for late-flowering cultivars. Although floral initiation occurs rapidly, low temperatures should be maintained for an additional 15–20 days after floral initiation.

Juvenility: The time of application of the cold treatment varies with cultivar. In general, cultivars classified as early-flowering have a short juvenile period and form few leaves while those classified as late-flowering have a longer juvenile period and form more leaves before the first flower bud (2). Some flowering types and their response to cold treatment are shown in the following table.

The effect of application time of cold treatment on *Matthiola incana* (temperatures of 50–55F for 14–21 days).[a]

| Cultivar | Timing | Cold treatment initiated | | Days to visible bud | Leaves at visible bud |
		Juvenility (days from sowing)	Mature leaves present		
'Brilliant'	Early	15	2	40	16
'Column'	Medium	38	10	70	—[b]
'Avalanche'	Late	57	—	86	42

[a]Adapted from (3,5,7).
[b]Dash (—) indicates that data are not available.

With most cultivars, regardless of flowering classification, the older the plant, the shorter the period of cold treatment needed. Vernalization of seed is of no benefit (4).

Field Performance

Stocks can only be field-grown successfully in areas of mild winters and/or cool summers. These areas include the West Coast, Arizona and parts of Florida.

Spacing: Space plants on 6–10" centers. A dense spacing such as 6" × 8" increases yield/ft^2 but potential problems due to disease and insects are also increased. Direct sowings may be as close as 3" apart but some thinning of seedlings should be done.

Support: Staking is only necessary if grown where temperatures are too high. Night temperatures should remain around 50F during the duration of the crop. If temperatures are consistently above 60F, support is necessary.

Greenhouse Performance

Stocks may be greenhouse-grown in the winter in all midwestern and northern areas. In the Midwest, holiday crops may be scheduled as shown in the following table.

Sowing times for holiday crops of *Matthiola incana* in the Chicago area (night temperatures of 45–50F; day temperatures of 55–60F).[a]

Flowering for . . .	Sow date
Christmas	Jul 15
Valentine's Day	Sep 1
Easter (late March)	Oct 1
Mother's Day	Dec 15
June weddings	Feb 25

[a] From (6).

Approximately 6–7 months are necessary for flowering in January to March unless supplemental lighting is used at the temperatures above. With later sowings, it is more difficult to maintain cool temperatures and quality suffers. Crop time can be significantly reduced if temperatures are raised; however, quality is also reduced.

Greenhouse spacing is 3" × 6" and 2 tiers of support are recommended (6).

Fertilization: Nutrition is critical for best growth and flowering. Stocks are sensitive to potassium deficiency and fertilizers such as potassium nitrate are most effective. Potassium deficiency causes leaves to die from the tip and margin to the base. The older leaves are most sensitive and the symptoms are most visible at flowering time.

Temperature: Seedlings should be grown at 60–65F until they have approximately 8–10 leaves (10–30 days, depending on cultivar) prior to lowering temperatures for the cold treatment. This length of the "warm" temperature influences the ultimate stem length (8). Seedlings started at low temperatures are dwarfed.

Night temperatures of 50F should be applied for a minimum of 3 weeks but preferably for 6 weeks. Once the cold treatment has been applied, temperatures should remain around 55–60F for the duration of the crop. Flower buds form after the fifteenth leaf on early-flowered forms if conditions are favorable. High temperatures (above 65F) result in weaker, taller plants and necessitate the use of support netting.

Light and photoperiod: Long days, using incandescent lights as a 4-hour night break or day extension (16 hours), are useful during or after the cold period. Incandescent lights, however, cause excessive elongation of the stem and should not be applied after the appearance of color on the flower buds (8).

Stage of Harvest

Stems should be harvested when ½ the flowers in the inflorescences are open. Stems should be immediately placed in preservative and out of the sun. Do not allow cut stems to remain out of water or in the heat, for postharvest life will be significantly reduced.

Postharvest

Fresh: If stems are recut frequently, preservatives used and plants kept away from excessive heat, fresh flowers persist for 7–10 days.

Dried: Harvest flowers when fully open and hang in small bunches (3–5 stems) in a warm place. If dried rapidly, stocks retain their fragrance.

Storage: Stems may be stored dry for 2 days although wet storage is recommended. Storage temperatures should be 36–41F. Prolonged refrigeration results in loss of fragrance. Hold stocks in the dark to avoid stem elongation.

Cultivars

According to Jim Nau of Ball Seed Co., cultivar strains can be classified as either European/Japanese or Californian. European/Japanese strains are predominately used for greenhouse production and seldom have the stem strength and size necessary for field production. They are selectable for doubleness when grown in the greenhouse.

Unless cultivars have been selected for doubleness, most will be approximately 50% double. Growers may increase the chances of double flowers by removing slow-growing seedlings in the greenhouse. Double-flowered plants are slightly more vigorous and by removing the less vigorous seedlings, a greater percentage of doubles occurs. In general, differences between single- and double-flowered plants can be recognized through 4 separate observations. Doubles not only have earlier germination and more vigorous seedling growth than singles, but produce cotyledons which are larger and paler green than those of singles. By itself, any one observation cannot be relied on for accurate separation. Seedlings should be watered thoroughly 1 day prior to separation, which is accomplished 15–20 days after sowing. Separation should be done early in the morning and out of full sun because cotyledon color is easier to differentiate in the shade than in sunlight.

California strains are sold under various names such as Excelsior or Giant Excelsior (also called Ball series). They offer strong stems, 50–60% double flowers and are usually field-grown. They are generally sown directly to the field and selection for doubleness is not possible. The 2 strains, although many differences occur between them, are collectively known as "column" stocks. Occasionally the California forms are called "mammoth" stocks.

Field cultivars

Cheerful series (Japanese) grows 2–3' tall and plants are useful for field and greenhouse culture. A limited number of colors are presently available.

Excelsior strain (California) is available in single colors or as a mix. Single colors include 'American Beauty' (carmine-red), 'Avalanche' (white), 'Pacific Blue' (mid-blue), and 'Sweetheart Pink'. Height of the flowering plants is 2–3'.

Goddess series grows 2–3' tall and is offered in orchid, white and yellow.

Miracle series bears flowers of blue, crimson, gold, lavender, white and yellow.

Ultra strain (California) has been selected for doubleness. Plants are 2–2.5' tall and are useful for outdoor and greenhouse production. 'Crispy' and 'Madonna' are early and midseason white selections, respectively.

Greenhouse cultivars

Frolic series (Japanese) is available in 7 colors and a mix and grows 2–3' tall.

Nordic series has been bred especially for northern greenhouse conditions. Seven colors are offered.

Wonder series (Japanese) bears non-branching 2–3' tall flower stems and is 60–90% double. 'White Wonder' and 'Snow Wonder' have similar flowers but differently shaped foliage.

Xmas series (Japanese) grows 3' tall, bears non-branching mostly double flowers and is early to flower. Blue, purple ('Xmas Ocean'), red, rouge, pink, rose, ruby, white and violet are available.

Physiological Disorders

Short plants develop when the temperature is too low during the seedling stage. Sow seed when temperature is above 60F.

Blind plants likely result from an insufficient period of time below 60F or too long a period above 60F, and will fail to form flowers. This was more of a problem with earlier types than with today's cultivars.

"Skips" are flowers with blank areas in the middle of the inflorescence. This problem, which is more prevalent in northern growing areas, may be due to low light levels just after flowers have initiated.

Pests and Diseases

Bacterial rot (*Xanthomonas incanae*) produces a green water-soaked line on the stem of the seedling. Later the stem turns dark brown, cracks and the plant dies. Older plants may also be infected. When stems of older plants are cut open, a yellow liquid is clearly visible. The bacteria are seed-borne and most easily controlled by soaking the seeds in hot water (130F) for 10 minutes.

Club rot (*Plasmodiophora brassicae*) affects many plants in the Brassicaceae family. The disease is also known as slime mold because the feeder rots are often destroyed and slimy in appearance. The main roots develop abnormally and form swellings similar to crown galls. Plants die without flowering. Fungicides have been effective, but discarding infected plants may be the best solution.

Damping off of seedlings is caused by soil fungi which may be controlled with sterile soilless mixes and other standard sanitary procedures.

Downy mildew results in pale green spots on the upper surface of the leaves and downy mold on the opposite sides. The foliage wilts, the plants are stunted and the flowers develop poorly, if at all. Avoid crowding the plants and provide as much ventilation as possible. Sterilize all media.

Verticillium wilt (*Verticillium albo-atrum*) results in yellow basal leaves and severe stunting. Vascular tissues are often discolored and flowering is inhibited. Crop rotation and soil sterilization are essential in breaking the wilt cycle.

Diamondback moths, flea beetles and springtails are serious pests and cause significant damage to the foliage and flowers.

Reading

1. Biswas, P. K., and M. N. Rogers. 1963. The effects of different light intensities applied during the night on the growth and development of column stocks (*Matthiola incana*). *Proc. Amer. Soc. Hort. Sci.* 82:586–588.

2. Cockshull, K. E. 1985. *Matthiola*. In A. H. Halevy (ed.), *The Handbook of Flowering*, vol. 3. CRC Press, Boca Raton, FL. 363–367.

3. Heide, O. M. 1963. Juvenile stage and flower initiation in juvenile stocks (*Matthiola incana* R. Br.). *J. Amer. Soc. Hort. Sci.* 38:4–14.

4. Howland, J. E. 1944. Preliminary studies on low temperature vernalization of column stocks, *Matthiola incana*. *Proc. Amer. Soc. Hort. Sci.* 44:518–520.

5. Kohl, H. C., Jr. 1958. Flower initiation of stocks grown with several temperature regimens. *Proc. Amer. Soc. Hort. Sci.* 72:481–484.

6. Nau, J. 1990. Stock growing comments. In *Proceedings of 3rd National Conference on Specialty Cut Flowers*. Ventura, CA. 119–123.

7. Post, K. 1942. Effects of daylength and temperature on growth and flowering of some florist crops. Cornell Univ. Agr. Exp. Sta. Bul. 787:58–61.

8. _____ . 1955. *Florist Crop Production and Marketing*. Orange Judd, New York, NY.

9. Roberts, R. H., and B. E. Struckmeyer. 1939. Further studies on the effects of temperature and other environmental factors upon the photoperiodic responses of plants. *J. Agric. Res.* 59: 699–709.

Many thanks to Mr. Jim Nau for reviewing this section.

Nigella damascena	Love-in-a-mist	1.5–2'/1'
Blue, white	Mediterranean	Ranunculaceae

Nigella has handsome foliage and flowers, and although the cut flowers have been considerably successful on the local level, plants are mainly grown for the attractive seed pods. The pods may be dried and used in arrangements or potpourri.

Propagation

Sow seed directly to the field or bench. Approximately ¼ oz of seed yields 1000 seedlings. If sown directly to the field, sow at the rate of 0.3 oz/100 linear ft or 3–3.5 oz/1000 ft^2 (1,2,3). Germination occurs in 10–14 days. When sown in the greenhouse, maintain 60F. In southern locations (zone 7 and south), sowing may be accomplished in the fall, similar to larkspur (2).

Nigella damascena

Growing-on

Grow plants at temperatures of 60–65F and apply 50–100 ppm N at each irrigation. Photoperiod is of little consequence.

Environmental Factors

Nigella flowers are formed as plants mature and reach a certain number of nodes. Warm temperatures accelerate growth and flowering but temperatures above 80F should be avoided. Photoperiod has little effect on flowering.

Field Performance

Spacing: Space plants or thin seedlings to 6–9″ centers. When using successive sowings, use dense spacings. The tighter the spacing, the greater the opportunity of obtaining large terminal flowers.

Planting time: Sow or transplant 3 or 4 times every 2–3 weeks early in the season for best fruit production. The best pods are from the terminal flowers. Those from the laterals are smaller and less saleable.

Fertilization: Side dress with a granular fertilizer such as 10–10–10 or 8–8–8 approximately 3 weeks after direct sowing or transplanting to the field. Soluble fertilization may also be used at the rate of 300–500 ppm N applied every week.

Shading: In the South, shading (55% shade) is useful and longer stems result.

Greenhouse Performance

Temperature: *Nigella* may be produced with cool temperatures of 55–60F and bright light.

Scheduling: Seed sown in fall or early spring result in flowering plants approximately 9–12 weeks later.

Stage of Harvest

Flowers: Harvest when the flowers are fully colored but before the petals have totally separated from the center.

Seed pods: Harvest when the pods are turning purple-bronze. They are easily air-dried.

Postharvest

Fresh: The flowers persist for 7–10 days, particularly if a preservative is used and water is replaced often. Store at 36–41F only if necessary.

Dried: Flowers may be dried if harvested when fully open. Pods, harvested when they are green or purple, are air-dried and persist indefinitely. Do not strip the finely divided foliage.

Cultivars

Miss Jekyll strain is available in azure, dark blue, rose shades and white. 'Mulberry Rose' has flowers in rose shades and purple-striped seed pods.

Additional Species

Nigella hispanica (fennel flower) is about 2' tall and bears deep blue flowers with blood-red stamens. The fruit is not as inflated as *N. damascena* and has a crown of hornlike projections on the top.

N. orientalis has yellow flowers with red spots but is grown for the curious fruit. 'Transformer' bears yellow flowers and curious seed pods useful for those "artistic" arrangements.

N. sativa has bluish white flowers and grows about 18" tall.

Pests and Diseases

Damping off, aphids and spider mites can be serious problems.

Reading

1. Kieft, C. 1989. *Kieft's Growing Manual* . . . . Kieft Bloemzaden, Venhuizen, The Netherlands.

2. Nau, J. 1989. *Ball Culture Guide: The Encyclopedia of Seed Germination*. Ball

Seed Co., West Chicago, IL.

3. Seals, J. 1991. Some uncommon and common (but choice) cut flowers from seed for field growing. *The Cut Flower Quarterly* 3(2):13–14.

Many thanks to Mr. Don Mitchell for reviewing this section.

Oxypetalum caeruleum   Tweedia   12–20"/12"
Light blue   Argentina   Asclepiadaceae

A plant with exciting potential as a cut flower or a pot plant, tweedia is relatively unknown in the American market. The sky-blue color of the star-like flowers is unique but plants with such magnificently colored flowers must possess some problems. Milky sap, unappealing foliar fragrance and a twining habit offset the beauty of the cut stem. Plants may be grown in the greenhouse or under protection outdoors; the flowers discolor if rain falls upon them.

Propagation

Propagate by sowing seed in plugs or open seed trays at 68–72F under high humidity conditions. Approximately 0.7 oz of seed yields 1000 plants (2). It is not recommended that seed be direct-sown because significantly longer time is needed to germinate. Terminal shoot cuttings (2–3" long) may be rooted if seed supply is inconsistent.

Growing-on

Fertilize newly emerged seedlings or rooted cuttings with 50–75 ppm N from potassium nitrate and transplant to field when the root system fills a 3.5" pot or plug. Grow at approximately 70F average temperature.

Environmental Factors

Temperature: Temperature has the greatest effect on growth and flowering of tweedia. Temperatures above 60F are necessary for optimum growth, but temperatures above 86F result in long, lanky stems, aborted flowers and poor flower color. If plants are consistently grown below 60F, growth is significantly slowed and flowering is delayed.

The effect of temperature on flowering and growth of *Oxypetalum caeruleum* at initial harvest.[a]

Temperature (F)	Time to flower[b] (days)	Stem length (in)	Aborted flowers (%)
57	115	18.0	10
70	38	20.0	4
86	32	24.8	20

[a] Adapted from (1).
[b] Time between placing 8-week-old plants at specific temperature to harvesting of 3 flower stems.

Light: High light intensity is best for flowering; low light levels cause stretching and thinning of flower stems. Providing shade in high light areas may be useful to increase stem length.

Photoperiod: No effects on time to flower occur due to photoperiod but long days (>12 hours) result in extended internodes and therefore longer stems, as the following table shows. Also, less flower abortion occurs on plants subjected to long days and higher quality flowering stems are formed.

The effect of photoperiod on stem length of *Oxypetalum caeruleum*.[a]

Photoperiod (hr)	Internode length (in)	Stem length (in)
8	1.3	16.1
10	1.5	19.1
12	2.0	20.4
14	2.3	23.4

[a]Adapted from (1).

Field Performance

Flowers are susceptible to weather damage, particularly rain and wind. Greenhouse production is recommended but field production is possible if protection from the elements is provided. Support of plants is necessary in the South but not in the Northwest.

Yield in outdoor production is approximately 5–10 stems/plant the first year and may be doubled if plants are overwintered. Stem length is longest and stems are strongest if plants are well fertilized, temperatures of at least 65F are provided and some shading is present.

Fertilize with side dressing of N or with liquid fertility of 300–500 ppm N once a week.

Greenhouse Performance

Tweedia is well suited for greenhouse production; warm temperatures and protection of the flowers are a necessity for it. Space plants 6–9" apart and fertilize consistently with liquid or slow-release fertilizer. Plants may be grown in containers or ground beds. If temperatures are above 70F, support may be necessary.

Stage of Harvest

Flowers are indeterminate: flowers occur in the nodes of the stems, and the stems continue to produce additional leaves and flowers. Groups of 2–4 flowers (cymes) occur in each node.

Harvest when approximately 6 cymes are present. The first 1 or 2 should be open, the last showing color.

Postharvest

Flowers persist for 6–10 days depending on temperature and light. The stems exude a milky sap which, although messy, does not seem to reduce the vase life. Studies with various solvents, such as alcohol and hot water, showed that removal of the sap did not affect vase life. Use of silver thiosulfate did not significantly extend vase life.

Cultivars

'Heavenborn' is a selection which bears deeper blue flowers. Plants have been successful in Dutch greenhouses.

Pests and Diseases

Root rots under conditions of poor drainage and hot weather are not uncommon. Aphids, in particular, relish *Oxypetalum*. Otherwise, few pests bother the plants.

Reading

1. Armitage, A. M., N. G. Seager, I. J. Warrington and D. H. Greer. 1990. Response of *Oxypetalum caeruleum* to light, temperature and photoperiod. *J. Amer. Soc. Hort. Sci.* 115:910–915.

2. Kieft, C. 1989. *Kieft's Growing Manual* .... Kieft Bloemzaden, Venhuizen, The Netherlands.

Physalis alkekengi	Chinese Lantern	12–15"/15"
Orange fruit	China, Japan	Solanaceae

Physalis consists of approximately 100 species, the best known of which is the chinese lantern. Plants are known for their inflated, bright orange calyces which surround the fruit. The calyx is harvested, dried and persists for years. Plants may reseed themselves in many areas and act like a perennial. Other botanical names for the species are *P. franchetii* and *P. alkekengi* var. *franchetii*.

Propagation

Best germination occurs when seed is chilled 4–6 weeks at 40F then placed at 60–70F. Approximately 0.2 oz of seed yields 1000 seedlings (1). Germination may require as little as 7 days and as many as 30. Fresh seed may be sown at 60–70F without stratification but if stored for any length of time, moist stratification (40F) reduces germination time and increases uniformity.

Growing-on

Transplanting to 3–4" containers from the open seed pack is accomplished approximately 3 weeks from sowing. Seedlings should be grown in plug flats for 4–6 weeks. Plants should be grown at 55–60F. Fertilize once or twice per week with 150–200 ppm N from a balanced fertilizer. Overfertilization and warm temperatures result in leggy plants with poor stem strength. Transplant to the field 8–12 weeks after sowing.

Environmental Factors

Chinese lanterns flower as plants mature. No evidence exists that photoperiod is necessary for flower initiation. Warm temperatures and bright light result in faster flowering. Temperatures below 80F are best for production of largest fruit. Consistently high temperatures (above 80F) result in fewer flowers and small, poorly colored fruit.

Field Performance

Spacing: Space on 1' centers or 12" × 18". Sufficient space is required to allow for expansion of the fruit and proper coloration.

Irrigation: Plants are heavy water users and should not be allowed to dry out, especially when fruit is being formed.

Fertilization: Side dress in the spring with a balanced fertilizer (20–10–20, 10–10–10) and also when plants are in flower, but before fruits have matured.

Stage of Harvest

Harvest when the fruit is fully colored.

Postharvest

Fresh: If the fruit is used fresh, approximately 12–20 days of vase life may be expected.

Storage: Store stems bearing fruit in water at 36–41F if necessary. Recut the stems when first placed in storage.

Dried: Strip leaves and hang stems containing fruit, or place fruit and stems horizontally in a box or other container. They are gourmet food for mice so keep boxes sealed if mice are a problem.

Cultivars

'Gigantea' has larger fruit than the species but is not easy to locate.

Pests and Diseases

Several diseases occur on chinese lanterns, but if grown in favorable environments, diseases are seldom serious.

Bacterial wilt (*Pseudomonas solanacearum*) results in rapid deterioration of the foliage. Plants should be discarded and plant rotation practiced.

Leaf spotting by various species of *Phyllosticta* may be controlled by general foliar fungicides at 10- to 14-day intervals.

Skeletonizing of the fruit by various insects and fungi occurs if the fruit is left on the plant too long. The problem is worse in high-density plantings where air circulation is poor, fruit remains wet and light seldom penetrates. Use of landscape fabric around the plants is helpful in keeping the fruit off the ground.

Reading

1. Kieft, C. 1989. *Kieft's Growing Manual* . . . . Kieft Bloemzaden, Venhuizen, The Netherlands.

Salvia leucantha	Mexican Bush Sage, Velvet Sage	2–4'/3'
Purple, white	Mexico	Lamiaceae

Numerous salvias have cut flower potential but their ornamental properties have not been exploited. Some species are perennial (*S.* × *superba*) but most are native to warm areas of the world and should be treated as annuals. One of the most useful species for cut flower production is *S. leucantha*, velvet sage. Plants are relatively easy to grow in the field and greenhouse, the foliage is handsome and flower production is excellent.

Propagation

Velvet sage is easily propagated by terminal cuttings taken before flower buds have formed. Approximately 2–3" long cuttings may be rooted in a 1:2 ratio of peat/perlite mix in 7–10 days if placed at 70–75F and humid conditions. A sweat tent or a similar means of maintaining high humidity is better than intermittent mist.

Growing-on

Once plants are rooted, they may be transplanted to small containers prior to planting out in the field. Place plants under long days (>12 hours) and fertilize with 150–200 ppm N once or twice a week. If roots are well formed, plants may be transplanted to the field immediately as long as the threat of frost has passed.

Environmental Factors

Photoperiod: Velvet sage is a short day plant which helps to explain why flowers occur in the fall. Long days result in vegetative development and long stems, while short days cause flower initiation and development (2). Short days are necessary for both initiation and development. In areas of early frosts, such as the Northeast, there may be insufficient time for flower development.

Temperature: Warm temperatures are best for flower development. They are particularly vigorous in warm summers and may attain a height and width of 4'. Cool temperatures in late summer result in fewer flowers on smaller plants.

Field Performance

Spacing: Plants should be spaced no less than on 15" centers and as wide as 3' centers. Work at the University of Georgia showed that wide spacing resulted in more stems/plant than close spacing but stems/ft^2 decreased.

The effect of spacing on yield of *Salvia leucantha*.[a]

Spacing (in)	Stems/plant	Stems/ft^2
24	125	31.5
36	180	19.2
48	180	11.6

[a]From (1).

Velvet sage is a large, vigorous plant and spacing less than 15" apart should be avoided. Spacing greater than 3' centers is also unacceptable, not only because yield/ft^2 is reduced, but also because the brittle stems need surrounding plants for support.

Support: Plants are woody at the base. The main stems are sufficiently strong without support, but the secondary flower stems are brittle. A 2-tier support system is useful.

Greenhouse Performance

Salvia leucantha is an excellent plant for greenhouse production. Flowering is easy to control and forcing may take place year-round using a chrysanthemum schedule.

Space rooted cuttings 12" × 12" or 12" × 18" apart. Closer spacing may be used but air movement is unnecessarily reduced. Place cuttings under long days (>14 hours) and fertilize with 200 ppm N of a balanced fertilizer such as 20–10–20. Calcium nitrate and potassium nitrate should be rotated in the winter. For the first crop a single pinch is useful, but not necessary, when the shoots are about 4" long. Once the new shoots are 4–6" long, place plants under short days (<12 hours) until the flower buds are colored. Short days must be maintained until flower buds have colored; long days interrupt the development of the flowers. Maintain 60–63F night temperatures and 70–75F day temperatures. Reduce night temperatures to 55F about 1 week prior to harvesting (when flower buds are colored).

Harvest all stems from a single planting over a period of 1 week; do not wait for laterals to form as in the field. Yield is reduced compared to the field but harvesting is easier and subsequent plantings allow for extended harvests throughout the season. Place stems immediately in water with floral preservative. The leaves wilt readily and must be protected from heat and stress.

Crop time is approximately 11–15 weeks from planting. This includes 3–5 weeks LD and 8–10 weeks SD until harvest. These times vary with season and location.

Stage of Harvest

Flowers should be harvested when the white petals (corolla) emerge from the blue sepals (calyx) on the first 3–4 basal flowers.

Postharvest

Fresh: Flowers persist approximately 7 days in water with floral preservative added. The flowers tend to shatter, particularly if stems are out of water for any length of time. The use of STS as a 30-minute pulse prior to placing in preservative solution adds an additional 3–4 days.

Dried: Flowers are air-dried and make good dried flowers. The application of silica gel or glycerine may be useful.

Storage: Stems do not store well dry; the foliage declines more rapidly than the flowers. They may be stored wet for 3–4 days at 35–40F.

Cultivars

No cultivars are presently available, although a pure purple form may be found in botanical gardens.

Additional Species

Salvia farinacea (mealy-cup sage) bears wedgewood-blue flowers on 2' stems. Seed germinates in 2–3 weeks at 70–72F. 'Victoria' produces deep

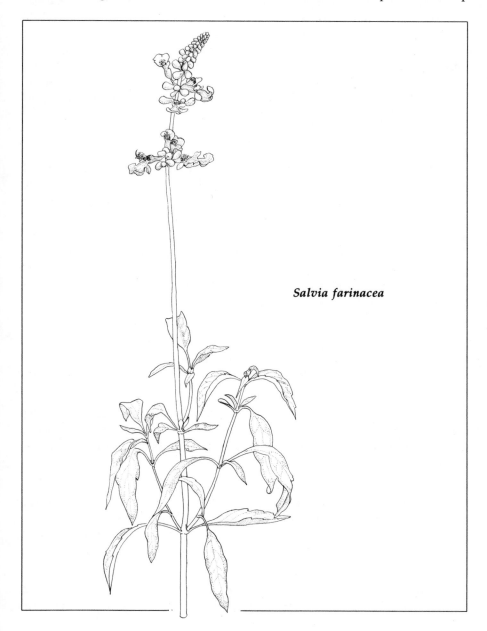

Salvia farinacea

violet-blue flowers which are useful fresh or dried.

S. guaranitica (anise-scented sage) grows 3' tall and bears dozens of dark blue flowers. Untested but has potential.

S. horminum (clary) is often used for dried flowers. They have brightly colored, veined bracts and dry well. Harvest when the bracts feel firm and papery. Remove large leaves and hang upside down.

'Indigo' ('Indigo Spires') appears to be a cross between *S. pratensis* (meadow sage) and *S. farinacea* (mealy-cup sage). Plants produce many 2–3' long branches of rich blue flowers. Propagate by terminal cuttings.

S. splendens (annual sage) is occasionally used. Colors include red, white, salmon and purple but red is the predominant color. Propagate by seed.

S. × *superba* (perennial hybrid sage) produces dozens of 18–24" long, blue to violet-blue flowers. 'Blue Queen' (violet-blue), 'Lubecca' (purple) and 'May Night' (indigo) are useful cultivars for cutting. Propagate cultivars by terminal cuttings; seed is available for *S.* × *superba*.

Pests and Diseases

Few pests and diseases occur on velvet sage. Aphids can be a problem. If the perennial sages are grown north of zone 7, disease is seldom a problem. However, if grown in areas of hot, humid summers, root rot may be common.

Reading

1. Armitage, A. M. 1987. The influence of spacing on field-grown perennial crops. *HortScience* 22:904–907.

2. Armitage, A. M. 1989. Photoperiodic control of flowering of *Salvia leucantha*. *J. Amer. Soc. Hort. Sci.* 114:755–758.

Scabiosa atropurpurea   Pincushion Flower   2–3'/2'
Blue   Southern Europe   Dipsacaceae

Grown almost entirely as a field crop, the annual *Scabiosa* provides a mix of flower colors on a season-long schedule. Plants are more tolerant of heat than the perennial types and may be grown further south. Perennial species, particularly *S. caucasica*, are also used as cut flowers and are discussed in the perennial plant section.

Propagation

Seed: Seed is often direct-sown to the field after the threat of frost has disappeared. Sow 0.5 oz/100 linear ft (1); if transplants are used, ½ oz of seed yields 1000 seedlings (2). Seed must be covered very lightly, if at all, because light enhances germination. Seed germinates in 10–12 days at 65–70F.

Growing-on

If sown in the greenhouse, grow plugs or trays at 50–55F for about 10–12 weeks from seeding (2). Warmer temperatures accelerate growth but plants tend to stretch. Fertilize lightly (50–100 ppm N) with potassium and calcium nitrate.

Environmental Factors

Photoperiod: Plants are long day plants. Flowering during the winter is enhanced with incandescent lights, either by daylength extension or by nightbreak lighting (4).

Temperature: Cool temperatures (below 55F) are best for plant growth (4). The combination of cool growing temperatures and LD significantly reduces flowering time. Well-rosetted (i.e., older) plants are more responsive to cool/LD conditions than seedlings (4).

Field Performance

Seed or transplant on 9–15" centers in full sun (3). The yield in trials at Athens, GA, was 14 stems/plant with an average stem length of 27.8" from July 3 to 20. Many more flowers were produced after that time, but stem length only averaged 15". Successive plantings (every 2–4 weeks until mid-summer) are necessary for optimum stem length and flower quality. Flowering occurs as days lengthen and temperatures increase.

Greenhouse Performance

Scabiosa atropurpurea is seldom greenhouse-grown due to poor quality under warm conditions and poor financial return. However, for an early spring crop, seedlings may be grown at 55–60F until rosettes have formed (10–12 weeks after sowing). Reduce night temperature to 50F and keep days as cool as possible. Long days (>16 hours) using 10–20 fc of incandescent light should be used throughout the crop cycle. Warmer temperatures result in thin stems. Flowering occurs approximately 4 months from sowing.

Stage of Harvest

Harvest the flower when almost fully open.

Postharvest

Fresh: Flowers persist for 5–7 days in water, an additional 3–5 days with flower preservative.

Cultivars

'Imperial Giants' comes in a mixture of colors and grows 2–3' tall.

QIS series is available in 3 separate colors (dark blue, salmon-pink and scarlet) and as a mix. Plants are 3' tall. The upright growth and uniformity of flowering are most useful for cut flower growers.

Additional Species

Scabiosa stellata (drumstick plant) is grown for its seed heads which may be dried. An interesting novel item.

Pests and Diseases

No pests and diseases particular to *Scabiosa* occur.

Reading

1. Kieft, C. 1989. *Kieft's Growing Manual* .... Kieft Bloemzaden, Venhuizen, The Netherlands.

2. Nau, J. 1989. *Ball Culture Guide: The Encyclopedia of Seed Germination.* Ball Seed Co., West Chicago, IL.

3. Post, K. 1955. *Florist Crop Production and Marketing.* Orange Judd, New York, NY.

4. Wilkins, H. F., and A. H. Halevy. 1985. *Scabiosa.* In A. H. Halevy (ed.), *The Handbook of Flowering,* vol. 5. CRC Press, Boca Raton, FL. 328–329.

Trachelium caeruleum	Throatwort	3–4'/3'
Blue	Mediterranean	Campanulaceae

The name *trachelium* comes from *trachelos* (neck), for these plants were supposed to be useful against diseases of the trachea. Give me a cough drop any day. Plants are excellent subjects for cut flowers and will overwinter in areas of Florida, the Gulf Coast and California. The many flowers are lavender to dark blue and are borne in panicles at the end of the stem. The color is in demand and plants should be produced more often in the greenhouse and field.

Propagation

Usually propagated from seed, both raw and pelleted seed is available. Seed is generally sown under intermittent mist in the greenhouse at 62–70F. Seed germinates in 14–21 days. Seed is small and therefore should not be covered. Approximately 1/28 oz (1 gram) of seed yields 10,000 transplantable plants (3).

Growing-on

Grow seedlings in large-volume plugs or 3" pots at 62F night, 70F days. Fertilize with 50–100 ppm N solution of a complete fertilizer when 2 true leaves have expanded. Increase fertilizer to 200 ppm N every other watering. As plants reach 3–4 leaves, reduce greenhouse temperature to 60–62F. Plants may be transplanted when large enough to handle.

Environmental Factors

Photoperiod: Plants flower faster under long days of at least 14 hours (1). Short days inhibit flowering.

Temperature: Plants are Mediterranean in origin and do not respond well to large fluctuations in seasonal temperature. During greenhouse growing, temperatures of 60–70F appear to be optimum. Field production is best in areas of cool nights and warm days.

Field Performance

Plants do poorly in the summer due to high heat in the southern half of the country and in many areas of the Midwest. Performance in the fall, winter

Trachelium caeruleum

and early spring is excellent in south Georgia and Florida. *Trachelium* may be grown in the summer in the Northwest and coastal California.

  Spacing: Space plants 9–18″ apart; the wider the spacing, the more breaks and the greater the yield/plant.

  Support: None needed unless high winds are a factor.

Greenhouse Performance

  Grow plants on a bench in 6″ pots or in a ground bed. Space pot to pot or on 12" centers in the ground bed. Fertilize with 100–200 ppm N during the fall and winter.

Grow with bright light and 55–60F night temperatures and 65–70F day temperatures. Warmer temperatures result in faster growth and flowering but also cause thinner stems and looser flowers.

Supplemental lights (sodium or metal halide) accelerate growth and flowering if used during the day (1). Place plants under 14- to 20-hour day conditions. Use either HID lamps (350–450 fc) for faster flowering or incandescent lamps (10–20 fc) when plants are approximately 8 weeks old.

Support (1–2 tiers) should be used with greenhouse-grown crops. Plants require 5–7 months to flower from seed.

Stage of Harvest
Harvest the stem when ¼ to ⅓ of the flowers are open (2).

Postharvest
Fresh: Fresh flowers, if harvested at the proper stage, persist for approximately 2 weeks in water. The addition of STS resulted in an additional 1–2 days but is not needed (2).
Dried: Flowers may be air-dried but lose their color.
Storage: Store in water at 40F for approximately 24 hours.

Cultivars
'Blue Umbrella' has lavender-blue flowers and is similar to the species, though perhaps a little more compact.

'White Umbrella' bears creamy white flowers. The flowers show petal blackening as they decline more readily than the blue forms.

Pests and Diseases
No particular pests or diseases are significant. Most problems are caused by hot temperatures and high humidity.

Reading
1. Armitage, A. M. 1988. Effects of photoperiod, supplemental light, and growth regulators on growth and flowering of *Trachelium caeruleum*. *J. Hort. Sci.* 63:667–674.

2. Bredmose, N. 1987. Post harvest ability of some new cut flowers. *Acta Hortic.* 205:187–194.

3. Kieft, C. 1989. *Kieft's Growing Manual* .... Kieft Bloemzaden, Venhuizen, The Netherlands.

Zinnia elegans   Zinnia   2–3'/2'
Various colors   Mexico   Asteraceae

Zinnias have been used as cut flowers for many years, and although they no longer have the appeal of lesser-known, more exotic species, they are useful as an inexpensive "cut and come again" filler crop. Their flowering season extends from April to October.

Propagation

Always propagated from seed. Most of the cut flower types are open pollinated but excellent F_1 cultivars have been developed. Approximately 1 oz of seed yields 1000 plants (4). Seed germinates in 3–5 days at 80–85F, 5–7 days at 70–75F. If seed is direct-sown (open pollinated types only), 0.5 oz/100 linear ft may be used (3).

Growing-on

Grow at 60–65F nights and 70F days. Soil should have a pH of 6.3–6.8. Fertilize with 100 ppm N at each irrigation. Greater concentrations of nitrogen should be avoided. Plant out after 5–6 weeks in the final container.

Environmental Factors

Photoperiod: Zinnias are quantitative short day plants. That is, they flower more rapidly under short days but eventually flower regardless of photoperiod (1). Daylengths of 12 hours or less stimulate flowering (1). Continuous LD produces the longest stems but delays flowering by about 3 weeks (2). A treatment of SD followed by LD produces flowers on the longest stem in the shortest time (2). From the commercial point of view, however, control of photoperiod is seldom practiced.

Light intensity: Zinnias are high-light plants and flower poorly on stretched stems under low winter intensities.

Temperature: Temperatures below 60F result in chlorotic foliage and delayed flowering.

Field Performance

Plants produce higher quality flowers if sequential plantings are used. Transplant or sow to the field every 2 weeks for 6 successive plantings. Transplants may be planted as soon as the last frost has occurred.

Space on 9–12" centers. No pinching or support is necessary.

Greenhouse Performance

Zinnias are seldom grown as cut flowers in the greenhouse. However, if forced in the greenhouse, grow at 65F night, 70F day. Fertilize at 150–200 ppm N using a balanced fertilizer source. Long days, from incandescent lamps (25 fc), can be applied for 2–4 weeks, followed by short days (<12 hours) until budded. Plants may then be placed under LD. Plant at least 3 successive crops, 2 weeks apart for winter flowers of the best quality. Supplemental light during the day is useful but may not be cost-effective.

Stage of Harvest

Harvest when pollen begins to form, that is, when flowers are fully mature. Flowers are best for the local market.

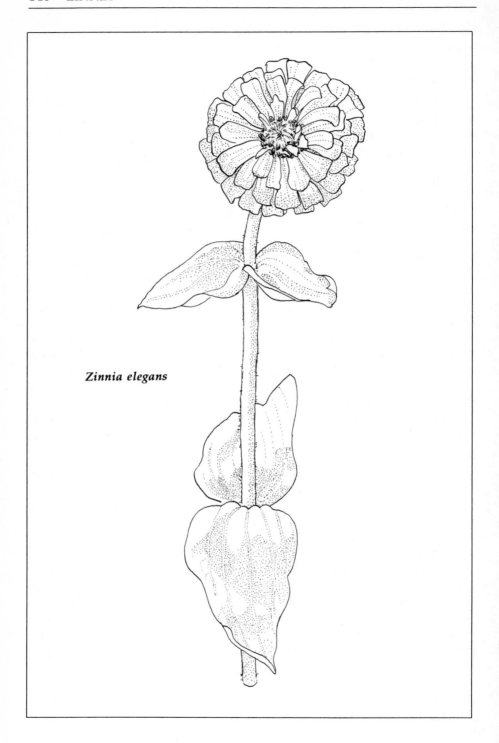

Zinnia elegans

Postharvest

Fresh: Flowers persist 7–10 days in preservative.

Storage: Flowers may be stored wet for 5 days at 36–38F (2).

Cultivars

Dahlia-flowered and cactus-flowered forms are often used for cut flowers. They are available as mixes only.

'Ruffles' is a fine F_1 cultivar available in mixed and 4 single colors.

'State Fair' is a popular, large-flowered, 2–3' tall cultivar and is often asked for by name.

Pests and Diseases

Numerous leaf spot organisms occur, including *Alternaria, Cercospora* and *Erysiphe*, the causal agent of powdery mildew. Powdery mildew is a greater problem when warm days are interwoven with cool, damp nights. Application of general-purpose foliar fungicides at 10-day to 2-week intervals helps to control the diseases.

Insects which feed on zinnias include blister and Japanese beetles, mites and aphids. Nematodes cause angular spots on the foliage and can be quite destructive.

Reading

1. Armitage, A. M. 1985. *Zinnia elegans* and *Z. angustifolia.* In A. H. Halevy (ed.), *The Handbook of Flowering,* vol. 4. CRC Press, Boca Raton, FL. 548–552.

2. Healy, W. 1991. Cut flowers: cut zinnias. *Georgia Commercial Flower Growers Assoc. Newsletter* 1(5):8–9.

3. Kieft, C. 1989. *Kieft's Growing Manual* .... Kieft Bloemzaden, Venhuizen, The Netherlands.

4. Nau, J. 1989. *Ball Culture Guide: The Encyclopedia of Seed Germination.* Ball Seed Co., West Chicago, IL.

ADDITIONAL ANNUAL SPECIES SUITABLE FOR CUT FLOWER PRODUCTION

Numerous annual species and cultivars can and have been used as cut flowers, either fresh or dried. From the commercial viewpoint, sufficient production must be possible under local conditions and vase life of fresh flowers should be at least 7 days. If fresh flowers are shipped, foliage and flowers must be capable of enduring the associated stress and look as good at the other end of the trip as they did prior to shipping. The following chart gives species not already discussed but with potential as cut flowers. Portions of the chart are adapted from Bullivant (1) and Seals (2).

Species	Common name	Exposure[a]	Use[b]
Ammobium alatum	Winged everlasting	Su,Ps	D
Anaphalis margaritacea	Pearly everlasting	Su	F,D
Anethum graveolens	Flowering dill	Su	F
Asclepias curassavica	Sunset flower	Su,Ps	F,Dp
Atriplex hortensis	Orache	Su	Ff
Brassica oleracea	Ornamental kale	Su	F
Bupleurum griffithii	Bupleurum	Su,Ps	F,D
Calendula officinalis	Calendula	Su,Ps	F
Capsicum annuum	Ornamental pepper	Su	Dp
Carlina acaulis	Silver thistle	Su	F,D
Catananche caerulea	Cupid's dart	Su	F,D
Chenopodium quinoa	Goosefoot	Su	D
Chrysanthemum segetum	Corn marigold	Su	F
Craspedia globosa	Golden drumstick	Su	F,D
Cynara cardunculus	Cardoon	Su,Ps	F,D
Dianthus chinensis	China pink	Su	F
Fibigia clypeata	Paper pumpkin seed	Su	Dp
Helipterum manglesii	Rhodanthe	Su	D
Helipterum roseum	Sunray everlasting	Su	D
Iberis amara	Rocket candytuft	Su,Ps	F,D
Jasione perennis	Shepherd's scabious	Su,Ps	F
Moluccella laevis	Bells-of-ireland	Su,Ps	F,D
Nicandra physalodes	Shoo-fly	Su	D
Papaver nudicaule	Iceland poppy	Su	F,Dp
Reseda odorata	Migonette	Su,Ps	F
Rudbeckia hirta	Gloriosa daisy	Su	F
Tithonia rotundifolia	Mexican sunflower	Su	F
Trachymene coerulea	Blue lace flower	Su,Ps	F
Vaccaria pyramidata	Rose cockle	Su,Ps	F
Xeranthemum annuum	Immortelle	Su	D
Zea mays	Ornamental corn	Su	D

[a] Su = full sun, Ps = partial shade.
[b] F = fresh flowers, D = dried flowers, Dp = dried fruit or pods, Ff = fresh foliage.

Reading

1. Bullivant, E. 1989. *Dried Fresh Flowers From Your Garden*. Pelham Books/Stephen Greene Press, London, U.K.

2. Seals, J. 1989. Extra special cut flowers from seed. In *Proceedings of 2nd National Conference on Specialty Cut Flowers*. Athens, GA. 59–80.

Perennials for Cut Flowers

Plants which persist in the ground and may be harvested for at least 3 years are referred to as perennials. Although many species may be raised from seed, many cultivars are also propagated by vegetative means. One of the advantages of producing perennials is the tremendous diversity of species useful as cut flowers. Many are little known to the consumer, therefore creating interest and profit for the grower. If bed preparation is accomplished properly prior to planting, little soil maintenance is necessary while the crop is in the ground. On the other hand, poor soil preparation will be paid for in reduced yield and quality for many years. In general, perennials return a meager yield the first year and don't start paying for themselves until the second and third year. In the southern half of the country, planting of most species should be accomplished in early fall to allow for strong root development before winter. In areas of heavy winter heaving, spring planting is best. If planted in the fall, the arrival of cold weather and short days are beneficial to many perennials and may result in some first-year production. In the case of most species, cold is necessary to break dormancy or initiate flowering. Because plants are in the ground for many years, it is essential to grow crops which are suitable for a given climate. Overwintering and/or heat stress are persistent problems if poor selection of species and cultivars occur. In this section, guidelines for outdoor production are provided for each species by means of a climatic zone range. The guidelines provide the southern and northern climatic zones where quality crops may be produced and are based on the hardiness zone map produced by the USDA in 1990 (see Appendix III). If crops are produced in a greenhouse, the map is irrelevant and need not be consulted. Greenhouse production guidelines have been included wherever possible and, if forcing indoors, the ability to provide cold temperatures and control photoperiod becomes important for many crops.

ACHILLEA TO *VERONICASTRUM*

In the following listings, the first line at each perennial entry provides the genus and species, followed by the common name and then the normal height/spread of the mature plant. The second line provides the flower color of the species, the country or region of origin, the botanical family to which the species belongs and finally the climatic zones where the plants may be cultivated. When more than one species in a genus is treated (as with *Achillea* and *Aster*), and when suggested readings refer to the genus as a whole, the readings appear at the conclusion of the last species entry.

Achillea spp.   Yarrow

Of the approximately 100 species, 4 are useful as commercial cut flowers. The best yellow-flowered forms are *A.* 'Coronation Gold' (coronation gold yarrow) and *A. filipendulina* (fern leaf yarrow). *Achillea millefolium* (common yarrow) is available in numerous colors; *A. ptarmica* (sneezewort) is a white-flowered species. A relatively new series, the Galaxy series (hybrids between *A. millefolium* and *A. taygetea*) also has potential for cut flower production. Other hybrid selections with 1.5–2.5′ long flower stems are also useful. Yarrows may be used fresh or dried. For me, sneezing and yarrow are synonymous and go together like popcorn and a movie, but not nearly as pleasant.

Achillea 'Coronation Gold'   Coronation Gold Yarrow   3–3.5′/3′
Yellow   Hybrid origin   Asteraceae   Zones 3–9

Coronation gold yarrow is a hybrid between *A. filipendulina* and *A. clypeolata*. No seed is presently available, although seed is occasionally offered which is most likely *A. filipendulina*. The gray-green foliage is fragrant (some say smelly) and flower heads are approximately 3″ wide, although 4–4.5″ wide inflorescences are not uncommon.

Propagation
Division: Plants may be divided any time after flowering. From a mature 3-year-old plant, up to 100 divisions may be made. Divisions should be sorted to size, with large crowns planted in the production bed, smaller ones planted in pots for growing-on or in a separate production area. Water divisions well.

Environmental Factors
Temperature: Cold is not necessary for flower development with cultivars which have *A. filipendulina* in their parentage. Plants are perennials and flower year after year as far south as south Florida indicating that cold temperatures are not critical. Temperatures below 40F, however, may help in

uniformity and plant vigor. The optimum duration of cold is not known but is likely less than 4 weeks. Plants have a wide range of temperature adaptability and are useful as cut flowers from Minnesota to Florida.

Photoperiod: No photoperiod control occurs. Plant maturity is more important for flowering than photoperiod.

Soil pH: Yield and stem length are better with a soil pH of 6.4 compared with 3.7 (4).

Field Performance

Longevity: 'Coronation Gold' produced consistent quality and yield for 5 years in the Georgia trials. On a 1' × 1' spacing, the following results were recorded.

Yield and stem quality of *Achillea* 'Coronation Gold' over time (Athens, GA).

Year	Stems/plant	Stems/ft^2	Stem length (in)	Stem diameter (mm)
1984	7	7.0	23.1	4.9
1985	41	41.0	25.4	4.6
1986	46	46.5	27.8	5.1
1987	45	44.6	28.5	4.8
1988	45	44.9	24.8	5.3

Similar results were obtained in trials in Burlington, VT. Two-year-old plants yielded 54 stems/plant, approximately 19" in length. In that trial, 2'× 2' spacing was used (7).

Stem length: Distribution of stem lengths over a 4-year period for plants on a 1' × 1' spacing is presented in the following table.

Stem length of *Achillea* 'Coronation Gold' over time.

Year	Stem length (%)		
	<10 in	10–20 in	>20 in
1984	3	96	1
1985	9	53	38
1986	3	36	61
1987	0	13	87
1988	0	5	95

Spacing: 'Coronation Gold' does not spread as aggressively as many other yarrows and high-density planting is not detrimental. The yield/plant increases as spacing distance increases but yield/ft^2 declines. Stem length also increases as spacing distance becomes smaller. The following table shows how spacing affects yield and stem length (based on work done at the University of Georgia) (1).

The effect of spacing on *Achillea* 'Coronation Gold'.

Spacing (in)	Stems/plant	Stems/ft^2	Stems >20 in (%)
12	46	46.5	61
24	74	18.6	50
36	119	13.2	32
48	158	9.9	42

Spacing closer than 1' apart is feasible if plants remain in production no more than 3 years. Close spacing results in additional root rot and foliar disease problems. In 1989, the sixth and last year of testing of 'Coronation Gold' at Athens, GA, plants originally spaced 2' × 2' yielded 58 stems/plant and 16 stems/ft^2 with an average stem length of 22.3". Plants originally spaced 3–4' apart in 1984 yielded 97 stems/plant with an average stem length of 23.7".

Guideline for Foliar Analyses

At field trials in Athens, GA, foliage was sampled from vigorously growing healthy plants when flower buds were visible, but prior to flower opening. These are guidelines only and should not be considered absolute standards. Based on dry weight analysis.

(%)						(ppm)				
N	P	K	Ca	Mg		Fe	Mn	B	Al	Zn
					'Coronation Gold'					
2.9	0.24	3.15	0.70	0.18		210	33	35	156	30

Stage of Harvest

Flowers should not be harvested until pollen is visible on the inflorescence. Stems harvested prior to pollen shed have unsatisfactory shelf life.

Postharvest

Fresh: Flowers persist about 7–12 days in water if harvested at the proper stage (2).

Dried: Yarrow can be hung upside down to air-dry. Flowers, however, will shrivel if picked too early. Good results with small numbers of stems are obtained by placing the stems in 1–2" of water and allowing the water to evaporate in the drying area (9).

Achillea filipendulina   Fern Leaf Yarrow   3–4'/2'
  Yellow   Caucasus   Asteraceae   Zones 3–9

Fern leaf yarrow is the common "yellow yarrow" of gardens and cut flowers. The bright yellow inflorescences are up to 4" across and held on longer stems than 'Coronation Gold'. Plants differ from 'Coronation Gold' by having green rather than gray-green foliage, brighter yellow flowers and fewer breaks. It is popular for its ease of culture, strong tall stems and availability from seed or crowns.

Propagation

Seed: Seed germinates within 7–14 days at 65–70F and high humidity. Cover the seed lightly. Approximately 1/64 oz of seed yields 1000 seedlings (6).

Division: Plants should be divided early in the spring but may be divided any time after flowering.

Growing-on

Transplant to 2–4" pots or large cell packs approximately 3 weeks after sowing. Temperatures of 55–60F are optimum for growing-on. Fertilize with 100 ppm N until ready to transplant to the field.

Environmental Factors

Temperature: As with 'Coronation Gold', cool temperatures are useful only for quality and uniformity. Plants are tolerant of warm temperatures and may be grown as far south as central Florida. They also do well in cool climates and are the leading yellow yarrow in northern European countries. Fern leaf yarrow may be a better choice than 'Coronation Gold' in northern states due to the longer stem lengths.

Photoperiod: Photoperiod does not significantly affect flowering.

Field Performance

Spacing: 1' × 1' or 12" × 18" between plants and 2–3' between rows.

Yield: Fewer stems are produced compared with 'Coronation Gold' but stem lengths are generally longer.

Yield and stem quality of *Achillea* 'Coronation Gold' and *Achillea filipendulina* 'Parker's Variety' (Athens, GA; second year data; spacing 1' × 1').

Cultivar	Stems/plant	Stem length (in)
'Coronation Gold'	46	25
'Parker's Variety'	30	31

Longevity: Plants are productive for 3–5 years.

Stage of Harvest   See *Achillea* 'Coronation Gold'.

Postharvest   See *Achillea* 'Coronation Gold'.

Cultivars

'Cloth of Gold' is a popular gold-flowered cutting form. Stems are 2–3' long and flowers are 3–4" wide.

'Gold Plate' also has large, golden yellow flowers and long stems.

'Parker's Variety' has long 2–3' stems and 3–4" wide, deep yellow flowers.

Few differences between these cultivars occur in the field and all are suitable.

Achillea millefolium	Common Yarrow	2–2.5'/3'
White Europe	Asteraceae	Zones 2–9

Common yarrow is a mat-forming species with deeply cut, dark green foliage. The flower heads are small and arranged in flattened inflorescences (corymbs). The native species is predominately creamy white, but pink, rose, mauve and bicolor cultivars are available. Plants spread rapidly and beds fill in within 2 years after planting. They are highly productive and may be propagated readily.

Propagation

Seed: Seed germinates in 10–15 days under humid (sweat tent or mist bed), warm conditions (70–72F). The small seed should be covered lightly with vermiculite or clean sand. Approximately 1/64 oz of seed yields 1000 seedlings (6).

Division: Plants may be divided at any time, but preferably in early spring or immediately after flowering. Even root pieces (essentially root cuttings) reproduce a new plant. A 2- to 3-year-old plant yields hundreds of single crown divisions. Once divisions have been taken, place in a propagation bed for growing-on.

Growing-on

If seedlings are planted in plugs, grow for 3–5 weeks at 55–65F in full light. Fertilize with 50–100 ppm N to maintain green foliage. Do not overfertilize, or plants become spindly. Transplant to field when plants are large enough to be handled.

If seeds are sown in a seed flat, transplant seedlings after the first true leaves have formed to cell packs. Grow on as with plugs.

Divisions should be sorted by size; large divisions may be directly transplanted to the field, the smallest ones may be placed in pots or cell packs and grown-on in the greenhouse or cold frame.

Achillea millefolium

Environmental Factors

Cold is not necessary for optimum flower development, although 3–4 weeks of 40F temperatures contribute to uniformity and stem quality. Plants are particularly cold hardy and are common from the prairies of Canada to the Piedmont of Georgia. Stem strength and flower color is enhanced by cool night temperatures and stems are of higher quality in the North than in the South.

Field Performance

Longevity: Plants are tenacious and spread rapidly. They are long-lived perennials and productive for 3–5 years. They require division every 2–3 years to rejuvenate the planting, otherwise plants become less vigorous and yield declines.

Yield and stem quality of *Achillea millefolium* 'Rose Beauty' over time (Athens, GA; planted fall, 1984; spacing 1' × 1').

Year	Stems/plant	Stems/ft^2	Stem length (in)	Stem diameter (mm)
1985	14	13.9	27.0	3.3
1986	42	42.3	31.5	3.4
1987	36	35.6	38.1	4.4

Stem length: Stem length distribution at Athens, GA, over a 3-year period is found in the following table.

Stem length of *Achillea millefolium* 'Rose Beauty' over time (spacing 1' × 1').

Year	Stem length (%)		
	<10 in	10–20 in	>20 in
1985	6.7	16.8	77.5
1986	3.8	9.2	86.9
1987	0.0	0.0	100.0

Spacing: Common yarrow spreads aggressively and forms a dense mat. Any semblance of spacing in our trials disappeared by the third year and even those spaced 3 feet apart were a solid mat at that time. As the following table shows, flowering stems/plant increased as spacing distance increased but stems/ft^2 declined. A 12" spacing is recommended.

The effect of spacing on yield and stem quality of *Achillea millefolium* (planted in 1984; data from 1986).

Spacing (in)	Stems/plant	Stems/ft^2	Stems >20 in (%)
'Rose Beauty'			
12	42	42.3	90
24	91	22.7	83
36	107	11.9	91
'Cerise Queen'			
12	94	94.1	68
24	143	35.7	42
36	185	20.5	58

Fertilization: Plants need little additional fertilizer if planted in organic soils. High rates of nitrogen result in rapid vegetative growth at the expense of flower development. If planted in pots, however, higher rates of nitrogen and potassium should be supplied compared to that required with field production (3).

Guideline for Foliar Analyses

At field trials in Athens, GA, foliage was sampled from vigorously growing healthy plants when flower buds were visible, but prior to flower opening. These are guidelines only and should not be considered absolute standards. Based on dry weight analysis.

N	P	K	Ca	Mg		Fe	Mn	B	Al	Zn
		(%)						(ppm)		
				'Lilac Beauty'						
2.76	0.34	5.04	0.85	0.19		127	62	32	49	47
				'Paprika'						
3.08	0.43	5.56	0.75	0.19		135	60	29	54	48
				'White Beauty'						
2.66	0.43	5.15	0.96	0.19		147	68	30	65	37

Stage of Harvest

Flowers should not be harvested until pollen is visible on the inflorescence. Stems should be harvested in the coolest part of the day, such as the morning.

Postharvest

Fresh: Shelf life in water or appropriate preservative is only 3–4 days at room temperature. Place stems in warm water immediately to aid in water uptake. The use of silver thiosulfate (STS) only slightly increases postharvest life. Stems placed directly in a cooler (40F) may be held for about 1 week.

Dried: See *Achillea* 'Coronation Gold'.

Cultivars

Many cultivars are available from seed but variability from seed is great. Some of the more useful cultivars for cut flower production follow.

'Cerise Queen' is one of the most popular cultivars and bears cherry-red flowers.

'Fire King' has deep red flowers, although they fade with age and hot weather.

'Jambo' bears medium yellow flowers on 15–18" long stems.

'Lusaka' has white flowers on vigorous, 18" tall plants.

'Nukuru' produces purple-and-white, bicolored flowers.

'Rose Beauty' (var. *roseum*) bears pink flowers that are not as colorful as 'Cerise Queen' but are equally effective.

'Sawa Sawa' is becoming more popular due to its lavender-to-purple flowers on 18–20" tall stems.

Many other cultivars are becoming available to the American grower.

Some of the results of the first 2 years' production in trials in Athens, GA, and Watsonville, CA, are shown in the following table.

Yield and stem quality of *Achillea millefolium.*

Cultivar	Color	Year	Stems/plant		Stem length (in)	
			GA	CA	GA	CA
'Heidi'	Dark violet	1	15	21	11.8	21.0
		2	46	—[a]	20.6	—
'Kelwayi'	Dark red	1	26	25	14.5	38.0
		2	56	—	17.8	—
'Kelwayi'[b]	Dark red	1	20		16.2	
		2	60		21.0	
'Lilac Beauty'	Lilac	1	6	17	15.5	33.0
		2	51	—	18.0	—
'Lilac Beauty'[b]	Lilac	1	7		18.3	
		2	43		18.2	
'Paprika'	Red with	1	12	13	14.4	33.0
	yellow center	2	46	—	18.7	—
'Wesersandstein'	Light rose	1	11	21	14.4	33.0
		2	31	—	23.3	—
'White Beauty'	Creamy white	1	10	26	13.3	27.0
		2	28	—	19.2	—

[a]Dash (—) indicates that data are not available.
[b]Grown under 55% shade, GA only.

From the above data, it is obvious that first-year production in coastal California conditions results in higher yield and significantly longer stems than in Georgia. Unfortunately, the stem lengths were so short in year 2 in the California trials that no data were taken. Second-year yield and stem lengths in Georgia dramatically improved compared to first-year data.

I have tested the Galaxy series in Georgia. The series resulted from a cross (*A. millefolium* × *A. taygetea*) and various selections have occurred. They are similar in leaf shape and texture to *A. millefolium* but are not quite as rampant. The flower heads, however, are much larger and more colorful. Some of the cultivars available include 'Appleblossom' ('Apfelblüte'; mauve), 'Beacon' ('Fanal'; red), 'Great Expectations' ('Hoffnung'; pale yellow) and 'Salmon Beauty' ('Lachsschönheit'; salmon-peach).

Significant increase in yield and quality occurred the second year (1988) compared with the first (1987) in all cultivars and continued into 1990, particularly with 'Beacon' and 'Salmon Beauty'. Unfortunately, all cultivars fade badly, at least in the heat of a Georgia summer—a serious drawback to the series becoming a major cut flower. Flower stems arise from lateral breaks, resulting in many short stems, a problem more prevalent in the South than the North. 'Appleblossom' is a poor choice as a cut flower due to poor stem length. Cultivars were originally selected as garden plants, and their relative lack of height and propensity to fade may limit their usefulness as cut flowers in the United States. Shelf life, however, is better than for *A. millefolium*, and they dry well.

Summary of cut stem characteristics of *Achillea* Galaxy series over time (planted spring, 1987).[a]

Yield and quality	'Appleblossom'	'Beacon'	'Great Expectations'	'Salmon Beauty'
Summer 1987				
Stem length (in)	7.7	11.8	11.9	8.9
Stems/plant	13.0	18.0	25.0	11.0
Flower width (mm)	5.5	5.7	7.8	3.5
Summer 1988				
Stem length (in)	14.2	17.6	20.6	21.2
Stems/plant	53.0	50.0	63.0	89.0
Flower width (mm)	7.1	7.3	12.2	8.1
Summer 1989				
Stem length (in)	12.5	20.7	20.3	21.9
Stems/plant	42.0	127.0	151.0	157.0
Flower width (mm)	9.3	8.6	9.1	7.2
Summer 1990				
Stem length (in)	12.2	20.0	17.8	23.5
Stems/plant	57.0	188.0	203.0	171.0
Flower width (mm)	6.5	7.7	8.6	9.2

[a]Based on original planting of 50 plants. Significant increases in plant population occurred in subsequent years.

Achillea ptarmica

		Sneezewort	2–3'/3'
White	Europe	Asteraceae	Zones 3–9

Obviously someone with allergies gave the common name to this species. It comes from the use of the dried root for snuff, although the flowers are less allergenic than those of common yarrow. The creamy white flowers are held in terminal corymbs. *Achillea ptarmica* is less important commercially than *A. filipendulina* and *A. millefolium*, but interest in it is increasing. I think it is a poor cut flower crop compared with other available yarrows, however, yield is good, the crop continues into the fall and shelf life is better than the colored types.

Propagation

See *Achillea millefolium* for seed techniques. Tip cuttings are best for rapid growth (5).

Environmental Factors

Production under greenhouse conditions is best for cuttings taken in early February and grown at 60F (5). No photoperiod effect is known.

Field Performance

Yield: First-year harvest for Georgia and California and second-year harvest for Vermont are shown in the following table.

Yield and stem quality of *Achillea ptarmica*.

Location	Stems/plant	Stem length (in)
Athens, GA	13	12.2
Burlington, VT[a]	25	17.0
Watsonville, CA	19	27.0

[a]From (7).

Second-year harvest at Georgia was significantly higher, with over 100 stems/plant. Flowers were harvested until mid-November with an average stem length of 20″.

Greenhouse Performance

Sneezewort is greenhouse-grown in some European countries, although seldom produced in this way in the United States. In Finland, with supplemental lighting, flowers were harvested 12 weeks after planting for 3–5 weeks (8). The second harvest was also faster with supplemental lighting.

Stage of Harvest

Harvest when flowers are fully open.

Postharvest

Fresh: Flowers last 5–8 days in water.
Dried: Flowers may be air-dried.
Storage: Flowers may be stored wet for 2–3 days at 40F.

Cultivars

'Ballerina' is a relatively new cultivar with clear white flowers.

'The Pearl' ('Boule de Neige'; 'Schneeball') is the most common cultivar with profuse, buttonlike white flowers. Some of the flowers of 'The Pearl' may be single. May be raised from seed or cuttings.

Additional Species of *Achillea*

Achillea ageratum (sweet yarrow) has been used as a fragrant and medicinal herb for hundreds of years. The flower head is similar but about ⅓ the size of *A. filipendulina* 'Parker's Variety'. The species itself is not particularly useful as a cut flower, although 'Moonwalker' has been selected for its cut flower habit. Plants grow 2.5–3′ tall; the flowers are useful as fillers in a fresh bouquet and also dry well. Approximately 1/256 oz of seed yields 1000 seedlings. No cold treatment is needed, and if sown sufficiently early, plants flower the first year. 'Golden Princess' bears flat, golden inflorescences on 3–4' tall stems.

A. decolorans was used as a cut flower many years ago but is seldom seen today. The white flowers are useful for wreaths and fillers and are produced from late spring through summer.

Pests and Diseases of *Achillea*

Most yarrows are relatively pest- and disease-free, although downy and powdery mildew can be a problem.

Downy mildew results in small, yellow spots on the upperside of the leaves and white mold on the underside.

Powdery mildew results in white spots on both sides on the leaves.

Stem rot caused by *Rhizoctonia solani* may result in decay of the stem base. Application of fungicides and crop rotation alleviate the problem.

Reading for *Achillea*

1. Armitage, A. M. 1987. The influence of spacing on field-grown perennial crops. *HortScience* 22:904–907.

2. Blomme, R., and P. Dambre. 1981. {The use of outdoor flowers for cutting} Het gebruik van bloemen in openlucht als snijbloem. *Verbondsnieuws voor de Belgische Sierteelt* 25(15):681–685.

3. El-Kholy, S. A. 1984. Soil moisture and macronutrient effects on yield and quality of *Achillea millefolium* L. *Minufiya J. of Agr. Res.* 8:331–348.

4. Escher, F., and H. Ladebusch. 1980. {Cut flower plants: the influence of soil acidity on their growth} Schnitt-Stauden: Der Einfluss der Bodenversauerung auf ihre Entwicklung. *Gb + Gw.* 80(51/52):1135–1136.

5. Geertsen, V., and N. Bredmose. 1986. {Three new cut flowers for growing in early spring} Tre nye snitblomster til dyrkning i det tidlige forar. *Gertner Tidende* 102(18):574–575.

6. Kieft, C. 1989. *Kieft's Growing Manual* .... Kieft Bloemzaden, Venhuizen, The Netherlands.

7. Perry, L. 1989. Perennial cut flowers. In *Proceedings of 2nd National Conference on Specialty Cut Flowers.* Athens, GA. 155–162.

8. Sarkka, L. 1991. Wintertime production of *Achillea* and *Physostegia* with supplementary lighting and CO_2 enrichment. Abstract presented at 2nd International Symposium on Development of New Floricultural Crops, 17–21 September 1991, Baltimore, MD.

9. Vaughan, M. J. 1988. *The Complete Book of Cut Flower Care.* Timber Press, Portland, OR.

Aconitum carmichaelii

		Azure Monkshood	2–3'/3'
Blue	Central China	Ranunculaceae	Zones 2–6

Although this is one of the finest blue cut flowers available today, production in the United States is limited to coastal areas of California, the Northwest and the Northeast. The enlarged roots are extremely poisonous, containing significant amounts of aconite, and the foliage is only slightly less toxic. No taste tests need be conducted with this crop. Monkshood is well established in several European markets but is only sporadically available in the United States. One of the flower sepals is enlarged and resembles a hood, thus accounting for the common name. The flowers are held in terminal racemes and open in mid to late summer.

Propagation

Seed: Although many companies offer seed of monkshood, the seed is notoriously difficult to germinate. Seed develops a deep dormancy upon ripening and 12-month germination times are not uncommon (1).

To speed up the process, sow seed for all *Aconitum* species in moist, well-drained medium and place at 65–70F for 2–4 weeks. Transfer seed flat to 20–25F for 6–8 weeks. Avoid soil temperatures below 16F. Place in cool temperatures (45–55F) even if germination has occurred. Grow at cool temperatures until ready to transplant.

Sowing in the fall and placing the flats where they will be snow-covered during the winter is a cost-effective means of providing these conditions. Winter provides the cold, the melting snow in the spring is beneficial to reduce inhibitors and germination occurs in early spring. Germination is erratic and may require 2 years for 50–70% germination rates.

Division: Plants may be carefully divided in early spring. A piece of the enlarged root must be present. Division should not be done for at least 3 years after planting.

Environmental Factors

Temperature: *Aconitum* is a cool crop and does not perform well south of zone 6. Plants require moist, cool conditions for adequate establishment and summer temperatures in much of the country preclude high yields and quality. If plants are subjected to high temperatures, stems are weak and support is necessary. Performance is best in the Pacific Northwest and the Northeast.

Cold (32–35F) is necessary for flowering, although the duration of the cold period is not known. The tubers may be stored at 28F to delay flowering. Planting of frozen tubers may take place as late as early July for late fall flowering. Attempts to force *A. napellus* to flower earlier in the field using plastic tunnels only advanced flowering 4–5 days. Quality was unaffected (4).

Light: Grow in full sun; no photoperiodic effects are known.

Soil pH: Yield and stem length are greater at a soil pH of 6.4 than at 3.7 (2).

Aconitum carmichaelii

Field Performance

Longevity: Plants are long-lived perennials and are productive for at least 5 years. Replanting 20% of the area every year allows for a constant supply of flowers.

Spacing: Space at 18″ × 18″ or 2′ × 2′. Do not plant more than 3–4″ deep.

Yield: Eight to twelve flowers per mature plant is not uncommon.

Greenhouse Performance

Precooled tubers may be planted in ground beds or in 8–10″ pots. Temperatures should be approximately 45–50F for 6–8 weeks then raised to 55–60F during crop growth. Crops planted in late February flower in late May. Heating greenhouses to 40F for the entire duration can be successful, although flowering will be slower. Plants must be supported using mum support netting. Since this crop requires only low energy, it has excellent potential for winter cropping.

Stage of Harvest

Inflorescences (racemes) should be harvested when the first 1–3 basal flowers are open. If cut too early, flower buds will not open. Plunge immediately into flower preservative. 'Spark's Variety' should be cut with more open flowers than *A. napellus*.

Postharvest

Fresh: Monkshood persists 7–10 days in preservative, less in plain water. Keep from temperature extremes; temperatures below 45F and above 60F should be avoided. Flowers are susceptible to chilling injury, and blackening of flowers may occur if stored below 45F (5). Silver thiosulfate improves the vase life.

Dried: *Aconitum* may be air-dried and will persist for many months. Strip the foliage prior to hanging upside down. However, it may not be a good idea to preserve poison on a stem, regardless of how well it dries.

Cultivars

'Barker's Variety' and 'Kelmscott' have light blue and violet-blue flowers, respectively. Some authorities claim that these cultivars are derived from var. *wilsonii*.

var. *wilsonii* is 5–6' tall and bears dark blue flowers. Support is required.

Additional Species

Many differences of opinion concerning nomenclature of *Aconitum* exist. The following species of *Aconitum* are useful as cut flowers.

Aconitum × *arendsii* (arend's aconite) is relatively new and difficult to locate but bears the largest flowers and stoutest stems. It is sometimes listed as a cultivar of *A. carmichaelii* ('Arendsii'). The rich, dark blue flowers and strong, upright stems are excellent for flower production. If obtainable, it is the species of choice for the cut flower grower.

A. × *cammarum* is a name which covers a class of hybrids between *A. napellus* and *A. variegatum*. 'Bicolor' (blue and white), 'Blue Sceptre' (deep blue), 'Bressingham Spire' (violet-blue), 'Newry Blue' (dark blue) and 'Spark's Variety' (dark blue) are excellent cultivars with stiff, upright racemes. 'Bicolor' and 'Newry Blue' are sometimes sold as cultivars of *A. napellus*.

A. napellus (common monkshood) is the most popular species for cut flower production. The flower colors may wash out under warm temperatures. 'Roseum' ('Carneum') is a handsome, light pink cultivar.

A. orientale (oriental monkshood) has sulfur-yellow flowers but does not have the market potential of the blue-flowered species.

Pests and Diseases

Crown rot produces symptoms of leaf yellowing, plant wilt and rot at the crown where the stems emerge. It causes black streaks in the water conducting vessels of the stems and roots. Caused by *Sclerotinium delphinii*.

Mosaic virus causes yellow mottling and stripes on leaves. Plants should be culled.

Verticillium wilt, caused by *Verticillium albo-atrum* and *Cephalosporium* spp., results in leaves which fade to green-yellow, often on one side of the plant only. Leaves die, flowers are of poor quality and black-to-brown discoloration in the cut stem is apparent.

Reading

1. Armitage, A. M. 1989. *Herbaceous Perennial Plants: A Treatise on Their Identification, Culture, and Garden Attributes*. Varsity Press, Athens, GA.

2. Escher, F., and H. Ladebusch. 1980. {Cut flower plants: the influence of soil acidity on their growth} Schnitt-Stauden: Der Einfluss der Bodenversauerung auf ihre Entwicklung. *Gb + Gw.* 80(51/52):1135–1136.

3. Kalkman, F. C. 1983. Pretreatment improves the quality of summer flowers (in Dutch). *Vakblad voor de Bloemisterij* 38:26–29.

4. Loeser, H. 1986. {Forcing of cut perennials} Verfruhung von Schnittstauden. *Zierplanzenbau* 26(8):316.

5. Vaughan, M. J. 1988. *The Complete Book of Cut Flower Care*. Timber Press, Portland, OR.

Asclepias tuberosa   Butterfly Weed   2–3'/3'
Orange   Eastern North America   Asclepiadaceae   Zones 3–8

This species is native from Maine to Florida and as far west as Arizona. The bright orange flowers are held in umbels above the alternate leaves. Although orange is most common, flower color may occasionally range from red to yellow. The subsequent fruits are long and narrow and are also ornamental. They may be used as dried ornaments to augment bouquets of grasses and potpourri. It is one of the few members of the milkweed family that does not produce abundant quantities of milky sap and, therefore, is not as difficult to handle as other species of the family. As well, butterfly weed lacks the invasive qualities typical of many of its more obnoxious relatives.

Propagation

Seed: Fresh seed may be germinated without a great deal of difficulty. However, seed should be removed as a mass from the follicles when they turn yellowish brown and begin to split, but before the down is fluffy and visible (7). Check the follicles occasionally and allow to ripen naturally; seed is ripe when it turns brown. Do not allow follicles to split completely or seed will be lost. Immediately after collection, clean the seed by grasping the mass with one hand and gently sliding the clasped fingers of the other hand downward. A good firm tug separates the seed from the compacted down and eliminates the laborious job of cleaning individual seed (7).

If seed is purchased (a great deal easier than the above job), ½ to ¾ oz of seed yields 1000 seedlings (2). Sow the seed immediately or, if not possible, store the dried seed at 40F.

Asclepias tuberosa

Sow at 70–72F under high humidity; germination occurs within 30–90 days (1). Alternatively, seed may be placed in moist sand or paper wrap in the refrigerator (36–40F) for 60 days to reduce germination time and improve germination percentage.

Cuttings: Terminal stem cuttings can be taken in spring prior to flowering. Approximately 3–4" long cuttings should be stuck under a sweat tent or mist system. Rooting hormone is not necessary; rooting requires 4–6 weeks.

Root cuttings are an easier means of propagation. Cut the taproot into 2–3" long sections and place them vertically, maintaining polarity, in a well-drained, sterilized medium. Keep medium warm and moist.

Digging from the wild: Plants have a long taproot and survival percentage is very low when gathered from the wild. Don't even think about it!

Growing-on

Butterfly weed immediately begins taproot growth upon germination;

should it become potbound at any time, plantlets rapidly deteriorate. If seedlings are sown in a seed flat, transplant to 4" pots by the time the second set of true leaves appears. Provide bright light, temperatures near 65F and feed with 200 ppm N once a week using a complete fertilizer. Do not over-water; plants are more tolerant of drought than overwatering. Regardless of propagation technique, hold in pots only until vigorous growth occurs. Avoid damage to the taproot when transplanting. If the taproot is broken, the plant requires 2 years to recover, if it survives.

Environmental Factors

Temperature: Asclepias goes through a winter dormancy period and benefits from a chilling period (below 40F). However, winter-sown seed results in flowering during the summer, indicating that cold is not a require-ment for flowering (6). While not an absolute requirement, cold results in better quality of the first flower and enhances development of subsequent flowers.

If crowns are used, they may be sprouted in the greenhouse after cold storage at 38F for at least 12 weeks. Crowns stored for 16 weeks sprouted in 9 days while those which did not receive a cold treatment never sprouted (3). Prolonged cold storage also reduced the time to flower from 70 days for plants stored for 12–14 weeks to 56 days for those held for 16 weeks (3).

Photoperiod: Plants flower more rapidly under long days (LD). Forced under 9-hour photoperiods, plants did not flower due to flower abortion and blind shoots. Days-to-flower in a warm greenhouse was reduced by about 10 days for plants forced under 17-hour photoperiod compared to 13-hour (3). Long days also promote vigorous shoot extension, leaf production, more flowers per inflorescence and inhibition of lateral branching (3,4,5). The following table shows results of work done at Kansas State University (3).

The effect of cold treatment and photoperiod on flowers/inflorescence of greenhouse-forced *Asclepias tuberosa*.

Cold period (wk)	Photoperiod (hr)		
	13	15	17
12	131	213	143
14	219	214	113
16	216	146	224

Under short days (SD), plants remain short, leaves droop and plants appear wilted despite being fully turgid.

In the field, plants tolerate high temperatures and full sun to partial shade. Soils must be deep and well drained as the taproot is susceptible to root rots in poorly drained soils. Butterfly weed is one of the latest plants to emerge in the spring and care must be taken not to disturb the dormant crowns in the spring.

Field Performance

Longevity: Once plants are established, they are long-lived perennials and may be kept in the same bed for many years. Clump diameter increases with age and the number of flowering stems also increases. Three- to five-year production cycles are not uncommon.

Spacing: Space plants 18–24" apart. A 12" × 18" grid has also been used successfully. Plants commonly grow 3' tall by the second year; spacing closer than 18" results in additional insect and disease pressure. In our trial, average stem length of 22.1" occurred on our first harvest at 18" spacing.

Greenhouse Performance

Plant established seedlings or rooted cuttings in deep ground beds at about 2 plants/ft^2 (6–9" centers). Temperatures should be 50–55F in late spring and 60–65F as temperatures rise. Cuttings planted in January through March flower from May to June and continue until early fall. Plants may be started under short daylengths in the winter or spring, but daylength must be lengthened to force flowering. The use of incandescent lights to provide 14- to 16-hour LD by nightbreak lighting (4–6 hours during the middle of the dark period) is recommended for most flowers, best shoot length and earliest flowering. Cropping time in the greenhouse depends on season but is approximately 15–20 weeks from seed. If crowns are purchased, plant in sufficiently large containers and store at 38F for approximately 14 weeks. Remove cooled crowns to the greenhouse (60–65F). Emergence occurs within 5–7 weeks. Provide LD (14–16 hours) as above. Flowering occurs 60–80 days after cooling crowns.

Stage of Harvest

Harvest when ½ to ⅔ of the flowers are open; flowers do not open well once stems are cut. If fruits are to be harvested, harvest when green before they start to split.

Postharvest

Stems exude little or no milky sap (unlike other members of the family), thus no special heat treatments or dipping solutions are necessary for cut stems. However, plunge stems into water containing a preservative and store at 40–45F immediately upon cutting. Stems should be recut under water by the florist and consumer to provide additional shelf life. Silver thiosulfate has a beneficial effect on vase life. Average shelf life in water at room temperature is 5–8 days.

Cultivars

Few cultivars are available; however, seed propagation yields sufficient variation in flower color for selections to be made.

Additional Species

Asclepias curassavica (blood flower) is native to the West Indies and is occasionally offered as a cut flower. 'Red Butterfly' has deep red flowers and grows 2–2.5' tall. Seed may be direct-sown to the field. Plants should be grown in partial shade for best height and performance.

A. incarnata (swamp milkweed) has lovely pink and white flowers on 2–3' tall stems. Plants perform best in moist soils but also tolerate "normal" soils. Like butterfly weed, *A. incarnata* requires approximately 16 hours of daylight for flower initiation and flower development. 'Soulmate', a new introduction from the Netherlands, has rose-pink flowers and grows 2–3' tall. Postharvest life is 10–14 days without preservative.

Pests and Diseases

Spider mites are a major problem on butterfly weed, particularly in rich soils and where plants are grown too succulent due to overwatering or over-fertilization. Plants are less susceptible if neglected (i.e., do not feed or water heavily); however, miticides should be readied by late May in the South and mid-June in the North. Other significant pests are aphids and thrips.

Viruses result in bright green or yellow-green spots and lines on the foliage. Cull infected plants.

Reading

1. Armitage, A. M. 1989. *Herbaceous Perennial Plants: A Treatise on Their Identification, Culture, and Garden Attributes.* Varsity Press, Athens, GA.

2. Kieft, C. 1989. *Kieft's Growing Manual* .... Kieft Bloemzaden, Venhuizen, The Netherlands.

3. Lewnes-Albrecht, M., and J. T. Lehmann. 1991. Daylength, cold storage, and plant production method influence growth and flowering of *Asclepias tuberosa*. HortScience 26:120–121.

4. Lyons, R. E. 1985. *Asclepias tuberosa*. In A. H. Halevy (ed.), *The Handbook of Flowering*, vol. 5. CRC Press, Boca Raton, FL. 22–28.

5. Lyons, R. E., and J. N. Booze. 1983. Effect of photoperiod on first year growth of 2 *Asclepias* species. HortScience 18:575 (Abstr.).

6. Nau, J. 1989. *Ball Culture Guide: The Encyclopedia of Seed Germination.* Ball Seed Co., West Chicago, IL.

7. Phillips, H. P. 1985. *Growing and Propagating Wild Flowers.* Univ. of North Carolina Press, Chapel Hill, NC.

Many thanks to Dr. Robert Lyons for reviewing this section.

Aster spp.   Aster

The genus contains over 600 species of which 3–4 are useful as cut flowers. The main species used for cut flower production are *A. ericoides* (september aster), *A.* × *dumosus*, *A. novi-belgii* (michaelmas daisy), *A. novae-angliae* (new england aster) and hybrids of *A. ericoides*, *A.* × *dumosus* and *A. novi-belgii*. Most of the cut flower types flower in late summer or fall. Flower yield and stem length are less the first year than subsequent years, particularly in areas of warm summer temperatures. Growers in coastal California enjoy better yields and stem lengths the first year compared with eastern growers because of cooler summer temperatures. Asters are often used as fillers in mixed bouquets and occasionally as primary flowers in single-species bouquets.

Aster ericoides

Aster ericoides	September Aster		2–3'/2'
Various colors	North America	Asteraceae	Zones 3–7

The light green leaves of september aster are less than 2" long and occur on many branched stems. The flower heads are white, tinged rose and extremely numerous. They are popular as fillers for arrangements and bouquets and are in constant demand.

Propagation

All named cultivars are propagated by basal cuttings, often referred to as vegetative ground shoots (2). Terminal cuttings result in shorter plants than basal cuttings and should be avoided. Terminal cuttings, are used for pot plant cuttings, however. Place unrooted cuttings in peat/perlite or a comparably well-drained mix at 70–75F under a sweat tent or intermittent mist. Cuttings root in 7–14 days. Rooting hormone is useful but not necessary. Always root cuttings under a minimum of 16-hour days (2) using incandescent lights to keep plants vegetative.

Growing-on

Rooted cuttings may be planted immediately in the field or greenhouse but are usually grown-on prior to planting. If planting in the field, place in 3–4" pots under long days, and immediately fertilize with 75 ppm N using potassium nitrate. Grow at temperatures no higher than 60F. Approximately 2 weeks later, raise fertility level to 150 ppm N with a complete fertilizer at every irrigation. Plant in the field 3–5 weeks after potting. If planting in the greenhouse, rooted cuttings may be placed in the ground bed or bench immediately upon rooting and treated as above.

Environmental Factors

Although little scientific literature exists for *A. ericoides*, considerable information is available for other species (see *Aster novi-belgii*). In general, *A. ericoides* must go through a long day/short day sequence similar to other fall flowering asters. However, because *A. ericoides* flowers later in the fall than *A. novi-belgii*, this species either requires additional numbers of short days, or more likely, the short day photoperiod (i.e., number of hours of light per day) necessary for flowering is shorter than that needed by michaelmas daisy.

Temperature also plays a significant role in flowering. Plants remain vegetative if night temperatures are cool (40F) even at 12-hour photoperiods. However, they may bud up much earlier under warm nights (65F) and hot days even under long days (2). This is not uncommon in the South.

Field Performance

Plants may be planted out in the fall, early spring and as late as June. *Aster ericoides* is a short day plant and flowers in October through November in the East; it flowers earlier in the West, regardless of planting date. Dates in Athens, GA, ranged from October 10 to November 8 for second-year harvest. Planting later than mid-June may result in plants with insufficient stem length.

Spacing: Plant approximately 12" × 12" or 12" × 18".

Yield: Unfortunately little information on outdoor yields is available. However, the 2-year field performance of a number of cultivars, presented in the following table, may be useful.

Yield and stem quality of *Aster ericoides* (Athens, GA, and Watsonville, CA).

Cultivar	Color	Year	Stems/plant GA	Stems/plant CA	Stem length (in) GA	Stem length (in) CA
'Blue Wonder'	Blue	1	13	9	26.3	51.0
		2	20	92	25.8	50.0
'Constance'	White	1	10	13	20.7	40.0
		2	21	50	30.4	54.0
'Esther'	Pink	1	14	13	7.0	27.0
		2	24	28	24.1	30.0
'Monte Cassino'	White	1	17	17	20.4	38.0
		2	28	31	29.2	35.0

Especially with 'Blue Wonder' and 'Constance', the differences between California and Georgia trials were more dramatic the second year than the first. This is not uncommon, particularly when comparing the rarified growing conditions of Watsonville, CA, to the hot, humid conditions of Athens, GA.

Shading: Some cultivars benefit from the addition of shade, while others are adversely affected. The following table presents results from work at Athens, GA.

Yield was reduced under shade. Disease was also more prevalent under shade in the second year compared with the first, and therefore shade cannot be recommended. Some of the worst instances of disease occurred in hybrids such as 'Pink Star' and 'Rose Star'. Most likely, such outbreaks were due to poor ventilation and the fact that shaded plants do not dry out as rapidly after rain as those in full sun.

The effect of shade on yield and stem quality of *Aster ericoides*.

Cultivar	Shade level (%)	Stems/plant Year 1	Year 2	Stem length (in) Year 1	Year 2
'Blue Wonder'	0	13	20	26.3	25.8
	55	10	10	26.0	26.8
'Constance'	0	10	21	20.7	30.4
	55	5	17	22.5	24.2
'Monte Cassino'	0	17	28	20.4	29.2
	55	15	28	24.8	29.2

Greenhouse Performance

Aster ericoides can be forced for year-round production. Plants flower under short day conditions and grow vegetatively under long days, much like chrysanthemums. If forcing on a year-round schedule, it is necessary to have incandescent lamps and black cloth facilities for best uniformity and control of flowering time. Place rooted cuttings in 6–8" pots or in ground beds, and space 9" × 9" or 2 plants/ft². Fertilize with 50–75 ppm N from potassium nitrate. If natural daylength is less than 12 hours, use incandescent lights as day extension (photoperiod >14 hours) or as cyclic lighting. In general, a pinch is applied to the growing stems when they are 6–8" long. Allow 4–6 leaves to remain if possible. Fertilize with 150–200 ppm N using a complete fertilizer. Apply long days until stems attain a height of approximately 12–18". Short days may be artificially applied by black cloth during late spring through early fall when natural daylength is too long to naturally trigger flowering. Reduce fertilizer when SD begin; after 3 weeks of SD, terminate fertilizer and reduce watering to the point of plant wilt. Water to keep plants from wilting only; this "stress" results in flowers ready to be cut 4–7 weeks after the beginning of short days, depending on cultivar.

After harvesting, cut plants back to the ground, remove all partially cut stems and stubble and leach thoroughly with plain water. Place plants back in LD (>16 hours), thin to 4–6 stems/plant and start cycle once again. In highlight areas such as California, Florida, Colorado, or during the spring and summer cycles, 5–7 stems may be allowed to remain. Plants may be cropped for 12–15 months in this manner prior to discarding.

Temperatures of 60/70F night/day result in excellent vegetative and reproductive growth. Low night temperatures (below 55F) after SD result in erratic bud development and poor vase life. Terminal flowers open but the lateral flowers are delayed or may not open at all.

Stage of Harvest

Cut the stems when 2–4 flowers in the inflorescence have opened. Place immediately in water or floral preservative. Although the use of STS has been inconsistent, low concentrations may result in additional vase life with some cultivars.

Postharvest

Fresh: If placed immediately in water, stems persist for 8–12 days, depending on temperature.

Storage: Flowers may be stored in preservative in the cooler at 40F for approximately 5 days without loss in quality.

Dried: Flowers do not dry well.

Grading

No standard grades have been adopted in United States; however, the standards in Dutch auctions, outlined in the following paragraphs, may be of interest (1).

Class I stems are fresh, undamaged, free of pests and diseases and damage from same, free of chemical residues, free of brown flower centers, free from stems which have branches longer than 8″ and sufficiently straight and strong to carry the inflorescence.

Class II stems are reduced in quality in all categories, but one can reasonably expect them to have ornamental value after handling and that this quality will be retained for a reasonable amount of time.

In each of the 2 classes, ¼ of the flowers are open, and no more than a 10% variation in stem length is permissible. Five stems are included in each bunch.

Cultivars

'Blue Wonder' has blue flowers with a tinge of pink.

'Esther' has white flowers with a tinge of pink and is similar in growth habit to 'Monte Cassino'. Unfortunately, plants were less perennial in Athens, GA, than other cultivars, dying after 2 years.

'Monte Cassino' is the most popular cultivar, bearing clusters of small white flowers. Higher production and faster flowering (particularly under greenhouse conditions) are keeping 'Monte Cassino' ahead of the pack.

'San Carlos' and 'San Remo' are two recent white-flowered introductions. They are more floriferous and less light-sensitive than 'Monte Cassino'. They are better adapted to greenhouse than field production.

'White Wonder' is similar in growth habit to 'Blue Wonder' but has creamy white flowers.

Pests and Diseases

Aphids pierce the stem and leaves and secrete honeydew, the presence of which can result in the development of sooty mold.

Caterpillars ruin the foliage but are seldom a problem at time of flowering.

Powdery mildew causes a white mold on leaves and stems; it can decimate the crop.

Spittle bugs are more common on this species than other asters. A general-purpose insecticide is effective.

Many thanks to Mr. Jack Graham and Mr. Jeff McGrew for reviewing this section.

Aster novae-angliae	New England Aster	1–6'/3'
Aster novi-belgii	New York Aster, Michaelmas Daisy	1–6'/3'
Various colors	North America Asteraceae	Zones 3–7

The toothed leaves of new york aster are opposite and differ from the foliage of new england aster by being less pubescent (hairy). Flowering is earlier than *A. ericoides*, occuring in August and September. The culture of both species is similar. In warm areas, plants may also flower in the spring. This is due to the onset of warm weather and short photoperiods at that time. The flowers should be cut back and although stems are much shorter than those harvested in the fall, they may find a market as off-season fillers. Gloves should be worn when harvesting asters, particularly *A. novae-angliae* (new england aster). Sensitive individuals can develop contact dermatitis and allergic reactions from the foliage of many cultivars.

Propagation

Propagation is by vegetative basal cuttings (see *Aster ericoides*) or division. Two- to three-inch cuttings should be plunged in a mixture of peat/perlite and placed under a sweat tent or intermittent mist at 70–72F.

Growing-on   See *Aster ericoides*.

Environmental Factors

Aster novi-belgii has evolved into a highly regulated species in its flowering behavior. The species requires a specific sequence of chilling (vernalization) to break dormancy, long days (LD) for stem elongation, shorter days (SD) for flower initiation and finally very short days to induce dormancy. In nature, this sequence is satisfied by the chill of winter, the long days of spring and summer, the shortening days of late summer and finally the short days of late fall.

Vernalization: Plants should be chilled for 4–8 weeks at 40F. Vernalization causes the plants to be more responsive to subsequent photoperiod (LD, SD) (4). Vernalization also results in greater stem lengths of flowering shoots.

Photoperiod: Long days result in shoot elongation and are necessary for flowering. Even without chilling, LD promote flowering, although the number of flowers is significantly less than if chilling has been given (4). Approximately 4–5 weeks of LD of at least 18 hours are promotive but continuous lighting (24 hours) is even more effective. The number of LD cycles differs with cultivar; some may require up to 8 weeks of LD (4).

Short days are not particularly short for new england asters and new york asters. A SD of 14 hours is normal for many cultivars although some cultivars will even flower with 16-hour photoperiods. Daylengths less than 12 hours result in flower abortion and onset of dormancy and should be avoided (4).

Temperature: During the SD period, temperatures of 86F and 72F resulted in more flowers than 60F. Increasing temperatures and longer photoperiods (although still effectively SD) resulted in the greatest flower number (4). Low temperatures during SD caused a tendency to flower abortion.

Gibberellic acid: GA₃ substitutes for vernalization and LD, as long as the appropriate SD are given (4). Treatments are seldom applied commercially.

Field Performance

Grown-on rooted cuttings should be set out in early spring to June. Plants respond to the long day conditions of spring and summer and then shorter days of late summer. Late spring flowering can occur in the South, the flowers of which are useful to the market (see "Environmental Factors"). Normally, cultivars flower in late August through September, although some may flower as early as late July. Dates in Athens, GA, ranged from September 10 to October 10 for second-year harvest. Therefore, these asters fit well with *A. ericoides* because their early flowering combined with the late flowering of *A. ericoides* allows a long harvest period. In general, yield and stem length of first-year harvests are less than subsequent years, particularly in warm climates (see *Aster ericoides*). This can be explained by the relative lack of vernalization in these climates. In areas of the West Coast, where night temperatures in spring and early summer approach 40F, some vernalization occurs and shoots elongate even in the first year. Two-year yields and stem lengths of cultivars grown in Athens, GA, and Watsonville, CA, are shown in the following table.

Yield and stem quality of *Aster novae-angliae* (NA) and *Aster novi-belgii* (NB) (Athens, GA, and Watsonville, CA).

Cultivar	Color	Year	Stems/plant		Stem length (in)	
			GA	CA	GA	CA
'Alma Pötschke' (NA)	Pink	1	12	10	20.0	27.0
		2	35	44	26.0	27.0
'Blue Gown' (NB)	Blue	1	10	9	27.5	51.0
		2	22	31	26.5	38.0
'Climax' (NB)	Lavender-blue	1	10	11	22.0	51.0
		2	22	20	27.7	31.0
'Elta' (NB)	Lilac-blue	1	9	10	22.0	38.0
		2	—[a]	35	—	32.0
'Harrington's Pink' (NA)	Pink	1	12	9	28.0	28.0
		2	—	13	—	26.0
'Mt. Everest' (NB)	White	1	10	—	20.0	—
		2	16	26	27.0	43.0
'Rosa Sieger' (NA)	Salmon-red	1	10	12	21.0	27.0
		2	22	21	26.7	28.0
'Winston S. Churchill' (NB)	Red	1	15	20	21.0	33.0
		2	27	28	20.6	30.0

[a] Dash (—) indicates that data are not available.

First-year production data reveal that stem lengths in particular are significantly longer under coastal California conditions than in Georgia. Differences in data for the second year are not as large.

Spacing: Plant 12" × 12" for smaller cultivars and 12" × 18" for larger ones. In Vermont, a 2' × 2' spacing of *A. novi-belgii* 'Benary's Composition resulted in 44 stems/plant in the second year of production. The average stem length was 36" (3).

Shading: Some cultivars benefit from the addition of shade; others are adversely affected. In general, shade cannot be recommended due to the increased prevalence of mildew, root rot organisms and various other diseases. The following table presents first-year yield and stem lengths from work at Athens, GA.

The effect of shade on yield and stem quality of first-year aster cultivars (Athens, GA).

Cultivar	Shade level (%)	Stems/plant	Stem length (in)
'Blue Gown'[a]	0	5	18.1
	55	5	25.7
'Mt. Everest'[a]	0	10	14.4
	55	11	16.4
'Pink Star'[b]	0	11	12.8
	55	4	20.2
'Winston S. Churchill'[a]	0	12	14.0
	55	11	17.2

[a] Cultivar of *Aster novi-belgii.*
[b] Hybrid cultivar.

Disease was much more prevalent under shade in the second year compared with the first; data were not even taken the second year. Heavy shading (i.e., if plants receive less than 25 fc) can also result in devernalization of the plant.

Longevity: Although asters are a true perennial, disease problems render their long term commercial performance questionable. In some areas of Europe, California and Florida, plants are treated as annuals, even in full sun.

Greenhouse Performance

For greenhouse forcing, cuttings or clumps should be vernalized. Rooted cuttings should be cooled to 35–40F for 4–6 weeks. Plant in 6–8" pots or in ground beds at a spacing of 9" × 12" by the end of July. Photoperiods greater than 17 hours and temperatures of 60–65F should be maintained. Grow under LD until stems are 12–18" long (approx. 3–4 weeks) and then maintain a SD of 13–14 hours. Avoid daylengths less than 11 hours. Photoperiods can be manipulated with incandescent lamps and shade cloth. Temperatures during SD should average approximately 65F for longest stem lengths. Flowering time is 6–10 weeks after the beginning of SD treatment, depending on cultivar and temperature.

If noncooled cuttings are used, stems may be shorter and flowering delayed compared with cooled stems. Maintain cool temperatures during LD stage in the greenhouse for vernalization. Unheated greenhouses or plastic frames can be used for late spring and early summer crops. Cuttings planted in November or December will naturally be vernalized after approximately 6 weeks of temperatures below 40F. At that time, the LD-SD sequence described above may begin.

Guideline for Foliar Analyses

At field trials in Athens, GA, and Watsonville, CA, Foliage was sampled from vigorously growing healthy plants when flower buds were visible, but prior to flower opening. These are guidelines only and should not be considered absolute standards. Based on dry weight analysis.

(%)						(ppm)				
N	P	K	Ca	Mg		Fe	Mn	B	Al	Zn
				'Rosa Sieger' (GA)						
3.0	0.45	3.29	1.68	0.20		168	65	37	83	72
				'Climax' (GA)						
3.1	0.65	3.64	0.98	0.18		162	88	39	48	121
				'Climax' (CA)						
2.2	0.24	3.67	1.39	0.35		180	273	46	52	26

Stage of Harvest

Stems may be harvested when 2–4 flowers/inflorescence are open. Place in water immediately.

Postharvest

Fresh: Flowers persist for 5–7 days in water, longer in a preservative. Flowers are relatively insensitive to ethylene. In general, vase life of cultivars of new york aster (*A. novi-belgii*) is better than that of new england aster (*A. novae-angliae*) cultivars.

Dried: Flowers do not dry well.

Cultivars

The following are cultivars of *Aster novi-belgii*.

'Bonningdale White' and 'Bonningdale Blue' bear large white and blue flowers, respectively, on 3' tall plants.

'Fellowship' produces 1–1.5" wide, lilac-pink flowers.

'Gayborder Splendour' bears deep red flowers.

'Lassie' has light pink flowers.

'Lisette' produces lilac-pink flowers.

'Sailor Boy' bears dark blue, 1" wide flowers.

'White Ladies' produces 1–1.5" wide, white flowers.

Additional Species of *Aster*

Aster cordifolius is represented most often by the lavender-blue cultivar 'Ideal'. Plants are harvested in late September and early October in the Southeast. Second-year yield was 22 stems/plant with an average stem length of 32". Foliage was larger and less susceptible to mildew or rust than other species tested. A species with excellent potential.

A. × *dumosus* may have some possibilities as a cut flower. 'Heinz Richard' (deep purple flowers) and 'Kristina' (white flowers) are presently being tested. Unfortunately, vase life appears to be poor.

A. tataricus (tatarian aster) bears many ½ to ¾" wide, lavender-blue flowers in late fall (September and October in the Southeast). The plants attain 4–6' in size and are among the last of the asters to flower. They are most useful in southern states where a long autumn is normal.

Hybrid asters: Hybridized from various species, some of these asters are finding a place in specialty cut flower offerings and all are best grown in the greenhouse.

Butterfly series goes under such flighty names as 'Lilac Blue Admiral', 'Purple Monarch', 'Painted Lady' (pink) and 'Skipper' (dark pink). I have not tested these but they are supposed to have larger flowers than 'Monte Cassino' and stiff, erect stems.

Master series includes 'White Master', 'Pink Master' and 'Blue Master' (lilac-blue). They are similar in flower and habit to the Butterfly series. Both Butterfly and Master series appear to be excellent for greenhouse culture.

Star series of hybrid asters includes 'Pink Star', 'Rose Star', 'Snow Star' and 'White Star'. Flowers are smaller than new england asters and new york asters but larger than those of *A. ericoides*. They do not appear particularly heat tolerant and also require good drainage.

Pests and Diseases of *Aster*

Leaf spots are caused by many leaf-spotting fungi including *Alternaria* spp., *Cercospora asterata*, *Leptothyrium doellingeriae*, and *Septoria* spp. Spray at weekly or 10-day intervals with sulfur or copper fungicide, particularly in rainy seasons.

Downy mildew is prevalent in the Midwest and South.

Powdery mildew is more prevalent in the lower leaves of many asters. The disease usually develops in late August to mid-September.

Rust is caused by various organisms including *Coleosporium solidaginis* and *Puccinia asteris*. Infected plants dehydrate, turn brown and remain stunted. Some cultivars are more susceptible than others. For example, 2 of the most susceptible cultivars in trials in Georgia were 'Snow Star' and 'Pink Star', whereas 'Rose Star' was not affected.

Reading for *Aster*

1. Anon. 1990. Regulations for supply of cut flowers, Dutch auctions 1990. Pathfast Publishing, Frinton-on-Sea, U.K.

2. McGrew, J. 1990. Personal communication.

3. Perry, L. P. 1989. Perennial cut flowers. In *Proceedings of 2nd National Conference on Specialty Cut Flowers*. Athens, GA 155–161.

4. Schwabe, W. W. 1985. *Aster novi-belgii*. In A. H. Halevy (ed.), *The Handbook of Flowering*, vol. 5. CRC Press, Boca Raton, FL. 29–41.

Many thanks to Ms. Fran Foley, Mr. Jeff McGrew and Mr. Jack Graham for helping with the data and reviewing this section.

Astilbe × *arendsii*

Astilbe × *arendsii*	False Goat's Beard		2–4'/2'
Various colors	Hybrid origin	Saxifragaceae	Zones 3–7

Because it requires low maintenance and is shade tolerant, *Astilbe* has become a popular garden plant, and the cut flowers gain more acceptance with consumers every year. Flowers, ranging from white to purple to red, are borne in widely branched panicles. The genus has been greatly enhanced by the hybrids which were raised by Georg Arends of Ronsdorf, Germany, and many subsequent breeders. Cultivars of various heights and flower colors abound, as well as those with green and bronze foliage.

Propagation

Many commercial cultivars are available as a result of tissue culture, though growers may still raise additional plants from seed or division.

Seed: Seed is not available for most cultivars; however, seed of hybrids may be purchased in various shades or tones (e.g., Rose Tones). The seed is tiny (384,000 seeds/oz) and should be covered lightly. Seed germinates in 3–4 weeks if placed at 70–73F under mist or sweat tent.

Division: Named hybrids are best propagated by dividing the rootstock. Plants are lifted and divided into 1- or 2-eyed pieces in late fall after foliage dies back. Root pieces sold in the spring by commercial propagators can be stored over the winter in moist sphagnum at 33–35F (5). Growers wishing to increase their own cultivars should divide in the fall or early spring every 3–5 years. A 1- or 2-eyed division should provide a 5- to 8-eyed crown after 1 growing season (5).

Growing-on

Grow seedlings at 60–65F for 6–8 weeks and transplant to 4" pots when seedlings can be handled without damage. Small divisions should be potted into 4" containers immediately. Fertilize propagules with 50 ppm N from a complete fertilizer for 4 weeks and raise to 100 ppm N as plants grow more rapidly. Reduce temperature to 55–60F until plants are ready for the field. Green plants (i.e., non-flowering) may be put in the field 14–16 weeks after sowing, 4–6 weeks after taking divisions.

In all but the coolest areas of the country (e.g., Pacific Northwest), partial shade is required in the field. If sufficient and constant moisture can be maintained, the need for shade becomes less critical.

Environmental Factors

Astilbe requires a cold treatment to flower and should be allowed to go dormant. White-flowered cultivars such as 'Avalanche' and 'Deutschland' require at least 9 weeks at 40F but only 6 weeks are necessary for the red cultivars 'Fanal' and 'Red Sentinel' (1). Lower temperatures (32–35F) are also used to break dormancy (5). Long photoperiods (14 hours) result in taller flower stems than short photoperiods (8 hours) (5). Consistent moisture is essential for optimum yield and stem length. If plants dry out dramatically, plant longevity and flower quality are reduced.

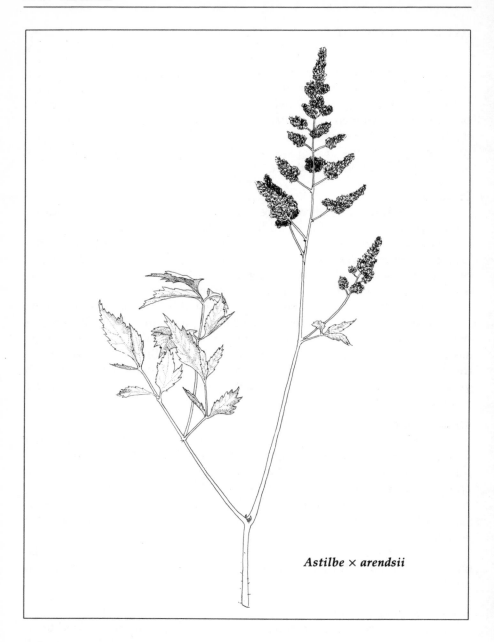

Astilbe × *arendsii*

Field Performance

Longevity: Under proper conditions, plants are long-lived and need not be replaced for 3–5 years. However, if placed in areas where consistent moisture cannot be provided, plants rapidly deteriorate. Longevity is also enhanced where cooler summer conditions prevail. Production is insignificant the first year but begins in earnest the second to third year.

Yield and stem quality of *Astilbe* × *arendsii* **'Bridal Veil' over time (spacing 1' × 1').**

Year	Stem/plant	Stem length (in)
1986	2.3	15.4
1987	4.6	18.0
1988	6.4	18.5

Spacing: Space at 10" × 12" or 12" × 15" spacing. Plants do not spread rapidly and original spacings are maintained throughout the productive life of the planting.

Greenhouse Performance

Precooled crowns may be planted in 6–10" pots or in ground beds with a density of approximately 1 plant/ft². Some reports suggest that crowns should be given a 1-hour hot water bath (140–150F) prior to forcing. Plants which were subjected to this treatment had more foliage and flowers were of a higher quality (3).

Grow initially at 45–50F and allow temperatures to rise to 55–60F as outdoor temperatures rise. Little or no fertilization is necessary during the forcing stage (6). Provide long days with incandescent lights during winter and early spring months for longest stem length. Constant moisture is necessary. Shade plants after April. Crop time is 10–18 weeks depending on cultivar and forcing temperatures.

Stage of Harvest

Inflorescences should be harvested when ½ to ¾ of the flowers are open. The uppermost buds should be swollen and showing color. Flower buds harvested when the panicles are less than half open do not develop further when placed in water, and develop only slightly more in a preservative solution (4). Allow at least 1 lower leaf per harvested stem to remain on the mother plant for continued development of the storage root (5).

Postharvest

Fresh: Flowers require significant attention throughout the postharvest chain. They persist longest when pretreated by placing cut stems in 130F water, cooling to room temperature, sleeving in paper and placing in floral preservative. Flowers so treated persisted 12 days compared to 2–4 days in room temperature water (2). Fresh flowers are sensitive to ethylene and must be isolated from fresh fruit or other ethylene-producing tissue. Ship stems in water. Pulsing with STS reduces damage by ethylene (4).

Storage: Plants may be stored for 7–10 days at 33–40F. Leaves senesce more rapidly than the flowers.

Dried: Both flowers and seed heads can be air-dried, preferably in an upright position, and will last indefinitely. For drying, harvest when all the flowers are open or only a few buds remain at the tip of the panicle.

Cultivars

Many cultivars are available; the following are useful as cut flowers. All are hybrids and may be listed under *Astilbe* × *arendsii*, *A.* × *hybrida*, *A.* × *japonica*, *A.* × *rosea* or *A.* × *thunbergii*.

Color	Cultivar	Plant height (in)
Pink	'Bressingham Beauty'	36–40
	'Erica'	30–36
	'Europa'	18–24
	'Gloria Rosea'	25–30
	'Granat'	24–30
	'Peach Blossom'	24–30
	'Venus'	24–30
Magenta	'Amethyst'	36–40
	'Dusseldorf'	20–24
	'Gloria Purpurea'	25–30
	'Jo Ophurst'	36–40
Rose-pink	'Bonn'	18–24
	'Cattleya'	36–40
	'Gloria'	24–30
	'Ostrich Plume'	30–36
	'Rheinland'	24–30
Red	'Fanal'	15–18
	'Glow'	18–20
	'Koblenz'	18–24
	'Red Sentinel'	36–40
White	'Bridal Veil'	18–24
	'Deutschland'	24–30
	'Snowdrift'	24–30
	'White Gloria'	15–18

Additional Species

Astilbe chinensis, *A.* × *japonica* and *A. davidii* are some of the species which were hybridized to produce the various hybrids. The species are difficult to locate in the United States and have limited color selection. They are useful for cut flower production if they can be located in sufficient quantity.

A. simplicifolia 'Sprite' has pale, shell-pink flowers but the plant is only about 18" tall. The seed heads, however, are most handsome and have potential in a cut flower program. Dry flower stems in water.

A. taquetii 'Superba' has 3–4' tall, magenta flowers in narrow, erect panicles. The seed heads are particularly upright and attractive. The use of this late-flowering species extends the cropping time of *Astilbe*.

Pests and Diseases

Few diseases affect *Astilbe*; however, some leaf spotting may occur.

Powdery mildew is caused by *Erysiphe polygoni*; a white mold appears on the undersides of the foliage. Defoliation occurs in serious cases.

Wilt is generally the result of *Fusarium* spp. and may be alleviated by placing healthy plants in *Fusarium*-free soil.

Gray mold results when humidity is high and healthy stems become infected with *Botrytis cinerea*. If plants are well spaced and growing vigorously, little botrytis occurs.

Japanese beetles are the most serious insect pest of *Astilbe*.

Reading

1. Beattie, D. J., and E. J. Holcomb. 1983. Effects of chilling and photoperiod on forcing Astilbes. *HortScience* 18(4):449–450.

2. Kalkman, E. C. 1986. Post-harvest treatment of *Astilbe* hybr. *Acta Hortic.* 181:389–392.

3. Latta, R., and C. F. Doucette. 1932. Insect control stimulates growth. *Flor. Rev.* 70(4806):11–13.

4. Sacalis, J. N. 1989. *Fresh (Cut) Flowers for Designs: Postproduction Guide* I. D.C. Kiplinger Chair in Floriculture, The Ohio State Univ., Columbus, OH.

5. Stimart, D. P. 1989. Strategies of growing fresh cut flowers of *Astilbe, Liatris,* and *Paeonia*. In *Proceedings of Commercial Field Production of Cut and Dried Flowers.* Univ. of Minnesota, The Center for Alternative Crops and Products, St. Paul, MN. 121–132.

6. Wilkins, H. F. 1985. *Astilbe.* In A. H. Halevy (ed.), *The Handbook of Flowering,* vol. 1. CRC Press, Boca Raton, FL. 521–522.

Many thanks to Dr. Dennis Stimart for reviewing this section.

Astrantia major		Masterwort	2–4'/3'
White, pink	Austria	Apiaceae	Zones 4–6

The unique flowers are greenish white with a pale green collar consisting of narrow segments. The flowers are tiny but grouped together in a dense head. The collar (bracts) under the head gives the whole flower a starry appearance. Flowers are best produced in areas of cool summers and cool night temperatures; they are poor crops under warm growing temperatures.

Propagation

Seed: Sow seed in moist medium and place at 60–65F for 2–4 weeks. Seed flats should then be placed at about 30–35F for a minimum of 4–6 weeks. After the cold treatment, put flat in cold frame or a greenhouse at 50–55F. Alternating temperatures are beneficial for germination.

Growing-on

Grow seedlings at 55F for 4–6 weeks. Fertilize with 50–75 ppm N from potassium nitrate then increase to 100 ppm N of a complete fertilizer. High nitrogen results in poorly colored flowers. Plant in the field as soon as ground is workable. Spacing of 12" × 12" is appropriate. Plants flower the second year.

Field Performance

Constant moisture is nece' sary for best growth. Yields in the Netherlands were reported as approximately 7 flowers/ft^2 the first year and 10–12 flowers/ft^2 the following year. Plants may require support the second year.

Longevity: Three to five years of production is normal for *Astrantia*.

Stage of Harvest

Harvest time is critical for *Astrantia*. Harvest when the uppermost flowers are open; if harvested too early, plants will wilt and flowers will not open (similar to yarrow). If harvest is further delayed, vase life will suffer.

Postharvest

Fresh: Flowers persist for 5–7 days in water (2).

Dried: Flowers may be dried with silica gel and shrink less with desiccants than by air-drying alone (1). Cover the bottom of a box with silica gel or borax. Carefully work the crystals between the petals and lay the stems in the box. Once stems are in place, cover with additional desiccant and leave for 5–6 days (1).

Cultivars

'Involucrata' (ssp. *involucrata*) has a collar of pink bracts. A selection of ssp. *involucrata* with extra-long bracts is sometimes offered under the name of 'Shaggy', a most apt name.

'Primadonna' is a seed-propagated cultivar with 24–30" stems bearing many rose-red flowers.

'Rose Symphony' bears rosy red flowers.

'Sunningdale Variegated' has variegated foliage, but the flowers are similar to the species.

Additional Species

Astrantia carniolica is available as 'Rubra', a purple- to maroon-flowered plant. Plants are a little shorter than *A. major* and have darker foliage.

A. maxima bears wonderfully handsome, pink flowers on vigorous plants. Unfortunately, the price for plants is high due to lack of supply. When prices decline, more flowers should appear in the market.

Pests and Diseases

Aphids are the most common pests although thrips and spider mites can also be a problem. If plants are allowed to dry out, physiological problems such as leaf margin die-back occur.

Reading

1. Bullivant, E. 1989. *Dried Fresh Flowers From Your Garden*. Pelham Books/Stephen Greene Press, London, U.K.

2. Vaughan, M. J. 1988. *The Complete Book of Cut Flower Care*. Timber Press, Portland, OR.

Astrantia major

Campanula persicifolia

		Peach-leaf Bellflower	2–3'/3'
Blue	Europe	Campanulaceae	Zones 3–6

One of the best bellflowers for cut flowers, it is very popular in European and California markets. The long, unbranched stems bear racemes of 1–2" wide, bell-shaped, purple-blue flowers.

Propagation

Seed: Seed is small and should be lightly covered with fine sand or a thin blanket of vermiculite. Germinate at 60–65F under sweat tents or intermittent mist. Seedlings emerge in 14–21 days. Approximately 1/56 oz of seed yields 1000 seedlings (4).

Division: Divide crowns in spring or after flowering.

Growing-on

If planted in seed flats, seedlings should be transplanted to 3–4" pots or packs when the second set of true leaves emerge. If sown in plugs, sow in large containers (288s or less). Grow at 55–60F until 3–4 leaves emerge, then place in cold frame or unheated greenhouse for a minimum of 6 weeks. Plant to the field in the fall.

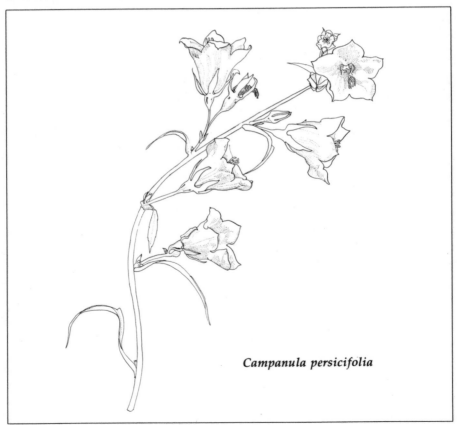

Campanula persicifolia

Environmental Factors

Little literature is available for *C. persicifolia*, but information concerning flowering of *C. fragilis* (8), *C. isophylla* (5), *C. medium* (7) and *C. pyramidalis* (9) provides some useful guidelines to flowering control.

Temperature: All perennial campanulas benefit from a cold treatment, usually supplied by natural winter cold. In recent research work, storage of crowns for 12 weeks at 40F was necessary to induce flowering in *C. persicifolia* (3). Cold was not necessary to break dormancy (i.e., leaves were formed) but was needed to induce flowering (3). In *C. pyramidalis*, only 6 weeks at 43F were necessary for 80% of the stems to be vernalized (9). A cold period of 10–12 weeks at 40F or below is recommended (1).

Photoperiod: *Campanula persicifolia* appears to be day neutral and, once the cold treatment has been satisfied, flowers under long or short days (3). In other species, however, long days (LD) are necessary for flowering after vernalization (7,8,9). A daylength of 15–17 hours results in the greatest flowering for other species but some cultivars may respond with critical LD of 13–14 hours. Short days should be avoided because plants will become devernalized (i.e., lose the beneficial effects of cold treatment).

Gibberellic acid: GA does not appear to substitute for either the LD or low temperature requirement of *Campanula*.

Field Performance

Location: Insufficient cold is supplied in zones 7b–11. Peach-leaf bellflower is a cool-season crop and performs far better in areas of cool summer nights. It performs best on the West Coast and north of zone 7. Production in zone 7 and south results in tall, spindly stems whose quality cannot compete with stems grown further north or from Europe.

Longevity: Plants are long-lived and production continues for at least 3 years. Divide ⅓ of the crop every year.

Spacing: Space plants 12" × 12" or as little as 9" × 12". Sub-irrigation is necessary for close spacing. Provide support netting for straight stems.

Forcing: After enough cooling has been provided (see "Environmental Factors"), portable polyethylene frames may be used to raise temperatures for earlier flowering.

Greenhouse Performance

Cool crowns for 12 weeks at 40F (3). The evergreen rosettes are subject to fungal diseases during cooling; using 20–50 fc of incandescent lights for at least 8 hours and applying fungicides during the cold treatment alleviates the problem. Precooled crowns may be planted in gallon pots or in ground beds in January at a spacing of 10" apart, 6" between rows. Long days (>16 hours) are not necessary but may be applied after cold treatments are completed to produce taller plants (3). If greenhouse temperatures are maintained at approximately 60F, flowering occurs about 8 weeks later. If temperatures are 50–55F, an additional week is required. Provide constant fertilization with 75–100 ppm N of a complete fertilizer. Support is necessary for stems of the best quality. Warm temperatures and high nitrogen levels result in tall, spindly plants.

Stage of Harvest

Harvest when 1–2 flowers of the inflorescence are open. The best stage of harvest is when the flower buds are colored and considerably swollen (6).

Postharvest

Fresh: Stems persist 8 days in water and 16 days in Carnation Chrysal™, a flower preservative (2). Flowers open from bottom to top. Leaves tend to deteriorate before flowers.

Dried: Flowers do not dry well.

Cultivars

'Alba' has white flowers and may be seed-propagated.

'Grandiflora' has large, deep blue flowers.

'Moerheimii' bears double, white flowers.

'Telham Beauty' produces some of the largest flowers in the species and is one of the most popular cultivars.

Additional Species

Campanula glomerata (clustered bellflower) produces clusters of bell-shaped, violet-blue flowers atop the 1–2' tall stems. Approximately 1/25 oz of seed yields 1000 seedlings (4). Cold is also required for flowering. Spacing of 12" × 12" is sufficient. Vase life is approximately 9 days in water. 'Acaulis' has pale blue flowers. 'Alba' produces white flowers. 'Joan Elliott' (purple) is a dwarf, vegetatively propagated cultivar that is more suited to the garden than it is for cut flowers. 'Superba' has large, blue flowers and is one of the best cultivars for cut flowers.

C. pyramidalis (chimney bellflower) grows to 5' tall and is an excellent cut flower. The bell-shaped flowers are clustered together in a pyramidal inflorescence. The species is a lavender-blue color but a white form, var. *alba*, is also available. If grown from seed, use approximately 1/128 oz/1000 seedlings (3). Seed germinates in 3 weeks at 65–70F. Plants forced in the field or greenhouse need 11 weeks of cold at 40–45F followed by 15-hour days (8).

Pests and Diseases

Aphids should be controlled to reduce problems of sooty mold.

Botrytis and leaf spot can be problems in areas of high summer rains.

Crown rot (*Pellicularia rolfsii*) results in rotting of the crown. It develops under moist soil conditions and warm temperatures. A grayish white discoloration of the base of the stems (*Sclerotinia sclerotiorum*) also occurs and causes decay and falling over.

Sclerotinia rot results in white mold followed by large dark spots on the foliage. The disease usually occurs in humid greenhouses with little air circulation. Similar results occur in dense plantings in the field under rainy weather.

Rust (*Coleosporium campanulae*) can be a serious problem on the underside of *C. persicifolia*. The foliage is covered with orange or reddish brown pustules. Leaves dehydrate and plants are stunted. Other organisms are *Puccinia campanulae* and *Aecidium campanulastri*.

Spider mites are worse on plants which are highly fertilized.

Reading

1. Bartels, A. 1990. *Bartels Grower Guides*. Aalsmeer, The Netherlands.

2. Blomme, R., and P. Dambre. 1981. {The use of outdoor flowers for cutting} Het gebruik van bloemen in openlucht als snijbloem. *Verbondsnieuws voor de Belgische Sierteelt* 25(15):681–685.

3. Iversen, R. R., and T. C. Weiler. 1989. Forcing the issue: a guide to forcing garden perennials into bloom for flower show exhibitions. *Amer. Nurseryman* 169(8): 95–103.

4. Kieft, C. 1989. *Kieft's Growing Manual* .... Kieft Bloemzaden, Venhuizen, The Netherlands.

5. Moe, R., and O. M. Heide. 1985. *Campanula isophylla*. In A. H. Halevy (ed.), *The Handbook of Flowering*, vol. 2. CRC Press, Boca Raton, FL. 119–122.

6. Vaughan, M. J. 1988. *The Complete Book of Cut Flower Care*. Timber Press, Portland, OR.

7. Wallensiek, S. J. 1985. *Campanula medium*. In A. H. Halevy (ed.), *The Handbook of Flowering*, vol. 2. CRC Press, Boca Raton, FL. 123–126.

8. Zimmer, K. 1985. *Campanula fragilis*. In A. H. Halevy (ed.), *The Handbook of Flowering*, vol. 2. CRC Press, Boca Raton, FL. 117–118.

9. _____ . 1985. *Campanula pyramidalis*. In A. H. Halevy (ed.), *The Handbook of Flowering*, vol. 2. CRC Press, Boca Raton, FL. 127–130.

Many thanks to Dr. Leonard Perry for reviewing this section.

Centaurea macrocephala   Golden Basket Flower   3–4'/3'
Yellow   Caucasus   Asteraceae   Zones 2–6

Basket flower is a large-leafed plant which produces abundant large, bright yellow flowers which are particularly useful dried. They are common in European markets and find their way to this country mainly as imports. *Centaurea macrocephala* is a well-known garden plant and cut flowers have been enjoyed by the home gardener for many years.

Propagation

Seed: Germinate under high humidity and 68–72F soil temperature. Research has indicated 86% germination in 5–10 days under the above conditions (4). Approximately 2 oz of seed yield 1000 seedlings. Some growers direct-sow although transplants are generally more successful.

Division: Plants may be divided in spring or fall.

Growing-on

Seedlings and small divisions should be transplanted to large cell packs or 4" pots as soon as they can be handled. Grow at 50–65F; avoid temperatures above 75F. Fertilize with 100–150 ppm N from a complete fertilizer; do not exceed 200 ppm N.

Environmental Factors

Temperature: It is not well established if cold is necessary for flower development in this species. No vernalization is necessary for *C. cyanus*, *C. moschata* or *C. americana* (3). The above species are all annuals, and lack of vernalization is not unexpected. No vernalization was necessary for flowering of *C. montana* (mountain bluet) a perennial in most of the country (2). For other perennial species such as *C. macrocephala*, cold is likely beneficial, if not absolutely necessary.

Photoperiod: Most *Centaurea* species appear to be LD plants and flower more rapidly under daylengths of 14 hours or more.

Gibberellic acid: Weekly spray applications of 25 ppm GA for 9 weeks caused flowering of *C. montana* even under SD (2), although too much GA or too many applications resulted in weak distorted stems.

Field Performance

Location: Plants are more productive and flowers are of a superior quality when grown in areas of cool nights and bright days. Field production is best north of zone 7. Research results at the University of Georgia have been disappointing, likely due to excessive summer temperatures and humidity.

Longevity: Plants are long-lived perennials. Once established, 3–5 years of production is possible. Planted from seedlings or small divisions in the fall, production will be negligible the first season. Production peaks in the second to third year from planting.

Spacing: Plants are large and require sufficient space to reduce insect and disease pressure. Space plants 18–24" apart.

Stage of Harvest

Harvest when flowers are ½ to ¾ open. Place in warm water immediately.

Postharvest

Fresh: Flowers persist about 1 week in a preservative solution. The foliage, however, persists for less time, particularly if preservative is not incorporated.

Storage: Flowers may be stored for 1–2 weeks at 38–40F.

Dried: *Centaurea* flowers may be air-dried. Strip the leaves and hang upside down. Flowers may also be dried in silica gel (5). The handsome spherical fruit has shiny brown scales and may be picked immediately after the flower dies.

Cultivars

No cultivars are available.

Additional Species

Centaurea americana (american basket flower) and *C. moschata* (sweet sultan) are annuals; see section on annuals for information.

C. montana (mountain bluet) is a perennial species with deep blue flowers. No vernalization is required but LD (4–6 hours of nightbreak incandescent lights) can be used to induce flowering (1). Seed requires 7–14 days to germinate at 68–72F.

C. pulchra is similar to *C. macrocephala* but has rosy red flowers and is slightly smaller. Unfortunately, plants are difficult to locate. 'Major' has larger flowers than the species.

Pests and Diseases

Stem rots are caused by *Phytophthora cactorum, Sclerotinia sclerotiorum* and *Pellicularia filimentosa*.

Wilt is caused by *Fusarium* spp., similar to wilt occurring on annual aster (*Callistephus*).

Spider mites are a major problem in warm summers. Leaf and flower fungal diseases such as botrytis are worse if overhead irrigation is used.

Reading

1. Cox, D. A. 1986. Containerized herbaceous perennial production: forcing *Centaurea montana* for early spring flowering by night-lighting. In *Proceedings of SNA Research Conference*. 21:73–75.

2. _____ . 1987. Gibberellic acid induced flowering of containerized *Centaurea montana* L. *Acta Hortic*. 205: 233–235.

3. Kadman-Zahavi, A., and H. Yahal. 1985. *Centaurea cyanus*. In A. H. Halevy (ed.), *The Handbook of Flowering*, vol. 2. CRC Press, Boca Raton, FL. 169–173.

4. Pinnell, M., A. M. Armitage and D. Seaborn. 1985. Germination needs of common perennial species. Univ. of Georgia Research Report 331, Athens, GA.

5. Vaughan, M. J. 1988. *The Complete Book of Cut Flower Care*. Timber Press, Portland, OR.

Many thanks to Dr. Douglas Cox for reviewing this section.

Centranthus ruber		Red Valerian	2–3'/3'
Red, pink, white	Europe	Valerianaceae	Zones 5–7

Plants grow in ditches, walls, cliffs and roadsides throughout northern Europe but are only recently being discovered by American growers as a cut flower. Easily grown and readily marketable, the fragrant flowers occur in terminal clusters (cymose panicles) in shades of pink, red and white.

Propagation

Seed: Germination occurs in 2–3 weeks if seed is placed at 65–70F.

Approximately ¼ oz of seed yields 1000 seedlings (2).

Cuttings: Terminal stem cuttings are used by perennial plant growers but seldom used commercially by cut flower growers.

Growing-on

Grow seedlings at 60–65F under natural daylengths. Apply 50–100 ppm N from a complete fertilizer. Plants may be placed in the field 8–10 weeks after sowing (3).

Environmental Factors

Plants flower the first year from seed indicating that a cold treatment is not necessary. They do not perform well where temperature fluctuates a great deal during the year. That is, they are better suited for coastal areas than areas with hot summers or very cold winters. Performance in Athens, GA, (zone 7b) was disappointing.

Field Performance

Few field data are available, but plants often occur on limestone areas in their native habitat (1). The use of lime in the beds is therefore recommended. Soils rich in nutrients are not necessary and result in tall, rather spindly plants. Eight to ten flowers/plant should be attainable. Plants should be spaced approximately 12" apart. Flowers normally occur in May through July.

Greenhouse Performance

There is no reason why flowers could not be forced in a greenhouse during the winter. Sow in late summer to early fall, space 9–12" apart, fertilize lightly (100–150 ppm N) and grow at 55/65F night/day temperatures. At least 1 tier of support, possibly 2, is necessary. If supplemental light is available, plants would no doubt benefit. Flowering occurs 16–18 weeks from sowing (3).

Stage of Harvest

Harvest when the first flowers in the inflorescence are fully open. The use of floral preservative is recommended.

Postharvest

Fresh: Flowers persist 7–10 days in preservative.

Storage: Not recommended, but flowers may be placed wet at 40F for 3–5 days.

Cultivars

'Albus' (white), 'Coccineus' (deep red) and 'Roseus' (rosy red) are available as separate colors from seed. A mix is also offered.

'Pretty Betsy' is a selection from 'Coccineus' that grows 2–3' tall.

'Snowcloud' has been introduced as a white valerian by Kieft Seed Co. of Venhuizen, The Netherlands. Plants are 3' tall and somewhat fragrant.

Centranthus ruber

Pests and Diseases

No pests and diseases particular to *Centranthus* have been noted.

Reading

1. Armitage, A. M. 1989. *Herbaceous Perennial Plants: A Treatise on Their Identification, Culture, and Garden Attributes.* Varsity Press, Athens, GA.

2. Kieft, C. 1989. *Kieft's Growing Manual . . . .* Kieft Bloemzaden, Ven-huizen, The Netherlands.

3. Nau, J. 1989. *Ball Culture Guide: The Encyclopedia of Seed Germination.* Ball Seed Co., West Chicago, IL.

Cirsium japonicum		Japanese Thistle	2–3'/2'
Red, pink	Japan	Asteraceae	Zones 3–7

This tough plant is one of the few ornamentally useful thistles for fresh cut flowers. Flowers are available most of the year if greenhouse and field production are practiced. The dark green foliage is prickly and not a favorite with my harvest crew, nor will it be with yours. The flower heads are dark red or pink. Production is best in areas of cool temperatures, although production in zone 7 is fair, if not spectacular.

Propagation

Seed: Seed sown under intermittent mist or a sweat tent at 60–65F will germinate in 7–14 days. Approximately ⅛ oz of seed yields 1000 seedlings (2). Seed is sometimes direct sown at the rate of 3–3.5 oz/1000 ft² (3), but germination is inconsistent when direct-sown.

Division: Plants may be divided after 2 years' growth.

Growing-on

Transplant from 288s to cell packs or 4" pots after 4 weeks, or as soon as seedlings can be handled. Fertilize sparingly (75 ppm N) for the first 2 weeks then raise to 100–150 ppm N. Grow at 55–60F until ready to transplant to the field (approx. 7 weeks from sowing) (3). Divisions may be planted in 4" pots and grown-on for 4–6 weeks in a cold frame.

Environmental Factors

Plants do not require a cold period for flowering. Many species of thistle are long day plants but little response to photoperiod has been found with *C. japonicum*.

Field Performance

Longevity: In general, 2–3 years of production are normal. Plants may be divided for rejuvenation.

Spacing: Space plants 12" × 12" or 9–12" between plants with 6–9" rows in the bed.

Yield: Yield of japanese thistle in Athens, GA, is provided in the following table.

Yield and stem quality of *Cirsium japonicum* (Athens, GA).

Year	Stems/plant	Stems/ft²	Stem length (in)
1987	8	7.6	27.9
1988	13	12.6	38.4

Greenhouse Performance

Plants may be forced in heated greenhouses during the fall, winter and spring. Sowings in July result in flowers by December if grown in 55–65F houses. Flowers continue through April. Seed may be sown every 4 weeks for best quality. Greenhouse crops generally are used as annuals only.

Guideline for Foliar Analyses

At field trials in Watsonville, CA, foliage was sampled from vigorously growing healthy plants when flower buds were visible, but prior to flower opening. These are guidelines only and should not be considered absolute standards. Based on dry weight analysis.

(%)						(ppm)				
N	P	K	Ca	Mg		Fe	Mn	B	Al	Zn
				'Rose Beauty'						
2.6	0.19	2.24	0.60	0.29		462	130	14	208	21

Stage of Harvest

Flowers should be harvested when the flowers are open. If cut too soon, flowers will not persist well.

Postharvest

Fresh: Flowers persist for approximately 1 week when placed in floral preservative.

Storage: Flowers may be held temporarily at 36–41F but storage is not recommended (4).

Dried: Flowers may be dried by cutting the flowers as soon as they come into full bloom and hanging upside down. Flowers may be sprayed with clear plastic if any sign of shattering occurs (1).

Cultivars

'Lilac Beauty' bears lavender flowers on 2–3' tall stems.

'Pink Beauty' has pink flower heads on 2–2.5' tall stems.

'Rose Beauty' has carmine-red flower heads on 2–2.5' stems.

Pests and Diseases

Leaf spots, caused by *Cercospora* and *Phyllosticta* species, result in black leaf spots. More prevalent under humid, wet conditions.

Reading

1. Kasperski, V. R. 1956. *How to Make Cut Flowers Last*. M. Barrows and Co., New York, NY.

2. Kieft, C. 1989. *Kieft's Growing Manual* .... Kieft Bloemzaden, Venhuizen, The Netherlands.

3. Nau, J. 1989. *Ball Culture Guide: The Encyclopedia of Seed Germination*. Ball Seed Co., West Chicago, IL.

4. Vaughan, M. J. 1988. *The Complete Book of Cut Flower Care*. Timber Press, Portland, OR.

Delphinium elatum **hybrid**

Delphinium hybrids

Delphinium hybrids		Delphinium	3–4'/3'
Various colors	Hybrid origin	Ranunculaceae	Zones 2–7

A mainstay in the cut flower industry, delphiniums have been grown for many years. They consist of hybrids mainly from *D. elatum* and *D. grandiflorum*. Cultivars belonging to *D. × belladonna* are characterized by having lateral stems that produce open flowers only slightly later than the terminal stem and are more airy and open than other hybrid cultivars. Hybrid cultivars produce flowers on the central stalk which, if removed, are followed by flowers on lateral stems. They are more classical in appearance and flower over a longer period of time. Many parents are involved in the hybrids thus reducing differences between the two forms. In the southern states, delphiniums are field-planted in fall for spring flowering and treated as an annual. In the North, plants may be in production for up to 3 years. Numerous cultivars are available through seed and vegetative propagation.

Propagation

Seed: Lightly cover the seed and chill it (35–40F) for 2–4 weeks, after which temperatures of 65–70F may be used for germination. Germination begins after 2 weeks but is erratic and may continue for another 2–3 weeks.

Cuttings: Take 3–4" long terminal cuttings of new shoots arising from the base of the plant. The base of the cutting should be solid, not hollow. They may be rooted under mist or a sweat tent in sand/peat or peat/perlite mixture in 3–4 weeks.

Growing-on

Grow seedlings at 50–55F in the greenhouse or in cold frames and transplant when large enough to handle. Cuttings should be transplanted to 4–5" pots as soon as rooted and grown until ready for planting. Seed sown in January will be ready for transplanting in March or April for northern growers; seed should be sown in July for plants to be moved outdoors by October for southern growers. Growers in coastal central and northern California, Oregon and Washington can plant out as late as June for flowering in September. Summer temperatures are too warm in other parts of the country to attempt such late plantings.

Environmental Factors

Temperature: Plants benefit from, but do not have an absolute requirement for, cold temperatures. That is, plants will flower the first year from seed without being exposed to chilling temperatures but flower yield and quality will be enhanced if chilling is provided. Approximately 6 weeks at temperatures of 35–40F satisfy the vernalization requirements of most delphiniums (4). Therefore fall planting is recommended for all areas of the country. Temperatures above 70F reduce flower yield and size. Night temperatures of 50–60F are optimum for growth of delphinium.

Photoperiod: Long days hasten flowering, increase stem length and improve quality in most delphiniums, particularly the belladonna forms (4).

Field Performance

Spacing: Plant at a density of 1' × 1' if used as an annual; 12" × 18" if more than 1 year of production is anticipated.

Yield: Five to six flowering stems/plant should be realized the first year from elatum hybrids. Up to 12 shorter stems may be harvested from belladonna types.

Irrigation: Hollow stems remain on the plant after harvesting and overhead irrigation must be avoided. Otherwise, stem rot could become a serious problem.

Support: Support may be necessary for the elatum hybrids but not generally for the belladonna hybrids. However, as temperatures rise, stems tend to fall over and support is useful for late harvests.

Forcing: Plastic greenhouses or frames can be moved over the outdoor crop in late February and flowering occurs approximately 30–40 days earlier than in nature.

Greenhouse Performance

Seedlings or cuttings transplanted in August may be flowered in a cool greenhouse by January. Incandescent lighting to provide long days (>12 hours) accelerates flowering. Two to three croppings may be cut from each plant. Harvesting will finish when cool greenhouse temperatures can no longer be maintained. Temperatures above 75F should be avoided; long spindly stems result otherwise. Similarly, fertilizer concentrations greater than 100–150 ppm N should be avoided.

Guideline for Foliar Analyses

At field trials in Watsonville, CA, foliage was sampled from vigorously growing healthy plants when flower buds were visible, but prior to flower opening. These are guidelines only and should not be considered absolute standards. Based on dry weight analysis.

(%)						(ppm)				
N	P	K	Ca	Mg		Fe	Mn	B	Al	Zn
					'Pacific Giants'					
3.2	0.33	3.52	2.86	0.70		617	59	18	517	35

Stage of Harvest

Harvest when ¼ to ⅓ of the flowers on the stem are open. Place cut stems immediately in water.

Postharvest

Fresh: Vase life in water is 6–8 days (4) but is significantly enhanced by pulsing cut stems with a preservative containing silver thiosulfate (STS). Flowers of delphinium are sensitive to ethylene and if not treated with STS, they shatter readily. Stems may be stored upright in water for 1–2 days at 38–41F (2).

Dried: Some cultivars of belladonna hybrids may be air-dried but most dried "delphiniums" are actually larkspur. True delphiniums, however, may be dried if cut before the bottom flowers drop. If picked after that time, ⅔ of the flowers will end up as confetti (1). After leaves have been stripped, the inflorescence should be hung in small bunches upside down. When the flowers feel papery, they should be stood upright to finish drying. The closed flowers may partially open again to provide a more natural look (1).

Cultivars

Dozens of cultivars are available through seed producers and perennial plant growers. Additional cultivars are constantly being introduced by European breeders.

Hybrid cultivars

'Blue Triumphator' bears deep blue flowers on 3–4' tall stems.

'Camaraderie' has veined and picotee flowers, mostly in pastel shades. The stems are 4–5' tall.

Magic Fountain series is offered by many seed producers but is smaller and less statuesque than Pacific hybrids. Numerous colors are available, however, and stems are handsome.

Pacific hybrids (Giant Pacific Court hybrids) are 4–5' tall and include 'Astolat' (lavender-pink), 'Black Knight' (dark purple), 'Galahad' (white) and 'King Arthur' (dark blue). All have double flowers and most are available from seed.

D. × belladonna

'Belladonna' bears blue flowers.

'Bellamosa' has deep blue flowers.

Beverly Hills series grows 4–5' tall and is available from seed or in plugs in salmon, scarlet or yellow flowers. Susceptible to overwatering and powdery mildew.

'Casa Blanca' produces white flowers.

'Clivenden Beauty' has light blue flowers.

'Princess Caroline' is a new introduction from the Netherlands and has been most impressive in California trials. Flowers are salmon-pink and are borne on long, strong flower stems. Should be used as a greenhouse crop only.

'Volkerfrieden' ('International Peace') bears deep blue flowers on 3–4' stems. Plants flush up to 3 times a year and may be planted as close as 6" apart in the greenhouse.

Additional Species

Delphinium cardinale 'Scarlet Butterfly' has scarlet-red flowers; 'Yellow Butterfly' bears bright yellow flowers. *Delphinium nudicaule* has orange-red flowers and *D. semibarbatum (D. zalil)* has yellow blossoms. None have the classic style and grace of the hybrids, but they may find a niche in the delphinium market. They are available from seed.

Pests and Diseases

Black spot of foliage caused by *Pseudomonas delphinii* results in large black spots on stems and leaves. Good air circulation and low humidity are helpful in reducing incidence of the disease. Cull infected plants.

Crown rot causes the plant to wilt and fall over. Application of general fungicide when plants are young is recommended.

Powdery mildew can infect plants when weather is wet and cloudy.

Reading

1. Bullivant, E. 1989. *Dried Fresh Flowers From Your Garden.* Pelham Books/Stephen Greene Press, London, U.K.

2. Nowak, J., and R. M. Rudnicki. 1990. *Postharvest Handling and Storage of Cut Flowers, Florist Greens, and Potted Plants.* Timber Press, Portland, OR.

3. Sacalis, J. N. 1989. *Fresh (Cut) Flowers for Designs: Postproduction Guide* I. D.C. Kiplinger Chair in Floriculture, The Ohio State Univ., Columbus, OH.

4. Wilkins, H. F. 1985. *Delphinium.* In A. H. Halevy (ed.), *The Handbook of Flowering,* supp. CRC Press, Boca Raton, FL. 89–91.

Many thanks to Mr. Jack Graham for reviewing this section.

Dianthus barbatus   Sweet William   1–2'/2'
Various colors   Southern Europe   Caryophyllaceae   Zones 3–7

Although technically a biennial (plants flower after 2 years, then die), sweet william may reseed itself and persist for more than 2 years. Sweet william requires a cold period in order to flower; plants are therefore often planted in the fall. In the field, seeds may be planted in fall and flowering will occur the next spring in some cultivars. New colors and cultivars more suited to cut flower production are constantly being introduced.

Propagation

Seed: Plants may be direct sown in the fall at 0.1 oz/100 linear ft (2) or sown in the greenhouse. Seed sown at 65–70F under intermittent mist or a sweat tent germinates in 7–10 days (3). Cover seed very lightly or not at all.

Cuttings: Plants may be propagated by stem cuttings, but this is seldom practiced.

Growing-on

Plants raised in the greenhouse should be sown in late summer and grown at 55–60F if possible. Fertilize with 100–150 ppm N using a balanced fertilizer. Plants should be ready to place in the field in 8–10 weeks.

Environmental Factors

Temperature: Most cultivars require vernalization and seedlings seldom flower without exposure to chilling (1). Flower initiation occurs only after the cold treatment has been fulfilled (1). The cold treatment consists of 40F for approximately 12 weeks but seedlings usually must be grown for 12 weeks or more before they are responsive to the cold (1). Unrooted cuttings can be vernalized during the rooting process, but results are contradictory (1). The use of supplemental light to enhance the rooting of cuttings reduces the amount of chilling needed (1). If high temperatures (above 100F) occur immediately after the cold treatment, the benefit of the cold treatment disappears (devernalization) (1).

Photoperiod: Although little effect on flowering occurs due to photoperiod, fully vernalized plants flower slightly earlier under short days compared to long days (1). The use of LD may produce a higher percentage of flowering plants if vernalization is insufficient (1).

Field Performance

If direct sown, seedlings should be thinned to 6–8" in the row (4). Yields of 4–10 stems/plant are not uncommon. Transplants should be placed in the field sufficiently early to allow establishment of the plants before the arrival of cold weather. If planted in the spring or summer, flowering will not occur until the following spring.

Greenhouse Performance

Because sweet william is a cool-loving plant, the greenhouse may be maintained at 45–50F; it is therefore relatively inexpensive to force sweet william into flower. Plants (seedlings or cuttings) should be grown for 8–12 weeks at 55–60F before applying the necessary cold treatment. When plants have sufficient roots and leaves, temperatures should be reduced to 40–45F. Plants flower as temperatures increase in the spring.

Stage of Harvest

Harvest when 10–20% of the flowers in the inflorescence are open.

Postharvest

Fresh: The use of STS enhances vase life. Flowers persist 7–10 days.
Storage: Flowers may be stored dry at 34–36F or wet at 40F for 7–10 days.

Cultivars

Single and double forms are available. Most are 18–24" tall and available in single or mixed colors.

'Diadem' bears single, crimson flowers with a pale eye.

'Double Mix' consists of double flowers in a wide range of colors.

'Giant White' produces large, white flowers.

Messenger series is an early-flowering mixture of single flowers.

'Newport Pink' is an exceptional cultivar with deep salmon-pink, single flowers.

'Nigricans' has dark crimson, single flowers with bronze foliage.

Parachute series consists of early single-flowered forms. Red with green leaves, red with bronze foliage and white-flowered selections are available.

'Pride of Park Avenue' is a mix of 18–24" tall flowers with excellent yields and field performance. Selected by Bob Pollioni.

'Super Duplex' bears double flowers in a mix of colors.

Additional Species

Dianthus caryophyllus (carnation) is greenhouse-grown throughout the world but is not included in the context of this "specialty" book. Five spray types in the Gipsy series, however, are available: 'Gipsy' (lavender-pink), 'Giant' (larger but otherwise similar to 'Gipsy'), 'Pink', 'Bright Eye' (white with dark pink eye) and 'Dark Eyes' (large carmine eye). They may be planted outdoors in areas of moderate winters (survive to 15F) or grown in a cool greenhouse.

D. knappii (yellow pinks—an oxymoron?) and *D. plumarius* (cottage pinks) are presently used or have potential as cut flowers.

Hybrid carnations: Numerous hybrids of *D. barbatus* with other species have been bred for bedding plant and pot plant use but are not useful for cut flower production, particularly in the field. However, a few excellent cultivars have arrived from Japan.

'First Love' produces flowers which change from white to soft pink and finally to rose-pink. Plants do not require cold to flower and can be forced year-round, although warm temperatures (above 80F) should be avoided. Generally greenhouse-grown at 55/65F night/day temperatures. Plants are spaced 9" apart and flower 100–110 days from sowing.

Miss series is seed-propagated and generally sown in late summer or fall for spring flowering and planted to the field or greenhouse when plants have about 6 leaves. Plants require cold temperatures for best performance, therefore temperatures in the greenhouse should be lowered (35–40F) when plants have produced 10–15 leaves. Cool temperatures are necessary for 40–50 days, after which plants are grown at 45/65F night/day conditions. In the field, plants can withstand 15F if properly acclimated. 'Miss Biwako' bears rose-red flowers on 2' tall stems. 'Miss Kobe' has magenta-purple blooms, and 'Miss Kyoto' produces pink flowers.

Pests and Diseases

Many of the diseases of carnations also infect sweet william. Do not grow sweet william and greenhouse carnations in the same bench. In the field, a number of diseases are particularly destructive to sweet william.

Rust, caused by *Puccinia arenariae*, can be a serious disease and is particularly destructive to the lower foliage.

Wilt results from *Fusarium oxysporum* var. *barbati* and manifests itself in a yellowing of new growth. Leaves point downward and plants are stunted. Remove the infected plants and sterilize infected soil.

Reading

1. Cockshull, K. E. 1985. *Dianthus*. In A. H. Halevy (ed.), *The CRC Handbook of Flowering*, vol. 2. CRC Press, Boca Raton, FL. 430–432.

2. Kieft, C. 1989. *Kieft's Growing Manual* .... Kieft Bloemzaden, Venhuizen, The Netherlands.

3. Nau, J. 1989. *Ball Culture Guide: The Encyclopedia of Seed Germination*. Ball Seed Co., West Chicago, IL.

4. Post, K. 1955. *Florist Crop Production and Marketing*. Orange Judd, New York, NY.

Echinacea purpurea   Purple Cone Flower   3–4'/3'
Purple   Eastern United States   Asteraceae   Zones 3–8

Native from Pennsylvania to Georgia to Louisiana, the species may be cultivated over a wide range of environmental conditions. Drooping, mauve-purple ray flowers are attached around a copper-brown cylindrical disc atop 3–4' tall stems. The flowers may be sold fresh but often the petals are removed and the disc is sold as a dried flower.

Propagation

Seed: Seed germinates in 15–20 days if sown at 70–75F and in the light under mist or a sweat tent (3). Cooler temperatures result in slower and less uniform germination. Stratification at 40F for 4 weeks has also been shown to enhance germination (2). Approximately ⅓ to ½ oz of seed yields 1000 seedlings (4).

Division: Plants may be carefully divided in the spring or fall. Division may be accomplished every 3 years.

Cuttings: Take 1–3" long root cuttings in early spring and insert upright in a loose sand/peat mix (60/40, v/v). Cuttings may also be laid flat and barely covered with medium.

Growing on

If seedlings are grown in plugs, grow for 4–6 weeks in full sun at 60–65F before transplanting to cell pack, 4" pot or field. Fertilize with 50–100 ppm N constant liquid feed using a complete fertilizer. If grown in seed flats, transplant to cell packs as soon as seedlings can be handled without damage (usually approx. 5–6 weeks).

Divisions and root cuttings should be sorted to size; large propagules may be transplanted directly to the field, smaller ones may be placed in pots or cell packs and grown-on in the greenhouse or cold frame.

Environmental Factors

Cold is not necessary for flower initiation and development, although stem length and yield are greater when at least 6 weeks of temperatures at 40F are provided. Little difference in stem length occurs between northern and southern plantings. No photoperiod responses are known.

Field Performance

Longevity: Three to five years of performance should be expected.

Spacing: Space plants from as close as 15" × 15" to as much as 2' × 2'. Plants spaced closer than 15" centers are more prone to foliar disease. If spaced greater than 2' apart, plants may require support. Research in Burlington, VT resulted in 15 stems/plant at a spacing of 2' × 2'. The average stem length was approximately 31" (1).

Stage of Harvest

If sold as fresh flowers, harvest when petals are expanding and place in preservative. If used as a disk flower only, additional time on the plant is useful to color the disk and to allow easier removal of the petals. Place at 40F after harvest.

Postharvest

Fresh: Petals of the species (not necessarily the cultivars) tend to droop regardless of the timē of harvest. This property detracts from the beauty of the flower and consumers may regard the flower as wilting simply due to the nature of the flower. Flowers last 7–10 days in preservative solution.

Dried: After removal of the petals, the disk may be hung to dry and will last indefinitely.

Cultivars

'Alba' has creamy white flowers which contrast well with the copper-brown cone. Plants may be propagated from seed.

'Bright Star' is 2.5–3' tall and carries rose-pink flowers on stiff stems. Plants are vegetatively propagated.

'Magnus' is a seed-propagated, 3' tall cultivar with large, deep purple flowers.

'Robert Bloom' has intense cerise flowers. It is more commonly available in Europe than in the United States.

'White Lustre' has warm white petals surrounding an orange-brown cone. Other colors are also available in the Lustre series.

Additional Species

Echinacea angustifolia is a western species with a similar cone, but the petals are straplike and are not useful as fresh flowers.

E. pallida (pale cone flower) has narrow, drooping petals and is most useful as a dried cone.

Pests and Diseases

Leaf spots caused by *Cercospora rudbeckiae* and *Septoria lepachydis* result in marginal necrosis followed by blackening of leaves. Treat with a general-purpose foliar fungicide.

Reading

1. Perry, L. P. 1989. Perennial cut flowers. In *Proceedings of 2nd National Conference on Specialty Cut Flowers*. Athens, GA. 155–161.

2. Phillips, H. R. 1985. *Growing and Propagating Wild Flowers*. Univ. North Carolina Press, Chapel Hill, NC.

3. Pinnell, M., A. M. Armitage and D. Seaborn. 1985. Germination needs of common perennial seeds. Univ. of Georgia Research Report 331, Athens, GA.

4. Seals, J. 1991. Some uncommon and common (but choice) cut flowers from seed for field growing. *The Cut Flower Quarterly* 3(2):13–14.

Many thanks to Dr. Leonard Perry for reviewing this section.

Echinops bannaticus

Echinops bannaticus	Globe Thistle		3–5'/3'
Blue	Southern Europe	Asteraceae	Zones 3–8

Grown for the metallic blue, globular flowers, *E. bannaticus* (often sold as *E. ritro*) is useful as a fresh and dried cut flower. The foliage, green on top and gray-green beneath, has pointed lobes but is not prickly. The flower heads, consisting of many single flowers each surrounded with bristly bracts, are coarse and somewhat difficult to handle.

Propagation
Seed: Sow seed in greenhouse under mist or sweat tent at 65–70F. Seed germinates in 14–21 days and may be transplanted to 3.5–4" containers 2–3 weeks later. Approximately 1 oz of seed yields 1000 seedlings (2).

Division: Divide plants in spring or in summer after flowering. A portion of the root must accompany the vegetative division. Plantlets naturally occur around the main stem.

Cuttings: Take a 1–2" long piece of healthy root in the spring and place vertically in rooting medium in warm moist location. New shoots appear within 2–3 weeks.

Growing-on
Temperature in the greenhouse should be 55–65F. Avoid temperatures above 70F. Fertilize plantlets with 50–100 ppm N until large enough to transplant to the field (6–8 weeks). If plants are left in greenhouse longer than 8 weeks, transplant to a larger container to minimize root restriction.

Environmental Factors
Temperature: Cold is necessary for best flowering. Plants will not flower uniformly unless a cold treatment is provided, usually by winter. Most rapid development occurs if crowns are provided with at least 6 weeks at 40F (1). Hot summers reduce the quality of stems and flowers, particularly the intensity of the blue color. Cooler summers intensify the color and reduce foliar chlorosis but also result in reduction in stem length. The cold hardiness makes this useful as far north as the prairie provinces of Canada.

Photoperiod: After vernalization, plants flower most rapidly under LD (>16 hours). Plants, however, are taller under LD than SD (8 hours) (1).

Field Performance
Longevity: Globe thistle is a long-lived perennial and will be productive for many years. For commercial growers, 3–5 years of flower production are possible.

Yield and stem quality of *Echinops bannaticus* 'Taplow Blue' over time (planted fall, 1984; spacing 2' × 2'; full sun).

Year	Stems/plant	Stems/ft^2	Stem length (in)	Stem diameter (mm)
1	1	0.4	27.0	6.5
2	4	1.0	38.4	7.2
3	5	1.3	38.3	6.8
4	7	1.8	33.2	6.4

Spacing: Plants grow 3–5' tall and spread equally wide over time. If plants are to remain in the ground longer than 3 years, space 2 feet apart. If plants are to be removed in 3 years or less, spacing may be reduced to 18" centers.

Shading: Plants are normally grown in full sun in the North but shade is beneficial in the South (zone 7 and below).

The effect of shade on yield and stem quality of *Echinops bannaticus* 'Taplow Blue' (Athens, GA; average of 2 years' production).

Shade level (%)	Stems/plant	Stem length (in)
0	5	33
55	7	43
67	6	36

The addition of shade cloth is beneficial not only for yield and stem length but also for the protection it provides from winds and rain. In the North, the same benefits may be gained with 20–30% shade material.

Greenhouse Performance

For best greenhouse production, cool potted crowns for 6 weeks at 40F followed by 12 weeks in the greenhouse at 60F under 16- to 24-hour photoperiod (1). Incandescent lamps may be used to provide LD.

Stage of Harvest

Flowers should be harvested when ½ to ¾ of the globe has turned blue. Flowers on inflorescences harvested too early fail to open. Leaves decline more rapidly than the flowers.

Postharvest

Fresh: Flowers persist for 6–12 days in water although foliage persists for only about 5 days.

Storage: Placing flowers in a 40F cooler results in intensified color. Stems may be stored wet for 7–10 days.

Dried: Air-dry by hanging bunches upside down. Do not strip leaves. If harvested too late, the globe will shatter.

Cultivars

'Taplow Blue' has more intense blue flowers than the species. It is the most popular cultivar of the genus and is often sold as a cultivar of *E. ritro*.

Additional Species

Echinops commutatus and *E. sphaerocephalus* grow up to 6' in height and have green leaves, gray stems and large white flower heads.

E. ritro is similar to *E. bannaticus*. 'Veitch's Blue' is common in Europe.

Pests and Diseases

Crown rot (*Pellicularia rolfsii*) infects roots and crown, often the result of waterlogged soils.

Reading

1. Iversen, R., and T. Weiler. 1989. Forcing the issue: a guide to forcing garden perennials into bloom for flower show exhibitions. *Amer. Nurseryman* 169(8):95–103.

2. Kieft, C. 1989. *Kieft's Growing Manual* .... Kieft Bloemzaden, Venhuizen, The Netherlands.

Echinops bannaticus

Eryngium planum

Eryngium planum		Flat Sea Holly	2–4'/3'
Blue	Eastern Europe	Apiaceae	Zones 3–8

One of the smaller-flowered sea hollies, *E. planum* is nevertheless a most useful and decorative cut flower. It is one of the most economical sea hollies to ship because the relatively small flowers allow more stems to be placed in the shipping container. The small, blue flowers are arranged in a tight globose head and each inflorescence is subtended by bracts which turn metallic blue in the summer. The sea hollies tolerate saline conditions and are cold hardy throughout the country.

Propagation

Seed: Ripe seed of *Eryngium* should be collected from stock plants and sown immediately in a loose mixture of sand and vermiculite or other seed medium. Seed enters a dormancy phase rapidly after harvest, and purchased seed takes many months for germination. In the following work, seed was germinated under intermittent mist at 70–72F.

Germination of *Eryngium planum* over time.[a]

Age of seed (months)	Germination (%)
Fresh	55
1	48
2	32
3	6
4	5
5	0
6	1

[a]Adapted from (1).

For purchased seed, sow in seed trays, cover lightly with soil and place in a cold frame, unheated greenhouse or outside under snow; germination occurs the next spring. Another season of warmth and cold, however, is necessary to germinate all viable seed. Approximately 0.7–1 oz of seed yields 1000 seedlings (2). *Eryngium alpinum* (alpine sea holly) germinates less uniformly and more slowly than *E. planum*.

Division: Plantlets are formed at the base of plants and may be carefully removed.

Cuttings: Root cuttings are an excellent means of propagation. Remove 2–4" long sections of mature root and place upright in containers of porous medium. Containers should be placed in a warm area (68–75F) and kept moist.

Growing-on

Grow at 55–60F and avoid temperatures above 70F. Fertilize sparingly (50–100 ppm N) until large enough to transplant to the field or bench. Seed-propagated material may be transplanted 5–8 weeks after emergence. The medium-to-large divisions should be grown for 3–4 weeks before placing in the field. Small divisions can be placed in growing-on beds for a year before being placed in the production area. Plantlets tolerate full sun in the greenhouse in spring, winter and fall, but shade is necessary in the summer.

Environmental Factors

Cold is necessary for flowering and temperatures of 40F or below may be provided by winter, cold frames or unheated greenhouses. Hot summers are tolerated but the metallic blue color of the flowers, stems and bracts is not as intense as those grown under cool summer nights. Plants grown north of zone 5 are of high quality, but stem lengths are shorter than those grown further south. *Eryngium* is sensitive to overwatering and well-drained soils must be provided.

Field Performance

Longevity: Sea holly is a long-lived perennial and flower production continues for many years. For commercial growers, 3–5 years of production are easily obtainable. However, yield declines after approximately 3 years, although stem length and diameter are not seriously affected over time, as the following table shows.

Yield and stem quality of *Eryngium planum* over time (planted fall, 1984; spacing 2' × 2'; full sun).

Year	Stems/plant	Stems/ft²	Stem length (in)	Stem diameter (mm)
1985	3	0.6	30.4	9.1
1986	6	1.4	32.4	9.4
1987	9	2.1	36.2	9.2
1988	6	1.5	37.0	8.9
1989	5	1.3	37.1	8.9

Spacing: Plants grow 2–4' tall with equal spread. If plants are to remain in production for more than 3 years, space 2' apart. If plants are to be removed at the end of the third year, spacing may be reduced to 18" centers.

Shading: Plants are usually grown in full sun in the North but are occasionally shaded in the South. Performance is reduced with shade, although flower color is enhanced.

The effect of shade on *Eryngium planum* (spacing 2' × 2').

Shade level (%)	Stems/plant	Stem length (in)
0	7	37.0
55	5	35.4
67	1	40.1

The addition of shade cloth is useful for wind and rain reduction, but the decrease in yield is too great to warrant it.

Guideline for Foliar Analyses

At field trials in Athens, GA, foliage was sampled from vigorously growing healthy plants when flower buds were visible, but prior to flower opening. These are guidelines only and should not be considered absolute standards. Based on dry weight analysis.

(%)						(ppm)				
N	P	K	Ca	Mg		Fe	Mn	B	Al	Zn
4.05	0.63	3.36	1.19	0.47		257	84	28	83	61

Stage of Harvest

Flowers should be harvested when the entire flower head, including bracts, turns blue.

Postharvest

Fresh: Flowers persist 10–12 days in water although foliage lasts only 5–8 days.

Storage: Placing flowers in 40F coolers results in intensified color. Stems may be stored for 7–10 days at 38–40F.

Dried: Air-drying is successful but drying in a desiccant such as silica gel preserves more color.

Cultivars

'Blue Ribbon' is similar to the species but more compact.

Additional Species

Eryngium alpinum (alpine sea holly) is the most popular species in Europe. It bears larger bracts than *E. planum* and is more ornamental. Shipping quality is not as good, however. Cultivars include 'Blue Star' (deep blue) and 'Superbum' (larger bracts).

E. amethystinum is popular in the United States.

E. bourgatii is also used for cut flowers.

Pests and Diseases

Leaf spots are common; treat with general-purpose foliar fungicide.

Reading

1. Pinnell, M., A. M. Armitage and D. Seaborn. 1985. Germination needs of common perennial seeds. Univ. of Georgia Research Report 331, Athens, GA.

2. Seals, J. 1989. Some uncommon and common (but choice) cut flowers from seed for field growing. *The Cut Flower Quarterly* 3(2):13–14.

Gypsophila paniculata

Gypsophila paniculata	Baby's Breath		2–4'/3'
White	Northern Asia, Europe	Caryophyllaceae	Zones 3–7

One of the mainstays of the cut flower industry, baby's breath is grown for its airy panicle of single and double flowers. Production occurs in the field and year-round in greenhouses. Some cultivars have been selected for their double flowers and some for their gray-green foliage. In warmer areas of the country, such as Florida, *Gypsophila* is grown as an annual, while in Michigan and California, it is produced as a perennial.

Propagation

Seed: Seed is used for a few cultivars ('Snowflake' for one) and the wild species, but most cultivars are propagated vegetatively due to variability of the seedlings and quality of resultant plants. If seed is used, approximately ¼ oz yields 1000 plants.

Grafting: Double-flowered cultivars were grafted on the rootstock of the more vigorous, single *G. paniculata*. Although still occasionally used, the practice is very labor-intensive and expensive and has all but disappeared.

Cuttings: Vegetative cuttings taken in the summer root in 10–14 days under mist and warm temperatures. Cuttings are more uniform and healthy, and flower production is equal to that of grafted plants.

Tissue culture: Most commercial propagation today is done by stem tip culture.

Growing-on

Plants should be grown under short days, high light and cool temperatures (50–55F) until plants are large enough to be planted to the field or greenhouse bench. Cool temperatures result in better branching than warmer (58–62F) temperatures.

Environmental Factors

Photoperiod: *Gypsophila* species are long day (LD) plants and flowering is inhibited by short days (SD). In general, the critical photoperiod for flowering is 12–14 hours for most cultivars (4). Plants must have at least 12 nodes before LD are perceived (5). Under normal growing conditions, this occurs 3–5 weeks after transplanting. The more LD cycles received, the more flowers produced. Also, the longer the photoperiod the earlier the flowering (7). Stem length and quality are greatest at 16- to 18-hour photoperiods (5).

Temperature: Night temperatures of approximately 55F are necessary in order for plants to respond to subsequent long days. If temperatures are below 55F, LD induction will not be perceived (7) and plants remain vegetative. At approximately 55F, all plants flower but flowering is significantly delayed compared with plants grown under warmer temperatures (6,8). Day temperatures should be maintained by setting venting temperature to 77F.

Rooted cuttings cooled at 32–35F in the dark for 7 weeks become vernalized (7). The cooling treatment results in plants flowering regardless of daylength.

**The effect of cooling rooted cuttings on flowering of
Gypsophila paniculata.[a]**

Treatment	Flowering (%)		Flowering stems/plant	
	SD	LD	SD	LD
Noncooled	0	71	0	15.3
Cooled[b]	80	97	15.3	28.5

[a]From (7).
[b]Cuttings were cooled at 33F in the dark for 7 weeks.

This use of precooled clumps allows flower production in cool green-houses under natural winter daylengths and promotes winter flowering of field grown plants in Florida. Plants may also be cooled at 50–54F for 7 weeks if sufficient light is provided for green leaves (7). Plants which have been cooled have more flowers under LD compared with those which have had no vernalization.

Carbon dioxide: CO_2 is effective in promoting growth and development (7).

Light intensity: The number of flowers increases with an increase in light intensity. Lack of light is often a limiting factor in the northern greenhouse during the winter.

Gibberellic acid: GA can substitute for the warm temperatures necessary for plants to respond to subsequent LD but does not substitute for LD (7). That is, plants respond to LD even below 55F if GA (500 ppm) is applied.

Field Performance

Natural flowering is from late spring through late summer, with 2–3 flowering flushes obtained. In California, flowering starts in early spring, continues into the fall but significantly declines in the winter. Yield of approximately 5–6 stems/plant is normal in winter production; 20–25 stems/plant occur under field conditions in the summer, depending on cultivar. An earlier crop may be forced in the field with plastic frames to warm air and soil and incandescent lamps to provide 16-hour days. Stems of plants grown under northern production are usually longer than stems produced in the South because of longer photoperiods in the summer.

Spacing: Plant on 18–24" centers with 1–2' between rows.

Longevity: Plants may be kept in production for 2–3 years although precooled plants may be set out every year from March to June. In Florida, precooled clumps are planted from September to February for winter and early spring production. After flowering, plants are removed.

Shading: Shading is not necessary.

Soil: Soil must be well drained for best production; plants do poorly if placed where the water table is high. Soil low in calcium and magnesium should be liberally fertilized with dolomitic lime. *Gypsophila* absorbs large amounts of those elements (see "Guideline for Foliar Analyses").

Greenhouse Performance

Gypsophila can be produced year-round, but the main time for greenhouse culture is for winter and spring production.

Cuttings: Cuttings may be planted in August and September and grown at 60–70F until plants have at least 12 nodes (3–5 weeks). Double-row spacing may be used in which plants are spaced 18–20" apart and rows are 3–3.5' apart. Long days of at least 16 hours should then be provided at least until flower stalks are visible. Continuous lighting (24 hours) is better than 16-hour lighting, but nightbreak lighting and cyclic lighting may also be used. Incandescent bulbs are best for photoperiodic lighting. Do not allow temperatures to drop below 55F. If precooled crowns or cuttings are used, LD treatments are not necessary for flowering, but weaker stems may result.

Light: In northern climates, the use of sodium HID during early development enhances subsequent flower yield and quality (3). Approximately 6 weeks of high pressure sodium lighting (93 moles m^{-2} s^{-1}; 600 fc) applied after pinching resulted in flowers approximately 10 weeks after pinching (2). The number of flowering stems and quality of stems and flowers are highly correlated to light intensity in northern climates. In the South, high intensity lighting is not as useful as in the North.

Fertilization: Few recommendations exist for fertilization in the greenhouse. Except for magnesium and calcium, nutritional requirements of *Gypsophila* are not high. The use of 100–150 ppm N and K once or twice a week is sufficient.

Guideline for Foliar Analyses

At field trials in Athens, GA, foliage was sampled from vigorously growing healthy plants when flower buds were visible, but prior to flower opening. These are guidelines only and should not be considered absolute standards. Based on dry weight analysis.

(%)						(ppm)			
N	P	K	Ca	Mg	Fe	Mn	B	Al	Zn
'Bristol Fairy'									
3.72	0.68	2.15	5.32	1.30	287	70	29	159	76

Stage of Harvest

For the fresh flower market, stems should be cut with 60–70% of the flowers open. For drying, 80–90% of the flowers should be open. For immediate local sale of fresh flowers, 80–90% flowers open is also appropriate. Plants may also be harvested in tight bud (5–10% open) if placed in a bud-opening solution (see "Postharvest").

Postharvest

Fresh: Flowers persist for 5–7 days in water, longer in a preservative. Water should be clean and adjusted to pH 3.5. Since *Gypsophila* is sensitive to ethylene and bacterial contamination, use of silver thiosulfate (STS) and a germicide is recommended. Pretreatment with STS for 30 minutes and sub-sequent placement in a preservative solution of 1.5% sucrose and 200 ppm Physan-20™ (a germicide) results in excellent vase life. The use of a combination STS/preservative solution results in a one-solution system for post-harvest treatment. For bud opening, place stems in a solution containing 200 ppm Physan-20™ and 5–10% sucrose. Place in rooms at 70F, 50% relative humidity and 100 fc of light. Flowers should open in 2–3 days (1).

Dried: Two methods are commonly used. In the first method, flowers are air-dried upright in a container of water with the water just covering the cut ends. Room temperature should be approximately 50F (9).

In the second method, flowers are dried in a solution of 1 part glycerine to 2 parts water (6). The plants can be removed from the glycerine solution when beads of moisture form on the leaf surface (9). Stems should then be dried upside down in a well-ventilated room.

Storage: Stems should not be stored dry for more than 2 days unless absolutely necessary. 'Bristol Fairy' may be stored a little longer than other cultivars, approximately 3 days. In the preservative solution mentioned above, stems with 50% of flowers open persist for up to 3 weeks if held at 33–35F.

Cultivars

'Bristol Fairy' has double, white flowers and is still the standard cultivar.

'Flamingo' is a popular cultivar in Europe and is becoming more available in the United States.

'Floriana Mist' and 'Floriana Cascade' were developed from clones of 'Bristol Fairy' by researchers at the University of Florida and Purdue University. They flower more consistently under short days and cool nights than 'Bristol Fairy' (10).

'Perfecta', more vigorous and with larger white flowers than 'Bristol Fairy', is one of the most widely used cultivars in the United States.

'Pink Fairy' is a double-flowered, pink selection.

'Red Sea' bears double, rose-pink flowers.

'Single' is the native baby's breath and is seed-propagated.

'Snowflake' ('Double Snowflake'; 'Schneeflocke') is propagated from seed and bears 50–60% double flowers.

Additional Species

Gypsophila elegans may be used as a short-stemmed filler. The stems are only 9–15" long but the many pink or creamy white flowers fill the plant. May be propagated from seed (4 oz yield 1000 plants) or cuttings. Treat plants as an annual crop.

G. oldhamiana bears pink to deep pink, fragrant flowers in a large, 9–12" long panicle. Plants are native to northeast Asia and Korea and are hardy to zones 4–5.

Pests and Diseases

Crown gall (*Agrobacterium gypsophilae*) results in soft, nodular galls about

1" in diameter. This disease was much more prevalent on grafted plants than on plants propagated from cuttings or seed because it was often spread with the grafting knives. Avoid propagation from infected plants, and dip plants and knives in a bacterial solution.

Blight from *Botrytis cinerea* causes ash-gray spots to develop on buds and stems.

Damping off (*Pythium debaryanum, Pellicularia filamentosa*) results in rotting at the soil line followed by stem rot and topple.

Red spider mites and thrips can be a problem, particularly in perennial crops.

Reading

1. Evans, R. Y., and M. S. Reid. 1990. Postharvest care of specialty cut flowers. In *Proceedings of 3rd National Conference on Specialty Cut Flowers.* Ventura, CA. 26–44.

2. Hicklenton, P. R. 1986. The effect of supplemental lighting on winter flowering of transplanted *Gypsophila paniculata. Can. J. Plant Sci.* 66:653–658.

3. ———. 1987. Flowering of *Gypsophila paniculata* cv. Bristol Fairy in relation to irradiance. *Acta Hortic.* 205:103–111.

4. Krogt, T. M. van der. 1982. Betere bloeispreiding in *Gypsophila* door teeltplaning. Bloemistry 6:34–35.

5. Kusey, W. E., Jr., T. C. Weiler, P. A. Hammer, B. K. Harbaugh and G. J. Wilfret. 1981. Seasonal and chemical influences on the flowering control of *Gypsophila paniculata. J. Amer. Soc. Hort. Sci.* 106:84–88.

6. Moe, R. 1988. Flowering physiology of gypsophila. *Acta Hortic.* 218:153–158.

7. Shillo, R. 1985. *Gypsophila paniculata.* In A. H. Halevy (ed.), *The Handbook of Flowering,* vol. 3. CRC Press, Boca Raton, FL. 83–87.

8. Shillo, R., and A. H. Halevy. 1982. Interaction of photoperiod and temperature in flowering control of *Gypsophila paniculata* L. *Scientia Hortic.* 16(4):385–393.

9. Vaughan, M. J. 1988. *The Complete Book of Cut Flower Care.* Timber Press, Portland, OR.

10. Wilfret, G. T., T. C. Weiler, B. K. Harbaugh and P. A. Hammer. 1986. 'Floriana Mist' and 'Floriana Cascade' gypsophila. *HortScience* 21:160–161.

Many thanks to Mr. Whiting Preston, Mr. Bob Pollioni and Dr. Peter Hicklenton for reviewing this section.

Limonium spp.   Statice, Sea Lavender

Approximately 200 species of annuals and perennials exist in this genus, although only a handful are used commercially. Two of the most useful annuals—*L. sinuatum* (a major species) and *L. suworowii*—are discussed in the section on annuals.

Limonium tataricum (*Goniolimon tataricum*) and *L. latifolium* are the major perennial species; considerable information is available on *L. altaica* as well, which is similar to *L. tataricum*. Other perennial species suitable for cut flower production are *L. bellidifolium* (*L. caspium*) and *L. gmelinii*.

Limonium peregrinum (also known as *L. roseum*), *L. perezii* and *L. sinense* are all half-hardy sub-shrubs. Of these, *L. peregrinum* does best in a greenhouse. Popular hybrids include *L.* 'Beltlaard', *L.* 'Misty Blue', *L.* 'Misty Pink' and *L.* 'Saint Pierre'.

Limonium altaica

| | | Altaica Statice | 2–2.5'/2' |
| Lavender | Asia | Plumbaginaceae | Zones 6–8 |

This species was provided to our program by Dr. Mark Roh of the United States Department of Agriculture. He found them in a greenhouse in Japan and we have grown them since 1985. The basal leathery leaves are glossy green and ovate, and the flowers are faintly odoriferous. Stems arise in early to midsummer with clouds of lavender to light blue. This species is similar in response to the environment and similar in growth to the other perennial statice species, *L. tataricum* and *L. latifolium*.

Propagation

Seed: Seed is difficult to locate but not particularly difficult to germinate. Sow seed lightly and place under mist or sweat tent at 70–72F. Germination occurs within 10–14 days.

Division: Plants may be cut apart carefully, retaining as much root system on plantlets as possible. Plantlets recover slowly and little production occurs the first year from division. Spring division is best if plantlets are to be replanted immediately. Otherwise, divide in fall and grow in greenhouse for 3–4 weeks; overwinter in cold frames or unheated greenhouses.

Cuttings: The best method of vegetative propagation is by root cuttings. Cut 1–3" long pieces of the fleshy roots. The thickest roots may be placed upright in sandy soil while the thinner ones may be placed horizontally and covered lightly. Cuttings are most successful in early spring but fall cuttings may also be used.

Growing-on

Grow seedlings and small divisions in the greenhouse under full light and 55–65F, temperatures. Grow for 6–8 weeks or until ready for transplanting. Large root divisions may be placed immediately in nursery beds, but smaller divisions require growing in the greenhouse or cold frame.

Environmental Factors

Cold treatment is necessary for best flower production. Hot summers have no detrimental effect on yield or quality, although flower color is more striking under cool nights. No photoperiod response has been evident in our trials.

Limonium latifolium and L. tataricum produce few flowers the first season from seed indicating that a vernalization period is probably necessary. Therefore, it appears that cool temperatures, followed by warm temperatures and LD are necessary for flowering in perennial statice.

Field Performance

Longevity: Limonium altaica has been in production in the Georgia trials for 4 years without any decline in yield.

Yield and stem quality of Limonium altaica over time (Athens, GA; spacing 2' × 2'; planted fall, 1985).

Year	Stems/plant	Stems/ft^2	Stem length (in)	Flower head diameter (in)
1986	8	2	10.8	7
1987	25	6	16.6	11
1988	28	7	18.0	11
1989	35	9	17.2	12

Spacing: Plants need not be spaced more than 2' × 2', and 1' centers are adequate. We have seen few disease or insect problems, so tight spacing should not be a problem.

Shading: Grow under full sun. Light shade may result in longer stems; however, stem diameter is not as strong.

Guideline for Foliar Analyses

At field trials in Athens, GA, foliage was sampled from vigorously growing healthy plants when flower buds were visible, but prior to flower opening. These are guidelines only and should not be considered absolute standards. Based on dry weight analysis.

(%)						(ppm)				
N	P	K	Ca	Mg		Fe	Mn	B	Al	Zn
3.85	0.40	3.60	0.48	0.40		129	47	22	102	36

Stage of Harvest

Flowers should be harvested when approximately 80% of the flower head has opened. Harvesting too early results in poor opening and small flower heads; harvesting too late results in discoloration. Place stems in floral preservative immediately after harvesting.

Postharvest

Fresh: Flowers persist in water or preservative for 3–4 weeks. With annual statice, gibberellic acid treatment increased vase life (see Limonium sinuatum). Flowers should be placed in a warm solution containing gibberellic acid plus 30 ppm silver nitrate and held at 68F until the desired degree of opening has been attained. At that time, place at 40F (4).

Dried: Hang stems upside down in a cool, well-ventilated room. Dried flowers last 1–2 years.

Cultivars

No cultivars of *L. altaica* are available; however, 'Emile' appears to have some *L. altaica* in its parentage. 'Emile' bears rosy lavender flowers and grows approximately 2–2.5' tall. Flowers produce only a faint odor.

Limonium perezii	Perez Statice, Seafoam Statice	1–2'/1'
Blue, white Canary Islands	Plumbaginaceae	Zones 8–10

Seafoam statice has large, leathery basal leaves and produces coarse, blue and white inflorescences. Plants are perennial in zones 8–11 (almost a weed in southern California) and in zone 7 with mulch, but they can be grown as annuals in most of the United States. Drainage must be excellent if plants are to be perennial.

Propagation

Seed germinates in 5–14 days if planted at 70–72F. Purchase clean (rubbed) seed. Although a little more expensive, clean seed facilitates seeding and reduces frustration. If seed is soaked in water for 24 hours prior to sowing, germination is enhanced (3). Approximately 1/16 oz of seed yields 1000 seedlings. Plants may also be divided, particularly if plants are perennial.

Growing-on

Transplant to cell packs or 4" pots as soon as seedlings can be handled. Fertilize with 75–100 ppm N using potassium nitrate or a complete fertilizer and maintain temperatures at approximately 65F. Plants may be placed in the field as soon as threat of frost has ended. Approximately 8–10 weeks from seed to field transplant are common.

Environmental Factors

Little information has been published about this species. Flowers are produced the first year from seed but likely LD and warm temperatures promote flowering, similar to annual statice (*L. sinuatum*), which see. If sown early, flowers produce some flowers the first year.

Field Performance

Plants perform better in Mediterranean climates than in eastern or southeastern climes. First-year results from trials at the University of Georgia resulted in only 5 stems/plant, averaging 19.7" long. Plants did not overwinter.

Guideline for Foliar Analyses

At field trials in Athens, GA, and Watsonville, CA, foliage was sampled from vigorously growing healthy plants when flower buds were visible, but prior to flower opening. These are guidelines only and should not be considered absolute standards. Based on dry weight analysis.

(%)						(ppm)				
N	P	K	Ca	Mg		Fe	Mn	B	Al	Zn
					(GA)					
3.38	0.52	2.20	0.72	0.54		86	77	17	77	260
					(CA)					
3.18	0.33	2.33	0.49	0.56		123	79	17	64	102

Stage of Harvest
Harvest when approximately 80% of the flower head has opened.

Postharvest
Fresh: Flowers persist for 10–14 days in water, slightly longer in floral preservative.
Storage: Plants may be stored dry for 4–5 days at 35–38F.
Dried: Flowers may be air-dried upside down in a well-ventilated room.

Cultivars
'Atlantis' is a seed-propagated cultivar which has darker blue flowers than the species. Plants grow 2–3' tall.

Additional Species of *Limonium*
Limonium gmelinii (siberian statice) bears lilac-blue flowers on 2' tall stems. Hardy to zone 4 (maybe 3), flowers are formed in midsummer starting the second year.

L. latifolium and *L. tataricum* (*Goniolimon tataricum*) are used as perennial statice flowers and can be treated like *L. gmelinii*. Little or no flower production occurs the first year from seed. Flowers are cut when 75% of the inflorescences are open (1).

Hybrids between *L. latifolium* and *L. bellidifolium* (caspia statice) produce lacy flower heads, have no offensive odor and are up to 4' tall. 'Saint Pierre' and 'Beltlaard' (less upright than 'Saint Pierre') and the Misty series ('Misty Blue', 'Misty Pink' and 'Misty White') are offered from these hybrids. Plants of the Misty series produce up to 20 stems/plant about 4 months after planting (2). They make exceptional greenhouse subjects but suffer in field culture in most areas of the country.

L. sinense 'Stardust' has proven to be an excellent plant in field trials at the University of Georgia. The handsome flowers are light yellow with white eyes and plants are perennial at least as far as zone 7b (north Georgia). Harvest begins in early June and continues until early August. First-year yields were 10 stems/plant at 13.5" in length; the second-year yields were 20 stems/plant and stem length was 18.7". The third yield fell back to 10 stems/plant but stem length increased to 20.1". A species with great potential as a cut flower.

Pests and Diseases of *Limonium*

Botrytis can appear at any time but is more prevalent under cool, wet conditions.

Leaf spots may be caused by numerous fungal species. Spray regularly with general foliar fungicide and pick off infected leaves when spots first appear.

Rust can also be a serious problem.

Fungal root rot as a result of wet soils can decimate all statice species. Maintaining good drainage is essential.

Reading

1. Hodgkin, G. W. 1992. Growing German statice. In *Proceedings of 4th National Conference on Specialty Cut Flowers.* Cleveland, OH. 33–37.

2. Jenkins, J. 1992. New and different flower crops. In *Proceedings of 4th National Conference on Specialty Cut Flowers.* Cleveland, OH. 44–45.

3. Kieft, C. 1989. *Kieft's Growing Manual* .... Kieft Bloemzaden, Venhuizen, The Netherlands.

4. Steinitz, B., and A. Cohen. 1982. Gibberellic acid promotes flower bud opening on detached flower stalks of statice (*Limonium sinuatum* L.). *HortScience* 17:903–904.

Lysimachia clethroides   Gooseneck Loosestrife   2–2.5'/3'
White   China, Japan   Primulaceae   Zones 3–8

Plants are easily grown and spread rapidly. Excellent flowers may be produced as far south as zone 7, but in zone 8 (south Georgia, Florida), although production is adequate, flower stems are thinner and flowers smaller. Flowers appear in late spring (zone 7) or summer (north of zone 7).

Propagation

Seed: Seed should be barely covered and placed at 65–68F. Germination is erratic. Once seed has germinated, place in a cooler area.

Division: Plants roam freely and the rhizomes may be easily divided after flowering.

Growing-on

Transplant to cell packs or 4" pots as soon as seedlings can be handled. Grow at 50–60F for 6–8 weeks with as much light as possible. Fertilize lightly with 50–100 ppm N of a complete fertilizer. Transplant to field in fall or early spring.

Environmental Factors

Cold is necessary to break dormancy in rhizomes. Although 6 weeks of 40F result in shoot emergence, rhizomes subjected to 12 weeks of cold (40F) emerge much more rapidly. Long days (>16 hours) after emergence are necessary for flower initiation and development (1).

Lysimachia clethroides

Field Performance

Spacing: Plant on 12″ centers. Plants fill in rapidly and, within 2 years, cover the planting area. Support netting is necessary.

Yield: Two-year yields and stem lengths are shown in the following table. Yields and stem length in the second year were much better than the first. Stem length in California was longer than in Georgia for both years; however, yield was almost double in Georgia in year 2.

Yield and stem quality of *Lysimachia clethroides* (Athens, GA, and Watsonville, CA).

Year	Shade level (%)	Georgia Stems/plant	Georgia Stem length (in)	California Stems/plant	California Stem length (in)
1	0	12	15.8	8	27.0
2	0	39	27.6	20	42.0
2	55	30	34.9	—[a]	—

[a]Dash (—) indicates that data are not available.

In the third year at Athens, GA, yield rose astronomically as plants spread with wild abandon. The yield for the original 48 plants was 6030 stems, an average of 126 stems/original plant! The stem length averaged 40" in the full sun. We thought the place would be carried away with loosestrife.

Shade: As the data in the preceding table from the University of Georgia show, although plants grown under 55% shade had longer stems, yield was reduced by 9 stems/plant. Stem diameters were no different under shade or sun.

Greenhouse Performance

To force *Lysimachia* in the greenhouse, approximately 13 weeks are required after cooling rhizomes (1). Space cooled rhizomes on 12" centers in greenhouse beds, or transplant in 6–10" pots and space pot to pot until leaves touch. Stems emerge in approximately 3½ weeks at 60F. At this time, 16- to 24-hour LD should be given with incandescent lights (20–50 fc). First flowers open in about 10 weeks (1). Fertilize with 100–150 ppm N of complete fertilizer.

Stage of Harvest

Harvest when flowers in the inflorescence are ⅓ to ½ open. This occurs when about 10 flowers are open. If placed in a complete preservative (e.g., Floralife™), flowers may be harvested when the majority of flower buds are white but not open.

Postharvest

Fresh: Work conducted at the University of Georgia showed that flowers cut at the proper stage of harvest persisted for 12 days in Floralife™ and Rogard™, 2 available postharvest products, but lasted only 5 days in water. The differences were like night and day. Various concentrations of STS were ineffective. Sugar concentrations were better than water but not as effective as the floral preservatives tested.

Storage: Store flowers at 36–41F whenever possible.

Cultivars

No cultivars of *L. clethroides* are used in cut flower production.

Additional Species

Lysimachia punctatà (yellow loosestrife) has yellow flowers in the nodes along the stem and is useful as a cut flower. Flowers are borne in whorls along the stem. Plants are about 2' tall.

L. vulgaris, also known as yellow loosestrife, has ½" wide, yellow flowers with orange dots clustered in panicles (like *Phlox paniculata*). Plants are 2–3' tall.

Pests and Diseases

Few problems occur if plants are provided with well-drained soils and full sun exposure.

Reading

1. Iversen, R., and T. Weiler. 1989. Forcing the issue: a guide to forcing garden perennials into bloom for flower show exhibitions. *Amer. Nurseryman* 169(8):95–103.

Paeonia **hybrids**		Peony	2–3'/3'
Various colors	China, Japan	Ranunculaceae	Zones 2–7

The result of hybridization with *P. lactiflora*, *P. officinalis*, *P. mollis* and others, peonies have long enjoyed popularity as a cut flower. Hundreds of acres were produced in the Midwest during the 1930s. Plants are long-lived and 5- to 30-year field production is not uncommon. All growth originates from an underground crown. The stem buds or eyes are formed at the top of the crown and are the beginning of next year's growth. Single- and double-flowering cultivars and early-, mid- and late-flowering cultivars are available.

Propagation

Plants are purchased as divided crowns and transplanted directly to the field. Five-eye pieces are best, although 3-eye pieces readily develop into flowering size (6). Remove threadlike roots prior to planting. Planting is best done in the fall; early spring planting is appropriate if fall-harvested roots were cold stored during the winter.

Environmental Factors

Photoperiod: Buds of peonies are vegetative in early summer and flower initiation commences in July and August, depending on cultivar. Both terminal and lateral buds are initiated by late fall, before the onset of dormancy. Peonies go dormant as early as late August, but most cultivars persist until late October. Short days do not trigger dormancy as in other perennials, and experiments have shown that plants go dormant regardless of photoperiod (9).

Temperature: No exact data are available concerning optimum length of cold or temperature necessary to break dormancy. Although peonies flower in northern latitudes where freezing temperatures occur, they also perform well in central California and northern Georgia where frost is not a constant guest during the winter. Flower bud dormancy may be broken with as little as 4 weeks at 43F, but increasing time to 6 weeks or lowering temperature to just above freezing for 4 weeks increases the number of flowering shoots (9). Stimart (7) states that approximately 600 hours at 32–36F are necessary to break dormancy.

Flower production declines as temperatures rise, and temperatures above 70F result in faster decline of flowers.

Field Performance

Planting: The buds (eyes) of the rootstock should not be planted deeper than 2″ below the soil surface. Deep planting inhibits flowering (4). Planting should be accomplished in the fall.

Spacing: Plants should be planted no closer than 2′ × 2′. If row planting is used, 2–3′ spacing between plants and 4′ wide rows are common (6). Closer spacing reduces longevity.

Disbudding: Lateral flowers are often disbudded to increase size of primary flower and to provide longer stems. Disbud approximately 3 weeks prior to blooming. Terminal flower buds may also be removed resulting in a spray of lateral flowers.

Longevity: Flower production peaks in the third through tenth year in the North. In southern areas, plants may have to be rotated a little earlier. Divide or replace plants when yield is significantly less than the previous year.

Shading: Peonies should be planted in full sun but will tolerate partial shade, particularly in the South. Reduction in flower number and size is indicative of too much shade.

Fertilization: Side dress peonies (8–8–8) in the fall and once in the spring after stems have emerged.

Forcing: Flowering may be advanced by covering with plastic tunnels in late winter.

Yield: Depending on cultivar, 8–12 flower stems/plant can be realized. Cut only ⅓ of possible stems or allow at least 3 leaves to remain on the plant after cutting the stem (5). Removal of too much foliage reduces vigor in subsequent years. Stem length depends on cultivar and the amount of cold. Stem length in Fremont, CA, averaged 10″, in Pantego, NC, 18″; stems in the upper Midwest were 2–3′ long (6).

Greenhouse Performance

Plants in which dormancy has been broken with cold temperatures can be forced in the greenhouse in 8 weeks at 60–65F night temperatures (9). Crowns dug from the field on November 1 in Minnesota were stored at 32–40F until the cold treatment had been satisfied (late December), then placed in a 65F greenhouse; shoots emerged and flowering occurred without problem.

Since flowers initiate before the onset of dormancy, it is possible that plants simply must attain a certain size or leaf area to stimulate the formation of additional flower buds. Another possible environmental signal to force initiation of new buds may be the lessening of daylength, since peonies are generally vegetative in summer but have finished initiation of terminal and lateral buds by September (9). If additional flower buds were forced early, then plants would still likely require a dormant period and cold treatment to overcome the dormancy. Most forced peonies are presently replanted or discarded after flowering.

Stage of Harvest

Double-flowered types should be further developed than single forms, and red cultivars should be more developed than whites (5). As a general rule-of-thumb, however, flowers should be harvested when the first true color appears on top of the tight bud. Allow as much foliage to remain on the plant as possible; reducing the foliage at harvest results in poorer production in subsequent years.

Postharvest

Fresh: Flowers persist up to 10 days if harvested in the bud stage but if already open, they persist for only 5 days (8). Fresh flowers are best maintained at 36–41F at all times. Flowers harvested when first showing color or at loose calyx stage may be stored dry at 32–34F for up to 4 weeks (3,9). Lower leaves should be removed from the cut stem.

Dried: Flowers may be air-dried, although they tend to shrink considerably. When flowers are almost dry, smooth out the outer petals until the flower regains its original shape (2). Flowers may also be dried in a microwave. Cover with warm silica gel and microwave for 1–3.5 minutes, depending on the fleshiness of the flowers. Freeze-drying of peonies is also recommended.

Storage: Flowers may be stored dry after being placed in water for 2–3 hours at 36F. Remove from the water and stand upright in 32–36F at 75–80% humidity. Storage of 4 weeks is reported (7). Flowers must be dry, or fungal growth will occur.

Cultivars

Many cultivars are available from specialist peony producers. For southern growers, selection of cultivars that flower in early and midseason is recommended over late-season cultivars (1). Similarly, single and semi-double cultivars result in fewer disease problems than fully double cultivars. If fully double cultivars are grown, select early and midseason cultivars. Cultivars which are recommended for cut flower production follow. The color given is the predominant color in the flower, not necessarily the only color; some flowers are flecked, spotted, edged or blushed with additional colors.

Color	Cultivar	Form	Timing
White	'Baroness Schroeder'	Double	Medium
	'Charlie's White'	Double	Early
	'Elsa Sass'	Double	Late
Pink	'Angel Cheeks'	Double	Medium
	'Honey Gold'	Double	Medium
	'James Pillow'	Double	Late
	'Mister Ed'	Double	Early
	'Monsieur Jules Elie'	Double	Early
	'President Taft'	Double	Late

continued

Color	Cultivar	Form	Timing
	'Raspberry Sundae'	Double	Early
	'Sarah Bernhardt'	Semi-double	Medium
	'Sweet Sixteen'	Double	Medium
	'Top Brass'	Double	Medium
Red	'David Harum'	Semi-double	Medium
	'Felix Supreme'	Double	Medium
	'Karl Rosenfield'	Double	Medium
	'Renato'	Double	Late

Pests and Diseases

Botrytis or gray mold is caused by *Botrytis paeoniae* and affects flowers, particularly double forms, during periods of wet weather. Botrytis can infect the entire plant, causing it to turn black. Control by removing any infected parts in summer and fall. Fungicides are applied when leaves begin to unfurl and a second application may be applied 10–14 days later. If additional sprays are needed, apply at 10- to 14-day intervals.

Leaf spots, caused by numerous fungal species, result in spots of varying sizes and colors. Red spots or measles (*Cladosporium paeoniae*) cause small, circular, discolored spots which eventually run together. The undersurface becomes light brown, the upper, dark purple. Remove all infected tissue as soon as spots are visible. Apply general foliar fungicide as above.

Root rots caused by soil-inhabiting fungi cause decay at the base of the plant.

Stem rot (*Sclerotinia sclerotiorum*) results in sudden wilt and stem rot. The large, black sclerotia develop inside the infected stems. Remove and dispose of infected plants.

Northern root-knot nematode (*Meloidogyne* spp.) can be particularly destructive. Nematocides and soil fumigation are useful, but if infestation is severe, the only solutions may be planting where peonies have never been or relocation of the nursery.

Virus organisms can cause ringspot, circular areas consisting of concentric bands of alternating dark and light green. Unlike other viruses, plants are not dwarfed. Control by removal and disposal. Dwarfing of plants is caused by leaf curl virus, Le Moine virus and crown elongation virus. Control is similar to ringspot virus.

Reading

1. Armitage, A. M. 1989. *Herbaceous Perennial Plants: A Treatise on Their Identification, Culture, and Garden Attributes*. Varsity Press, Athens, GA.

2. Bullivant, E. 1989. *Dried Fresh Flowers From Your Garden*. Pelham Books/Stephen Greene Press, London, U.K.

3. Heuser, C. W., and K. B. Evensen. 1986. Cut-flower longevity of peony. *J. Amer. Soc. Hort. Sci.* 111:896–899.

4. Nehrling, A., and I. Nehrling. 1960. *Peonies, Outdoors and In*. Heathside Press, New York, NY.

5. Post, K. 1955. *Florist Crop Production and Marketing.* Orange Judd, New York, NY.

6. Stimart, D. P. 1989. Peonies. *The Cut Flower Quarterly,* 1(4):5–7.

7. _____ . 1992. Strategies of growing fresh cut flowers of *Liatris* and *Paeonia.* In *Proceedings of 4th National Conference on Specialty Cut Flowers.* Cleveland, OH. 45–54.

8. Vaughan, M. J. 1989. *The Complete Book of Cut Flower Care.* Timber Press, Portland, OR.

9. Wilkins, H. F., and A. H. Halevy. 1985. *Paeonia.* In A. H. Halevy (ed.), *The Handbook of Flowering,* vol. 4. CRC Press, Boca Raton, FL. 2–4.

Many thanks to Dr. Dennis Stimart and Mr. Roy Klehm for reviewing this section.

Phlox paniculata

	Summer Phlox		3–4'/3'
Various colors	North America	Polemoniaceae	Zones 3–8

Phlox has been used as a cut flower for many years because of its vigorous growth, wide selection of flower colors and large inflorescences. Two major problems still plague summer phlox: the incidence of powdery mildew on many cultivars and the premature shattering of flowers after harvest. Less mildew-susceptible cultivars and species such as spotted phlox, *P. maculata,* are being incorporated into cut flower programs.

Propagation
Propagation is accomplished by specialty perennial growers from root cuttings, stem cuttings or division.

Growing-on
Generally, roots or propagules are directly placed in the field, with little or no additional growing time necessary. If roots are received too early, they may be stored in moist sphagnum moss at 40F. If potted plants are received, they may be placed in 45F greenhouses until ready to plant out.

Planting in the fall is best for cut flower growers, although planting in early spring is also acceptable.

Environmental Factors
Temperature: In work with *P. paniculata* 'Fairy's Petticoat', no cold treatment was necessary to break dormancy, but cold resulted in accelerated flower development and taller plants than those that did not receive cold (1). Normally, this is provided by winter temperatures.

Photoperiod: Summer phlox is a long day plant, the critical photoperiod is between 8 and 16 hours. All plants of 'Fairy's Petticoat' flowered when provided with 16- and 24-hour days but no flowering occurred under 8 hours, regardless of cold treatment (1).

Field Performance

Spacing: Space plants approximately 12" × 15" or as wide as 2' centers. Sufficient spacing is required to allow good air movement, a necessity for reducing incidence of powdery mildew.

Yield: The first harvest, after fall planting, results in 3–6 stems/plant. Yield increases the second year to 5–10 stems, depending on cultivar. The following table provides data from 2 years of harvests in Watsonville, CA.

Yield and stem quality of *Phlox paniculata* (Watsonville, CA).

Cultivar	Year	Stems/plant	Stem length (in)
'Amethyst'	1	12	17
	2	10	44
'Bright Eyes'	1	4	17
	2	6	38
'Lilac Time'	1	5	27
	2	8	48
'Snowdrift'	1	6	24
	2	8	45

This table demonstrates the effect of maturity on *Phlox*. Summer phlox is a clump-forming species and, as plants mature, the additional vigor is translated into longer and stronger stems, not necessarily additional yield.

Greenhouse Performance

Two- to three-year-old roots are best for greenhouse forcing. Root divisions generally require 6–8 weeks to become established. Plants may be purchased or dug, but the roots should always be cooled for more uniform flowering. After cooling roots and crown for 6 weeks at 40F, place plants under 16- to 24-hour photoperiod (incandescent lamps at 20–50 fc) (1). Use good ventilation and fungicides to reduce incidence of disease. Under 60F temperatures, plants flower in approximately 12 weeks. If plants are potted on August 15, cold storage can begin on October 15. Greenhouse forcing begins on December 1 and flowers may be cut around March 1 (1). Fertilize with a complete fertilizer at 150–250 ppm N every irrigation or with 500 ppm N once a week.

Stage of Harvest

Harvest when ½ the flowers are open on the inflorescence (2). Flowers are sensitive to ethylene and must be stored where ethylene is not present. STS does not appear to enhance flower longevity (1).

Postharvest

Fresh: Flowers persist 5–7 days in floral preservative.
Storage: Stems may be stored wet at 38F for 1–3 days (2).
Dried: Flowers do not dry well.

Cultivars

Many cultivars exist and I list but a few useful for cut flower production:

Pink

'Bright Eyes' is one of the most popular cultivars and has pale pink flowers with a crimson eye.

'Dresden China' produces pastel pink flowers with a deeper rose-pink eye.

'Eva Cullum' has large heads of clear pink flowers with a dark red eye. Plants are only 2–2.5' tall.

'Fairy's Petticoat' bears large heads of pale pink flowers with darker eyes.

'Rose Joy' has rosy pink flowers and stands approximately 3' tall.

'Windsor' produces deep pink flowers.

Purple, lavender

'Amethyst' bears purple flowers on 3–4' tall stems.

'Ann' is a late bloomer with large, lavender flower heads.

'Lilac Time' has lilac flowers with a white eye on 3–4' tall plants.

'Progress' has pale violet blossoms with a darker eye.

'The King' is approximately 3' tall and bears deep purple flowers.

'The Prince' has light violet flowers.

Salmon, red

'Othello' has deep red flowers with a long blooming time.

'Sir John Falstaff' bears large inflorescences of salmon-pink.

'Starfire' has striking, cherry-red flowers.

'Tenor' produces large, red flower heads.

White

'Blue Ice' is only 2.5' tall and bears white flowers with a blue eye.

'Mount Fuji' ('Mt. Fujiyama') bears large, pure white flower heads.

'Prime Minister' produces white flowers with a red eye and grows 3' tall.

'Snowdrift' ('Schneerausch') bears white flowers on 3–4' tall plants.

'White Admiral' has large, clear, white flower heads.

Additional Species

Phlox × *arendsii* (arend's phlox) is a hybrid between *P. paniculata* and *P. divaricata* (woodland phlox). Woodland phlox is only 12–15" tall but is not as susceptible to mildew. Arend's phlox may provide a robust plant with good disease resistance and is a potentially good hybrid for Midwest and southern growers. Cultivars include 'Anja' (red-purple flowers), 'Hilde' (lavender flowers) and 'Suzanne' (white flowers with a red eye).

P. maculata (spotted phlox) is rapidly gaining popularity as a cut flower. Plants are less susceptible to powdery mildew than *P. paniculata* and are available in 3 colors. Stems 2.5–3' tall may be harvested. Cultivars include 'Alpha' (rose-pink flowers with the hint of a darker eye), 'Delta' (white flowers with a pink eye), 'Miss Lingard' (white with pale yellow eye), 'Omega' (white flowers with lilac eyes) and 'Rosalinde' (dark pink flowers).

These are better cut flower species for areas where mildew is a problem.

Pests and Diseases

Leaf spots are caused by many different fungi. Dark brown, circular spots up to ¼" in diameter with light gray centers occur, followed by leaves which dry up and die prematurely. Use of sulfur helps reduce the incidence of leaf spots.

Powdery mildew is caused by *Erysiphe cichoracearum* and *Sphaerotheca humuli*, and results in a white coating on the foliage. Although the fungi do not cause permanent damage, the leaves become terribly discolored. Use of fungicides is essential starting around mid-June.

Crown rot from *Puccinia, Sclerotium* and *Thielaviopsis* can result in significant losses. Sterilizing soils inhibit these soil-borne fungi.

Mites, thrips and nematodes feed on phlox and may be controlled with appropriate spray materials. In the case of stem nematodes, plants should be discarded, soil disinfected and crops rotated.

Reading

1. Iversen, R. R. 1989. *Greenhouse Forcing of Herbaceous Garden Perennials.* Ph.D. Dissertation, Cornell Univ., Ithaca, NY.

2. Nowak, J., and R. M. Rudnicki. 1990. *Postharvest Handling and Storage of Cut Flowers, Florist Greens, and Potted Plants.* Timber Press, Portland, OR.

Physostegia virginiana

Physostegia virginiana		Obedient Plant	3–4'/3'
Purple-pink	North America	Lamiaceae	Zones 3–9

Physostegia is a popular cut flower in European, Japanese and North American markets. The whorled flowers are held in upright spikes above opposite, slightly toothed foliage. Plants are rhizomatous and spread freely and rapidly, particularly in rich soil. Its common name is derived from the fact that the flowers retain the position into which they are pushed, a useful characteristic for flower arrangers and decorators.

Propagation

Seed: Germination is erratic and may take from 3 weeks to many months. For best uniformity, sow seed in moist seed flats or plugs and place at 35–40F for approximately 6 weeks. Remove from cold and place in 70–72F greenhouse. Germination occurs in 20–25 days (1); therefore, seed flats should not be discarded too early. Approximately 1/10 oz of seed yields 1000 seedlings (5).

Division: Plants are rhizomatous and spread rapidly. The easiest method of propagation is to divide plants in the spring, retaining roots with each propagule. Plants may be divided after 1 year in the field. Root cuttings are also successful.

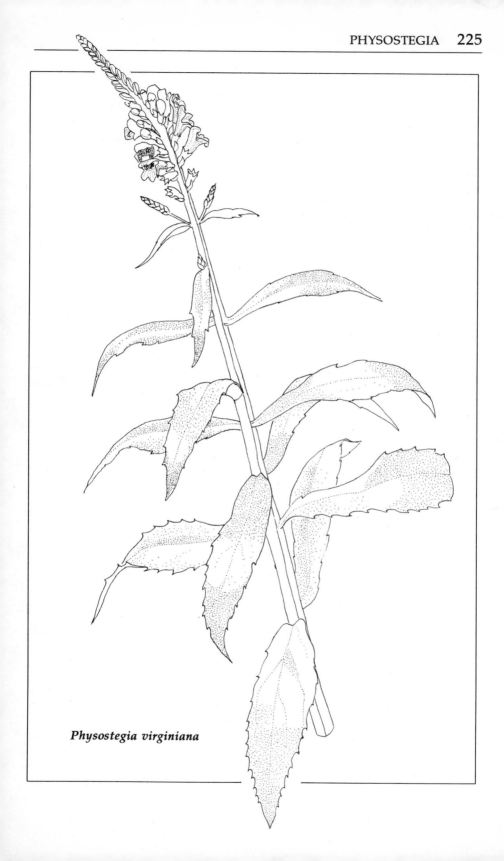

Physostegia virginiana

Growing-on

Large divisions may be transplanted directly to the field, small divisions should be placed in 4–5" pots for additional growth. Grow seedlings and divisions at 50–60F in cold frames or cool greenhouses until ready for transplant to the field. Plants grow more rapidly at 70F but internode elongation may occur. Fertilize sparingly with 100 ppm N using calcium nitrate and potassium nitrate.

Environmental Factors

Temperature: Work with *P. virginiana* 'Alba' demonstrated that cold is not necessary to break dormancy of the rhizome. However, the cold normally associated with winter temperatures seems to synchronize flower development (3). Plants given a 12-week cold treatment were taller than those provided with 6 weeks of cold (3).

Photoperiod: *Physostegia* is a long day plant, the critical daylength lying between 12 and 16 hours (2,3). If provided with LD, plants flowered regardless of presence or absence of a cold treatment. However, when plants were provided with 12 weeks at 40F, 80% flowered. This shows that cold can substitute for the LD, an occurrence not uncommon in LD plants. The critical photoperiod is probably shorter for 'Alba' than 'Bouquet Rose'. 'Alba' flowers in late June and July in north Georgia, while 'Bouquet Rose' does not flower until late August and continues through mid-September.

Field Performance

Longevity: Obedient plant is long-lived and may be expected to produce well for 3–5 years. However, plants become very dense after 2–3 years of production and should then be divided and rejuvenated.

Yield and stem quality of *Physostegia virginiana* 'Alba' over time (spacing 1' × 1').

Year	Stems/plant	Stem length (in)	Stem diameter (mm)
1	13	29.4	7.5
2	26	30.9	7.5
3	14	29.0	6.7

Yield was significantly reduced in the third year for 'Alba', but not with 'Bouquet Rose'.

Yield and stem quality of *Physostegia virginiana* 'Bouquet Rose' over time.

Year	Stems/plant	Stem length (in)	Stem diameter (mm)
1	12	40.2	8.6
2	24	63.6	8.9
3	30	76.2	9.0

Stem lengths are considerably longer with 'Bouquet Rose' than 'Alba' at the same spacing.

The effect of cultivar on stem length (spacing 2' × 2').

Cultivar	Stem length (in)	Stem length (%)		
		<2 ft	2–3 ft	>3 ft
'Alba'	30.9	11.6	54.1	34.3
'Bouquet Rose'	63.6	0.4	1.9	97.7

Additional details on stem distribution of 'Bouquet Rose' are shown in the following table.

Stem length of *Physostegia virginiana* 'Bouquet Rose' (spacing 2' × 2').

Stem length (in)	Stem length (%)		
	3–5 ft	5–6.5 ft	>6.5 ft
63.6	35.1	61.6	3.3

In Watsonville, CA, trials of various cultivars of *P. virginiana* were conducted; the results follow. In general, yield and stem length were excellent, but less so in California than in Georgia. That is a change!

Yield and stem quality of *Physostegia virginiana* (Watsonville, CA).

Cultivar	Year	Stems/plant	Stem length (in)
'Bouquet Rose'	1	17	33
	2	25	54
'Summer Snow'	1	10	22
	2	16	46
'Summer Spire'	1	18	27
	2	20	52

Spacing: Plants may be spaced 1' × 1', but because plants fill in rapidly, yield declines after 3 years. Spacing at 18–24" centers is best for tall cultivars such as 'Bouquet Rose' and 'Summer Snow', but 'Alba' may be planted on 12" centers to increase yield/ft^2.

The effect of spacing on yield and stem quality of *Physostegia virginiana* 'Alba' (second season in production).

Spacing (in)	Stems/plant	Stems/ft^2	Stem length (in)
12	26	26	37.4
24	43	10	35.6
36	50	6	33.9

The distribution of stem lengths due to spacing was also affected; spacing plants greater than 2' apart resulted in fewer long stems.

The effect of spacing on stem length of *Physostegia virginiana* 'Alba'.

Spacing (in)	Stem length (%)		
	<2 ft	2–3 ft	>3 ft
12	5	54	41
24	12	54	34
36	18	69	13

Greenhouse Performance

Rhizomes should be provided with 6 weeks at 40F in order to provide more uniform flowering. Cold is not necessary if uniformity is of little importance. Space rhizomes in 6–8" pots or a 9" × 12" spacing in greenhouse beds. Provide 16-hour LD and 60F average temperature once cooled rhizomes are in the greenhouse. Under New York conditions, flowering will begin approximately 12 weeks later (3). Work conducted in the winter in Finland showed that 16 weeks was required (6).

Guideline for Foliar Analyses

At field trials in Athens, GA, foliage was sampled from vigorously growing healthy plants when flower buds were visible, but prior to flower opening. These are guidelines only and should not be considered absolute standards. Based on dry weight analysis.

(%)						(ppm)				
N	P	K	Ca	Mg		Fe	Mn	B	Al	Zn
					'Alba'					
2.72	0.32	1.25	1.00	0.37		242	66	27	50	198

Stage of Harvest

Flowers may be cut when the spikes are fully elongated but before individual flowers are open, although allowing 3–4 flowers to open does not reduce shelf life significantly. Harvesting when more basal flowers are already declining reduces shelf life by 3–4 days. Pink flowers have better shelf life than white flowers because the white flowers turn brown as they decline and become unsightly. Pink flowers abscise in the same manner but the browning is significantly less visible.

Postharvest

Fresh: Stems should be immediately plunged in preservative in the field to increase longevity. Place stems in cooler (40F) as soon as possible. The use of pulses of silver thiosulfate (STS) and 5% sucrose reduces shattering significantly. Too much STS (>2 mM) results in browning of petals and leaf margins. Flowers persist approximately 6 days without preservative or STS treatment, but with proper treatment (STS, preservative, sugar) vase life of 14 days is realistic. Work with *P. purpurea* showed that flowers stored dry for 1 week at 32F and treated with preservative and STS persisted for 8 days compared with a 4-day vase life when stems were not treated once removed from cold storage (4). The same study showed that if flowers were held dry at relatively warm temperatures (72F), vase life was not subsequently affected unless flowers remained warm and dry for up to 8 hours. However, even though stems appear relatively resilient, they should go into preservative as soon as possible.

Dried: Flowers do not dry well.

Cultivars

'Alba' (var. *alba*) has milky white flowers on 2' stems. Flowers are produced 4–6 weeks earlier than pink cultivars.

'Bouquet Rose' ('Rose Bouquet') has rose-pink flowers on 3–5' stems.

var. *rosea* flowers a little earlier than 'Bouquet Rose' and bears rose-pink flowers on 3' stems.

'Summer Snow' is the most popular white-flowered form with 3–4' tall, white spikes in early to late summer. Flowers appear about the same time as pink cultivars and are taller than var. *alba*.

'Summer Spire' has pink-red flowers on 3–3.5' tall stems.

'Vivid' is the most popular garden form with compact stems and vivid purple flowers. The stems are only 12–15" tall and are more difficult to market because of short stems.

Additional Species

Physostegia purpurea, which bears purple-magenta flowers, is native to the southwestern United States but has become naturalized across the southern states. It may have potential because of its relatively early flowering. In South Carolina, flowers are harvested in late April and May. Combining *P. purpurea* and *P. virginiana* allows for a longer harvest of flowers. No other species are used for cut flower production.

Pests and Diseases

Crown rot (*Pellicularia rolfsii* and *Sclerotinia* spp.) invades through roots or lower stem wounds and causes rapid wilting. Sterilizing soil prior to planting offers the best control.

Reading

1. Armitage, A. M. 1989. *Herbaceous Perennial Plants: A Treatise on Their Identification, Culture, and Garden Attributes*. Varsity Press, Athens, Ga.

2. Cantino, P. D. 1982. A monograph of the genus *Physostegia* (Labiatae). *Contributions From the Gray Herbarium* 211:1–105.

3. Iversen, R. R. 1989. *Greenhouse Forcing of Herbaceous Garden Perennials*. Ph.D. Dissertation, Cornell Univ., Ithaca, NY.

4. Kelly, J. W., and T. W. Starman. 1990. Postharvest handling of *Physostegia purpurea* cut flowers. *HortScience* 25:552–553.

5. Kieft, C. 1989. *Kieft's Growing Manual* .... Kieft Bloemzaden, Venhuizen, The Netherlands.

6. Sarkka, L. 1991. Wintertime production of *Achillea* and *Physostegia* with supplemental lighting and supplemental CO_2 enrichment. Abstract presented at 2nd International Symposium on Development of New Floricultural Crops, 17–21 September 1991, Baltimore, MD.

Many thanks to Dr. John Kelly for reviewing this section.

Platycodon grandiflorus

Platycodon grandiflorus		Balloonflower	2.5–3'/2'
Blue	China, Japan	Campanulaceae	Zones 3–8

Balloonflower has become more popular as a cut flower in recent years. The bulging flower buds and lovely blue flowers provide unique, long-lasting flowers.

Propagation
Division: Plants have long taproots. The crown may be divided as long as sufficient root is taken with the crown section. If replanted immediately, few problems occur. Division may be accomplished in the spring after the foliage has emerged. Do not divide more than once every 3 years.

Seed: Some excellent cultivars are available and seed propagation is a reliable means of increasing stock. Seed, sown in plugs or trays and placed at approximately 70F, germinates in 10–20 days. Approximately 1/10 oz of seed yields 1000 seedlings (2).

Growing-on
Three to five weeks are needed to transplant to final container, depending on whether seedlings are in open trays or plugs. Approximately 10 weeks between sowing and the time plants will be ready to place in the field are recommended (3), although plants may be planted out earlier. Plant to the field in the fall.

Environmental Factors
Temperature: *Platycodon* requires a cold treatment to break crown dormancy (1). At least 6 weeks at 40F are necessary but 12 weeks result in more rapid flowering. Plants tolerate outdoor temperatures as far south as north Florida and north to New England.

Photoperiod: Plants are day-neutral and flower approximately the same time regardless of photoperiod (1).

Field Performance
Spacing: Space long taproots 12–18" apart. Plants will form large clumps within 3 years.

Yield: Approximately 5 flower stems are formed after the first winter, up to 15 stems on mature, well-developed specimens. Flowering occurs in mid to late summer and continues for about 4 weeks.

Longevity: Plants are long-lived and should remain productive for at least 5 years.

Support: Stems of the species and other tall cultivars require support. This is a necessity in the South and recommended in the North.

Greenhouse Performance

Plant 1-year-old, bare roots in ground beds (12" centers) or in deep, 6–7" pots. Provide 6 weeks of 40F cold treatment, making sure that the medium remains moist. The cold treatment may be given in an unheated greenhouse, cold frame or preferably in cold storage chambers. After 6 weeks, plants should be placed in 60F houses. Stem emergence will occur in about 4 weeks (1). (*Platycodon* is notoriously slow to emerge in the field or greenhouse; don't give up too early.) An additional 9 weeks are necessary for flowering. Natural photoperiod is sufficient. Approximately 30 days are necessary between visible flower bud and open flower (1).

Stage of Harvest

Harvest when 2–3 flowers are open on the flower stem (3).

Postharvest

Fresh: Flowers persist 5–7 days in preservative.

Cultivars

var. *albus* ('Albus') has white flowers with yellow veins on 3' tall stems.

'Double Blue' bears deep blue, double flowers on 2' tall plants.

Florists series is available in dark blue, pink and white and has been developed for the specialty cut flower trade.

Fuji series is a seed-propagated strain bred for cut flowers. Flowers are available in pink, white and blue. Plants grow 2–3' tall.

'Hakone Blue' is a tall, double-flowered form also available from seed.

'Komachi' is a flowerless flower. The buds swell but never open. It is interesting enough to have found a following, but don't bet the farm on it. A white form is also available and likely other cultivars with similar flower habit will be developed.

'Shell Pink' may be grown from seed and bears shell-pink flowers on 2–2.5' tall stems.

Pests and Diseases

Few pests affect this plant; enjoy it.

Reading

1. Iversen, R. R. 1989. *Greenhouse Forcing of Herbaceous Garden Perennials.* Ph.D. Thesis, Cornell Univ., Ithaca, NY.

2. Kieft, C. 1989. *Kieft's Growing Manual* .... Kieft Bloemzaden, Venhuizen, The Netherlands.

3. Nowak, J., and R. M. Rudnicki. 1990. *Postharvest Handling and Storage of Cut Flowers, Florist Greens, and Potted Plants.* Timber Press, Portland, OR.

Scabiosa caucasica		Perennial Scabious	2–2.5'/2'
Blue, white	Caucasus	Dipsacaceae	Zones 3–7

A number of species are useful for cut flowers; however, *S. caucasica* is the only perennial species. Flowers of the annual *S. atropurpurea* (pincushion flower) are also useful and discussed in the section on annuals.

Propagation

Seed: Seed sown at 65–70F under intermittent mist or sweat tents germinates in 10–18 days. Approximately 2 oz of seed yield 1000 seedlings (1).

Division: Plants may be divided after 2–3 years in the field.

Growing-on

Plants may be transplanted 3–4 weeks after sowing and should be grown at 55–58F until ready to transplant to the field. Fertilize with 75–100 ppm N for the first 2 weeks then raise to 125 ppm N with a complete fertilizer. Transplant prior to flowering, approximately 10–12 weeks from sowing. Plants which have been divided may be moved immediately to 4" pots for 2–3 weeks prior to planting in the field.

Environmental Factors

Temperature: *Scabiosa caucasica* appears to have a critical temperature and photoperiod for flowering. Under winter and SD conditions, stem elongation does not occur over 65F (4). Apparently, *S. caucasica* requires some cooling at temperatures below 40–45F whereas the annual, *S. atropurpurea*, does not (see annual section).

Photoperiod: Flowering occurs more rapidly under LD. Larger plants are more responsive to LD treatments than seedlings.

Field Performance

Plants produce more flowers of higher quality in areas of cool summers and cold winters. Quality of the cut flowers decline south of zone 7, although precooled plants may be used for winter production in Florida.

Spacing: Space plants 18" × 18" or 12" × 12". Spacing as wide as 2' centers has also been used. In Burlington, VT, 13 stems/plant were harvested from 2-year-old plants of *S. caucasica* 'Fama' spaced 2' apart. The approximate stem length was 27" (2).

Longevity: Plants are productive for 3–4 years, but 2–3 years are normal.

Shading : Not necessary.

Forcing: Field plants covered with clear single plastic were forced earlier than uncovered plants. Night temperatures were 40-43F (3).

Greenhouse Performance

Plants forced for winter production should be sown in July and August and grown under SD at 50–55F for 4–6 weeks. Long days (>14 hours), by day extension or nightbreak lighting with 4 hours of incandescent lights, should then be provided. Flowering occurs 8–12 weeks after the beginning of

Scabiosa caucasica

LD treatment. Night temperatures below 55F must be maintained; otherwise, weak stems result.

Guideline for Foliar Analyses

At field trials in Watsonville, CA, foliage was sampled from vigorously growing healthy plants when flower buds were visible, but prior to flower opening. These are guidelines only and should not be considered absolute standards. Based on dry weight analysis.

(%)						(ppm)				
N	P	K	Ca	Mg		Fe	Mn	B	Al	Zn
					'Fama'					
2.81	0.22	2.11	0.20	0.36		400	116	27	332	19

Stage of Harvest

Flowers may be harvested as soon as flower color is visible.

Postharvest

Fresh: Fresh flowers remain viable for 5–8 days.
Storage: Flowers may be held wet at 36–41F.
Dried: Flowers do not dry well.

Cultivars

'Blue Perfection' has fringed, lavender-blue flowers and stands 2' tall.

'Bressingham White' has larger white flowers than 'Miss Wilmott' and is an excellent cultivar.

'Clive Greaves' has light blue flowers on 2–2.5' tall stems.

'Compliment' ('Kompliment') is 20–24" tall with dark lavender flowers.

'Fama' bears large, lavender-blue flowers with silver centers. Plants are approximately 2' tall.

'House's Hybrids' are a mixture of blue and white shades.

'Miss Willmott' is a white cultivar on 2–2.5' stems.

'Perfecta' has lavender-blue flowers on 2–3' tall stems.

'Perfecta Alba' has white flowers.

'Pink Mist' produces double, pink flowers on 2' stems.

'Stäfa' bears dark blue flowers on 2–2.5' tall stems.

Additional Species

Scabiosa ochroleuca (cream scabious) has creamy yellow flowers and makes a good, although short-lived, species for cut flower production. Under proper conditions, plants grow 6' tall. This is also known as *S. columbaria* var. *ochroleuca*.

Pests and Diseases

Powdery mildew (*Erysiphe polygoni*), root rot (*Phymatotrichum omnivorum*) and stem rot (*Sclerotinium sclerotiorum*) are fungal diseases which infect scabious. Fungal sprays and sterilized soils offer some protection.

Beet curly top virus results in foliar deformation. Dispose of plants at first sign of infection.

Reading

1. Kieft, C. 1989. *Kieft's Growing Manual* .... Kieft Bloemzaden, Venhuizen, The Netherlands.

2. Perry, L. P. 1989. Perennial cut flowers. In *Proceedings of 2nd National Conference on Specialty Cut Flowers*. Athens, GA. 155–162.

3. Plomacher, H. 1980. Plants grown under plastic for cutting: *Scabiosa caucasica*. *Zierpflanzenbau* 80:17.

4. Post, K. 1955. *Florist Crop Production and Marketing*. Orange Judd, New York, NY.

Solidago hybrids

Solidago hybrids	Goldenrod		2–3'/3'
Yellow	North America	Asteraceae	Zones 3–8

To refer to *Solidago* as a useful plant 5 years ago would bring chuckles at best, or outright derision. However, goldenrod is a handsome cut flower, exhibiting ease of culture and excellent vase life. Market resistance to goldenrod is declining, albeit slowly, and sales potential is strengthening. New cultivars with different colors and more compact growth habit are most helpful. A major drawback to goldenrod production, however, is its susceptibility to rust.

Propagation

Seed: Seed of numerous taxa (not hybrids) may be sown at 68–72F and germinates in 2–3 weeks. Seed is small and approximately 1/50 oz of seed yields 1000 seedlings, depending on species (2).

Cuttings: Terminal cuttings may be rooted at any time but preferably prior to flower initiation.

Division: Field-grown plants may be divided after 2–3 years.

Growing-on

Grow seedlings at 50–60F with 100 ppm N using a complete fertilizer. Plants should be grown in LD (>14 hours). Divisions may be placed in 4" pots and grown for 2–3 weeks under LD prior to planting out. Plants may be field-planted when green in the fall or early spring.

Environmental Factors

Temperature: No cool treatment is necessary for flowering.

Photoperiod: *Solidago canadensis* (canadian goldenrod), one of the parents of the hybrids, is a SD plant for flower initiation but also responds to SD by becoming dormant (5). Flowers initiate when plants are provided with 14 hours of light but remain vegetative under 16-hour photoperiods. Twelve-hour photoperiods result in poorly developed inflorescences. Very short photoperiods (8 hours) result in flower abortion and dormancy. Thus, in the field in the annual cycle of changing daylengths, vegetative growth and shoot elongation are promoted by LD; then as days shorten in late summer, flowering occurs; and finally as autumnal equinox is approached and passed, dormancy ensues (5). Plants grow taller under LD and application of SD inhibits stem extension.

Field Performance

Spacing: Grow plants on a 12" × 12" or 12" × 18" spacing.

Longevity: To maintain quality, crop should be replanted every 2–3 years.

Pinching: Not necessary the first year but recommended in successive years.

Support: Not necessary the first year but recommended for taller cultivars in subsequent years.

Yield: Three years' data are shown in the following table.

Yield and stem quality of *Solidago* over time (Athens, GA, and Watsonville, CA).

Location	Year	Stems/plant	Stem length (in)	Stem diameter (mm)
		'Strahlenkrone'		
Athens, GA	1	7	17.5	4.7
Watsonville, CA	1	5	27.0	5.0
Athens, GA	2	44	19.6	4.5
Watsonville, CA	2	—[a]	—	—
Athens, GA	3	17	20.3	4.3
Watsonville, CA	3	—	—	—
		'Super'		
Athens, GA	1	5	18.0	4.5
Watsonville, CA	1	10	33.0	5.0
Athens, GA	2[b]			
Watsonville, CA	2	18	35.0	5.0

[a] Dash (—) indicates that data are not available.
[b] Plants died over the winter of a rust infection.

Shading: Shading results in higher incidence of disease, lower yield and no benefit to stem length or diameter. Second-year data with 'Strahlenkrone' showed that shade resulted in 22 stems/plant (44 in sun), stem length of 16.9" (19.6" in sun) and no difference in stem diameter. Obviously shade is not recommended.

Greenhouse Performance

Flowers can be forced in the winter and spring by manipulating temperature and photoperiod lighting. Cuttings should be planted at 12" × 12", grown at 65F and fertilized with 100 ppm N. Long days (>16 hours) should be applied to extend stem length and delay flowering. Plants may be pinched when new growth occurs. When new shoots are approximately 18" long, photoperiod should be shortened to 12–14 hours to initiate flowers. Crop time is 10–16 weeks from planting of cuttings, depending on temperature and cultivar. Crowns, dug from outside in February through April, will flower in May and June in a 65–70F greenhouse.

Guideline for Foliar Analyses

At field trials in Athens, GA, and Watsonville, CA, foliage was sampled from vigorously growing healthy plants when flower buds were visible, but prior to flower opening. These are guidelines only and should not be considered absolute standards. Based on dry weight analysis.

(%)						(ppm)				
N	P	K	Ca	Mg		Fe	Mn	B	Al	Zn
				'Strahlenkrone' (GA)						
3.6	0.46	3.82	0.87	0.30		202	115	24	43	68
				'Super' (CA)						
2.7	0.27	4.71	1.23	0.43		200	282	30	43	25

Although nitrogen and phosphorus were relatively low for 'Super' in California trials, the resulting stems were of excellent quality.

Stage of Harvest

Harvest inflorescence when approximately ½ the flowers are open (3).

Postharvest

Fresh: Flowers persist 7–10 days in water.
Storage: Flowers may be stored dry for up to 5 days at 36–41F (6).
Dried: Cut when flowers are fully open, then dry standing up (1).

Cultivars

'Baby Gold' is used more as a garden plant than a cut flower because it is more dwarf than other available cultivars. However, the flower color is excellent and the flowers hold up well. Research in Burlington, VT, on 2-year-old plants showed 21 stems/plant (spacing 2' × 2') with an approximate stem length of 24" (4).

'Praecox' bears bright yellow flowers and is a selection of *S. virgaurea* that flowers in early summer and fall. This is a popular cultivar in Europe.

'Strahlenkrone' is an exceptional yellow cultivar and grows about 2–2.5' tall.

'Super' has lemon-yellow flowers on 2–3' tall stems. Though one of the most handsome goldenrods I have seen, it is unfortunately highly susceptible to rust and doesn't do well with poor drainage. Losses in our trials were close to 100%.

'Tara' has medium yellow flowers and robust habit.

'Yellow Submarine' may be a hybrid between *Solidago* and × *Solidaster*. The flowers are deep yellow and the vigorous plants grow 2–3' tall. They have been one of the best performers in the trials at Georgia.

Additional Species

Solidago caesia (wreath goldenrod) has dark yellow flowers atop 3' tall, bluish, wiry stems. Flowers occur in the fall and may be used to extend flowering time of *Solidago*. It is an unusual goldenrod and may find a niche in the cut flower market.

S. odora (sweet goldenrod) has yellow flowers on 3' tall stems. The benefit of this species is in the fragrance of the foliage, which smells like anise when crushed.

Pests and Diseases

Powdery mildew caused by *Erysiphe polygoni* results in white fungi on the undersides of the leaves and the stems.

Rust, caused by *Coleosporium asterum*, is the most serious disease of goldenrod. Rust-colored pustules cover the foliage and stems in late summer. Because pine trees act as an intermediate host, plant *Solidago* well away from stands of pine trees. No effective control is known, although spraying with zinc-based fungicides appears to provide some control.

Reading

1. Bullivant, E. 1989. *Dried Fresh Flowers From Your Garden.* Pelham Books/Stephen Greene Press, London, U.K.

2. Kieft, C. 1989. *Kieft's Growing Manual* .... Kieft Bloemzaden, Venhuizen, The Netherlands.

3. Nowak, J., and R. M. Rudnicki. 1990. *Postharvest Handling and Storage of Cut Flowers, Florist Greens, and Potted Plants.* Timber Press, Portland, OR.

4. Perry, L. 1989. Perennial cut flowers. In *Proceedings of 2nd National Conference on Specialty Cut Flowers.* Athens, GA. 155–162.

5. Schwabe, W. W. 1986. *Solidago.* In A. H. Halevy (ed.), *The Handbook of Flowering,* vol. 5. CRC Press, Boca Raton, FL. 338–340.

6. Vaughan, M. J. 1989. *The Complete Book of Cut Flower Care.* Timber Press, Portland, OR.

× *Solidaster luteus*

| | | Solidaster | 2–2.5'/2' |
| Yellow | Hybrid origin | Asteraceae | Zones 4–8 |

× *Solidaster* (the × refers to an intergeneric cross and is silent) is an intergeneric cross between a goldenrod and aster. Flowers are light yellow to lemon-yellow and have excellent vase life. Rust is still a serious problem.

Propagation

Plants must be vegetatively propagated, generally from terminal cuttings or division.

Growing-on

Grow cuttings at 60–65F under long day conditions (>15 hours) until large enough to plant out in the field or greenhouse. Fertilize with 75–100 ppm N of a complete fertilizer.

Environmental Factors

Photoperiod: Plants appear to initiate faster with short days (13–14 hours). Long days (>16 hours) result in stem extension.

Temperature: Cold temperatures do not appear to be necessary for flowering.

Field Performance

Spacing: Plant 12" × 12" or 12" × 18" apart.

Support: Use 1–2 layers of support netting.

Pinching: Pinch plants at least once in early spring.

Longevity: Replace plants after 3 years of production, depending on disease severity.

Shading: No shade is recommended.

Yield: Three years' data are shown in the following table.

Yield and stem quality of × *Solidaster* over time (Athens, GA, and Watsonville, CA).

Location	Stems/plant	Stem length (in)	Stem diameter (mm)
Year 1			
Athens, GA	5	16.9	4.4
Watsonville, CA	5	25.0	5.0
Year 2			
Athens, GA	7	19.4	4.0
Watsonville, CA	9	37.0	4.5
Year 3			
Athens, GA	17	27.6	4.2

Greenhouse Performance

Space cuttings 12" × 12" or 9" × 12" in ground beds or in 6–10" pots. Place under long days (>16 hours) and pinch when plants are 6–8" tall. Provide SD (13–14 hours) when stems are approximately 18" tall. Plants may be flowered year-round by manipulating photoperiod. Fertilize with 150–200 ppm N approximately twice a week.

Stage of Harvest

Harvest when ⅓ of the flowers are open.

Postharvest

Fresh: Stems persist 7–10 days in water, 3–4 days longer in preservative.
Storage: Stems can be held for 5–6 days out of water at 36–41F.
Dried: Harvest in full flower; flowers may be air-dried standing up.

Cultivars

'Lemore' is sometimes listed as a cultivar of × *Solidaster*. Plants have yellow flowers and are about 2' tall. It is often sold as a cultivar of *Solidago*.

Pests and Diseases

A hybrid of *Solidago* and *Aster*, × *Solidaster* is susceptible to their numerous diseases. See *Solidago* and *Aster*.

Rust remains the most serious threat and can result in total loss of the crop.

Thalictrum delavayi   Yunnan Meadow-rue   3–6'/3'
White, mauve   Western China   Ranunculaceae   Zones 3–7

Plants, also known as *T. dipterocarpum,* bear small but delicate flowers that are useful as fillers and may be substituted for baby's breath. The best cultivar is 'Hewitt's Double' whose flowers consist of lilac sepals and creamy yellow stamens produced in a 2–3' long inflorescence (panicle).

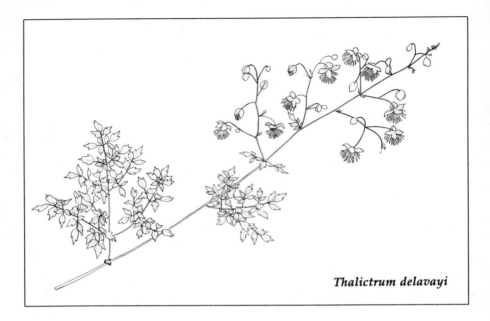

Thalictrum delavayi

Propagation

Seed: Sow thinly on fine medium at 60–65F; seed normally germinates within 2–3 weeks. If germination does not occur in 3 weeks, place the seed flat at 40F for 2–4 weeks. Approximately 1/5 oz of seed yields 1000 seedlings (2).

Division: Plants may be divided every 3–4 years.

Growing-on

Transplant seedlings when they are large enough to handle. Divisions and seedlings should be grown at 50F for 6–8 weeks before placing in the field. Fertilize with 100 ppm N using a complete fertilizer. Larger divisions may be planted immediately in the field.

Field Performance

Limited data are available on field performance; however, nylon or wire mesh must be used to separate the flowers from each other. They otherwise become terribly entangled, and damage occurs to flowers and to those trying to extricate them. Spacing should be no closer than 18" × 18".

Stage of Harvesting

Flowers should be harvested when most of the flowers are open. Unopened flowers do not develop well if cut in bud stage.

Postharvest

Fresh: Flowers persist for approximately 1 week in preservative.

Storage: Store at 36–41F for up to 1 week (3); however, storage is not recommended.

Dried: Harvest in full flower, strip foliage and dry standing up to maintain shape (1). Flowers retain their color for only a few months but they are useful fillers for large arrangements. Stems may also be hung upside down to dry (1).

Cultivars
'Album' bears white flowers.

'Hewitt's Double' is the best cultivar for cut flowers. Its double flowers are less likely to shatter, and ship better than the species.

Additional Species
Thalictrum aquilegifolium (columbine meadow-rue) has fuller flowers and occurs in purple and white. Plants are summer-hardy to zone 7 but winter-hardy to zone 4. It is an excellent species for the South. 'White Cloud' is an exceptional white-flowering cultivar.

Reading
1. Bullivant, E. 1989. *Dried Fresh Flowers From Your Garden.* Pelham Books/Stephen Greene Press, London, U.K.

2. Kieft, C. 1989. *Kieft's Growing Manual* .... Kieft Bloemzaden, Venhuizen, The Netherlands.

3. Vaughan, M. J. 1989. *The Complete Book of Cut Flower Care.* Timber Press, Portland, OR.

Veronica longifolia

Veronica longifolia	Long-leaf Veronica		2–3'/2'
Blue	Europe, Asia	Scrophulariaceae	Zones 4–8

Numerous *Veronica* species are available from perennial plant growers but *V. longifolia* is most suitable for the cut flower trade. Plants are robust, relatively winter-hardy and tolerate warm summers well. The main problem as a cut flower is that flowers on the bottom of the inflorescence decline before the top flowers are open. The stage of harvest and postharvest procedures become particularly important with this plant.

Propagation
Most cultivars are propagated by division or terminal cuttings. However, the species and a few cultivars may be seed-propagated. The small seed should be lightly covered and placed at 68–72F. Germination occurs in 2–3 weeks. Approximately 1/50 oz of seed yields 1000 seedlings (1).

Growing-on
If small propagules are received or seedlings are being grown prior to planting in the field, initially place at 58–65F and lower the temperature 2–4F after 2–3 weeks of growth. Fertilize sparingly (75–100 ppm N once a week) until plants are sufficiently large to plant to the field.

Environmental Factors

Temperature: Little is known about the effects of cooling. However, for some cultivars, cooling is not necessary as shown by flowering the first year from seed. Yields of field plants, however, are lower in first-year plants (after 1 winter) than in 2-year-old plants. This is probably due to maturing of plants more than cooling. While plants tolerate hot summer temperatures, they also perform well in the Northeast and the West.

Photoperiod: Plants begin flowering naturally in late spring in the South, early summer in the North and flower sporadically through the summer months. Photoperiod appears to be of little importance, but LD may play a role in forcing greenhouse plants.

Field Performance

Spacing: Space plants on 12″ centers or 12–18″ apart.

Yield: Field studies at Georgia on *V. longifolia* 'Schneeriesen', an excellent white-flowered cultivar, are shown in the following table.

Yield and stem quality of *Veronica longifolia* 'Schneeriesen' over time (spacing 15″ × 15″; Athens, GA).

Year	Shade level (%)	Stems/plant	Stem length (in)	Stem diameter (mm)
1	0	50	16.8	3.0
2	0	84	21.4	3.3
2	55	26	30.0	3.9
3	0	30	28.7	5.0

Second-year yield of a blue-flowered cultivar, 'Blauriesen', was 31 stems/plant with an average stem length of 20″.

Shading: The preceding table demonstrates why shade cannot be recommended. Although stem length and diameter benefitted from the presence of 55% shade cloth, yield was much reduced. One of the reasons for the large difference in yield between sun and shade was because of the longer harvest time for plants in full sun. Those in shade were harvested from May 14 to July 3, whereas those in full sun were harvested well into October. If the additional late summer harvests were not counted, then full sun plants yielded 40 stems/plant in the same time as shade plants produced 26 stems.

Greenhouse Performance

No relevant information concerning the forcing of *Veronica* exists but placing plants under 16–18 hours may accelerate flowering. Long photoperiods may be accomplished with 60 watt incandescent lamps at 20–50 fc. Temperatures of 60/70F night/day are sufficient, although lower temperatures (50–55F) may be used. This is similar to schedules for other summer-blooming perennials and may be pertinent for *Veronica*.

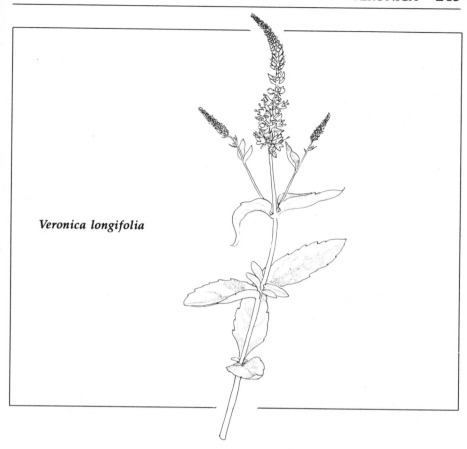

Veronica longifolia

Guideline for Foliar Analyses

At field trials in Athens, GA, foliage was sampled from vigorously growing healthy plants when flower buds were visible, but prior to flower opening. These are guidelines only and should not be considered absolute standards. Based on dry weight analysis.

(%)						(ppm)				
N	P	K	Ca	Mg		Fe	Mn	B	Al	Zn
'Schneeriesen'										
2.9	0.35	1.20	0.58	0.23		82	30	11	30	57

Stage of Harvest

Harvest when approximately ½ the flowers on the inflorescence are open (2). Place immediately in preservative in the field. The inflorescences decline rapidly if too many flowers are already open. Store at 36–41F and keep away from fresh fruit or senescing flowers as *Veronica* is ethylene-sensitive.

Postharvest

Fresh: If plants are harvested at the proper stage of development, they persist for approximately 7 days. Recut the stems prior to shipping and again upon receipt by buyer. They do not ship exceptionally well and may be best grown for the local market.

Storage: Storage is not recommended, but stems may be kept at 36–41F if necessary (3).

Dried: Flowers do not dry well.

Cultivars

'Blauriesen' bears lavender-blue flowers on 2–2.5' tall stems. There is little difference between this and 'Foerster's Blue'; some authorities consider them synonymous.

'Foerster's Blue' is approximately 2' tall and bears deep blue to lavender-blue flowers.

'Schneeriesen' is a wonderful plant for both garden and cut flower use. Flowers are fairly clean. All white forms, however, appear to decline more rapidly than the blue-flowered forms; senescence is more visible on a white inflorescence than on a blue inflorescence. Both 'Schneeriesen' and 'Blauriesen' are available from seed. They flower the first year and have performed exceptionally well.

Additional Species

Veronica spicata is somewhat useful, but generally plants are too short and compact for use as cut flowers. 'Sightseeing' is a seed-propagated mix of white, pink and blue flowers on 18–24" long stems and may be useful as a cut flower.

V. subsessilis, sometimes sold as *V. longifolia* var. *subsessilis*, is an excellent form for cut flowers. Plants are 2–3' tall and bear lilac-blue flowers.

V. virginica (culver's root) is properly known as *Veronicastrum virginicum*, and is discussed under that name.

Pests and Diseases

Leaf spots can result in ragged-looking leaves. They are caused by *Septoria veronicae* as well as other fungi and may be controlled by fungicidal sprays. Start the spray program in early June and continue once every 3 weeks with a general fungicide. Aphids and thrips are the major pests of *Veronica*.

Reading

1. Kieft, C. 1989. *Kieft's Growing Manual* .... Kieft Bloemzaden, Venhuizen, The Netherlands.

2. Nowak, J., and R. M. Rudnicki. 1990. *Postharvest Handling and Storage of Cut Flowers, Florist Greens, and Potted Plants*. Timber Press, Portland, OR.

3. Vaughan, M. J. 1989. *The Complete Book of Cut Flower Care*. Timber Press, Portland, OR.

| *Veronicastrum virginicum* | | Culver's Root | 3–4'/2' |
| White | Eastern United States | Scrophulariaceae | Zones 3–8 |

Often referred to as *Veronica virginica,* culver's root is closely related to *Veronica.* Flowers of the species are light blue but the white-flowered var. *album,* is the best form for cut flowers.

Propagation

Seed: Seed may be germinated in 2–3 weeks if placed at 65–70F under mist. Approximately 0.02 oz of seed yields 1000 seedlings (1).

Division: Divide plants after 2–3 years.

Cuttings: Terminal cuttings (2–3" long) should be taken in early summer or fall. Roots form in 2–3 weeks.

Growing-on

Grow plants in cell packs or 4" pots at 55–65F. Fertilize with 75–100 ppm N using potassium nitrate or calcium nitrate. Plant in the field in early fall or early spring.

Environmental Factors

No photoperiod responses have been shown with *Veronicastrum.* Plants have to attain a certain leaf area or maturity prior to flowering. Plants tolerate warm temperatures, but stem strength is better in areas where summer nights fall below 70F.

Field Performance

Spacing: 12" × 18" or 12" × 12". Flowers branch considerably, particularly near the top of the flowering stem, and a high-density spacing (<12") results in flowers chafing against each other, resulting in some damage.

Pinching: Pinching out the center flower results in the lateral breaks flushing at the same time. The resulting inflorescence is more handsome and eye-catching than stems in which the center flower is not removed.

Longevity: Plants persist at least 3 years. Approximately ⅓ of the crop should be planted and replaced each year.

Support: Not necessary in cool areas but useful in the Midwest and South after the first year.

Yield: Limited data are available but the following table provides the results of trials in Georgia and California.

Yield and stem quality of *Veronicastrum virginicum* 'Album' over time (Athens, GA, and Watsonville, CA).

Location	Year	Stems/plant	Stem length (in)	Stem diameter (mm)
Athens, GA	1	19	22.7	3.5
Watsonville, CA	1	8	33.0	6.0
Athens, GA	2	43	27.2	5.0
Watsonville, CA	2	11	29.0	9.0
Athens, GA	3	48	40.2	5.5

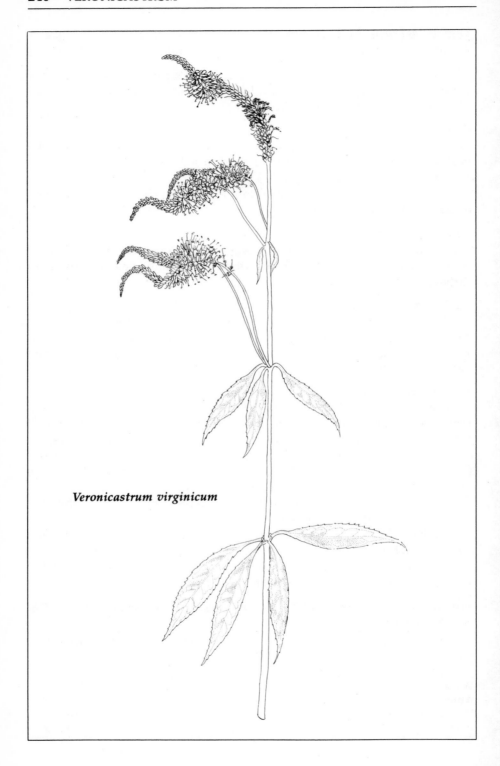

Veronicastrum virginicum

Obvious differences include higher yield in Georgia than California, but stems were stronger, as measured by stem diameter, in California than in Georgia. Stem strength in Georgia, however, was certainly adequate.

Shading: Shading is not recommended. At the University of Georgia, second-year harvests of plants grown in full sun compared with those under 55% shade resulted in longer stems but reduced yield of plants grown under shade.

The effect of shade on yield and stem quality of *Veronicastrum virginicum* 'Album' (Athens, GA).

Year	Shade level (%)	Stems/plant	Stem length (in)	Stem diameter (mm)
1	0	19	22.7	3.3
1	55	6	20.0	2.8
2	0	43	27.2	5.0
2	55	19	32.9	4.5

Stage of Harvest
Stems should be cut when the inflorescence is approximately ⅓ open. This occurs when less than 10 flowers are open. If cut too early, the foliage will decline before all the flowers open. The secondary flowers should be showing color.

Postharvest
Flowers persist for 7–10 days in floral preservative. One of the problems with *Veronicastrum* is the incidence of marginal leaf browning. In work conducted at the University of Georgia, flowers cut at early bud stage persisted for 10 days in Rogard™, a flower preservative, but only 4–5 days in water. Leaf browning was also significantly reduced. Silflor™, a silver-containing product of Floralife Company resulted in approximately 8 days of vase life. The use of sugar solutions (2.5–5%) also helped reduce the incidence of leaf browning.

Cultivars
'Album' (var. *album*) has creamy white flowers and a much-branched inflorescence.

Pests and Diseases
Downy mildew (*Peronospora grisea*) results in pale spots on the top of the foliage. The undersides are covered with a grayish mildew.

Leaf spots (*Septoria veronicae*), small, violet-to-brown, circular spots, occur in varying sizes on the top of the foliage. The spots may run together and result in a scorched appearance. Use a general-purpose fungicide.

Reading
1. Kieft, C. 1989. *Kieft's Growing Manual* .... Kieft Bloemzaden, Venhuizen, The Netherlands.

ADDITIONAL PERENNIAL SPECIES SUITABLE FOR CUT FLOWER PRODUCTION

Numerous perennials may be used as cut flowers but for the most part, little production or postharvest information is available. Gaps in information, however, are being filled in rapidly; as other specialty crops enter the market, pieces of the puzzle are coming together. The following table includes equally valuable additions to the cut flower mix already discussed. Portions of the chart are adapted from Seals (1).

Species	Common name	Exposure[a]	Use[b]
Agapanthus spp.	African lily	Su	F
Anaphalis margaritacea	Pearly everlasting	Su,Ps	D
Aquilegia × *hybrida*	Columbine	Ps	F
Armeria pseudarmeria	Giant sea pink	Su	F,D
Baptisia australis	Blue indigo	Su	F
Carlina acaulis	Silver thistle	Su	F,D
Catananche caerulea	Cupid's dart	Su,Ps	F
Cephalaria gigantea	Giant scabious	Su	F
Chelone obliqua	Turtle-head	Su	F
Chrysanthemum parthenium	Feverfew	Su,Ps	F,D
Chrysanthemum × *superbum*	Shasta daisy	Su	F
Coreopsis grandiflora	Tickseed	Su	F
Digitalis purpurea	Foxglove	Ps	F
Doronicum plantagineum	Leopard's bane	Su	F
Gaillardia × *grandiflora*	Blanket flower	Su	F
Gaura lindheimeri	Gaura	Su	F
Gentiana asclepiadea	Gentian	Su,Ps	F
Helenium autumnale	Autumn sunspray	Su	F,D
Helianthus angustifolius	Swamp sunflower	Su	F,D
Heliopsis helianthoides	Heliopsis	Su	F,D
Heuchera 'Raspberry Ripple'	Tall alum	Su,Ps	F
Iris spuria	Spuria iris	Su	F
Kniphofia uvaria	Red hot poker	Su	F
Lobelia cardinalis	Cardinal flower	Su,Ps	F
Lobelia siphilitica	Giant blue lobelia	Su,Ps	F
Lychnis chalcedonica	Maltese cross	Su,Ps	F
Monarda didyma	Bee balm	Su,Ps	F
Papaver somniferum	Opium poppy	Su	F
Primula vialii	Cone primrose	Ps	F
Rudbeckia 'Goldsturm	Yellow cone flower	Su	F
Salvia patens	Gentian sage	Su	F
Salvia × *superba*	Perennial hybrid sage	Su	F
Sedum 'Autumn Joy'	Stonecrop	Su	F
Sidalcea malviflora	Checkerbloom	Su,Ps	F
Verbascum chaixii	Mullein	Su,Ps	F
Viola odorata	Sweet violet	Ps	F

[a]Su = full sun, Ps = partial shade.
[b]F = fresh flowers, D = dried flowers.

Agapanthus hybrid

Reading

1. Seals, J. 1989. Extra special cut flowers from seed. In *Proceedings of 2nd National Conference on Specialty Cut Flowers*. Athens, GA. 59–80.

Bulbous Species for Cut Flowers

Many species useful for cut flowers are propagated from underground structures such as bulbs, corms, rhizomes and tubers. All are referred to as "bulbous species." Numerous advantages may be cited for growing bulb species, some of which include ease of planting, uniqueness of flower forms and above all, ease of harvesting. Most bulbous species produce 1–2 flower stems (scapes) per bulb the first year, and the leafless flower stems are relatively easy to harvest, compared to annuals and perennials. Bulbous species do not branch a great deal; therefore, they may be planted close together, increasing yield/ft². Many species, although perennials in a garden situation, are replaced every year. This allows mistakes in spacing, cultivar selection, weed control and other problems to be corrected after 1 year, a difficult procedure with perennials. Most importantly, the market is relatively strong for many bulb flowers. Anemones, lilies and liatris are well established while cultural methods for, and cultivars and species of, little-known crops such as ornamental onions, *Triteleia*, *Ornithogalum* and calla lilies are rapidly improving. Also, there is little doubt that as we turn our heads, another half-dozen cultivars of tulips and daffodils lie waiting to be discovered.

Some growers of field crops shy away from bulbous species. For them, the disadvantages of growing bulbous crops outweigh their advantages. The cost of bulbs, while inexpensive when purchased in bulk, are far more costly than seed and often more expensive than cuttings or divisions of vegetatively propagated material. The cost of the initial material necessitates a high return for each stem, not always possible in the reality of the market place. Some species must be grown as annuals and the difficulty of removing all the used bulbs and associated bulblets, offsets and foliage is more than many growers wish to do. The remnants may resprout and act as additional weeds. While soil sterilization is useful, it is not always possible.

However, in the long run, the market dictates the production of any flower. Within this chapter are some handsome species with wonderful potential as cut flowers, in the field or in the greenhouse.

ACIDANTHERA TO ZANTEDESCHIA

In the following listings of bulbous plants, the first line at each entry provides the genus and species, followed by the common name and then the normal height/spread of the mature plant. The second line provides the flower color of the species, the country or region of origin, the botanical family to which the species belongs and finally the climatic zones where the plants may be cultivated. When more than one species in a genus is treated (as with *Allium*), and when suggested readings refer to the genus as a whole, the readings appear at the conclusion of the last species entry.

Acidanthera bicolor	Abysinnian Gladiolus		3–4'/3'
White with purple throat	Ethiopia	Iridaceae	Zones 7–10

Considered by some to be synonymous with *Gladiolus callianthus*, this is an excellent fragrant cut flower with numerous, 3" wide flowers along the scape. Approximately 5 flowers are formed on the spike and open from the bottom to top, as does *Gladiolus*. Although some authorities consider it a species of *Gladiolus*, most bulb catalogues still list it as *Acidanthera*, and there it shall stay. The "bulb" is a small tunicated corm, about ½" wide. Corms are inexpensive and the shelf life is reasonable, if not exceptional. Corms of *Acidanthera* should be handled as an annual in most areas of the country.

Environmental Factors

Photoperiod: Photoperiod likely has an effect on flowering time and LD may be beneficial.

Temperature: Little information has been published on *Acidanthera*, but its close taxonomic relationship with *Gladiolus* and similar flowering patterns suggest a certain sameness. Temperature affects the rate of development and crop timing (see section on *Gladiolus*). *Acidanthera* does not require cold for flowering and temperatures below 40F should be avoided.

Field Performance

Spacing: Space 3–4" apart (up to 16 corms/ft^2).

Longevity: Bulbs should be grown as annuals because yield is reduced significantly after the first year. Although yield is diminished in subsequent years, stem length and diameter are not adversely affected.

Yield and stem quality of *Acidanthera bicolor* 'Muralis' over time (Athens, GA; planted fall, 1985).[a]

Year	Scapes/corm	Stem length (in)	Stem diameter (mm)
1	1.2	28.6	8.0
2	0.6	32.2	7.5
3	0.5	34.4	7.5

[a]Adapted from (1).

If one wishes to replant corms, lift in late fall and overwinter in dry, warm (60–65F) conditions in a well-ventilated area. In zones 7b and south, corms may be left in the ground but, as seen in the preceding table, yield declines each season. Bulbs are sufficiently inexpensive and should be replanted every year.

Planting time: In the North, corms may be field-planted after the last frost date. In the South, corms may be planted in the fall. Plants normally flower in late summer in the South and fall in the North. When corms were planted at different times between November and March, few differences occurred in yield and stem quality.

The effect of planting date on harvest, yield and stem quality of *Acidanthera bicolor* 'Muralis'.[a]

Month of planting	Survival (%)	Flowers/bulb	Initial harvest	Stem length (in)	Stem diameter (mm)
Nov	98	1.2	Jul 2	28.9	8.2
Feb	97	1.3	Jul 2	28.3	8.5
Mar	84	0.8	Jul 11	28.1	7.7

[a]Adapted from (1).

The harvest persisted for approximately 22 days regardless of planting date.

Guideline for Foliar Analyses

At field trials in Athens, GA, foliage was sampled from vigorously growing healthy plants when flower buds were visible, but prior to flower opening. These are guidelines only and should not be considered absolute standards. Based on dry weight analysis.

(%)						(ppm)				
N	P	K	Ca	Mg		Fe	Mn	B	Al	Zn
				'Muralis'						
2.5	0.29	1.54	0.47	0.16		110	32	15	27	50

Calcium deficiency during production results in brittle stems which break when harvested, a disorder known as *topple*.

Stage of Harvest

Harvest when 1–2 flowers are open; other flowers will open in a preservative solution. The earlier the preservative is applied, the longer the vase life.

Postharvest

Fresh: Flowers persist for 5–7 days at room temperature in a commercial preservative. Most commercial preservative solutions are effective and should be used for rehydration of stems.

Storage: Flowers should be stored at 40–45F in an upright position. Flowers may be stored 6–8 days at these temperatures. Lower temperatures result in injury and prevent flower opening. Leaving lights on in the storage area helps to open buds.

Little information has been published on postharvest methods of *Acidanthera*, but since it is so closely related to *Gladiolus*, see "Postharvest" section on *Gladiolus*. Stem tips of *Acidanthera* bend if placed on their sides; they should be maintained upright unless refrigerated throughout the market chain. The problem is not as severe as with gladioli.

Cultivars

'Muralis' has larger flowers and stronger stems than the species.

Pests and Disease

Rust and thrips disfigure the foliage and are common, serious problems. Voles and other rodents can be serious pests. Problems inherent with gladiolus production should be considered when producing *Acidanthera*.

Reading

1. Armitage, A. M., and J. M. Laushman. 1990. Planting date and in-ground time affect cut flowers of *Acidanthera* . . . . *HortScience* 25:1236–1238.

Allium spp.   Ornamental Onion

The genus consists of 300–500 species widely distributed over the Northern Hemisphere, many of which are useful for cut flowers. The pungent smell of onion is present in all species to varying degrees, but is only truly noticeable on most species when stems are cut, damaged or crushed. The principal cut flower species in cultivation are *A. giganteum* and *A. sphaerocephalon*, although *A. aflatunense, A. caeruleum, A. christophii, A. moly* and *A. triquetrum* are also grown. The genus has it all; plants are easy to grow, have handsome flowers, bear long stems and are relatively insect and disease resistant. All that is needed is a decent name. *Ornamental onions* does not convey a warm feeling of beauty and romance but rather suggests purple-skinned circles on display in a salad bar. *Chives* is no better. To allow for better marketing, a better name is needed. Any suggestions?

Allium giganteum

Allium giganteum		Giant Onion	3–4'/3'
Purple	Himalayas	Liliaceae	Zones 3–9

The most common onion for cut flowers, stems may be found in most major markets in the spring and early summer. The globe-shaped bulb is 2–3" across and up to 12" in circumference making it one of the largest bulbs in the genus. Small, ¼" wide flowers are clustered close together in a 4–5" lilac-purple ball (umbel) on top of a naked 3–4' long stem. Well-grown flowers are particularly eye-catching and demand excellent prices. However, the bulbs are expensive relative to other *Allium* species and flowers must realize high prices to be profitable.

Propagation

Seed: Seed requires 3–5 years to reach flowering size. Seed should be sown lightly in a cold frame or other cool semi-protected area. Germination is erratic and seed may require up to 1 year for complete germination.

Division: Bulbs split readily and may be divided and replanted in the field immediately. Flowering occurs the second year.

Environmental Factors

Temperature: Experimental evidence suggests cold is necessary for flowering (5). In warm climates where little or no cooling occurs, bulbs may be precooled at 40F for 8–10 weeks prior to planting (3). Plants begin to go dormant while in flower and dormancy is complete within 3 weeks of harvest. No irrigation is necessary once dormancy is complete.

Field Performance

Bulb size: Use bulbs which are 8" (20 cm) in circumference.

Spacing: Space bulbs 9–12" apart and 4" below the surface for best yields.

Planting time: In most climatic zones, bulbs may be planted in the fall, although early spring planting may be practiced. Planting in October through January did not affect yield in zone 7b.

In general, each bulb yields a single stem and occasionally a shorter second stem. Foliage may be damaged by spring frosts but flowers are unaffected. The foliage declines before the flowers are harvested.

The general performance overview which follows is adapted from De Hertogh (3).

Location	Zone	Initial harvest	Duration of harvest (days)	Stem length (in)
Ottawa, ON	4	Jun 18	30	46
East Lansing, MI	5	Jun 27	23	44
Washington, DC	7	May 10	18	44
Raleigh, NC	8	May 26	9	44
San Francisco, CA	9	Jul 5	30	28

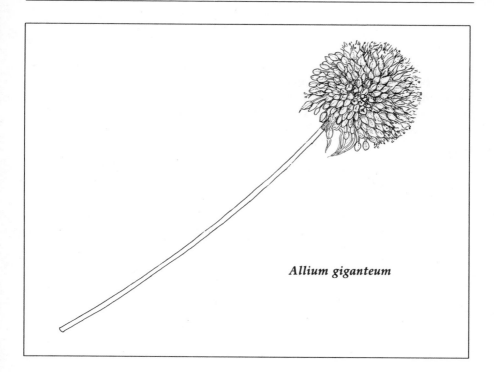

Allium giganteum

Harvest times are generally earlier and are shorter as plants were grown further south. The consistently cool climate in San Francisco resulted in a delay of flower harvest.

Longevity: Commercial production is possible for 2–3 years. In trials in north Georgia, flowering declined after 2 years and was dismal the third.

Shading: Not necessary; full sun is best.

Stage of Harvest

Flowers should be harvested when ½ the flowers are open. The remainder naturally open in any normal postharvest solution. Place flowers in a 36–43F cooler after harvesting. Storage has a negative effect on vase life, reducing marketable time after stems emerge from coolers (4).

Postharvest

Fresh: Stems have a vase life of appproximately 14 days (6).

Storage: Stems may be stored up to 7 days after 6 weeks of storage (6). Stems should be recut after flowering and placed in a preservative solution of pH 4.0.

Cultivars

No cultivars are available.

Allium sphaerocephalon   Drumstick Chives   2–3'/2'
Purple   Western Europe to Iran   Liliaceae   Zones 3–9

In early summer, the young, oval, 2" wide flower heads are green and purple but mature to a deep purple. The many-flowered inflorescences consist of bell-shaped flowers. The oval bulbs may be planted in the fall. Each bulb produces many offsets in the summer and can almost become weedy in some areas.

Propagation
Seed: Seed requires 2–4 years to reach flowering size. Seed should be sown lightly in a cold frame or other cool semi-protected area. Seed may require up to 1 year for germination.

Division: Offsets are routinely formed and may be divided after 1–2 years. Separate sizes by diameter and replace larger ones in the production area.

Environmental Factors
Cold does not appear to be necessary for flowering. Bulbs, once dug, may be stored at room temperature prior to planting. Bulbs planted in Georgia in March received little or no cold and soil temperatures did not fall below 40F. Dormancy occurs approximately 4 weeks after flowering.

Field Performance
Bulb size: The optimum size is bulbs which are 2–3" (5/6 or 6/7 cm) in circumference (3).

Spacing: Space 1" apart and 4" below the soil surface.

Planting time: No differences in yield, harvest times or stem length occurred when bulbs were planted in November or December. Stem diameter was only slightly affected by the later planting.

The effect of planting date on harvest, yield and stem quality of *Allium sphaerocephalon.*[a]

Month of planting	Scapes/bulb	Initial harvest	Duration of harvest (days)	Stem length (in)	Stem diameter (mm)
Nov	1.1	Jun 4	10	27.4	7.2
Dec	1.2	May 31	13	26.6	6.4

[a]Adapted from (1) .

In other locations, harvest times and stem lengths in Nova Scotia, Canada (zone 5), East Lansing, MI (zone 5) and Fayetteville, AR (zone 7) were June 22/26", July 1/24" and May 15/12", respectively (3).

Longevity: *Allium sphaerocephalon* is productive for 2–3 years before problems with diseases and offset production reduce yield.

Yield and stem quality of *Allium sphaerocephalon* over time (Athens, GA; spacing 8″ × 8″).[a]

Year	Stems/bulb	Stem length (in)	Stem diameter (mm)
1	1.2	27.5	6.8
2	2.5	22.4	5.5
3	0.5[b]	20.0	5.2

[a]Adapted from (1).
[b]Bulbs infected with *Sclerotium cepivorum* (bulb rot).

Spacing: Space bulbs 2–4″ apart. De Hertogh (3) recommends 1″ apart and we have had success with bulbs spaced as far as 8″ apart.

Shading: Not necessary.

Stage of Harvest

Flowers should be harvested when the bottom 3–4 whorls of flowers are open. This represents between ¼ and ½ of the flowers open. Flowers continue to open if placed in clean water. Place stems in cooler (40F) only if necessary, as cold storage reduces shelf life.

Postharvest

Fresh: Stems have a vase life of approximately 10–14 days in water.

Storage: Flowers may be stored in water up to 4 weeks at 32–35F (3).

Dried: Wait until nearly all flowers are open (some seed may be formed from the basal flowers) (2). Stems may be hung upside down but that is not necessary (2).

Cultivars

No cultivars are commercially available.

Additional Species of *Allium*

Allium aflatunense (persian onion) has similarly ball-shaped flowers, but plants are significantly shorter (2–3′ tall) than *A. giganteum*. Space bulbs 2–3″ apart and 4″ below the surface. Longevity and performance are poor south of zone 7. Bulbs must be precooled at 41F for 8–10 weeks prior to planting south of zone 7. Average stem length in zones 4–7 is approximately 26″ (3). South of zone 7, stems are shorter. Bulbs are readily available and relatively inexpensive.

A. caeruleum (*A. azureum*; blue globe onion) has grasslike foliage and deep blue flowers. Stem length averages approximately 18″ and inflorescences are 1–2″ in diameter. Plant 2–3″ apart and 4″ below soil surface. Treat as annuals in most of the country.

A. christophii has metallic blue, many-flowered umbels on 6–8″ tall plants. The flowers are handsome and dry well; however, the stem length may be too short for wholesale markets. Flowers do not ship well and are best grown for local markets.

A. 'Globemaster' bears deep purple, rounded flower heads on 2–3′ tall plants. It is a hybrid between *A. christophii* and *A. elatum*. Recently raised in the Netherlands, bulbs are not commonly available and are expensive. The hybrid appears to have exceptional potential for the cut flower trade.

A. stipitatum is similar to *A. giganteum* but much less available in this country. The var. *album* is a white form.

A. thunbergii produces rose-lilac flowers in the fall which persist on the plant until frost. If the flowers are not harvested, they literally dry on the plant. Although flowers are only 12–15" tall, the late flowering habit and drying ability make this a potential species for cut flowers. Bulbs are winter-hardy to at least zone 5b.

Pests and Diseases of *Allium*

Bulb rot, caused by *Sclerotium cepivorum*, causes abortion and destruction of the flowering stem and eventual death of the bulb. Tips of the leaves begin to turn yellow and finally brown. The bulbs are covered in a mat of white mycelia, on which appear small black sclerotia. Destroy infected bulbs.

Reading for *Allium*

1. Armitage, A. M., and J. M. Laushman. 1990. Planting date and in-ground time affect cut flowers of *Acidanthera* .... *HortScience* 25:1236–1238.

2. Bullivant, E. 1989. *Dried Fresh Flowers From Your Garden.* Pelham Books/Stephen Greene Press, London, U.K.

3. De Hertogh, A. A. 1989. *Holland Bulb Forcer's Guide.* 4th ed. International Flower Bulb Center, Hillegom, The Netherlands.

4. Kalkman, E. C. 1984. Storage has a negative influence on the vase life of *Allium* and *Eremurus*. *Vakblad voor de Bloemisterij* 39:33.

5. Rees, A. R. 1985. Miscellaneous bulbs. In A. H. Halevy (ed.), *The Handbook of Flowering,* vol. 1. CRC Press, Boca Raton, FL. 306–308.

6. Sacalis, J. N. 1989. *Fresh (Cut) Flowers for Designs: Postproduction Guide* I. D. C. Kiplinger Chair in Floriculture, The Ohio State Univ., Columbus, OH.

Alstroemeria **spp.**   Peruvian Lily   3–4'/2'
Various colors   South America   Amaryllidaceae   Zones 8–10

The popularity of *Alstroemeria* continues unabated in florists shops throughout the world. Most flowers are greenhouse-grown in Europe, South America and England, but significant greenhouse production occurs in the northern tier of the United States; field production is popular in coastal California. All commercial cultivars are hybrids whose parentage is not well known; however, *A. aurea, A. ligtu, A. pelegrina, A. pulchra* and *A. violacea* are of major importance. The environmental responses of the parents greatly affect the responses of the hybrids; therefore, cultivars do not always react to the environment similarly. Most breeding has taken place in the Netherlands and England and growers must pay royalties based on square footage or number of plants in production.

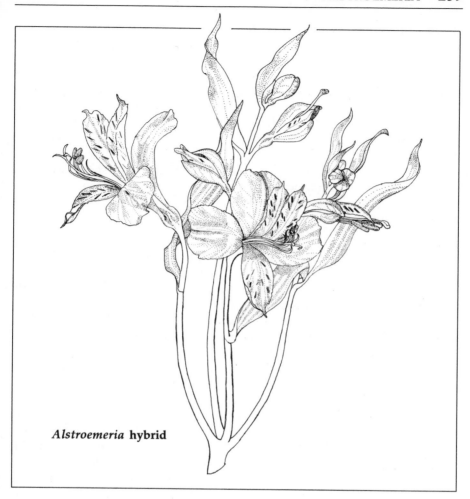

Alstroemeria hybrid

Shoots arise from a rhizome which has fibrous and fleshy storage roots. The rhizome is extremely important because it is the site which perceives temperature, and changes in temperature result in plants being vegetative or reproductive. Depending on cultivar, *Alstroemeria* can be flowered year-round but flowering is heaviest in spring and early summer. However, outdoor production in California is excellent in fall and early spring, with some flowering in the winter.

Environmental Factors

Temperature: For some cultivars, cold treatment of planted rhizomes is an absolute requirement for flowering (2). Treatment with 40F for 6 weeks is most effective; however, initiation still occurs at 55F, although slower (4). Newer cultivars are not as sensitive to low temperatures as the older cultivars. Soil temperatures are more important than air temperature for *Alstroemeria*; if soil temperature is maintained below 60F, plants continue to flower, regardless of air temperature (2). Dry-stored rhizomes do not respond to cool temperature treatments (7), thus they must be planted for temperature to be effective. Soil temperatures above 70F inhibit flower initiation. If plants have been subjected to inductive temperatures, flowering is reduced if they are given subsequent temperatures above 63F (3). This is referred to as devernalization of the rhizome. For continuous production of flowers, plants should be grown around 48F and under 16-hour photoperiod. Maintaining the plants in a vegetative mode occurs with 70–80F temperatures (7).

Photoperiod: Long days result in faster flowering than short days. The optimum photoperiod appears to be 12–14 hours; more than 14 hours decreases total shoot production. The LD treatment is not effective unless rhizomes have been subjected to cool temperatures (2).

Field Performance

Soil: Soil should be well drained with a pH of 6.0–6.5.

Covering: Many growers provide a clear plastic covering or low density shade cloth over the top and on the side towards the prevailing winds. Plants are expensive and some protection from wind and rain is good insurance.

Spacing: Space plants on approximately 18" centers or 18" × 20" in 2 rows in a 3' wide bed. Correct spacing depends on cultivar.

Planting: Bury rhizomes at the same depth as in the pot (or in the liner). Plant so that the growing point is headed into the center of the bed. Carefully spread roots out when planting. The fat storage roots are necessary for continuous flowering and should be handled with respect.

Support: Provide at least 2 tiers of support mesh. They may be raised as the shoots grow. Place the bottom layer approximately 1' above the soil.

Harvesting: Usually stems are pulled, not cut. Remove with a rapid, upward pulling motion. However, not all stems should be pulled all the time. Many of the butterfly types do not produce sufficiently strong stems and are cut. Similarly, when young plants start to flower, stems should be cut to reduce chances of removing the rhizome. Some people report skin rashes when handling *Alstroemeria*. Use of gloves and long-sleeved shirts is recommended.

Thinning: Thin vegetative shoots as often as possible to result in longer flowering. No more than 30% of the shoots should be removed at one time.

Scheduling: In many cases, rhizomes arrive in November, are potted and placed in a greenhouse until April and then planted to the field. Flowering begins in June, but the early flowers are removed to strengthen the plant. Yield peaks in August from April planting. Rhizomes planted in August start to flower in October. However, peak flowering occurs in March and April.

Yield: Approximately 100 stems/plant each year is a reasonable expectation for field-grown *Alstroemeria*, depending on cultivar and spacing. Plants spaced in 3' wide rows produce higher yield/plant than those on 2' rows.

Greenhouse Performance

Environmental needs: Use ground beds for best production. Rhizomes should be immediately planted 3–4" deep and at 16" × 20" or 20" × 24" spacing (1). Use 2 rows per 3' wide planting bed. Provide cool soil temperatures (below 60F; 55F is optimal) for at least 6 weeks. If planted in the summer, vegetative growth will commence, followed by flower initiation due to cool temperatures in the fall and winter. The cooling requirement should be completed by mid-December in northern states. Provide 14- to 16-hour photoperiods once the 6 weeks of cooling have been completed. The long days during the winter may be provided by day extension or by providing 4–5 hours of incandescent light during the night. Provide high light intensities in the winter; if necessary, HID lamps should be used. They facilitate increased growth as well as providing a long day during the winter. Remove vegetative shoots every month once flowering begins.

Fertilization: Continuous applications of calcium nitrate and potassium nitrate at 400–500 ppm N and K are recommended (1).

Harvesting: Pull, don't cut, flowering stems from the rhizome, except with young plants.

Timing: Rhizomes planted from August to December have peak production in March and April.

Stage of Harvest

Pull stems when the first flowers are fully colored and the majority are showing color. For long distance shippers, stems may be harvested when the first buds are swollen and about to open.

Postharvest

Fresh: Flowers will continue to open for approximately 10 days; however, the foliage may start to yellow earlier. The use of STS and other preservatives enhances flower longevity and reduces leaf yellowing.

Storage: Flowers may be stored wet for 2–3 days at 38–40F (5) or dry at 33–35F for up to 1 week (6).

Dried: *Alstroemeria* flowers do not dry well.

Cultivars

Numerous cultivars exist, most of which have evolved from European sources. The following list provides a few cultivars useful for cut flowers. Consult your sales representative for the most recent cultivars.

'Butterscotch' (bronze)	'Ostara' (lavender)
'Harlequin' (orange)	'Regina' (pink)
'Harmony' (bronze)	'Rosario' (pink)
'Jacqueline' (pink)	'Walter Remming' (white/orange)
'King Cardinal' (red)	'White Wings' (white)
'Mandarin' (orange)	

Pests and Diseases

Normal pathogens such as *Botrytis, Pythium* and *Rhizoctonia* spp. affect plants, but no diseases specific to *Alstroemeria* occur. It is essential to provide adequate ventilation and spacing for plants. Aphids, spider mites and whiteflies can be a problem.

Reading

1. De Hertogh, A. A. 1989. *Holland Bulb Forcer's Guide*. 4th ed. International Flower Bulb Center, Hillegom, The Netherlands.

2. Healy, W. E., and H. F. Wilkins. 1981. Interaction of soil temperature, air temperature and photoperiod on growth and flowering of *Alstroemeria* 'Regina'. *HortScience* 16:459.

3. _____ . 1982. The interaction of temperature on flowering of *Alstroemeria* 'Regina'. *J. Amer. Soc. Hort. Sci.* 107:248–251.

4. _____ . 1985. *Alstroemeria*. In A. H. Halevy (ed.), *The Handbook of Flowering*, vol. 1. CRC Press, Boca Raton, FL. 419–424.

5. Nowak, J., and R. M. Rudnicki. 1990. *Postharvest Handling and Storage of Cut Flowers, Florist Greens, and Potted Plants*. Timber Press, Portland, OR.

6. Sacalis, J. N. 1989. *Fresh (Cut) Flowers for Designs: Postproduction Guide* I. D. C. Kiplinger Chair in Floriculture, The Ohio State Univ., Columbus, OH.

7. Vonk Noordegraff, C. 1975. Temperature and daylength requirements of *Alstroemeria. Acta Hortic.* 51:267–274.

Many thanks to Ms. Fran Foley and Dr. Will Healy for reviewing this section.

Anemone coronaria	Poppy Anemone	8–15"/8"
Various colors	Mediterranean	Ranunculaceae	Zones 6–9

The production of anemones for cut flowers has been practiced for many years. Flowers are produced in the cool season—spring in the field or winter in the greenhouse—and are not tolerant of warm conditions. Active selection and breeding of anemones has resulted in numerous cultivars and many colors. The market is strongest prior to Mother's Day; demand decreases after that date.

Propagation

Tubers: Anemones are not usually propagated by the grower but can be divided if clumps are large.

Seed: Sow seed on top of soil and place at 55–60F. Germination occurs in 10–14 days. Plugs are available for certain cultivars through plug specialists.

Growing-on

Seedlings should be fertilized lightly (50–75 ppm N) and placed in high light and cool temperatures (45–55F).

If tubers are to be planted, soak tubers for 12–48 hours in water prior to planting.

Environmental Factors

Temperature: Poppy anemones are only winter-hardy to zone 6, perhaps to zone 5 if sufficient mulch is applied. Warm temperatures during production inhibit flowering and result in poor quality flower stems. Therefore, field production is mainly practiced in Mediterranean climates or in areas with mild winters and cool springs in the United States. Cold treatment (vernalization) of the tubers, however, is useful, but not necessary, to accelerate flowering and increase percentage flowering. Tubers may be soaked in water for 48 hours and either exposed to 33F for several weeks prior to planting or sprouted in polyethylene bags at 35–48F for 6–7 weeks prior to planting (6,8). Such treatments, however, may reduce flower yield (6). Natural vernalization occurs in the field if tubers are planted in the fall in mild winter climates or in early spring elsewhere. High temperatures signal the onset of dormancy.

Photoperiod: Photoperiod studies are not clear-cut, but it appears that SD accelerate flowering and LD result in early termination of flowering (4,5). Under normal flowering times, natural SD occur during flowering.

Field Performance

Tuber size: Use 4/5 cm tubers (2). Since tubers cannot be easily measured, use at least 1-year-old tubers to be confident they are of sufficient size. Tubers greater than 5 cm in circumference should be avoided; as some growers have learned the hard way, "such monsters should be put straight on the fire, they are worth neither time nor space for their planting" (3).

Spacing: Plant tubers 1" apart and 1" below the surface.

Planting time: The best planting time for tubers is in the fall in zones 7–9 and in early spring further north. Late planting results in significant decrease in yield and quality. The following table shows the effect of different planting times in zone 7b (Athens, GA).

The effect of planting date on harvest, yield and stem quality of *Anemone coronaria* 'De Caen' (Athens, GA).[a]

Month of planting	Survival (%)	Flowers/corm	Initial harvest	Duration of harvest (days)	Stem length (in)
Nov	96	10.2	Feb 27	65	9.5
Dec	89	4.8	Mar 30	33	7.4
Jan	25	1.1	Apr 15	17	5.4
Feb	20	0.2	Apr 30	5	5.5

[a]From (1).

It is obvious from the preceding table that early planting is essential, at least in zone 7. The delay of first harvest date as a result of late planting caused flowers to emerge as weather became warmer. Warm weather shortens duration of harvest and decreases stem length, diameter and flower diameter.

Planting zones: In other locations, flowering time and stem lengths of 'De Caen' were May 20/10" (Glencoe, IL, zone 5), May 2/12" (Washington, DC, zone 7) and Jan 27/6" (Baton Rouge, LA, zone 9) (2). Data based on planting from October to December.

Longevity: Anemones should be treated as annuals for commercial production. Research in which tubers remained in place for 3 years showed that productivity declined after the first year.

Yield and stem quality of *Anemone coronaria* tubers in the field over time.[a]

Year	Tuber survival (%)	Stems/corm	Stem length (in)
1	90	6.5	10.0
2	30	7.0	9.3
3	20	5.4	8.5

[a]Adapted from (1).

Although the number of stems/tuber and stem length were only slightly affected, the survival of tubers was dramatically reduced each year. Survival was affected by warm summer soil temperatures, diseases and pests. This work was done in Georgia, but most growers in the United States find that yearly renewal of tubers is necessary for best production and quality (2).

Shading: Shading results in longer stem lengths. In research at Georgia, stems of De Caen hybrids were approximately 9" and 12" long under full sun or 67% shade, respectively (2). Yield was unaffected.

Tubers vs. plugs: Tubers often do not germinate as well as growers would like, even when they are soaked, and field planting of seedlings (plugs) may be practiced. The use of plugs results in better stands of plants; the yield and quality of cut stems are not affected.

Greenhouse Performance

Greenhouse production in northern states occurs in winter months in cool greenhouses. Commercial production in the South is difficult because of warm day temperatures in the winter. Most growers plant plugs in ground beds or 4–6" pots. Space approximately 6" apart and maintain temperatures below 55F.

Stage of Harvest

Some recommendations suggest that flowers should be harvested after they have opened and closed once or twice. This is difficult to monitor, however, and most growers harvest flowers when the petals (actually sepals) have started to separate from the center but are not fully open.

Postharvest

Fresh: Bud-cut flowers open well in water alone and persist for 4–6 days. Additional vase life occurs if pulsed with silver thiosulfate (STS) for 15–30 minutes. Transfer stems to warm water (80–100F) containing 1–2% sugar (6).

Recut the base of the stems with each transfer.

Storage: Flowers may be stored dry at 38–44F for 1–2 days, after conditioning for 24 hours at 75F in a solution of STS plus 5.5 oz/gal (40 g/liter) of sugar or 100 ppm hydroxyquinoline sulfate plus 1.4 oz/gal (10.2 g/liter) of sugar (7).

Dried: Flowers may be dried in a microwave (9). Place the flowers on approximately 2" of warm silica gel and cover with additional gel. Heat for 1–3.5 minutes, depending on the fleshiness of the flowers.

Cultivars

Cleopatra series is a recent introduction and is mainly recommended for the greenhouse. Available from seed, plants bear 18–24" long scapes. Flowers are available in single colors and a mix.

De Caen hybrids are the most popular field-grown anemones and consist of single, saucer-shaped flowers. They are available as a mix or as single colors.

'Mona Lisa' is a recent introduction, mainly used in the greenhouse trade. The stems are longer than 'De Caen' and the vase life is better. In the field, they flower a little later than 'De Caen'.

St. Brigid hybrids have semi-double to double flowers. They are also available as a mix and as single colors.

'St. Piran' has long stems of single and semi-double flowers available in a mix.

Additional Species

Anemone × *fulgens* grows from a tuber like *A. coronaria* and is treated similarly (2). The most popular cultivar is 'St. Bavo'.

A. × *hybrida* hybrids are effective cut flowers, but vase life is short. However, flowers occur in late summer and fall, an important time for field flowers.

Pests and Diseases

Numerous leaf spots and tuber rots are caused by various fungi. Apply appropriate fungicides after the foliage has emerged.

Reading

1. Armitage, A. M., and J. M. Laushman. 1990. Planting date and in-ground time affect cut flowers of *Acidanthera* . . . . *HortScience* 25:1236–1238.

2. De Hertogh, A. A. 1989. *Holland Bulb Forcer's Guide*. 4th ed. International Flower Bulb Center, Hillegom, The Netherlands.

3. Genders, R. 1960. *Bulbs All the Year Round*. Faber and Faber, London, U.K.

4. Kadman-Zahavi, A., and A. Horovitz. 1980. Acceleration of dormancy in the poppy anemone by long days (in Hebrew). *Hassadeh* 51:434–435.

5. Kadman-Zahavi, A., A. Horovitz and Y. Ozeri. 1984. Long-day induced dormancy in Anemone coronaria L. *Ann. Bot.* 53:213–217.

6. Maia, N., and P. Venard. 1971. La vernalization de bulbes d'anemones.

P.H.M. Rev. Hortic. 146:17–21.

7. Nowak, J., and R. M. Rudnicki. 1990. *Postharvest Handling and Storage of Cut Flowers, Florist Greens, and Potted Plants.* Timber Press, Portland, OR.

8. Twisk, D., and M. De Roy. 1962. Is bloevervroeging van anemonen en ranonkels mongelik? *Weekbl. Bloembollcult* 73:484–485.

9. Vaughan, M. J. 1988. *The Complete Book of Cut Flower Care.* Timber Press, Portland, OR.

Brodiaea laxa see *Triteleia laxa*

Crocosmia × *crocosmiiflora*   Crocosmia, Montbretia   2–2.5′/2′
Various colors   Hybrid origin   Iridaceae   Zones 5–9

An underused cut flower, crocosmia provides many flowers on thin spikelike inflorescences (racemes). The flowers are 1.5–2″ long and occur in several handsome colors.

Propagation
One- to two-year-old corms may be purchased from bulb suppliers. Seed requires approximately 2 years to reach flowering size.

Growing-on
Plant corms immediately to the field.

Field Performance
Spacing: Space corms 3″ below the soil surface and 6″ apart. In warmer parts of the country, corms multiply rapidly and colonize the area. Most cormels, however, are too small to flower.

Planting time: South of zone 5, corms may be planted in January.

The effect of planting date on harvest, yield and stem quality of *Crocosmia* × *crocosmiiflora* (Athens, GA).[a]

Month of planting	Flowers/corm	Initial harvest	Duration of Harvest (days)	Stem length (in)
Jan	1.3	Jul 2	30	25.7
Feb	0.8	Jul 15	25	20.2
Mar	0.8	Jul 21	21	20.0

[a]Adapted from (1).

Later planting extends flowering time but does not significantly affect yield. Stem length, however, is reduced as corms are planted later in the season. North of zone 5, corms may be planted as soon as field conditions warrant.

Longevity: North of zone 5, corms should be lifted in the fall (similar to *Gladiolus*), graded, and replanted in the spring. In southern and coastal climates, crocosmia may be considered a 2- to 3-year crop.

Yield and stem quality of *Crocosmia* × *crocosmiiflora* over time (Athens, GA).[a]

Year	Stems/corm	Stem length (in)	Stem diameter (mm)
1	0.9	22.2	4.9
2	1.2	16.0	4.7
3	2.0	20.0	4.5

[a]Adapted from (1).

Corms did not produce well in the fourth year; this species may therefore be treated as a 2- to 3-year crop where corms overwinter. Corms are inexpensive and may be replanted each year if so desired.

Stage of Harvest

The first few flower buds at the base should be showing color but need not be open (3).

Postharvest

Fresh: Fresh stems persist 7–10 days. They are sensitive to ethylene and must be stored away from fruits and vegetables (3).

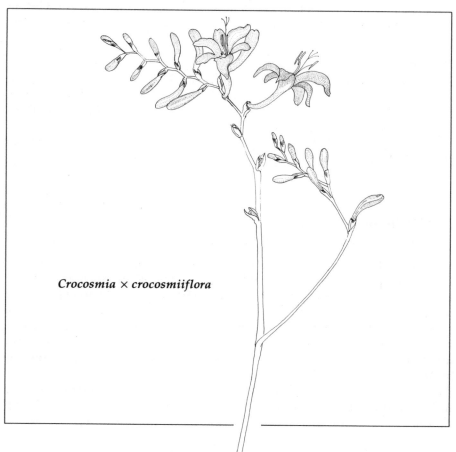

Crocosmia × *crocosmiiflora*

Storage: Stems may be stored dry for up to 4 days at 34–37F, although storage in water is recommended (3).

Dried: Flowers may be air-dried upside down in small bunches in a warm, dry place. The straplike leaves are also useful and provide a fresh look to a dried arrangement. If bunches are hung with plenty of air circulation, they retain their original color (2).

Cultivars

Many cultivars are available and additional ones are constantly appearing from Europe.

'Citronella' has small (1.5" long) lemon-yellow flowers.

'Emily McKenzie' has large (2" long) orange flowers with a crimson throat.

'Lucifer', a hybrid clone, bears deep orange-red flowers and grows well on both sides of the Rocky Mountains.

'Solfatare' produces apricot-yellow flowers on 2' tall stems.

'Spitfire' has red and yellow bicolored flowers on 3' tall stems.

Additional Species

Crocosmia masonorum has 3' long flower stems, narrow foliage and bright orange-red, upright flowers. 'Firebird' bears fiery orange-red flowers with a bright yellow throat.

Reading

1. Armitage, A. M., and J. M. Laushman. 1990. Planting date and in-ground time affect cut flowers of *Acidanthera* . . . . *HortScience* 25:1236–1238.

2. Bullivant, E. 1989. *Dried Fresh Flowers From Your Garden*. Pelham Books/Stephen Greene Press, London, U.K.

3. Vaughan, M. J. 1988. *The Complete Book of Cut Flower Care*. Timber Press, Portland, OR.

Dahlia **hybrids**   Dahlia   2–5'/3'

Various colors   Hybrid origin   Asteraceae   Zones 7–10

Dahlias have experienced a significant resurgence in popularity and are field-produced from Minnesota to Florida. Additional production occurs in Europe and Japan. Today's cultivars resulted from hybridization of *D. pinnata* and *D. coccinea* and probably other species. Dahlias emerge from tuberous roots and bear tall, often hollow stems, opposite leaves and terminal inflorescences. Although numerous colors and flower shapes occur, most cultivars are classified as single, in which showy florets surround a central disc of smaller, yellow florets, and double (or decorative), in which the colored florets predominate. Tubers must be lifted in northern states but may remain in the ground for up to 3 years in southern areas (zones 7–10). A good product for the local market because flowers do not ship well.

Dahlia hybrid

Propagation

Most growers purchase roots from specialty suppliers but dahlias may be propagated by seed, tubers or stem cuttings. For seed germination, maintain 80–85F, cover lightly and place in an area of high humidity. Germination occurs in 10–12 days. Terminal cuttings can be taken from actively growing plants, however, the best results arise from tubers forced in the greenhouse in the winter. New shoots arise in about 2 weeks when greenhouse temperatures remain between 50–60F. Select 2–3 node cuttings and place in a well-drained medium in a humid environment at 65–72F. Tubers may be divided but tubers themselves cannot produce new buds. A piece of the old stem with a bud attached must be taken with each piece of tuber.

Growing-on

Transplant seedlings or cuttings to 4–6" pots and grow at 60–68F. Plants may be placed in the field as soon as danger of frost is over.

Environmental Factors

Photoperiod: Daylength has a direct influence on flowering and tuber formation. Long days (approx. 14 hours, depending on cultivar) cause faster flower initiation and if daylengths are very short (8 hours), flowers often fail to open. A large volume of research on various cultivars suggests that the percentage of flowering plants and the total production of flowers are optimized in daylengths of 13–15 hours (2,3). Daylengths of less than 11 hours and greater than 16 hours had a deleterious effect. Some cultivars fail to flower when daylengths are greater than 16 hours (3,4). Short days (12 hours or less) result in tuber formation for most cultivars (7,10).

Temperature: Night temperatures of 50–86F do not affect flower initiation, but flower development proceeds more slowly at cooler temperatures (6). The greatest influence of cold temperatures is the breaking of tuber dormancy. If tubers spend at least 40 days at 32F, dormancy is broken and normal shoot production occurs (5).

Field Performance

Planting time: Place tubers or started plants in the field after all threat of frost. Late frosts will check the emerging foliage and result in significantly delayed flowering. Unsprouted tubers may be planted earlier but if planted when the soil is too cold, sprouting is delayed.

Spacing: Space 2' apart. More dense spacing results in tangled stems and poor air circulation, resulting in greater disease problems. Planting up to 3' apart results in more flowers and less disease but is an uneconomical use of space.

Support: Many systems are used, but all cutting types require support. Four-foot-tall bamboo canes (usually each plant is provided with 3 canes forming a triangle with the plants tied into the triangle), wire cages or 2–3' tall wire runs which keep the plants from falling over are used.

Mulch: Dahlias are shallow-rooted and a root mulch should be liberally applied. Pine straw, bark, peat moss, manures or lawn clippings may be used.

Fertilization: Side dress with a complete granular fertilizer such as 10–10–10 when tubers begin to sprout. Liquid fertilizer (300–600 ppm N) once every 2 weeks is sufficient in most climates.

Pinching: Pinching the terminal shoot encourages the development of the many side shoots. The result is the production of more flowers over the long run, although initial flowering is delayed by 1–2 weeks. Pinch approximately 2" of growth when plants are about 2' tall. However, some growers choose to harvest the central flower, which is the largest and earliest. This is strictly based on the price obtained for the earlier, larger flower against the delay of axillary flowers.

Disbudding: Most varieties bear flowers with small side buds beneath the center bud (like a chrysanthemum). Removal of the lateral flower buds causes larger flowers; allowing them to remain results in a spray inflorescence. Disbudding requires significant labor and some skill.

Yield: Yield is highly dependent on cultivar; however, yields of 30 flowers/plant are not uncommon. Flowers are generally harvested in early summer and may continue to flower until frost.

Longevity: In the South where tubers are left in the ground, 3-year production from the same tuber is not uncommon. If tubers are lifted and stored properly, then they may be used for up to 5 years.

Lifting: In northern states and Canada, tubers should be lifted after the first frost. Lift, clean and store dry tubers in a well-ventilated room at 45–50F.

Refer to lifting of *Zantedeschia* (calla lily) tubers for additional guidelines.

Greenhouse Performance

With proper manipulation of photoperiod and temperature, dahlias may be forced year-round. When tubers arrive, plant immediately. If unable to plant, place tubers in the shipping container in the cooler at 45–50F.

Planting: Plant in large containers (12" diameter) or ground beds. Water in well and keep soils moist.

Light and photoperiod: High light levels are required for best dahlia growth and winter production often requires supplemental lighting. Shade may be needed for summer production. Provide daylengths of 11–14 hours; never allow daylengths to fall below 8 hours. Long days of 16 hours may delay flowering but otherwise will not likely be detrimental (1). Nightbreak lighting (4 hours of lighting) can be used (1).

Temperature: Provide minimum night temperatures of 63–65 F (1); day temperatures of 73–77F are recommended. Avoid temperatures greater than 80F or quality will be reduced. The crop may be slowed down if temperature is lowered to 55F. This is particularly useful when flower buds are in color before the market is ready.

Pinching: Similar to field-grown plants, dahlias may be pinched for additional flower production. However, non-pinched plants may be spaced more closely together than pinched plants.

Scheduling: Depending on cultivar, plants flower approximately 9–13 weeks from planting the tuber. The later the planting date, the more rapid the flowering.

Stage of Harvest

Dahlias should be harvested when the flowers are ¾ to fully open, but before the outer petals begin to decline. If cut too early, dahlias may fail to open, even in opening solutions. Flowers which do eventually open are often of poor quality. After harvest, immerse stems in warm water (130F) (8).

Postharvest

Fresh: Dahlias persist for 3–5 days in water, 7–10 days if an opening solution is used (8,9).

Dried: Dahlias are best dried in silica gel or sand, they shrink when air-dried. In sand, flowers may take from several days to 4 weeks to dry (9).

Storage: Flowers can be stored wet at 37–40F, but storage should be avoided whenever possible.

Shipping: Always ship in water or preservative.

Cultivars

Check with your supplier concerning cultivars. Dahlias are divided into various classes and some classes may be more useful in a particular market than others.

Class	Description
Single-flowered	Single row of ray petals.
Anemone-flowered	Usually disc flowers and ray flowers of different colors.
Collarette	One or more series of ray flowers. Above each series, a ring of florets (the collarette) only half the length of the rays occurs, usually in a different color. May be single-, peony- or double-flowered.
Peony-flowered	Usually 2–3 series of ray flowers and a single disc.
Decorative	Flower heads fully double, showing no central disc. A popular cut class.
Pompon	Similar to doubles but smaller.
Cactus	Flower heads fully double, the margins of the flowers thin and elongated.

Pests and Diseases

Dahlias are subject to viruses, insects and a host of disease organisms. Growing dahlias requires a preventative spray program for mildews, leaf spots and Japanese beetles. Southern growers, in particular, must spray conscientiously, especially following afternoon thunderstorms.

Reading

1. De Hertogh, A. A. 1989. *Holland Bulb Forcer's Guide.* 4th ed. International Flower Bulb Center, Hillegom, The Netherlands.

2. Durso, M., and A. A. De Hertogh. 1977. The influence of greenhouse environmental factors on forcing *Dahlia variabilis* Willd. *J. Amer. Soc. Hort. Sci.* 102:314–317.

3. Konishi, K., and K. Inaba. 1964. Studies on flowering control of dahlia. I. On optimum day-length. *J. Jap. Soc. Hortic. Sci.* 33:171–180.

4. _____. 1966. Studies on flowering control of dahlia. III. Effects of day-length on initiation and development of flower buds. *J. Jap. Soc. Hortic. Sci.* 35:73–79.

5. _____. 1967. Studies on flowering control of dahlia. VII. On dormancy of crown-tuber. *J. Jap. Soc. Hortic. Sci.* 36:131–140.

6. Mastalerz, J. W. 1976. Garden dahlias may have potential as a greenhouse crop. Daylength controls flower initiation. Pennsylvania Flower Growers Bul. 287(1):4–6.

7. Moser, B. C., and C. E. Hess. 1968. The physiology of tuberous root development in dahlia. *Proc. Amer. Soc. Hort. Sci.* 93:595–603.

8. Nowak, J., and R. M. Rudnicki. 1990. *Postharvest Handling and Storage of Cut Flowers, Florist Greens, and Potted Plants.* Timber Press, Portland, OR.

9. Vaughan, M. J. 1988. *The Complete Book of Cut Flower Care.* Timber Press, Portland, OR.

10. Zimmerman, P. W., and A. E. Hitchcock. 1929. Root formation and flowering of dahlia cuttings when subjected to different day lengths. *Bot. Gaz.* 87:1–13.

Thanks to Mr. and Mrs. Ken and Suzie Cook for reviewing this section.

Achillea filipendulina 'Parker's Variety'

Acidanthera bicolor 'Muralis'

Aconitum × *arendsii*

Aconitum carmichaelii var. *wilsonii*

Aconitum napellus

Ageratum houstonianum 'Blue Horizon'

Agrostemma githago 'Milos'

Allium aflatunense

Allium sphaerocephalon

Alstroemeria 'Walter Remming'

Amaranthus caudatus var. *atropurpureus*

Anemone coronaria 'Mona Lisa'

Antirrhinum majus (mix)

Antirrhinum majus 'Liberty Pink'

Asclepias tuberosa

Aster 'Pink Star'

Astilbe 'Bonn'

Astilbe 'Ostrich Plume'

Astilbe 'Rheinland'

Astrantia major

Buddleia davidii 'Black Knight'

Callistephus chinensis

Callicarpa americana

Campanula persicifolia

Campanula glomerata 'Superba'

Carthamus tinctorius 'Lasting Orange'

Caryopteris incana

Celosia argentea var. *plumosa* (mix)

Centaurea americana 'Jolly Joker'

Celosia argentea var. *spicata* 'Flamingo Feather'

Centaurea macrocephala

Centranthus ruber

Cirsium japonicum 'Rose Beauty'

Cornus alba

Consolida ambigua (double mix)

Cosmos bipinnatus 'Sensation Pink'

Crocosmia × *crocosmiiflora*
'Emily McKenzie'

Dahlia 'Cheerio'

Delphinium 'Blue Triumphator'

Delphinium 'King Arthur'

Dianthus barbatus (mix)

Dianthus 'First Love'

Echinacea purpurea

Echinacea purpurea

Echinacea purpurea 'White Lustre'

Echinops bannaticus 'Taplow Blue'

Emilia javanica (mix)

Emilia javanica

Eryngium planum

Euphorbia marginata

Eustoma grandiflorum 'Yodel Blue'

Freesia × *hybrida*

Gladiolus hybrids at harvest

Godetia amoena (Grace series)

Gomphrena globosa 'Lavender Queen'

Gomphrena 'Strawberry Fields'

Gypsophila paniculata 'Perfecta'

Helianthus annuus 'Sunrich Lemon'

Helianthus annuus 'Goldburst'

Helichrysum bracteatum 'Bright Bikini'

Hydrangea quercifolia 'Snowflake'

Ilex verticillata 'Winter Red'

Iris 'White Cloud'

Lavatera trimestris 'Mont Rose'

Liatris spicata

Lilium in the field

Limonium altaica

Limonium sinuatum 'Heavenly Blue'

Lysimachia clethroides

Lunaria annua

Matthiola incana

Narcissus 'Ice Follies'

Nerine sarniensis 'Salmon Supreme'

Nigella damascena

Ornithogalum saundersiae

Oxypetalum caeruleum 'Heavenborn'

Paeonia 'Charlie's White'

Paeonia officinalis

Phlox paniculata 'Starfire'

Physalis alkekengi

Physostegia virginiana 'Bouquet Rose'

Platycodon grandiflorus var. *albus*

Polianthes tuberosa 'Mexican Single'

Ranunculus asiaticus

Ranunculus asiaticus

Salix chaenomeloides

Salvia leucantha

Scabiosa caucasica 'Pink Mist'

× *Solidaster luteus*

Solidago 'Strahlenkrone'

Thalictrum aquilegifolium 'White Cloud'

Trachelium caeruleum 'Blue Umbrella'

Triteleia × *tubergenii* 'Queen Fabiola'

Tulipa 'West Point'

Tulipa 'White Triumphator'

Veronica longifolia 'Schneeriesen'

Veronicastrum virginicum 'Album'

Zantedeschia 'Black Magic'

Zinnia elegans 'Ruffles' (mix)

Freesia × *hybrida* Freesia 12–15"/9"
Various colors Hybrid origin Iridaceae Greenhouse

Although significant field production occurred in southern California from the 1950s through the 1970s, problems with disease and insects reduced productivity. Precooled freesias are still produced in Florida as a winter crop but most production occurs in protected structures. Plants are native to the Cape Province of South Africa. In their native habitat, corms sprout in the fall and flower in winter at temperatures around 46–50F (4).

Propagation

Seed: Seed sown at 60–66F soil temperature in the dark germinates in approximately 3 weeks and may be transplanted to pots or flats 1–2 weeks later (4).

Corms: Most growers purchase freesia corms produced in the United States or the Netherlands.

Environmental Factors

Temperature: Temperature is the main trigger for flower initiation and development. Freesias initiate flowers at 40–68F but 54–60F is optimal (4,7). Temperatures above 70F should be avoided because no flowers will initiate (6). Temperatures greater than 61F hasten flower stem development once flowers have initiated but the time savings is often offset by a reduction in flower quality. Abnormal inflorescences develop in which the flowers are more widely spaced on the spike, fewer flowers occur per spike and flower stems are shorter (4). The entire crop is best forced at temperatures of 54–60F.

Corms: Bulb specialists pretreat corms for 10–13 weeks at 86F prior to shipping (4). Corms must be ordered well in advance to ensure proper treatment by the bulb distributor.

Photoperiod: Temperature is more important than photoperiod, particularly as temperatures increase (7). However, flower initiation is enhanced by SD while flower development (stage after initiation) is enhanced by LD (5). Short days increase the number of flowers per raceme, length of stem and number of lateral flower stems (2,5).

Greenhouse Performance

Corms: If corms cannnot be planted immediately upon arrival, store at 55F, high relative humidity and no ventilation (1). Plant 5–7 cm corms in well-drained, fluoride-free soil, pH 6.5–7.0, with the tops of the corms approximately 2" below the surface. Space corms about 2–3" apart (90–110 corms/100 ft^2 of bed) (1). Provide at least two layers of mesh support system over the bed.

After planting, corms may be grown at 70F days and 65F nights until 5–7 leaves are visible. At that time, lower temperatures so soil temperature is 50–55F. Low soil temperatures limit production to winter months in much of the country unless soil cooling is used when temperatures become warm.

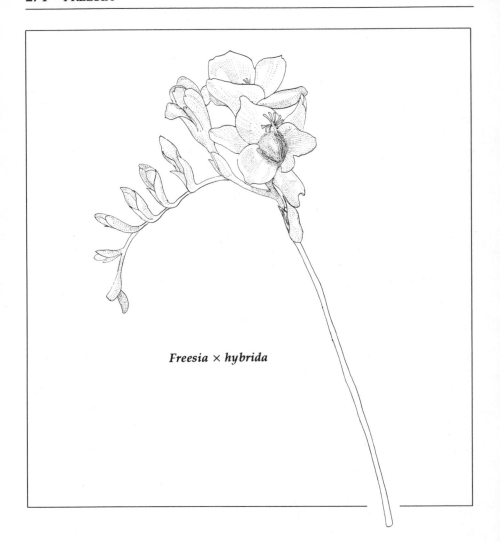

Freesia × *hybrida*

Warmer temperatures result in problems discussed under environmental factors. Provide as much light as possible. Fertilize with 200 ppm N with a complete fertilizer such as 20–20–20 every other week (1).

Flowering generally starts 110–120 days after corms are planted and persists for 4 weeks (1). Corms must be staggered for long-term flower production.

Seedlings: Seedlings are transplanted when they are 2–3″ tall (4–5 weeks from sowing) and grown at 70F days and 65F nights until 6–8 leaves are visible (4). Lower to continuous 50–55F soil temperatures for flower initation and development. Follow similar cultural practices outlined for corms.

Stage of Harvest

Harvest when first flower is beginning to open and at least 2 additional flowers are showing color (8).

Postharvest

Fresh: Flowers persist approximately 1 week (9). Freesias are susceptible to ethylene and should be kept away from fruit or other ethylene sources. An 18-hour pulse with a preservative solution to which sucrose has been added at the rate of 2 lb/gal should be done in the dark at 70F and 85% relative humidity (3). The treatment will increase flower size and allow more flowers to open.

Immature flowers (cut before the first flower has opened) should be held in a preservative solution containing 4% sucrose (3).

Avoid fluoridated water (3).

Dried: Freesias may be dried with silica gel desiccant (9). They do not air-dry well.

Storage: Flowers may be stored dry at 32–35F and high relative humidity (90%) for 7 days (8). They may be held longer in water at 33–35F. Freesias should be stored upright as they are geotrophic (bend upward). Prior to shipping, stems may be pulsed with 200 ppm 8-HQC plus 20% sucrose for 24 hours at 70F and 60% relative humidity (10).

Freesias should not be placed in the same solution with cut narcissus.

Cultivars

Many cultivars are available in an array of colors and with single or double flowers. Consult a bulb specialist for available cultivars for your area.

Pests and Diseases

Botrytis and aphids are the most common problems. Dip corms on arrival into an appropriate fungicide to reduce incidence of botrytis and apply proper aphicides when necessary.

Reading

1. De Hertogh, A. A. 1989. *Holland Bulb Forcer's Guide.* 4th ed. International Flower Bulb Center, Hillegom, The Netherlands.

2. DeLint, P. J. 1969. Flowering in *Freesia*: Temperature and corms. *Acta Hortic.* 14:125–131.

3. Evans, R. Y., and M. S. Reid. 1990. Postharvest care of specialty cut flowers. In *Proceedings of 3rd National Conference on Specialty Cut Flowers.* Ventura, CA. 26–44.

4. Gilbertson-Ferriss, T. L. 1985. *Freesia × hybrida.* In A. H. Halevy (ed.), *The Handbook of Flowering,* vol. 3. CRC Press, Boca Raton, FL. 34–37.

5. Gilbertson-Ferriss, T. L., and H. F. Wilkins. 1978. Flower production of *Freesia hybrida* seedlings under night interruption lighting and short day influence. *J. Amer. Soc. Hort. Sci.* 103:587–591.

6. Gilbertson-Ferriss, T. L., H. F. Wilkins, and R. Hoberg. 1981. Influence of alternating day and night temperature on flowering of *Freesia hybrida. J.*

Amer. Soc. Hort. Sci. 106:466–469.

7. Heide, O. M. 1965. Factors controlling flowering in seed-raised *Freesia* plants. *J. Hort. Sci.* 40:267–284.

8. Nowak, J., and R. M. Rudnicki. 1990. *Postharvest Handling and Storage of Cut Flowers, Florist Greens, and Potted Plants.* Timber Press, Portland, OR.

9. Vaughan, M. J. 1988. *The Complete Book of Cut Flower Care.* Timber Press, Portland, OR.

10. Woodson, R. M. 1987. Postharvest handling of bud-cut freesia flowers. *HortScience* 22:456–458.

Gladiolus spp.	Gladiolus		1–3'/1'
Various colors	Hybrid origin	Iridaceae	Zones 8–10

Gladioli can hardly be considered a specialty cut flower. Glads have been produced for many years and are well established as a mainstream cut flower. A staggering volume of spikes are produced in this country as well as Europe, South America and Israel. Two main types of gladioli are used. Standard types produce 1 spike/corm with up to 30 large flowers/spike; miniatures may produce several stems per corm. The largest production areas are in Florida and Michigan, but smaller growers can still find a niche for good quality stems by producing spikes in the time window between the Florida and Michigan production seasons (June, early July).

Propagation

All flowers are produced from corms by specialist propagators. Corms are direct-planted to the field after the last frost. Some growers use the same corm for up to 3 years, but most growers replant each year.

Environmental Factors

All gladioli are vegetative when planted and flowers are initiated after a certain number of leaves are formed. The number of leaves formed differs with cultivars and the exact time of flower development depends on water balance, light and temperature. The flowering shoot emerges after the last leaf; generally 8–10 leaves are formed in most cultivars. Gladioli which do not flower are referred to as "blind." Blind mature gladioli are plants in which the flowers were formed but aborted, a phenomenon known as blasting. Blasting is a result of poor light conditions or drying out of the developing plants.

Light and photoperiod: Low light and short days during winter production increase the incidence of flower blasting. The plants are most sensitive to low light and SD during the first to fifth leaf stage (reduced flower percentage) and the fourth to sixth leaf stage (increased flower blasting). Long days, either natural or by applying nightbreak lighting in the greenhouse or field, reduce the incidence of blindness and improve the length and quality of the spikes

Gladiolus hybrid

(3,7). Long days, however, may delay flowering in some cultivars. Corm development continues during SD but is arrested when LD are applied and does not continue until after flowering (9). In summary, high light and long days are best for flower production of gladioli. During winter production, day extension of 4–5 hours or a night break of 2–4 hours is used in the field or greenhouse (3,10). Miniature and standard cultivars respond positively to supplemental photoperiodic lighting (2).

Temperature: Temperature affects the rate of floral development and therefore the rate of flowering. Summer-grown gladioli bloom in about 70 days, while the same cultivars require approximately 130 days to flower in the winter. Low night temperatures (33–38F) cause flower blasting when light intensities are low. Chilling during the day inhibited flowering but did not cause blasting. High temperature blasting is usually the result of poor water balance (plants dry out) and not temperature per se (8).

Corms may be stored by growers after curing and cleaning. Corms are placed at about 40F for 60–90 days (6).

Water: Water stress affects the developing flowers much more than the corm. Therefore, drying out causes more flower blasting than actual damage to the plant itself. The stages immediately after planting and the 4–7 leaf stage (when flowers are developing) are the most sensitive to water stress (8).

Field Performance

Planting: Plant after all danger of frost has passed. Use #1 corms if winter planting; smaller sizes may be used for summer production (1). Corms may be placed as close as 2" apart with 4–5" of soil above. Although corms may be planted "corm to corm," the probability of disease increases with dense plantings.

Soil: Fresh or fumigated soils should be used and 2- to 3-year crop rotations are most important. Soil pH of 6.0–6.5 is best, and well-drained soils are necessary to reduce root and foliar problems.

Scheduling: Depending on cultivar and time of year, flowering occurs 60–100 days from planting (1).

Fertilization: Plants in sandy soils require more frequent fertilization than those in heavier soils. A complete fertilizer such as 5–10–10 or 5–15–5 applied at approximately 2 lb/100 row feet before planting and as a side dressing about 1 month later results in sturdier stems. An additional side dressing may be used when the spikes are visible (1) but is probably not needed in clay/loam soils.

Photoperiodic control: For growers producing a winter field crop, incandescent lights should be strung over the plants to provide long days. Sixty- or 100-watt bulbs spaced at a distance to provide 10–20 fc during the night are most effective. Provide 13-hour days by lighting from 1 hour before dusk until 10:00 or 12:00 PM, depending on natural daylength. Nightbreak lighting and cyclic lighting may also be used.

Lifting: Corms may be removed after the foliage has declined (approx. 8

weeks after flowering) or after first frost. Foliage should be removed and corms placed in trays with screen or slat bottoms. No more than 4 layers of corms are placed in the trays. Temperatures of 75–85F for 10–15 days are used for curing. Corms are stored at 40F, 70–75% relative humidity after curing. To avoid problems of digging, curing and storage, purchase new corms annually.

Greenhouse Performance

Plant corms in ground beds at a spacing of 5–8 corms per running foot. Provide LD (13–15 hours) with incandescent lights (10–20 fc) during late fall, winter, and early spring production. Temperatures should be maintained at 70/65F day/night throughout the crop. Higher temperatures may be used to accelerate leaf emergence and therefore flowering, but high temperatures are not necessary for high-quality flowers. Flowers occur 60–90 days after planting, depending on cultivar. Fertilize with liquid (nitrate forms of nitrogen are best) or granular fertilizers at planting and after 3–4 leaves have emerged.

Stage of Harvest

Cut when 1–5 flowers on the spike are showing color.

Postharvest

Fresh: Gladioli respond well to placing the cut stems in a preservative solution containing up to 20% sugar and a germicide. Allow stems to remain in solution overnight at 70F. The use of warm, deionized water is recommended for rehydration. Deionized water is best for gladioli because they are susceptible to fluoride levels as low as 0.25 ppm. Stems should be placed at 68–76F for maximum bud opening.

The tips of gladiolus stems are very prone to bending if placed on their sides. Unless they can be refrigerated throughout the market chain, they must remain upright during storage and transport.

Storage: Stems may be stored dry if conditioned with 10% sucrose solution plus STS at 68F for 24 hours. After conditioning, cool flowers to 38–40F, wrap in moisture proof paper and place in polyethylene bags. After storage, recut stems and place in an opening solution until flowers reach the desired flowering stage (4).

Wet storage is easier to accomplish if stems are placed in a floral preservative. Stems should be stored at 33–38F (5).

Cultivars

Many standard, hybrid and miniature gladioli are available. Discuss optimum cultivars with a reputable bulb salesperson.

Pests and Diseases

Insects: The main pests are thrips, red spider mites, aphids and wire worms.

The gladiolus thrips are most prevalent and damaging. They feed by rasping the foliage and flowers, giving a whitish gray appearance to the surface of the infected tissue. They feed mainly in cloudy weather, seldom in full sunlight. Infected flowers are discolored and spotted and eventually dry up as if burned (6). Corms may also be attacked and become sticky from the sap which oozes out as a result of the infestation. Apply an insecticide early in the growing season. If possible, refrain from spraying when flowers are open.

Wire worms are the larvae of click beetles and feed on the corms and roots, boring holes in the base of the foliage. Wire worms are reddish brown, long and narrow, with a hard, many-jointed shell (6). Infestations are more common and debilitating in heavy soils which lack adequate drainage. Well-drained, light soils reduce the presence of wire worms, and most soil insecticidal drenches are also effective.

Diseases: Botrytis dry rot, corm rot, hard rot, leaf and flower spot, fusarium rot and viruses affect gladioli.

Botrytis gladiolorum causes botrytis dry rot and is the most common cause of corm rot and leaf and flower spot in glads. The foliage turns brown so suddenly it appears as if the field has been burned. Infected spikes may appear healthy at harvest but rot in transit. Planting in a well-drained field, use of fungicides and roguing are control methods.

Corm rots can be caused by many organisms. *Penicillium gladioli* causes sunken, corky, red-brown lesions and is usually introduced through physical injury. Handle the corms carefully to avoid wounding. If corms are dug, ensure proper curing procedures have been carried out to cover any wounded tissue (see "Field Performance" for digging and curing recommendations). *Fusarium oxysporum* f. *gladioli* causes fusarium dry rot of corms. It is the most serious storage disease organism of gladioli corms. Infected areas appear as concentric water-soaked sunken spots, varying in color from very light brown to tan (6). Treatments vary from hot water treatments (128F) of cormels to roguing. It is essential that soils be well drained and sterilized in areas where infection has occurred. Drying and curing time must be accomplished prior to storage.

Leaf and flower spotting caused by *Curvularia trifolii* f. *gladioli* shows up as oval, tan spots on the leaves and stems. The spots may grow from pinhead size to an inch in diameter in a few days. Spots may be seen on both sides of the leaf and black powdery spores occur in the middle of the lesions. Flowers fail to open when the disease is advanced. Foliar fungicide may have to be applied every week to control the disease.

Viruses include cucumber mosaic and tobacco mosaic virus. Streaking of the foliage and flowers is a common symptom of infection. Most viruses are transmitted by infected tools, aphids or leafhoppers. Disinfecting tools and controlling the insects offer control of the viruses. Since viruses are carried over from one season to the next in the corms, infected corms should be discarded.

Reading

1. De Hertogh, A. A. 1989. *Holland Bulb Forcer's Guide.* 4th ed. International Flower Bulb Center, Hillegom, The Netherlands.

2. Halevy, A. H. 1985. *Gladiolus.* In A. H. Halevy (ed.), *The Handbook of Flowering*, vol. 3. CRC Press, Boca Raton, FL. 63–70.

3. McKay, M. E., D. E. Blyth and J. A. Tommerup. 1981. The influence of photoperiod and plant density on yield of winter-grown gladioli in Queensland. *Scientia Hortic.* 14:171–179.

4. Nowak, J., and R. M. Rudnicki. 1984. Cold storage of cut gladiolus spikes. *Rosliny Ozdobne*, Ser. B. 9:67–72. Skierniewice, Poland.

5. _____ . 1990. *Postharvest Handling and Storage of Cut Flowers, Florist Greens, and Potted Plants.* Timber Press, Portland, OR.

6. Pirone, P. P. 1970. *Diseases and Pests of Ornamental Plants.* Ronald Press, New York, NY.

7. Shillo, R., and A. H. Halevy. 1976. The effect of various environmental factors on flowering of gladiolus. II. Length of the day. *Scientia Hortic.* 4:139–146.

8. _____ . 1976. The effect of various environmental factors on flowering of gladiolus. III. Temperature and moisture. *Scientia Hortic.* 4:147–155.

9. _____ . 1981. Flower and corm development in gladiolus as affected by photoperiod. *Scientia Hortic.* 15:187–196.

10. Shillo, R., G. Valis and A. H. Halevy. 1981. Promotion of flowering by photoperiodic lighting in winter-grown gladiolus planted at high densities. *Scientia Hortic.* 14:367–375.

Iris hybrids

	Dutch Iris		1.5–2'/1'
Various colors	Hybrid origin	Iridaceae	Zones 8–10

Many iris are useful as cut flowers, but dutch iris are most widely grown. Dutch iris are hybrids between numerous bulbous species (*I. latifolia* var. *praecox* and *I. tingitana* among them), and dozens of cultivars exist. They are more commonly grown as a greenhouse crop in the United States where weekly schedules are fulfilled; however, field production is also possible in the southern states and on the West Coast.

Propagation

Dutch iris are true bulbs and offsets are formed after flowering. Offsets may be divided, cleaned, sized and replanted each summer. Most growers, however, treat the bulbs as annuals and discard them each year. This is particularly true for greenhouse production. Bulbs should be planted immediately upon arrival.

Environmental Factors

Temperature: High temperature is necessary for successful flower forcing. The temperatures and durations depend on where the bulbs are grown and when they are lifted. When lifted from warm soils, the heat requirement is partially fulfilled. Warm storage recommendations differ for various areas but are given for approximately 2 weeks. For example, bulbs grown in the Netherlands may be stored at 86–95F for 2 weeks followed by 3 days at 110F. In western Washington, bulbs are stored for 2 weeks at 90F; in the United Kingdom, temperatures of 86F for 2 weeks followed by 3 days of 110F are satisfactory (5).

After high temperatures are applied, low temperatures are necessary for flower initiation. In general, temperatures of 55F for about 6 weeks are recommended. Prolonged high temperatures can nullify the beneficial effects of the cool temperature treatment.

Field Performance

Bulb size: Bulb size should be greater than 8/9 cm for optimum flowering (2). Optimum bulb size varies with cultivar.

Spacing: Space bulbs 3–6" apart and 4–5" below the soil surface (2).

Planting time: Bulbs should be planted when soil temperature is 60F (2). Bulbs planted in the fall produce flowers in late spring and summer. Bulbs treated with ethylene will be the first to flower (5). The following table provides some information concerning planting time on 5 cultivars of dutch iris, planted approximately 6" apart at Athens, GA.

The effect of planting date on harvest, yield and stem quality of dutch iris (Athens, GA).[a][b]

Month of planting	Stems/bulb	Initial harvest	Duration of harvest (days)	Stem length (in)	Stem diameter (mm)
Nov	0.84	Apr 15	15	16.2	9.5
Dec	0.89	Apr 13	17	15.0	9.5
Jan	0.94	Apr 24	14	14.7	9.3
Feb	0.80	Apr 30	13	12.3	7.5
Mar	0.73	May 20	15	11.2	7.4

[a]Adapted from (1).
[b]Data are averages of 'Blue Ideal', 'Blue Ribbon', 'White Bell', 'White Cloud' and 'White Wedgewood'.

Notice that yield drops off after January, but little difference in yield occurred between November and January plantings. However, harvest was delayed after December and stem length and diameter were reduced as planting was delayed. It is obvious that, at least in zone 7b, planting after January cannot be recommended. This is likely due to rising soil and air temperatures in March through June, which reduced quality, or lack of sufficient cooling.

Longevity: Most growers replace bulbs annually, and even in areas where bulbs may be perennialized, late frosts can devastate emerging flowers. In areas where no frost occurs, bulbs must be precooled.

Greenhouse Performance

Use as large a bulb as possible. Small bulbs produce a high incidence of flower blindness. Apply a 30-minute preplant fungicidal dip to reduce *Penicillium* and *Fusarium*.

Temperature: Use 55F night temperature and 60–63F day temperatures. Avoid temperatures above 63F, particularly under short days or time of low light (2). Low night temperatures (near 50F) enhance postharvest life (4).

Fertilization: Fertilize weekly with calcium nitrate at approximately 350 ppm N.

Scheduling: Harvest occurs 6–8 weeks after planting in greenhouse.

Stage of Harvest

Cut all dutch iris except 'Blue Ribbon' ('Prof Blaauw') when the flower has fully emerged from the sheath. This is referred to as the "pencil" stage, when a pencil of color is visible. 'Blue Ribbon' should be cut when the falls begin to open (2).

Iris should be packed in bunches of 10 stems.

Postharvest

Fresh: When brought from the field, rehydrate flowers in warm (100F) water. Flowers persist for 2–5 days in water. Silver thiosulfate does little to extend vase life.

Storage: Flowers may be stored dry at 31–32F upright for no more than a week (6) or stored wet upright for 5–10 days at 32F. Prolonged storage time results in failure of flowers to open (3).

If flowers are conditioned in a solution containing 1.5 oz/5 gal citric acid and 1.5 oz/5 gal sucrose for 12 hours at 68F, the vase life of dry shipped flowers improves (4). The retailer or consumer should rehydrate iris in warm water (100F) for 3 hours (4).

Cultivars

Many cultivars are available; consult wholesale bulb catalogues or *Holland Bulb Forcer's Guide* (2) for details.

Pests and Diseases

Fusarium oxysporum (bulb rot) and *Penicillium* (blue mold) fungi infect the basal plate area of iris bulbs resulting in gray-brown tissue. They should be dipped in fungicide prior to planting. Use of sterile soil in greenhouse forcing is recommended.

Reading

1. Armitage, A. M., and J. M. Laushman. 1990. Planting date and in-ground time affect cut flowers of *Liatris* .... *HortScience* 25:1239–1241.

2. De Hertogh, A. A. 1989. *Holland Bulb Forcer's Guide*. 4th ed. International Flower Bulb Center, Hillegom, The Netherlands.

3. Evans, R. Y., and M. S. Reid. 1990. Postharvest care of specialty cut flowers. In *Proceedings of 3rd National Conference on Specialty Cut Flowers*. Ventura, CA. 26–44.

4. Nowak, J., and R. M. Rudnicki. 1990. *Postharvest Handling and Storage of Cut Flowers, Florist Greens, and Potted Plants*. Timber Press, Portland, OR.

5. Rees, A. R. 1985. *Iris*. In A. H. Halevy (ed.), *The Handbook of Flowering*, vol. 1. CRC Press, Boca Raton, FL. 282–287.

6. Sacalis, J. N. 1989. *Fresh (Cut) Flowers for Designs: Postproduction Guide* I. D. C. Kiplinger Chair in Floriculture, The Ohio State Univ., Columbus, OH.

Liatris spicata	Kansas Gayfeather		2–4'/2'
Purple, white	North America	· Asteraceae	Zones 3–9

Liatris has become a major cut flower in the United States and enjoys widespread cultivation in fields and greenhouses. Approximately 30 species and over 10 hybrid forms are known. Numerous species may be used as cut flowers but only *L. spicata* and *L. pycnostachya* are commonly produced. American consumers should thank the Dutch for aggressively introducing this native species to the American marketplace, but now it is time for American growers to take up the slack.

Propagation

Liatris corms (often referred to as tubers) may be divided and replanted in the field or greenhouse. Allow to cure (place in warm, well-ventilated area) for 3–7 days after dividing. Seed may be sown in soilless media at 75–78F and high humidity. Cuttings from newly emerged stems may be rooted in approximately 21 days. Vegetatively produced corms are more productive than those grown from seed (12,14).

Environmental Factors

Temperature: Cold temperatures are essential for flowering in *Liatris*. Storage of corms at 28–36F for 8–15 weeks results in a majority of flowering corms. Prolonged cooling also reduces the time to flower when forced in the greenhouse. For example, corms stored for 3 weeks at 32F flowered in 99 days from planting in the greenhouse while corms stored for 15 weeks flowered in 72 days (9).

Gibberellic acid: Soaking corms for 1 hour in 500 ppm GA_3 after a 5-week cold storage resulted in 100% flowering (16). Use of GA may partially substitute for the cold treatment. Cold treatment/GA dip combinations are particularly useful for early forcing dates.

Photoperiod: Flower initiation occurs regardless of photoperiod; however, plants respond to photoperiod through accelerated flowering and longer stems when given LD. If corms are provided sufficient cooling period, LD result in accelerated flowering. However, if plants receive a short cooling period, then SD enhances flowering (3). Similar interactions with forcing temperature were found if corms were forced in the greenhouse. At cool forcing temperatures (55F), LD hastened flowering but at warmer forcing temperatures, photoperiod had little effect (6). For greatest flower acceleration, LD (14 hours) should be applied in the first 5 weeks after emergence of the foliage. Long days also result in greater stem elongation regardless of cooling treatments or forcing temperatures (6,7).

Studies have shown that continuous LD after emergence reduced the number of flowers/corm (15). A short period of SD prior to application of LD may be useful to increase the number of flowers.

Field Performance

Spacing: Plant corms about 2–4" apart and plant 2–3" beneath the soil surface.

Corm size: Small corms result in poor yield and short stems. In general, the larger the corm, the more rapid the flowering and the higher percentage of flowering corms occurs (14). Use of 6/8 or 8/10 cm corms is recommended.

Planting time: Stored frozen corms may be planted at any time; however, differences in yield and stem length occur.

The effect of planting date on harvest, yield and stem quality of *Liatris spicata* (Athens, GA).[a]

Month of planting	Flowers/corm	Initial harvest	Duration of harvest (days)	Stem length (in)	Stem diameter (mm)
Nov	2.2	Jul 1	14	25.0	7.1
Dec	1.2	Jul 1	15	22.8	6.9
Jan	2.0	Jul 8	14	20.0	6.9
Feb	3.4	Jul 12	12	26.5	7.9
Mar	4.5	Jul 21	15	28.9	6.0

[a] From (2).

Three weeks' extension of flowering occurred when planting was delayed until March, but this was likely due to the increase in number of weeks of cold storage. No difference in harvest duration occurred due to planting date nor did any differences occur in subsequent years of production.

Longevity: *Liatris* can be considered perennial (at least 3 years of production) in most of the country. Continued corm growth from year to year results in increased yield and stem length each year.

Yield and stem quality of *Liatris spicata* over time (Athens, GA).[a]

Year	Flowers/corm	Stem length (in)
1	2.7	24.7
2	8.0	30.0
3	15.0	39.2

[a] Adapted from (1).

Liatris spicata may be productive for up to 5 years although partial replacement after 3 years is recommended. Work with *L. pycnostachya*, however, showed that 3 years' production was maximum (1).

Support: Support is necessary, especially after the first year. Use of 2 layers of floriculture netting is recommended. If stems topple, flowers turn up and become distorted.

Greenhouse Performance

Use large corms for greenhouse forcing, which may be accomplished year-round. Pot 3 corms in 6–8" pots or in ground beds, using sterilized soils to reduce soil fungi. Maintain soil temperatures as close to 60F as possible and place under short days (8–10 hours) for the first 2–3 weeks after emergence. Fertilize with 100–150 ppm N after foliar emergence. Use LD (14–16 hours) by extending the day or with nightbreak lighting after SD for maximum stem elongation and most rapid flowering. Temperatures of 65–68F should be used for forcing. Flowers may be harvested 60–70 days after emergence, depending on light intensity and temperature.

Guideline for Foliar Analyses

At field trials in Athens, GA, and Watsonville, CA, foliage was sampled from vigorously growing healthy plants when flower buds were visible, but prior to flower opening. These are guidelines only and should not be considered absolute standards. Based on dry weight analysis.

(%)						(ppm)				
N	P	K	Ca	Mg		Fe	Mn	B	Al	Zn
					(GA)					
2.7	0.20	1.16	1.49	0.45		207	163	24	59	94
					(CA)					
3.3	0.19	2.31	1.12	0.41		207	178	31	59	86

Stage of Harvest

Inflorescences may be harvested when 3–4 flowers have opened if stems are pulsed in a bud-opening solution. If no preservative is used after harvesting, stems should be harvested when at least ½ the flowers are open.

Postharvest

Fresh: Flowers treated with preservatives persist for 7–12 days (13). The foliage may decline more rapidly. Lower foliage must be removed prior to placing cut stems in solution.

A 24- to 72-hour pulse in a bud-opening solution which includes 5% sucrose has been recommended for tight cut flowers (11). However, a continuous supply (not pulsed) of 2.5–5% sucrose allows most flowers to open and significantly increases the vase life (4,8).

Storage: Stems may be stored about 1 week in water at 32–35F after pulsing, about 5 days dry (13). Good air circulation is necessary in the storage room because *Liatris* is susceptible to botrytis. For long term transport, flowers may be cut in tight bud stage and opened after arrival in a preservative solution or a solution of 1 ppm 8-HQC and 50 g/liter sucrose (10).

Dried: Allow all flowers on spike to open. Strip leaves and air-dry by hanging upside down in a well-ventilated area (5).

Cultivars

The only flower colors are purple and white. Purple colors are best filled by the species itself or 'Floristan Purple'. Other garden forms such as 'Kobold' are too short (12–18" tall) for cut flower production.

var. *alba* is white and similar to the species except for flower color.

'Floristan White' is an excellent, creamy white–flowered cultivar. The Floristan series may be raised from seed.

'Gloriosa' is a vigorous purple cultivar but not readily available in the United States.

Additional Species

Liatris callilepis is offered by a number of bulb growers. Taxonomically, *L. callilepis* is a synonym for *L. spicata* and plants should be treated the same. Some bulb specialists sell vegetatively propagated plants as *L. callilepis* and seed-propagated material as *L. spicata*.

L. pycnostachya is the only other species commonly used; it is a taller, coarser plant than *L. spicata*. In our trials in Georgia, stems were over 3' tall and plants only persisted 2 years. 'Eureka' is a selection developed by the University of Nebraska and the U.S. Soil Conservation Service. 'Eureka', to my knowledge, is not nationally available.

L. scariosa (tall gayfeather) is also useable in a cut flower program. 'September Glory' has purple flowers which open almost simultaneously and 'White Spires' has white flowers.

Pests and Diseases

Leaf spots (*Phyllosticta liatridis, Septoria liatridis*) result in brown-to-black spots on the foliage. Fungicides may be applied when plants are young.

Rusts may infect plants. Certain grasses and pine trees act as alternate hosts for liatris rust caused by *Coleosporium laciniariae* and *Puccinia liatridis*. Destroy infected plants.

Reading

1. Armitage, A. M. 1987. The influence of spacing on field-grown perennial crops. *HortScience* 22:904–907.

2. Armitage, A. M., and J. M. Laushman. 1990. Planting date and in-ground time affect cut flowers of *Liatris* .... *HortScience* 25:1239–1241.

3. Berland, M. 1983. *Growth and Flowering in* Liatris spicata. M.S. Thesis, Agr. University of Norway, Aas, Norway.

4. Borochov, A., and V. Karen-Paz. 1984. Bud opening of cut liatris flowers. *Scientia Hortic.* 23:85–89.

5. Bullivant, E. 1989. *Dried Fresh Flowers From Your Garden.* Pelham

Books/Stephen Greene Press, London, U.K.

6. Espinosa, I., W. Healy and M. Roh. 1987. Interactions of photoperiod and temperature on flowering of *Liatris*. *Acta Hortic.* 205:113–119.

7. Geller, Z. 1981. *Horticultural and Physiological Aspects in Growing of* Liatris spicata. M.S. Agr. Thesis, Hebrew University of Jerusalem, Rehovat, Israel.

8. Han, S. S. 1992. Role of sugars in bud development and vase life of cut *Liatris spicata*. *HortScience*. In press.

9. Moe, R., and M. Berland. 1986. Effect of various corm treatments on flowering of *Liatris spicata*. *Acta Hortic.* 177:197–201.

10. Nowak, J., and R. M. Rudnicki. 1990. *Postharvest Handling and Storage of Cut Flowers, Florist Greens, and Potted Plants*. Timber Press, Portland, OR.

11. Sacalis, J. N. 1989. *Fresh (Cut) Flowers for Designs: Postproduction Guide* I. D. C. Kiplinger Chair in Floriculture, The Ohio State Univ., Columbus, OH.

12. Salac, S. S., and J. B. Fitzgerald. 1983. Influence of propagation method and fertilizer rate on growth and development of *Liatris pycnostachya*. *HortScience* 18:198–199.

13. Vaughan, M. J. 1988. *The Complete Book of Cut Flower Care*. Timber Press, Portland, OR.

14. Waithaka, K., and L. W. Wanjao. 1982. The influence of corm source, age and size on growth and flowering of *Liatris*. In *International Horticultural Congress*, vol. 2. Hamburg, Germany. 1724. (Abstr.)

15. Zieslin, N., and Z. Geller. 1983. Studies with *Liatris spicata* Willd. II. Effects of photoperiod on stem extension, flowering and gibberellin content. *Ann. Bot.* 52:855–859.

16. Zieslin, N. 1985. *Liatris*. In A. H. Halevy (ed.), *The Handbook of Flowering*, vol. 3, CRC Press, Boca Raton, FL. 287–291.

Thanks to Mr. Jack Zoonveld for reviewing this section.

Lilium **hybrids**	Hybrid Lilies		3–8'/2'
Various colors	Hybrid origin	Liliaceae	Zones 3–7

A large genus including many species of garden lilies as well as those suitable for cut flowers. Many hybrid lilies are forced in the greenhouse or under some form of cover and have become an important cut flower in Europe and North America.

Propagation
All bulbs used for cut flowers are produced either in the Netherlands or northwestern United States. Hybridizers propagate by scaling, offsets and seed.

Growing-on
Bulbs should be given a 10- to 20-second preplant dip in a solution of

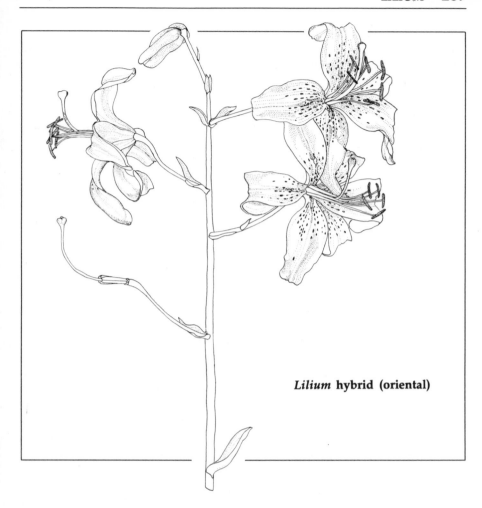

Lilium hybrid (oriental)

fungicides to prevent root rot complex associated with lilies (see "Pests and Diseases"). After treatment, immediately plant in the field or greenhouse. If bulbs must be stored, do not store longer than 10 days at 32–35F (1).

Environmental Factors

Temperature: All lilies require cold temperatures for flowering. Lilies harvested in late summer and fall are precooled at 35F for 6–8 weeks in moist peat moss. For later plantings, bulbs may be frozen at 30F after being precooled. After planting, warm temperatures result in faster forcing.

Light: Lilies need high light for best flowering, particularly if forced in the greenhouse during the winter months. Low light results in bud abortion and abscission.

Photoperiod: In easter lilies (*L. longiflorum*), application of LD can substitute for the cold requirement. The same relationship may be true with most liliaceous species (5).

Field Performance

Bulb size: Large bulb sizes are preferable to smaller sizes, but differences between species and cultivars occur. Bulbs ranging from 4–5" (10/12 cm) to 8–9" (20/22 cm) in diameter are used.

Spacing: Space bulbs 4–6" apart and 6" below the soil. Spacing depends on the width of the bulb.

Planting time: Lilies are generally planted in the fall although precooled bulbs may be planted in the spring in areas of insufficient cold.

Longevity: Most growers treat lilies as annuals, replanting after each crop, regardless of locale. However, flowers of 'Connecticut King' and 'Enchantment' were produced for 3 years under trials at the University of Georgia (zone 7b). Longevity depends on temperature, fertility, light and the amount of stem leaves allowed to remain on the plant after harvest. Bulbs planted in zone 8–10 are always treated as annuals.

Greenhouse Performance

Lily bulbs are harvested from August through October. Bulbs used for greenhouse forcing must receive at least 6 weeks (asiatic) and 8 weeks (oriental) of cold (35F), moist treatment. For later forcings and year-round flowering, bulbs should be frozen at 30F after being precooled for 6–8 weeks (1). Temperatures should not fall below 28F.

On arrival, bulbs should be planted immediately in sterile ground beds in a well-drained medium lacking superphosphate or perlite at a pH of 6.8–7.0. All cultivars can be forced for the spring (March through June) while some may be forced during the winter (December through March). Four crops may be produced on a year-round basis. Plant bulbs with at least 2" of medium above the bulb nose. Space large oriental lily bulbs (9" in circumference and greater) 6–7" apart; space small ones (7–8" in circumference) 5–6" apart. Asiatic lilies should be spaced at 4.5–6" for bulbs which are 7–8" in circumference, 3.5–4.5" apart for those which are 4–5" in circumference (1). More room between bulbs should be provided in the winter than the summer. If bulbs, on average, are planted on a 4" × 5" spacing, approximately 7 bulbs/ft² are needed.

High light is necessary for best greenhouse forcing and is often insufficient during the winter. Supplemental light is useful for areas of low light. During high light conditions in late spring and summer, shading is appropriate. Large changes in temperatures should be avoided and forcing temperatures of 55–63F are best. Temperatures above 70F are not necessary. During warm seasons, use of mulch helps to reduce soil temperatures. Fertilize with calcium nitrate and potassium nitrate (2 pounds and 1 pound per 100 gallons water, respectively) once a week (1).

Asiatic lilies require 8–10 weeks in the greenhouse, approximately 30–35 days to flower after reaching visible bud. Oriental lilies need 12–15 weeks in the greenhouse, approximately 50–55 days from visible bud to open flower (1).

Guideline for Foliar Analyses

At field trials in Watsonville, CA, foliage was sampled from vigorously growing healthy asiatic lilies when flower buds were visible, but prior to flower opening. These are guidelines only and should not be considered absolute standards. Based on dry weight analysis.

(%)						(ppm)				
N	P	K	Ca	Mg		Fe	Mn	B	Al	Zn
'Enchantment'										
2.0	0.12	2.51	1.09	0.30		63	30	17	60	25

Stage of Harvest

Cut when the first flower is fully colored, but not yet open. Open flowers are easily damaged in transit.

Postharvest

Fresh: The vase life of most cut lily flowers is 5–9 days, depending on cultivar and environmental conditions. Pulsing stems for approximately 20 minutes with a preservative containing STS extends vase life. Longer pulse times with more dilute STS are also effective (3). After pulsing, place stems in preservative solutions. Placing stems in a combination of STS and 10% sugar for 24 hours followed by placement in 50 ppm GA_3 greatly increases vase life of 'Enchantment' lilies (3).

Storage: Lilies may be stored dry at 33F for up to 4 weeks if initially pulsed for 24 hours with STS and 10% sucrose. Flowers should be wrapped in polyethylene film to reduce water loss during storage. Do not store more than 3 days without chemical pretreatment. An additional conditioning solution is an STS solution supplemented with sucrose at the rate of 5 oz/gal and 1000 ppm gibberellic acid (4). For wet storage, flowers are cut at bud stage, conditioned as above, and placed in containers of water at 32–34F. Flowers may be stored up to 4 weeks (4).

Cultivars

Many are available and additional ones appear every year. A number of hybrids performed well in field tests in Georgia ('Connecticut Lemonglow', 'Connecticut King', 'Enchantment') but the most extensive trialing of cut lily cultivars was done by De Hertogh (1,2) in greenhouses in North Carolina. Cultivars have been rated based on numerous characteristics. The following cultivars rated good to excellent in stem strength, an important consideration in cut stems. Those with asterisks are suitable for fall/winter forcing. Cultivars not mentioned may not have been tested or may not have scored as well in trials. Consult bulb growers and brokers for lists of other cultivars suitable for cut flower production.

Asiatic lilies
    'Amigos'* (dark yellow)
    'Avignon' (orange, red)
    'Bright Beauty' (light orange)
    'Carlaluppi' (yellow)
    'Chinook'* (salmon)
    'Cocktail'* (light lilac)
    'Connecticut King'* (yellow)
    'Crescendo'* (yellow)
    'Enchantment'* (orange)
    'Eurovision'* (orange)
    'Fiesta Gitana' (orange)
    'Flashlight' (orange)
    'Grand Paradiso' (orange, red)
    'Grand Prix'* (red)
    'High Style' (yellow)
    'Ladykiller'*(orange)

    'Medallion'* (yellow)
    'Moulin Rouge'* (red)
    'Roma'* (white)
    'Sun Ray' (yellow)
    'Yellow Giant' ['Joanna'] (yellow)
    'White Happiness'* (white)

Oriental lilies
    'Atlantis' (pink)
    'Casa Blanca' (white)
    'Gypsy Eyes' (red)
    'Journey's End'* (rose-red)
    'Mona Lisa' (pink)
    'Olympic Star' (red, white)
    'Star Gazer'* (rose)
    'Uchida' (rose)

Additional Species

Even with so many hybrids available, a few species are also used as cut flowers.

Lilium auratum (goldband lily) is an excellent cut flower. The best variety is var. *platyphyllum*, which has fragrant outward-facing white flowers with a band of gold on the inside.

L. formosanum (formosa lily) has demonstrated excellent stem strength and vigorous growth during field trials in Georgia. Its advantages are ease of growth, ease of propagation (plants sown in summer or planted in fall will flower the following summer) and stem strength. Disadvantages are lack of "exciting" colors and susceptibility to lily mosaic virus.

L. longiflorum (easter lily) also produces good cut flowers. The pot plant cultivars 'Ace' and 'Nellie White' have been joined by 'Harbor', 'Chetco' and 'Osnat'.

Physiological Disorders

Leaf scorch is usually associated with fluoride toxicity. Maintaining media free of fluoride and pH near 7.0 reduces the problem. Spraying susceptible cultivars daily with a 1% solution of pure calcium chloride until flower buds are visible may be helpful (1). Flower blasting and flower abscission result from high temperatures and low light intensity, respectively.

Pests and Diseases

Lily mosaic virus was a serious disease of lily bulbs but efforts to clean up propagation stock have considerably reduced its incidence, particularly on greenhouse-grown material. Yellowing and mottling appear on the leaves and they may become twisted and distorted. Aphids spread the disease from plant to plant. Discard bulbs if virus is present.

Root rot complex is a name given for a disease which discolors and rots roots. It is caused by a number of fungi including *Fusarium* and *Cylindrocarpon*. Bulbs should be dipped in appropriate fungicides for 10–30 minutes prior to planting. Fungicide combinations are described by De Hertogh (1).

Reading

1. De Hertogh, A. A. 1989. *Holland Bulb Forcer's Guide*. 4th ed. International Flower Bulb Center, Hillegom, The Netherlands.

2. De Hertogh, A. A. 1990. Research on forced flower bulbs focuses on improved quality and cultivars. *PPGA News*. 21(11):2–7.

3. Evans, R. Y., and M. S. Reid. 1990. Postharvest care of specialty cut flowers. In *Proceedings of 3rd National Conference on Specialty Cut Flowers*. Ventura, CA. 26–44.

4. Nowak, J., and R. M. Rudnicki. 1990. *Postharvest Handling and Storage of Cut Flowers, Florist Greens, and Potted Plants*. Timber Press, Portland, OR.

5. Rees, A. R. 1985. *Lilium*. In A. H. Halevy (ed.), *The Handbook of Flowering*, vol. 1. CRC Press, Boca Raton, FL. 288–293.

Narcissus **spp.**	Daffodil		18–24"/12"
Various colors	Spain, Portugal	Amaryllidaceae	Zones 3–9

Narcissus is forced for cut flowers for Valentine's Day through Mother's Day and may be produced in the greenhouse or field. Flowers have been divided into 11 classes, depending on parentage and morphological characteristics such as length of the trumpet or cup. Most cultivars used for cut flowers belong to the trumpet (class I) or large-cupped (class II) narcissus, although the tazetta forms (paperwhites), which require no cold for forcing, are also greenhouse-produced. Paperwhites may be field-produced only in nearly frost-free areas of the country.

Environmental Factors

Most daffodils require a warm–cool–warm temperature sequence: the initial warming occurs in the summer for flower initiation and the winter cool results in subsequent rapid growth and synchronous flowering once warm weather returns in the spring. For proper timing of cut flowers, controlled forcing facilities in which to store the bulbs are necessary. Generally, bulbs are first planted then stored at approximately 48F prior to warm temperatures for flower emergence. Daffodils are not as critical in their temperature requirements as tulips (which see) and planted bulbs may be stored in cold frames or under straw mulch outdoors to achieve these temperatures, but more uniformity and better timing are gained with controlled temperature facilities.

Narcissus hybrid

Field Performance

Bulb size: Use double-nosed daffodils or 12–16 cm rounds. It is difficult to measure the circumference of the bulb due to its shape.

Spacing: Plant approximately 6″ apart with 4–6″ of soil above the nose.

Planting time: In climatic zones 4–5, plant in September and early October; zones 6–7, in October and early November; zones 7–8, November and early December. In areas with little cold temperature (e.g., Florida, coastal California), precooled bulbs (cooled 8–10 weeks at 40F) should be planted in early December (1).

Longevity: In all but the warmest areas, daffodils will perennialize. Well-maintained bulbs should be productive for 3–5 years. At that time bulbs are lifted and separated.

Scheduling: The use of early- and late-flowering cultivars provides for a longer flowering period. Proper selection of cultivars can provide up to 8 weeks of harvest. Flowering begins in February in the South for early, small-flowered cultivars like 'February Gold' and early species such as *N. cyclamineus* and continues to late April for large-cupped cultivars. In the North, flowering is up to 4 weeks later.

Harvesting: Daffodils are often pulled rather than cut to ensure longest stem length.

Stem length: The difference in stem length between northern- and southern-grown bulbs is not nearly as large for daffodils as for tulips (which see). This is because cold is not as necessary for stem extension in daffodils as it is with tulips.

Fertilization: Two to three pounds of a complete granular fertilizer, such as 3–9–18 or 5–10–20, per 100 feet of row should be applied immediately after planting (1).

Greenhouse Performance

Most forcers treat daffodils in a way similar to tulips (which see). For the Valentine's Day market, bulbs are usually panned in October, stored at 48F until roots are visible through the drainage holes, transferred to 41F until shoots are 1–2″ tall and then placed at 33–35F until they are moved to the greenhouse bench. The total time in the cooler depends on the cultivar but is approximately 17 weeks, with a minimum cooling time of 15 weeks and maximum around 20 weeks (1). The greenhouse temperature (approx. 60F) and time in greenhouse (2–3 weeks) depend on cultivar and time of year. For market times before Valentine's Day, precooled bulbs must be purchased. For those interested in greenhouse forcing, the *Holland Bulb Forcer's Guide* by Dr. Gus De Hertogh provides specifics on cultivars and is essential reading (1).

Stage of Harvest

Single, large flowers should be harvested when closed, but with color showing. This is known as the goose-neck stage. The flowers should be at a 90–120° angle from the stem. For double-flowered cultivars, harvest when the flowers are just beginning to open.

Stems should be packed 10 to a bunch.

Postharvest

Fresh: Fresh flowers have a vase life of 4–6 days. Preservatives do not generally enhance the vase life of daffodils.

Storage: Flowers may be stored wet or dry. For dry storage, pack in polyethylene and store in open boxes in a cold room. Flowers may be kept 10 days at 32–33F, 8 days at 36–38F or 1–2 days at 50F (2). Flowers should be kept upright. If flowers arrive bent, they may be wrapped tightly in wet paper and placed in water under direct overhead light (3).

Hardening: Daffodils secrete a mucus which is detrimental to many other cut flowers such as roses, carnations, freesias and tulips. If daffodils are used in arrangements or stored with other flowers, they should be placed by themselves for 12–24 hours in clear water. Change the water at least once and wash the stems upon removal. If freshly cut flowers must be placed with other flowers, put daffodils in a bleach solution (5–7 drops of bleach per quart of water) for 1–5 hours (1). Rinse stems and place with other flowers.

Cultivars

Many cultivars are available. Consult a bulb specialist for best cultivars for your area. A list of recommended cultivars follows.

Class	Cultivar	Color (cup/perianth)	Timing[a]
Cyclamineus	'February Gold'	Yellow/yellow	VE
Double	'Cheerfulness'	White/gold	M
	'Flower Drift'	White/orange	M
	'Sir Winston Churchill'	White/orange	ML
	'Tahiti'	Yellow/red	M
	'White Lion'	White/yellow	M
Jonquilla	'Pipit'	Yellow/cream	M
	'Suzy'	Yellow/orange	ML
	'Trevithian'	Yellow/yellow	M
Large-cupped	'Carbineer'	Yellow/orange	ME
	'Carlton'	Yellow/yellow	E
	'Flower Record'	White/orange-red	ML
	'Fortune'	Yellow-orange/white	M
	'Ice Follies'	Light yellow/white	E
	'Salome'	White/pink	ML
	'St. Patrick's Day'	Yellow/yellow	M
Poeticus	'Actaea'	White/yellow-red	M
Small-cupped	'Amor'	White-yellow/orange	ME
	'Barrett Browning'	White/white-red	ME
Split Corona	'Cassata'	White/white	M
	'Orangery'	White/orange	M
Triandrus	'Thalia'	White/white	ML
Trumpet	'Bravoure'	White/yellow	M
	'Dutch Master'	Yellow/yellow	E
	'Golden Harvest'	Yellow/yellow	M
	'Las Vegas'	White/yellow	ME
	'Spellbinder'	Yellow/white	M
	'Unsurpassable'	Yellow/yellow	ME

[a] Timing is within class: VE = very early, E = early, ME = medium early, M = medium, ML = medium late, L = late.

Pests and Diseases

Basal rot, caused by *Fusarium*, infects the basal plate of the bulb and results in brown-colored decay. Cull infected bulbs and use a preplant fungicidal dip on others. The best preventive methods are excellent drainage and proper dry storage of bulbs.

Fire, manifested as reddish brown spots on leaves, flower and occasionally the bulb, can be troublesome. The spots are somewhat elongated, parallel to the veins. The disease occurs more often in warm, humid climates and after 2–3 days of rainy weather.

Aphids and bulb mites are the most serious pests for commercial growers of cut daffodils.

Reading

1. De Hertogh, A. A. 1989. *Holland Bulb Forcer's Guide*. 4th ed. International Flower Bulb Center, Hillegom, The Netherlands.

2. Nowak, J., and R. M. Rudnicki. 1990. *Postharvest Handling and Storage of Cut Flowers, Florist Greens, and Potted Plants*. Timber Press, Portland, OR.

3. Vaughan, M. J. 1988. *The Complete Book of Cut Flower Care*. Timber Press, Portland, OR.

Many thanks to Mr. Brent Heath for reviewing this section.

Nerine sarniensis

Nerine sarniensis	Guernsey Lily		18–24"/18"
Various colors	South Africa	Amaryllidaceae	Zones 9–10

Bulbs produce straplike leaves and an inflorescence consisting of a naked flower stem supporting an umbel of many 6-petaled flowers. The guernsey lily is not yet widely available, but demand as a greenhouse crop continues to increase in the United States. *Nerine sarniensis* also has exciting potential as an outdoor cut flower in warm areas of the country because it is summer-dormant. This means that flowers emerge in the fall prior to significant leaf expansion. Foliage appears in the fall, and leaves remain green if temperatures are not too cold. Once warm conditions occur, bulbs go dormant until the next fall. Their behavior is similar to species of resurrection lily, *Lycoris*. The other well-known species, *N. bowdenii*, is winter-dormant, similar to the tulip. Most outdoor flowering of *N. sarniensis* presently occurs in New Zealand. In the United States, plants are mainly produced in the greenhouse, although outdoor flowering may be accomplished in the southern and coastal states as bulbs become available.

Propagation

Bulbs produce many offsets which can be separated and replanted after grading. Purchasing clean material every year, however, is recommended. Most of the new cultivars are tissue-cultured.

Environmental Factors

Photoperiod: No photoperiodic responses are known.

Temperature: Temperature has the greatest effect on flower growth and development. Recent work showed that forcing temperatures around 70F produced higher quality flowers and more rapid flowering than 57F or 86F (3). Higher proportions of bulbs flowered at 70F than at 57F or 86F.

The effect of temperature on flowering of *Nerine sarniensis*.[a]

Temperature (F)	Flowering (%)	Bulbs with 2nd flower (%)	Time to flower (days)	Scape length (in)
57	34	0	128	14.0
70	95	42	90	15.2
86	0	0	—	—

[a]Adapted from (3).

Bulbs remained in 86F for 129 days without flowers; however, when transferred to 70F after that time, 70% of the bulbs flowered.

Shading: Flower quality and time to flower do not appear to be markedly influenced by light intensity, but scape length was longer on bulbs which received 55% shade (3). Prolonged use of heavy shade should be avoided as such a practice can result in poor bulb growth and subsequent flowering.

Field Performance
Bulbs 4–5 cm in circumference or larger should be used. Flowers appear in late summer through fall in the field. The use of shade in the field is recommended to avoid temperatures above 85–95F in areas of hot summer temperatures.

Greenhouse Performance
If bulbs have not been precooled, dry store bulbs at 36–38F for approximately 3 months. Plant in ground beds 6–9″ apart or in large pots, pot to pot. Maintain temperatures around 70F and provide high light. Flowers appear in 12–15 weeks. Some of the larger bulbs will produce a second flower 35–40 days after the first flower. Fertilize with 100–150 ppm N once or twice a week with a complete fertilizer. If bulbs are retained in their dormant state, maintain bulbs at approximately 50F and refrain from watering.

Stage of Harvest
Harvest when the first flower is just about to open. Stems should be packed 10 to a bunch.

Postharvest
Fresh: Flowers persist 10–14 days (2). Flowers are susceptible to chilling (1) and should be held no lower than 41F (2).

Storage: Flowers of *N. bowdenii* may be stored wet at 50F for 2–3 days (1). Flowers of *N. sarniensis* may be held dry for 4-5 days (2). Bulbs are generally stored at 36–38F. However, recent research in New Zealand suggests that warm temperature storage (86F) for several weeks results in faster flowering than for those bulbs that have been cold stored. More work is required before such warm temperature storage can be recommended.

Cultivars
Numerous cultivars have been produced by breeders in New Zealand.

Some of those useful for cut flowers include 'Cherry Ripe', 'Pink Distinction', 'Pink Fairy', 'Radiant Queen', 'Salmon Supreme' and 'Virgo'.

Additional Species
Nerine bowdenii is the most popular species for cut flowers and is widely produced in Europe.

N. flexuosa bears foliage which appears in flushes year-round, has no requirement for dormancy and may flower at any time.

Reading
1. Nowak, J., and R. M. Rudnicki. 1990. *Postharvest Handling and Storage of Cut Flowers, Florist Greens, and Potted Plants.* Timber Press, Portland, OR.

2. Vaughan, M. J. 1988. *The Complete Book of Cut Flower Care.* Timber Press, Portland, OR.

3. Warrington, I. J., N. G. Seager and A. M. Armitage. 1989. Environmental requirements for flowering and bulb growth in *Nerine sarniensis. Herbertia* 45(1&2):74–80.

Many thanks to Dr. Ian Warrington for reviewing this section.

Ornithogalum arabicum   Arabian Star Flower   18–24"/18"
White   Mediterranean   Liliaceae   Zones 8–10

Clusters of creamy white flowers with black centers are borne on 1–2′ tall stems. Their lack of winter hardiness and poor heat tolerance limit the production areas to the West Coast. Production is common in Mediterranean countries. Other species, such as *O. thyrsoides* (chincherinchee) and *O. saundersiae*, are also useful as cut flowers.

Environmental Factors
Photoperiod: No effects of photoperiod have been observed.

Temperature: The optimum temperature for flower initiation and development is 68–70F, after which 55F is best for completion of flower development and stem elongation. Highest quality flowers result from greenhouse temperatures of 55–62F.

Prolonged storage of bulbs at high temperatures (88–92F) retard the formation of flower buds, but subsequent development occurs when bulbs are transferred to lower temperatures (4). This is useful for scheduling flowers in the greenhouse. For example, 25–30 weeks at 88F followed by 2–4 weeks at 55F prior to planting results in late spring and early summer flowers. Early winter flowers require 45–50 weeks of warm storage.

Field Performance
Bulb size: Use large bulbs of 5.5–6.5″ circumference (14/16 cm) for greatest percentage of flowering. Bulbs less than 8 cm in circumference fail to

flower and only about 30% of bulbs 11 cm in circumference flower (4). See the following table for additional details.

The effect of bulb size on yield of *Ornithogalum arabicum*.[a]

Size of bulb		Flowering (%)	Flowers/ inflorescence
Wt (g)	Circumference (cm)		
6–8	7–8	0	—
8–13	8–9	5	13–19
12–22	9–11	20–30	18–23
20–60	11–15	70–95	22–26
50–100	15–20	100–120	25–29

[a]Adapted from (4).

Larger bulb sizes also result in increased flowers/inflorescence. However, very large bulbs tend to split (5) and should be avoided.

Spacing: Place bulbs 6–9" apart and cover with 4" of soil.

Longevity: Bulbs persist for 1–2 years, depending on location. On the West Coast or in Mediterranean climates, they may be left in the ground for 2 years but are generally treated as annuals. If grown in the East, bulbs must be lifted each year and treated as annuals. Trials in Georgia were disappointing; the majority of bulbs failed to survive, and for those that did survive, subsequent flower production was poor. Plants are essentially xerophytic and the winter and summer rain was likely to blame for the poor performance.

Greenhouse Performance

Purchase prepared bulbs (see "Environmental Factors") for winter and spring flowering. Place bulbs 6" apart in 8–10" pots or ground beds. The temperature and duration of storage has a direct influence on flowering time (see "Environmental Factors" and also discussion of *O. thyrsoides* under "Additional Species").

Fertilize with 75–100 ppm N from calcium nitrate after planting. Temperatures of 68–70F should be applied for 3–4 weeks followed by 58–62F until flowering.

Guideline for Foliar Analyses

At field trials in Watsonville, CA, foliage was sampled from vigorously growing healthy plants when flower buds were visible, but prior to flower opening. These are guidelines only and should not be considered absolute standards. Based on dry weight analysis.

(%)						(ppm)				
N	P	K	Ca	Mg		Fe	Mn	B	Al	Zn
2.0	0.25	3.59	2.08	0.30		82	10	24	60	37

Stage of Harvest

Harvest when the first flower is open if flowers are to be shipped long distances; approximately ¼ of the flowers may be open for local sales.

Postharvest

Fresh: *Ornithogalum* flowers have excellent vase life and persist over 2 weeks. Preservative is not necessary. Unopened flowers continue to open even in plain water.

Storage: Flowers of various species of *Ornithogalum* may be stored dry at 40F for 4–6 weeks in moisture-retentive boxes (3).

Dried: Flowering stems may be dried by desiccation. An equal mixture of borax and fine sand is best for drying. Place a thin layer of the borax/sand mixture in a container and lay the flowers on the layer. Gently pour a sufficient amount of desiccant over the stems to cover them. Cover the container. Drying takes 4–10 days (5).

Cultivars

The species is used for cut flowers.

Additional Species

Three other species are used for cut flowers.

Ornithogalum saundersiae bears 2–3' long stems which terminate in white flowers with dark eyes. A better choice for eastern growers than *O. arabicum*, it is far more tolerant of cold winters and hot summers.

O. thyrsoides (chincherinchee) is also native to South Africa and bears 12–30 pure white flowers on each 15–20" tall stem. Recent work by Dr. P. J. Jansen van Vuuren in South Africa showed that storage of bulbs at 40F for 14 weeks resulted in fastest flowering time; however, as storage temperature increased (to 86F), flowering time decreased (1). Storage temperatures of 86F inhibited flowering, and he demonstrated that bulbs could be stored for up to 6 months at 86–95F without detrimental effects on flowering (1). Outdoors, bulbs 4–5 cm in circumference produce an average of 1.5 inflorescences, bulbs 8–10 cm in circumference produced 4 inflorescences per bulb (3). For greenhouse production, 50–60F is used after planting. Plant in February and March for flowering in early June. Flowers should be harvested when the first flower opens and stems are pulled, not cut. Postharvest treatments are similar to *O. arabicum*. Cultivars include double-flowered 'Mount Blanc' and 'Mount Everest'. An excellent cut flower species.

O. umbellatum (star-of-bethlehem) carries 10–20 star-shaped white flowers with green stripes on 12" tall stems. This is one of the few useful *Ornithogalum* species for the eastern half of the country. Unfortunately, the common name, star-of-bethlehem, is also used for *O. arabicum*. Do not confuse the two when ordering bulbs; they are very much different.

Pests and Diseases

Leaf spots occasionally detract from the foliage and root rots may occur in wet soils.

Ornithogalum mosaic virus results in finely mottled, light and dark green foliage. More conspicuous mottling of gray and yellow occurs as the foliage matures. The virus is spread by aphids and is best controlled by reducing the aphid population.

Reading

1. Jansen van Vuuren, P. J. 1991. The influence of temperature on the flowering date of *Ornithogalum thyrsoides* Jacq. Abstract presented at 2nd International Symposium on Development of New Floricultural Crops, 17–21 September 1991, Baltimore, MD.

2. Nowak, J., and R. M. Rudnicki. 1990. *Postharvest Handling and Storage of Cut Flowers, Florist Greens, and Potted Plants.* Timber Press, Portland, OR.

3. Rees, A. R. 1985. *Ornithogalum.* In A. H. Halevy (ed.), *The Handbook of Flowering,* vol. 1. CRC Press, Boca Raton, FL. 300–301.

4. Shoub, J., and A. H. Halevy. 1971. Studies in the developmental morphology and the thermoperiodic requirement for flower development in *Ornithogalum arabicum* L. Hortic. Res. 11:29–39.

5. Vaughan, M. J. 1988. *The Complete Book of Cut Flower Care.* Timber Press, Portland, OR.

Ornithogalum thyrsoides

Polianthes tuberosa

Polianthes tuberosa		Tuberose	2–4'/2'
White	Mexico	Agavaceae	Zones 7–10

Tuberoses have been cultivated for many years and are well known for their sweet, heavy fragrance. Introduced in 1629, the species is represented today by cultivars with single or double flowers. Up to a dozen, waxy white, 2.5" long flowers occur along an erect, open spike. Rootstalks consist of tender bulblike tubers and must be lifted north of zone 7b (north Georgia), although if adequate mulch is employed, growers in climatic zone 7a may leave bulbs in the ground. Growers north of zone 7 must lift bulbs in the fall, store in a cool (40F) (3), dry area and replant in spring after danger of frost. Growers in the Northwest and coastal California may also leave bulbs in the ground.

Propagation

Tubers may be split after flowering and separated by size. Tuberoses increase by natural multiplication and large offsets may flower the following year. Smaller ones should be closely spaced in nursery rows for an additional year.

Environmental Factors

Photoperiod: No photoperiod effects have been reported.

Temperature: Tuberose grows best at a minimum temperature of 68F. High temperatures are necessary for flower bud initiation, continued differentiation and development (2).

Field Performance

Tuber size: Tubers from 6–8" around to as small as 3–4" are available. The smaller sizes may flower in the southern United States but are of little use in the North. Large tubers emerge slower but flower faster than smaller ones. Plant 9–12" apart and cover with 2–3" of soil.

Planting time: Tubers must be planted after danger of frost in northern areas. In areas of mild winters, they may be planted in the fall or early winter. To be on the safe side, plant no earlier than February, even in mild climates. Once established, bulbs can tolerate occasional freezing temperatures in the winter. Some information on planting dates from Athens, GA, follows.

The effect of planting date on harvest, yield and stem quality of *Polianthes tuberosa*.[a]

Month of planting	Flowers/bulb	Initial harvest	Duration of harvest (days)	Stem length (in)	Stem diameter (mm)
		'Mexican Single'			
Feb	0.8	Jul 2	87	43.7	8.3
Mar	1.1	Jul 22	67	36.9	7.4
		'The Pearl'			
Feb	0.9	Jul 16	73	33.2	8.9
Mar	1.1	Aug 1	58	35.0	9.3

[a]From (1).

Notice the duration of harvest. Tuberoses flower over a long period of time and flowers may be harvested for well over 8 weeks.

Longevity: If tubers remain in the ground (assuming they are hardy for the area), tuberose may be harvested for at least 3 years without division. The dead foliage may be used as a mulch in the winter. Remove mulch as soon as possible in the spring.

Yield and stem quality of *Polianthes tuberosa* over time (planted fall, 1985).[a]

Cultivar	Year	Stems/bulb	Stem length (in)
'Mexican Single'	1	0.9	40.0
	2	0.9	31.4
	3	1.5	30.5
	4	1.1	31.2
'The Pearl'	1	1.0	33.6
	2	2.7	27.4
	3	3.3	29.8
	4	2.5	31.2

[a]Adapted from (1).

The preceding table indicates that yield does not decline until the fourth year. Therefore, lifting and dividing should be accomplished during the third or fourth year. Stem length, however, was longest during the first year.

Greenhouse Performance

Warm temperatures (68–75F) are necessary to force tubers, which should be planted in ground beds. In one report, tubers of single-flowered cultivars planted on April 1 flowered on August 10, 132 days from planting when the average temperature was approximately 68F (2). The double forms are generally 3–4 weeks earlier under greenhouse conditions than the singles. Check with the bulb supplier for the availability of bulbs for winter forcing. Although bulbs received in the spring may be dry-stored at 40–50F until ready to plant, it is better to receive properly stored bulbs at the appropriate time from the supplier.

Stage of Harvest

Harvest when 2–4 flowers are open on the flower stalk and others are showing color. If necessary, they may be cut with as many as ½ to ¾ of the flowers open but the bottom flowers must not have started to fade.

Postharvest

Fresh: Fresh flowers persist up to 2 weeks during which time they continue to open (4). Faded flowers should be removed and stems recut as necessary. A flower preservative is useful for additional postharvest life. Single flowers appear to persist longer than doubles because the inner row of petals on double flowers darkens rapidly, thus discoloring the whole flower. Petals of single flowers also discolor but not as rapidly.

Dried: Single flowers do not dry well, doubles are only slightly better.

Storage: Flowers may be stored at 50F but not below 43F. If stored at too cool a temperature, flower buds do not open. Prolonged storage in cool rooms also reduces fragrance. Flowers may be stored dry for up to 3–4 days (4).

Cultivars

'Mexican Single' has waxy white, single flowers closely spaced on the flower stalk.

'The Pearl' is the most popular double-flowered form with twice the number of petals.

Pests and Diseases

Few problems affect tuberose. If field conditions are too wet, tubers disintegrate over the winter; therefore, good drainage is important. Nematodes can be a very serious problem: be sure to test soil prior to planting. Thrips can be a major problem in open flowers.

Reading

1. Armitage, A. M., and J. M. Laushman. 1990. Planting date and in-ground time affect cut flowers of *Liatris* .... *HortScience* 25:1239–1241.

2. Kosugi, K., and Y. Kimura. 1961. On the flower bud differentiation and flower bud development in *Polianthes tuberosa* L. *Tech. Bul. Fac. Agric. Kagawa Univ.* 12:230–234.

3. Post, K. 1955. *Florist Crop Production and Marketing.* Orange Judd, New York, NY.

4. Vaughan, M. J. 1989. *The Complete Book of Cut Flower Care.* Timber Press, Portland, OR.

Ranunculus asiaticus

		Ranunculus	1–2'/9"
Various colors	Mediterranean	Ranunculaceae	Zones 8–10

This species of *Ranunculus* is intolerant of extremes of heat or cold and is usually grown outdoors only in areas with a Mediterranean climate, such as southern and central coastal California. Some southern growers have had moderate success with it as a winter crop; however, winter rains result in tuber rot if the drainage is not excellent. Flowering generally takes place from late September and continues through March, depending on prevailing temperatures. Numerous areas in the East, particularly Long Island and New Jersey, were production centers in the 1940s and 1950s but little production occurs there today. In the greenhouse, production may take place anywhere cool temperatures and bright light occur. *Ranunculus* is a good companion crop for *Anemone coronaria* or carnation in the greenhouse.

Propagation

Tubers: Tubers may be purchased from bulb suppliers. In general, tubers smaller than 3/5 cm will not flower adequately. Tubers may be soaked in water overnight and provided with cold treatment if the grower so desires (see "Environmental Factors").

Seed: The small seed (39,000 seeds/oz), if sown at 50–60F, will germinate in 15–20 days. For the commercial flower grower, purchasing plugs from specialist plug growers is more sensible. Plugs may be planted immediately or grown on in a cool greenhouse (45–55F) until ready for planting.

Environmental Factors

Temperature: *Ranunculus* is a cool-loving plant and performs poorly if temperatures exceed 60F. Night temperatures of 45–50F are recommended (3).

Cold temperatures of 34–36F have been used on presprouted tubers (tubers soaked in water for 24 hours) to accelerate flowering. Research in France showed that when imbibed (soaked) corms were given a 14-day treatment of 36F, the time between planting and the production of the first 3 flowers was shortened by 4 weeks (3). More recent work in Italy found that storing tubers for 30 days at 50F resulted in faster flowering (126 days from planting tubers) compared with those stored at 36F (170 days) or those not cooled at all (190 days) (2). Before exposing tubers to cool temperatures, they should first be stored at 55–60F for 8–10 days.

Photoperiod: The highest percentage of tubers flower when placed under short day treatments (12 hours or less). Although long day treatments (>12 hours) accelerate flowering, neither the flower quality nor the yield are as high. Long days also result in greater tuberization. If plants are placed under 14-hour days or longer, 100% of the plants produce tubers but fewer than 40% produce flowers (3).

Field Performance

Tuber size: Best results occur with 5/6 cm tubers, although 3/5 cm tubers will flower.

Planting depth: Plant tubers with eyes up, approximately 1–2" below soil surface (1). The claw like appendages should be on the bottom.

Spacing: If using 3/5 cm tubers, plant approximately 5 tubers/ft^2 or approximately 5" apart. The largest tubers should be planted 7–8" apart (1).

Yield: Depending on cultivar and tuber size, 3–5 marketable stems/tuber are not uncommon. For the Victoria series, 4–6 stems/tuber were obtained the first year from plugs.

Longevity: Tubers are inexpensive and are usually treated as annuals. If grown from seed, they are always treated as annuals.

Greenhouse Performance

Plant tubers (or plugs) in a very well-drained soil in a raised bed. Planting can be started in September and continued until January. Maintain 45–50F night, 60F day temperatures and provide as much light as possible. Do not allow temperatures to exceed 60F for any length of time (1). If plants are grown too warm or if they dry out excessively, leaves yellow and short flowers small in diameter are produced. Maintain plants under natural photoperiod or as little as 8 hours of light. Avoid long days caused by light drift in the winter.

Fertilize plants weekly with approximately 200 ppm N and leach often to reduce soluble salts (1).

Tubers flower 60–90 days from planting, depending if they have been imbibed and/or vernalized prior to planting. Seed-grown plants flower 4–6 months from sowing. The lengthy time required for flowering from seed often dictates that seed cultivars be purchased as plugs.

Stage of Harvest
Cut flowers when buds show color and are about to open (4).

Postharvest
Fresh: Flowers persist in preservative for 5–7 days at cool room temperatures (60F).

Dried: Flowers may be air-dried by first stripping leaves and hanging upside down in small bunches. Drying by microwave is also practiced (5).

Storage: Flowers should be stored only if necessary at 34–36F in water with a preservative (5). They do not store well dry.

Cultivars
'Tecolote' has been used for cutting for many years. Plants bear 3–4" wide double flowers in a range of colors.

'Victoria' is an F_1 hybrid strain in which uniformity and flower shades are excellent. Available only from seed or plugs.

Pests and Diseases
Botrytis results in crown rot of the tuber. Do not plant too closely, provide good ventilation and do not overhead irrigate.

Various water molds such as *Pythium* and *Phytophthora* spp. result when drainage is poor. Tubers and roots are susceptible to these fungi. Be sure soils are exceptionally well drained.

Reading
1. De Hertogh, A. A. 1989. *Holland Bulb Forcer's Guide*. 4th ed. *International Flower Bulb Center*, Hillegom, The Netherlands.

2. Guda, C. D., and E. Scordo. 1989. Hybrid *Ranunculus* response to cold treatments on corm sprouts. *Herbertia* 45:56–60.

3. Horovitz, A. 1985. *Ranunculus*. In A. H. Halevy (ed.), *The Handbook of Flowering*, vol. 4. CRC Press, Boca Raton, FL. 155–161.

4. Nowak, J., and R. M. Rudnicki. 1990. *Postharvest Handling and Storage of Cut Flowers, Florist Greens, and Potted Plants*. Timber Press, Portland, OR.

5. Vaughan, M. J. 1989. *The Complete Book of Cut Flower Care*. Timber Press, Portland, OR.

Many thanks to Mr. Bob Pollioni for reviewing this section.

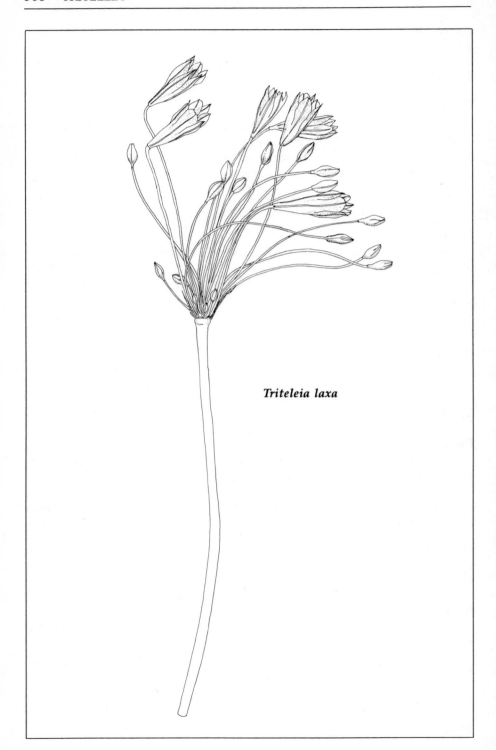

Triteleia laxa

Triteleia laxa

Triteleia laxa		Brodiaea	9–15"/6"
Blue	California	Liliaceae	Zones 6–9

This cormous species is still sold under the name of *Brodiaea laxa*, although it has been transferred to the genus *Triteleia*. The 2–5" wide inflorescence consists of 15–25 deep blue, tubular flowers. The individual flowers are up to 1¼" across, approximately 1" long and carried on 2–3" long pedicels. The species is native to California and southern Oregon but can also be produced in the eastern United States.

Propagation
One- to two-year-old corms can be purchased from reliable bulb suppliers. Seed can be purchased but requires 2 years to reach flowering size.

Growing-on
Corms should be immediately planted in the field. Seedlings may be grown-on in beds, pans or 4–5" pots in the greenhouse or propagation field.

Environmental Factors
Growth is affected by soil temperature. A sunny location where the soil warms up quickly in the spring is best. Photoperiod has little effect on flowering.

Treatment of corms with 20 ppm ethylene for 7 days resulted in reduction of time to sprouting and first flowering. The treatment also increased the number of flowers per inflorescence and the fresh weight of daughter corms. The length of the scape, however, was not affected (3).

Field Performance
Corm size: Use of 5/6 or 7/8 cm circumference corms is recommended (2).

Spacing: Space corms 3–6" apart and 4–5" below the surface.

Planting time: In zone 7b (Athens, GA), no difference in yield of corms planted after November was found. Few growth and flower differences occurred for any date, although yield was slightly reduced when planted as early as November. No differences in initial harvest date occurred due to planting time.

The effect of planting date on harvest, yield and stem quality of *Triteleia laxa*.[a]

Month of planting	Flowers/corm	Initial Harvest	Duration of harvest (days)	Stem length (in)	Stem diameter (mm)
Nov	0.8	May 27	7	8.7	4.7
Dec	1.4	May 21	13	12.0	3.9
Jan	1.0	May 29	8	9.9	2.7
Feb	1.3	May 27	13	11.7	3.1

[a]From (1).

Northern growers must wait until the ground thaws before planting. Corms may be lifted, cleaned and sorted to size after the foliage has disappeared or in the fall after the first freeze.

Yield and stem quality of *Triteleia laxa* over time (Athens, GA).[a]

Year	Stems/corm	Stem length (in)	Stem diameter (mm)
1	1.3	11.1	3.0
2	2.5	12.1	3.2
3	0.5	10.4	3.0

[a] From (1).

Longevity: In field tests in Georgia, corms persisted for 2 years.

The summer temperatures in north Georgia, combined with evening rainstorms, most likely reduced the corm numbers in the third year. *Triteleia* should be treated as a 1- or 2-year crop east of the Rocky Mountains.

Planting zones: Corms overwintered as far north as Nova Scotia, Canada (zone 5), but are not normally planted north of zone 6. Flowering time and stem lengths were July 20/16" (Nova Scotia, zone 5), June 25/14" (East Lansing, MI, zone 5), June 20/14" (Washington, DC, zone 7) and May 2/10" (Baton Rouge, LA, zone 9) (2).

Greenhouse Performance

Little information is available on greenhouse performance; however, data from California for flowers forced in greenhouses at 64/40F day/night temperatures are of interest. Without any ethylene treatment, corms required 104 days to sprout and 274 days to flower. With 20 ppm ethylene treatment for 7 days, corms sprouted in 78 days and flowered in 228 days (3).

Stage of Harvest

Harvest when 4–6 flowers are open. If insect pollination can be avoided (e.g., if plants are greenhouse-grown), allow 10–15 flowers to open prior to harvesting (4).

Postharvest

Fresh: Flowers persist 10–14 days in water (5), 1–2 additional days if preservative is used. Stems must be recut at each step of the postharvest chain. The white portion on the bottom of the stem should be removed. Stems may be stored dry for up to 4 days at 36–41F if necessary, although stems should be stored in water (5).

Dried: Flowers do not dry well.

Cultivars

'Queen Fabiola' is a hybrid between *T. laxa* and *T. peduncularis* and is properly classified as *T.* × *tubergenii*. Regardless of its taxonomic niche, it bears larger, darker blue flowers and is the principal cultivar available. The blue color is most intense in cool climates and fades rapidly as temperatures increase.

Pests and Diseases

Plants (corms) require excellent drainage or root and corm rots occur. Application of soil fungicide 1–2 weeks prior to planting reduces incidence of rot organisms.

Reading

1. Armitage, A. M., and J. M. Laushman. 1990. Planting date and in-ground time affect cut flowers of *Acidanthera* .... *HortScience* 25:1236–1238.

2. De Hertogh, A. A. 1989. *Holland Bulb Forcer's Guide.* 4th ed. International Flower Bulb Center, Hillegom, The Netherlands.

3. Han, S., A. H. Halevy, and M. S. Reid. 1990. Postharvest handling of brodiaea flowers. *HortScience* 25:1268–1270.

4. Nowak, J., and R. M. Rudnicki. 1990. *Postharvest Handling and Storage of Cut Flowers, Florist Greens, and Potted Plants.* Timber Press, Portland, OR.

5. Vaughan, M. J. 1988. *The Complete Book of Cut Flower Care.* Timber Press, Portland, OR.

Tulipa **spp.**   Tulip   12–30"/12"
Various colors   Asia Minor   Liliaceae   Zones 3–7

The origin of the modern tulip is not known although a long period of cultivation and selection occurred in Turkey and Iran prior to its introduction to Europe in the 16th century. Garden tulips have been divided into many different classes, based on parentage, flowering time (early, late) and flower form (single, double, lily-flowered). Cultivars for cut flowers include Darwin, Triumph, Rembrandt, double, peony- and lily-flowered. Essentially all bulbs come from the Netherlands and many flowers are also produced there. Flowers are produced for the early spring market (outdoor production) or in early January under greenhouse conditions. Greenhouse production generally requires controlled temperature forcing chambers, and, while all pre-greenhouse treatment may be accomplished outside in cold frames, controlled temperature facilities are necessary to meet a particular marketing period. For forcers growing bulbs in outdoor beds, the market may be affected slightly by cultural techniques, but the market date and flower quality essentially are under control of the prevailing temperatures.

Environmental Factors

Like *Narcissus*, tulips require an annual warm–cool–warm temperature sequence. In the field, this is provided by warm summer temperatures, followed by winter and spring to complete the sequence. The initial warm temperatures result in leaf differentiation and flower initiation. The cool treatment (13–20 weeks) causes acceleration of flowering, uniformity of flowering within the population and sufficiently long flower stems (6). The final warm treatment is necessary to force the flower to elongate and open.

Research has been conducted on many cultivars and optimal cooling and greenhouse forcing times have been determined for greenhouse forced bulbs (1).

Field Performance

Bulb size: The sole factor that is unequivocally related to flowering is bulb circumference (6). Bulbs below a critical size (depending on cultivar) will only form a single leaf and will not flower until the following year. Use 10/11 to 12/up cm circumference bulbs, depending on cultivar (1).

Spacing: Plant bulbs approximately 6" apart with 5–6" of medium above the nose.

Planting time: In most areas of the country, non-precooled bulbs should be planted in the fall. In the South (zones 6–7b; e.g., north Georgia), plant in October to November, in the North (above zone 6), in September and early October. In the deep south (e.g., Florida, south Texas, southern California), bulbs must be precooled (8–10 weeks at 40–45F) and planted in late November through December.

Longevity: Treat tulips as annuals, regardless of area or cultivar. In more northern areas, Darwin and Fosteriana hybrids provide some perennial performance.

Scheduling: The length of time tulips may be harvested depends on the use of early-, mid- and late-season cultivars. Also important is the length of winter temperatures below 45F and the rate of spring warming. If temperatures rise quickly in the spring, harvest time declines.

Trials conducted in different areas of the country in the 1960s by De Hertogh (1) provided some of the following results.

Average of 4-year cut tulip trials in various areas.

Location	Zone	Initial harvest	Duration of harvest (days)
College Station, TX	8	Feb 18	48
Pomona, CA	9	Feb 26	64
Corvallis, OR	9	Mar 12	64
Clemson, SC	7	Mar 14	38
Ames, IA	5	Apr 10	40
East Lansing, MI	5	Apr 15	40
St. Paul, MN	4	Apr 27	30
Hamilton, ON	5	May 1	32
Edmonton, AB	3	May 15	33

Notice that the duration of harvest is greatest in areas where less variation in temperatures occur (Northwest). In areas with "short springs," harvest time is shortest. The beginning of harvest follows appearance of spring in the country.

Stem length: The average stem length is shorter in warmer areas than in areas with cold winters (i.e., longer in the North than the South). This is

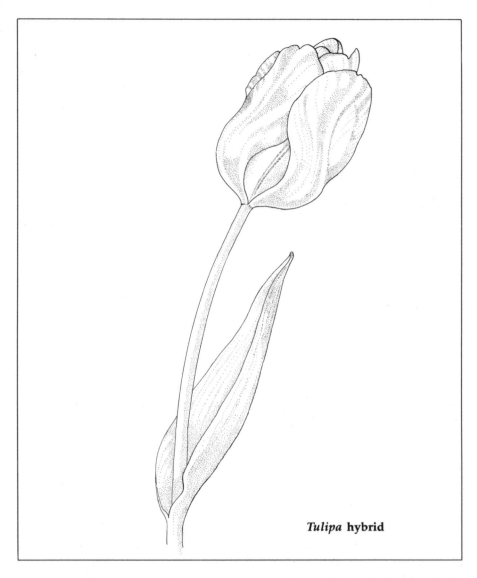

Tulipa **hybrid**

because cold is necessary for stem extension; less cold equals shorter stems.

Fertilization: Apply 2–3 pounds of a granular complete fertilizer (9–9–6, 8–8–8, 10–10–10) per 100 linear feet at planting and again upon shoot emergence.

Greenhouse Performance

Bulbs may be planted immediately upon arrival and stored in controlled facilities for the appropriate number of cold weeks for the cultivar used. For the Valentine's Day market, bulbs are usually panned in October, stored at 48F until roots are visible through the drainage holes, transferred to 41F until shoots are 1–2" tall and then placed at 33–35F until they are moved to the greenhouse bench. The total amount of time in the cooler depends on cultivar. For most, 16–17 weeks are optimum; 15 is minimum and 20–22 weeks is maximum (1). The greenhouse temperature (approx. 60F) and time in greenhouse (2–3 weeks) also depend on cultivar, locale and time of year. For market times before Valentine's Day, precooled bulbs must be used. For those interested in forcing in the greenhouse, the *Holland Bulb Forcer's Guide* by Dr. Gus De Hertogh (1) provides specifics on cultivars and is essential reading.

Stage of Harvest

Harvest Darwin tulip flowers when ½ of the flower is colored; others should be cut when the whole flower is nearly colored (5). Tulips must be harvested several times a day for optimum stage of harvest and optimum postharvest life.

Generally they are wrapped in bunches of 10 stems.

Postharvest

Fresh: Flowers persist 3–4 days in the opening stage, and a further week after they open (8).

Storage: Growers must wrap bunches after grading. If they are shipped immediately, they may be placed vertically in water. If they must be stored, place dry flowers at 32–35F (1).

Stems continue to grow for the first 24 hours in water and flowers bend toward the light. Growth regulators have been effective in reducing growth and bending after harvest. Solutions of 25 ppm ancymidol (A-Rest™) (3), 50 ppm ethephon (4) or the addition of benzyladenine (BA) (7) to the vase water for 2 hours have been tried, with mixed results.

Wholesalers should store tightly wrapped stems horizontally at 32–35F (1). If placed in water, recut about ¼" of the stem base and place in 6–8" of distilled water at 32–35F.

If flowers arrive bent, they may be straightened by wrapping them in wet paper and placing in water with light directly above (8).

Do not place tulips with daffodils. Daffodils exude a mucous substance which is toxic to many other species. Tulips and daffodils may be mixed if daffodils have been allowed to stand in water in separate containers for 24 hours (see *Narcissus*).

Cultivars

Many, many are used. Contact bulb specialists for colors and availability. Some of the more common forms and cultivars follow; see De Hertogh (1,2) for more complete cultivar listings.

Single, rounded petals

'Apeldoorn' (red), 'Paul Richter' (red), 'Rosario' (carmine-rose).

Double, rounded petals

'Monte Carlo' (yellow).

Parrot, fringed petals
'Fantasy' (pink), 'Flaming Parrot' (white, red).

Lily, pointed petals
'Aladdin' (red, yellow border), 'West Point' (yellow), 'White Triumphator' (white).

Pests and Diseases

Sterilize beds whenever possible to reduce incidence of soil-borne diseases such as those caused by *Rhizoctonia* and *Pythium* spp.

Botrytis (gray mold) results in grayish mold on the flower petals and stems. Use of fungicides and crop rotation help combat the problem. Overhead irrigation should be avoided.

Basal rot, caused by *Fusarium oxysporum*, results in red foliage, few roots and rotted bulbs. This is a problem which must be controlled by the bulb grower and should never enter the growers field. Always check the bulbs on arrival and check for a whitish mold and a foul smell. Infected bulbs feel soft beneath the outer covering and some may feel very light. If more than 10% of the bulbs are infected, the whole lot may have to be discarded.

Blue mold, caused by *Penicillium* spp., is generally not serious but bulbs should be dusted with a fungicide if placed in dry storage or drenched if immediately planted (1).

Flower rot often occurs with double-flowered forms which have been watered overhead and have not dried out. Provide good ventilation, particularly for double flowers.

Reading

1. De Hertogh, A. A. 1989. *Holland Bulb Forcer's Guide*. 4th ed. International Flower Bulb Center, Hillegom, The Netherlands.

2. _____ . 1990. Research on forced flower bulbs focuses on improved quality and cultivars. *PPGA News*. 21(11):2–7.

3. Einart, A. E. 1971. Reduction in last internode elongation of cut tulips by growth retardants. *HortScience* 5:459.

4. Nichols, R. 1971. Control of tulip stem extension. 1970 Annual Report, GCRI:74. Littlehampton, U.K.

5. Nowak, J., and R. M. Rudnicki. 1990. *Postharvest Handling and Storage of Cut Flowers, Florist Greens, and Potted Plants*. Timber Press, Portland, OR.

6. Rees, A. R. 1985. *Tulipa*. In A. H. Halevy (ed.), *The Handbook of Flowering*, vol. 1. CRC Press, Boca Raton, FL. 272–277.

7. Sytsema, W. 1971. De houdbaarheid van tulpen. *Vakblad v.d. Bloemisterij* 26(15):8–9.

8. Vaughan, M. J. 1988. *The Complete Book of Cut Flower Care*. Timber Press, Portland, OR.

Many thanks to Mr. Brent Heath for reviewing this section.

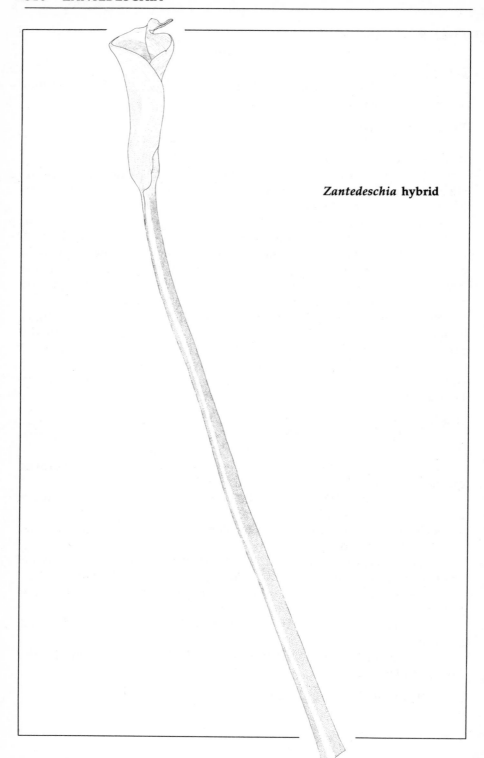

Zantedeschia hybrid

Zantedeschia **spp.**   Calla Lily   2–4'/2–3'
White, various colors   South Africa   Araceae   Zones 7–10

Six species are classified in the genus but significant selection and hybridization have taken place, resulting in numerous hybrids and cultivars. For simplicity's sake, callas may be thought of as "summer" or "winter" callas. The summer callas consist of disc-shaped, flattened rhizomes, deciduous foliage and green fruit. Species included as summer types are *Z. elliottiana* (yellow flowers, spotted leaves), *Z. jucunda* (yellow, spotted), *Z. albomaculata* (white, spotted), *Z. pentlandii* (lemon-yellow, usually unspotted) and *Z. rehmannii* (pink, usually unspotted). The colored hybrids have been developed from these species. Winter callas have elongated rhizomes, ever-green foliage and yellow-to-red fruits. They are represented by *Z. aethiopica* (white, unspotted), *Z. aethiopica* 'Green Goddess' (white with green spathe) and occasionally the dwarf white calla, *Z. aethiopica* var. *childsiana*. The winter callas have been very popular species but the deciduous, colored hybrids are most likely the future for cut flowers and potted calla lilies. Rhizomes are rapidly produced through tissue culture and division and are available from Florida, California and New Zealand. Rhizomes may be left in the ground in zones 7–10 but should be lifted further north.

Propagation

Seed: Seed propagation is generally limited to the true species and breeding programs. Flowers occur approximately 3 years from sowing (10).

Division: Although division is still a common method of increasing stock, micropropagation is becoming a more popular method for bulking up vegetative material. Division will continue to be used, however, until costs of micropropagation are reduced. Growers should not divide rhizomes before they are 2 years old and care must be taken not to introduce bacterial and viral diseases. Rhizomes should be lifted after foliage has died back. Lift care-fully from the field and remove soil, leaving roots to shrivel during curing. Divide with a sharp, sterile knife. Cure rhizomes in curing chambers for 10–14 days or until a protective skin develops. Curing chambers should be 70–80F, 70–80% humidity and have good air circulation. After curing, rhizomes should be stored at 68–70F for 6–8 weeks prior to planting (11). This assumes that dormancy has not been broken. If dormancy is broken after curing, 68–70F temperatures may reduce the ability of the rhizome to flower.

If rhizomes must be stored for a prolonged period, 45–48F will inhibit sprouting and maintain the health of the rhizome. Store in dry sawdust or peat moss. Do not store below 40F or rapid loss of flowering potential will occur. Rhizomes will be destroyed if temperatures fall below 32F (10).

Tissue culture: Tissue culture should only be carried out by competent laboratories. For those interested, see the articles by Cohen (2) and Welsh and Baldwin (11).

Environmental Factors

Light: Calla lilies do well in high-light areas, particularly if forced during the winter, but if forced outdoors during the summer, light intensity is seldom a problem. The use of shade during field production is most useful to extend the length of the flower scape (see "Field Performance"). Low light is sometimes a problem during greenhouse forcing in the winter months, resulting in etiolated leaves and flower stems.

Temperature: Temperature extremes, lack of water or root disturbance results in dormancy of rhizomes. In nature, dormancy of the colored callas normally occurs after flowering and is characterized by yellowing of foliage and rapid die back. White callas (*Z. aethiopica*) are evergreen.

Photoperiod: Flowering is not affected by photoperiod; however, plants grown under short days are shorter than those grown under long days. Flower buds form and develop under any condition favorable for vegetative growth (8).

Gibberellic acid: Gibberellic acid (GA) increases the number of flowers on all cultivars of colored calla lilies. Best results have been obtained with gibberellic acid when applied as a preplant dip to the rhizome, but success with rhizome spray has also been described (5). Inconsistent results have been reported from foliar application of GA.

A wide range of concentrations and application times have been recorded as preplant dips or rhizome sprays. A GA_3 quick dip of 25 ppm for 30 seconds, a GA_3 soak of 500 ppm for 10 minutes or a Promalin™ (GA_{4+7} and benzyladenine) soak of 50–100 ppm (GA equivalents) for 30 minutes have all been effective (11). Many growers have selected 50–100 ppm GA or Promalin™ as a dip (5–15 minutes) or spray to run off over rhizomes as soon as they are received.

If using 4% GA (check the concentration on the container), 1 level tablespoon of powder in a gallon of water makes approximately 150 ppm GA. If using 2% GA, 1 level tablespoon/gal of water makes approximately 75 ppm GA. With Promalin™ (1.8% GA) 1.5 tablespoons/gal of water provides approximately 100 ppm GA_{4+7}.

Field Performance

Planting: Plant rhizomes as soon as they arrive, but if storage is necessary, place at 50–65F until ready to plant. Check for incidence of soft rot (*Erwinia* spp.) and physiological problems such as chalking (see "Pests and Diseases").

Soil: Rhizomes are best forced in well-drained, sandy or silty loam, particularly if rhizomes are lifted every year. Clay soils result in poor aeration, poor drainage and a greater incidence of *Erwinia* infections. The importance of well-drained soils in reducing *Erwinia* spp. cannot be overemphasized. Clay soils are also difficult to clean from the rhizomes after lifting. Adjust pH to 6.0–6.5.

Fertilization: Fertilize sparingly as excessive nitrogen fertilizer results in leafy growth at the expense of flower production. A moderate application of complete fertilizer (100–150 ppm N) from emergence to flower color is often used.

Rhizome size: For colored callas, nearly all rhizomes 1.5–2" wide (4–5 cm) will flower whereas smaller rhizomes may require growing for an additional year prior to flowering. However, research showed that small rhizomes (1" wide) of Z. *elliottiana* and Z. *rehmannii* required the same time from planting to flower as large rhizomes (>2.5") (3). Treatment with GA is recommended for all sizes. Smaller rhizomes produce smaller flowers (3).

Spacing: Welsh and Baldwin (11) provide 2 spacing systems depending on whether or not tubers are lifted.

SYSTEM I Standard for greenhouse forcing, rhizome multiplication:
Lift annually;
4 rows/bed, rows and plants 8" apart;
43,000 rhizomes/acre (4 cm rhizomes).
SYSTEM II Standard for field production:
Lift after 2 years;
2 rows/bed, 8" between plants, beds 16" apart;
27,000 rhizomes/acre (4 cm rhizomes).

Golden State Bulb Growers of Watsonville, CA, provides the following minimum spacing recommendations based on rhizome size of colored callas (6).

Rhizome size (in)	Spacing when in field 2–3 years (in)	Spacing when lifted annually (in)
1.5–1.75	5 × 5	3 × 4
1.75–2	6 × 6	4 × 4
2–2.5	7 × 7	5 × 5
>2.5	8 × 10	6 × 8

Shading: The use of shade cloth or natural shade (e.g., pine trees) results in significant stem elongation of calla lilies. Work at the University of Georgia demonstrates the effect of shade on stem (scape) length. Shade was artificially provided by commercial shade cloth. Results will differ under different climates and latitudes.

The effect of shade on scape length of *Zantedeschia*.[a]

Cultivar	Shade level (%)	Scape length (in)
'Black Magic'	0	18.0
	55	22.8
'Majestic Red'	0	14.0
	55	24.4
'Pacific Pink'	0	14.4
	55	21.2
'Pink Persuasion'	0	15.2
	55	22.0

[a]From (1).

Harvesting: Flowers can be pulled or cut at the base of the stem. Pulling flowers results in extra stem length but scapes must be turgid. Flowers of sparsely rooted plants or plants irrigated improperly should be cut, not pulled. Harvest flowers in the cool of the day (see "Postharvest").

Scheduling: Research in Georgia and Minnesota showed that 4 cm spring-planted rhizomes required approximately 11 weeks to produce the first flower in the field (11).

Lifting: After the foliage declines, the rhizomes should be lifted, cleaned and cured. Rhizomes may be cured in the fall outdoors under shade or in a curing shed with good air circulation. See "Propagation" and the discussion there under division for more information on curing. After curing is complete, roots should be removed and rhizomes inspected for infection by *Erwinia* spp. Store rhizomes at approximately 68F. Prior to replanting, 8–10 weeks of storage should be provided—although some growers store as little as 6 weeks—depending on how completely the foliage has died down at harvest.

Greenhouse Performance

Rhizomes should be planted in ground beds 6–8" apart or 3 to an 8.5" pot (4). Well-drained soils are an absolute must for reducing the incidence of *Erwinia* infections. Pots may remain pot-to-pot until final 3–5 weeks. Rhizomes can remain in pots for harvesting and curing. After curing and when dormancy is broken, rhizomes may be reflowered.

Irrigation: White callas (*Z. aethiopica*) tolerate moist soils. Colored callas are less tolerant of wet soils than the white forms, but plants should not be allowed to wilt.

Temperature: Start plants at approximately 60–65F until sprouting. After sprouts have appeared, reduce night temperature to 55F for white callas and 60F for colored forms (4).

Scheduling: Callas normally flower approximately 9–12 weeks from planting but exact time depends on cultivar, planting date and duration of storage.

Guideline for Foliar Analyses

At field trials in Watsonville, CA, foliage was sampled from vigorously growing healthy plants of *Z. elliottiana* when flower buds were visible, but prior to flower opening. These are guidelines only and should not be considered absolute standards. Based on dry weight analysis.

(%)						(ppm)			
N	P	K	Ca	Mg		Fe	Mn	B	Al	Zn
3.9	0.34	3.9	0.96	0.23		300	193	13	90	94

Stage of Harvest

Flowers should be cut when the spathes unroll and are almost fully open to ensure good color expression.

Postharvest

Fresh: Cut stems should be placed in a conditioning solution for 8–12 hours (10). Flowers persist for 7–20 days depending on cultivar and environment. Flowers of var. *childsiana* remain unblemished for 10 days (7). Other flower problems include stem splitting and rolling. A sugar (2–5%) pulse may be used. Do not allow the stems to remain in the sugar or various microorganisms will proliferate. A dilute solution of chlorox may also be used for rinsing the sugared stem. Occasionally, flowers are sprayed with an antitranspirant if they are to be shipped a long distance, although no objective data have shown any benefit of this treatment.

Dried: Flowers may be dried in a microwave, but otherwise do not dry well.

Storage: Storage is not recommended; however, stems of *Z. aethiopica* may be stored wet at 38F for up to 1 week (7). Colored callas should be stored at 42–46F. Lower temperatures can result in chilling injury to the flowers. Stems are shipped dry and, if possible, cold.

Cultivars

Breeding programs in the United States and New Zealand have resulted in numerous cultivars useful for cut flowers. Along with the evergreen white-flowered *Z. aethiopica* and var. *childsiana*, deciduous hybrids of yellow, pink, green, red, and peach are available.

Cultivar	Color
'Black Eye Beauty'	Lemon-yellow with dark throat
'Black Magic'	Clear yellow with dark center
'Cameo'	Peach with dark throat
'Golden State Hybrid Yellow'	Golden yellow
'Mango'	Mango orange
'Pastel Magic'	Lemon-yellow with clear center
'Pink Persuasion'	Rose-pink with dark throat
Z. rehmanni var. *superba*	Light pink

'Black Magic' yielded 10–15, 2–3' long stems in the University of Georgia trials. Rhizomes have persisted for 3 years without lifting. While breeding continues for additional flower colors, breeding for *Erwinia* resistance remains an important challenge to the calla breeder.

Pests and Diseases

Bacterial soft rot (*Erwinia* spp.) is the most common and insidious disease organism. Growth is characterized by milky-colored, foul-smelling areas on the rhizome. The rhizome becomes soft at the infected areas. Caused by injury during handling and digging of the rhizome, outbreaks are more common in heavy, poorly drained soils. "Gentle" handling and proper curing techniques reduce incidence of the disease. Some growers dip cut rhizomes in a dilute solution (2%) of hydrogen peroxide for quick curing. There is no known chemical cure for *Erwinia* infections once established. Good drainage and aeration around the rhizome are vital for control of infection.

Blackspot (*Alternaria* spp.) occurs on the flower spathe when conditions are wet and humid. Iprodione (Rovral™) is effective in suppressing the fungus (9).

Pythium spp. also cause many problems. Even though *Zantedeschia* grows naturally in wet areas, overwatering—particularly if plants are grown in pots in the greenhouse—can cause yellowing of the leaves, stunted plants and poor flowering.

Chalking is a physiological disorder which is most prevalent in Z. *aethiopica* var. *childsiana* (dwarf white calla). During prolonged storage, the rhizomes develop a hard, chalky exterior resulting in poor sprouting and growth. If rhizomes are stored properly, chalking is much reduced.

Thrips and aphids can also be a problem.

Reading

1. Armitage, A. M. 1991. Shade affects yield and stem length of field grown cut flower species. *HortScience.* 26:1174–1176.

2. Cohen, D. 1983. Micropropagation of *Zantedeschia* hybrids. *Proc. Intl. Plant Prop. Soc.* 31:312–316.

3. Corr, B. E., and R. E. Widmer. 1991. Paclobutrazol, gibberellic acid, and rhizome size affect growth and flowering of *Zantedeschia. HortScience* 26:133–135.

4. De Hertogh, A. A. 1989. *Holland Bulb Forcer's Guide.* International Flower Bulb Center, Hillegom, The Netherlands.

5. Funnell, K. A., B. O. Tjia, C. J. Stanley, D. Cohen and J. R. Sedcote. 1988. Effect of storage temperature, duration, and gibberellic acid on the flowering of *Zantedeschia elliottiana* and Z. 'Pink Satin'. *J. Amer. Soc. Hort. Sci.* 113:860–863.

6. Golden State Bulb Growers. 1991. *Colored Callas: Guidelines for Cut Flower Growers.* Rev. ed. Watsonville, CA.

7. Plummer, J. A., T. E. Welsh and A. M. Armitage. 1990. Stages of flower development and post production longevity of potted *Zantedeschia aethiopica* 'Childsiana'. *HortScience* 25:675–676.

8. Post, K. 1936. Further responses of miscellaneous plants to temperature. *Proc. Amer. Soc. Hort. Sci.* 34:627–629.

9. Tjia, B. O., and K. A. Funnell. 1986. Post harvest studies of cut *Zantedeschia* inflorescences. *Acta Hortic.* 181:451–459.

10. Tjia, B. O. 1989. *Zantedeschia.* In A. H. Halevy (ed.), *The Handbook of Flowering*, vol. 6. CRC Press, Boca Raton, FL. 697–702.

11. Welsh, T. E., and S. Baldwin. 1989. Calla lilies: a New Zealand perspective. In *Proceedings of 2nd National Conference on Specialty Cut Flowers.* Athens, GA. 81–90.

Thanks to Mr. Keith Funnell, Mr. Tom Lukens and Mr. Eddie Welsh for reviewing this section.

ADDITIONAL BULBOUS SPECIES SUITABLE FOR CUT FLOWER PRODUCTION

Many other species may be used for field or greenhouse production although little information is available concerning cultural practices. The following chart lists but a few of them.

Genus	Common name	Exposure[a]	Use[b]
Arum	Arum lily (foliage)	Ps	F
Caladium	Caladium (foliage)	Ps	F
Convallaria	Lily-of-the-valley	Ps	F,D
Curcuma	Hidden lily	Su	F
Hippeastrum	Amaryllis	Su	F
Ixia	Ixia	Su	F
Lycoris	Resurrection lily	Su	F
Oxalis	Oxalis	Su,Ps	F
Vallota	Scarborough lily	Su	F

[a]Su = full sun, Ps = partial shade.
[b]F = fresh flowers, D = dried flowers.

Woody Species for Cut Flowers, Fruit and Foliage

Specialty cut crops encompass not only flowers from annual, perennial or bulbous herbaceous species, but the flowers, fruit, stems and foliage of woody plants as well. Cut stems of spring flowering plants such as forsythia, flowering cherry, crab apple and lilacs have dominated the woody flower field, but the fruit and foliage of holly, the leaves from magnolia and boxwood, and the twisted stems of contorted willow (*Salix matsudana* 'Tortuosa') have also been important. The number of species useful for cut purposes is endless, and growers are just beginning to notice their market potential. As with herbaceous plants, some species are being rediscovered, others are relatively new to the American horticulture industry and still others boast improved cultivars which are more adaptable to a cut stem program.

Unfortunately, research on postharvest problems of woody stems has largely been ignored, and questions about storage techniques, fruit and leaf abscission, postharvest solutions and potential for drying have been addressed by the trials and errors of a few foresighted producers, florists and wholesalers. They, along with European forcers, have created a market that will only improve with time. Literally thousands of woody branches and flowers are being imported to the United States from the Netherlands. Many problems, however, still beg solutions. Although some information is available concerning postharvest treatments, virtually none can be found about production of woody species for cut stems. Much of the production information provided in this section is therefore based on nursery production. While the production of plants for the landscape trade or for cut branches has many similarities, spacing, nutrition, pruning and cultivar selection can be significantly different.

In this chapter, though a few species are covered in depth, numerous others are but mentioned for lack of sufficient detailed information. I welcome additional information; the gaps are enormous.

BUDDLEIA TO SALIX

In the following listings of woody plants, the first line at each entry provides the genus and species, followed by the common name and then the normal height/spread of the mature plant. The second line provides the color of its flowers, fruit and/or stem, the country or region of origin, the botanical family to which the species belongs and finally the climatic zones where the plants may be cultivated. When more than one species in a genus is treated (as with *Cornus*), and when suggested readings refer to the genus as a whole, the readings appear at the conclusion of the last species entry.

Buddleia davidii		Butterfly-bush	5–10'/5–10'
Various colors	China	Loganiaceae	Zones 5–8

An excellent species for cut flowers, *Buddleia* bears flowers on new growth; therefore, plants may be cut heavily each year. Plants grow rapidly and can reach 5–8' tall in one season after being cut back the previous season. Although not always easily located, flowers are available in white, pink, lavender, purple and blue; additional species also have potential. The length of the inflorescence ranges from 6 to 30" long and is determined by the vigor of the plant; the more vigorous the vegetative growth, the larger the inflorescence.

Propagation
Seed: Seed requires no pretreatment. The use of intermittent mist or sweat tent and soil temperature of 70–75F results in rapid germination.

Cuttings: Collect cuttings from June through August and provide a quick dip of 1000–3000 ppm IBA (2). Remove rooted cuttings from the bench as soon as possible because cuttings rot rapidly with excess moisture.

Field Performance
Habit: Plants are large, multistemmed shrubs which can reach heights of 15', but 5–10' specimens are most common. In northern areas (Chicago, IL), plants are herbaceous perennials, dying back to the ground each year. North of zone 5, the usefulness of plants for cut flowers is marginal.

Transplanting: Plants transplant to the field easily; in fact, butterfly-bush is almost weedlike in its ability to withstand abuse. Rooted cuttings in plug trays are the most economical means of propagating and transplanting. From plugs, 4–5' tall plants can be produced the first year with approximately 10 stems/plant. Plants may also be planted from 1-gallon containers into moist, well-drained soil.

Spacing: No data are currently available. However, close spacing should be possible because plants can be severely cut back each season. A close spacing of 15 plants/20 linear ft may be used if plants are cut back to the ground in the fall.

Harvesting: Harvest stems as long as possible, remembering that a sufficient leaf area must remain to nourish the roots and provide next year's growth. Allow at least ⅓ of the plant height to remain, or harvest alternate branches. Stems should not be harvested mechanically due to the tenderness of the inflorescences.

Yield: The number of flowering stems depends on cultivar, severity of previous harvest and winter conditions. On a 3-year-old plant, 60–100 stems is not uncommon.

Greenhouse Performance

There seems to be little reason why *Buddleia* could not be forced out of season under greenhouse conditions. From observation of natural growing sequence, plants respond to long days and warm temperatures.

Stage of Harvest

Harvest when ½ the flowers on the inflorescence are open but before the open flowers have started to fade (3). Plants should be conditioned by placing stems in 80–100F water. If panicles are not turgid by the time the water cools, place stems in hot water a second time. Two to three changes may be necessary for thorough conditioning (3). Cutting stems under water may promote water uptake.

Postharvest

Fresh: Fresh flowers only persist 2–3 days if not well conditioned. This is the most limiting factor to the acceptance of *Buddleia* as a cut flower. Flowers will persist 5 to 8 days if properly conditioned. Paul Sansone, a successful grower in the state of Oregon, precuts under water, places the stems in a floral preservative and then moves them into the cooler. Flowers then persist for up to 10 days. White flowers decline more rapidly than other colors.

Dried: Large leaves should be removed and stems hung up to dry in a well-ventilated area. Flowers retain their fragrance even after drying (1).

Storage: Stems may be stored wet for 1–2 days at 38–40F (4).

Cultivars

Many are available, but some are more suitable for cut stems than others.

'Black Knight' has dark purple, highly scented flowers and is a vigorous grower.

'Dubonnet' bears rich purple flowers with a light orange throat. The panicles may be up to 14" long.

'Royal Red' bears purple-red flowers on 20" long panicles. An excellent "red" cultivar.

'White Bouquet' has 8–12" long panicles consisting of white flowers with an orange throat.

Additional Species

Buddleia × *weyeriana*, a hybrid between *B. davidii* and *B. globosa* is hardy in zones 7–9. The cultivars 'Sun Gold' and 'Golden Glow' bear yellow-orange and pale yellow-orange, fragrant flowers, respectively.

Pests and Diseases

Few pests bother butterfly-bush, although nematodes can be a nuisance in the South. Root rot, caused by *Phymatotrichum omnivorum,* has resulted in serious losses in Texas; however, it does not appear to be widespread.

Reading

1. Bullivant, E. 1989. *Dried Fresh Flowers From Your Garden.* Pelham Books/Stephen Greene Press, London, U.K.

2. Dirr, M. A. 1990. *Manual of Woody Landscape Plants: Their Identification, Ornamental Characteristics, Culture, Propagation and Uses.* 4th ed. Stipes Publishing, Champaign, IL.

3. Kasperski, V. R. 1956. *How to Make Cut Flowers Last.* M. Barrows and Co., New York, NY.

4. Nowak, J., and R. M. Rudnicki. 1990. *Postharvest Handling and Storage of Cut Flowers, Florist Greens, and Potted Plants.* Timber Press, Portland, OR.

Many thanks to Mr. Paul Sansone for reviewing this section.

Callicarpa americana   American Beautyberry   4–6'/3–6'
Purple, white fruit   United States   Verbenaceae   Zones 6–10

Noted for their magnificent purple or white fruit in the fall, the beautyberries are easily grown and have great potential as a cut stem. Of the approximately 40 species, 3 or 4 are available to American growers but this species is most useful for the berries (drupes). *Callicarpa americana* (american beautyberry; french mulberry) is native from Maryland to Georgia in the East, west to Arkansas and south to Mexico. It bears some of the largest and most ornamental fruit in the genus. Flowers are formed on new wood and the ¼" wide magenta fruit encircles the nodes in the top ⅓ of the stem. One of the chief advantages to growing any of the beautyberries is that flowers and fruit occur on new wood; stems may therefore be harvested almost to the ground.

Propagation

Cuttings: Softwood cuttings root in 7–14 days if placed in clean sand under intermittent mist (1).

Seed: Seed may be used but must be stratified for 30–60 days at 41F for best germination (1).

Field Performance

Habit: Plants are multistemmed shrubs. In north Georgia, plants reach a height of approximately 4' after being cut to within 1' of the ground the previous winter.

Transplanting: Plants are readily transplanted into well drained soils in the spring. Irrigation is necessary for good flowering and fruit production. Plants tolerate full sun to partial shade. Plants reach fruiting stage approximately 2–3 years after transplanting.

Spacing: No data are currently available. However, cutting back stems in the winter should allow for relatively close spacing. Research is presently underway to determine the influence of spacing on fruit production.

Fertilization: Excess fertility should be avoided once plants become productive. High rates of nitrogen result in reduced flowering and fruit production.

Harvesting: Harvest by cutting stems 6–12" from the ground. Fruit may fall off easily and harvesting must be done carefully to retain as much fruit as possible.

Yield: After about 2 years in the ground, approximately 30 stems are formed. Additional shoots form as plants mature.

Greenhouse Performance

No work has been conducted on forcing beautyberry out of season, but its annual growth rate and habit of fruiting on new wood suggest it could be greenhouse-forced. It is likely that long days and warm temperatures enhance flower and fruit production.

Stage of Harvest

Unfortunately, few data are available concerning harvest or postharvest techniques, but some preliminary studies were conducted at the University of Georgia. Early harvest (early October) may occur when the basal fruit clusters are fully colored and the terminal fruits are still green. Little additional fruit coloration occurs after harvest. Later harvests (mid-October to November) is better because all fruit is colored and many leaves have fallen.

Postharvest

Stems should be recut and immersed in hot water. Fruit persists for approximately 2 weeks (2). Stems may be stored at 32–36F for 2–4 days (2). Remaining foliage should be removed. The experiments at the University of Georgia showed that if stems are placed for 1–2 hours in a floral preservative, then placed in buckets without liquid, the foliage can be easily removed approximately 48 hours later. Once leaves are removed, place the stems back in water and store in a 32–36F cooler.

Cultivars

var. *lactea* is a white-fruited form. Fruit is beautiful initially but discolors as it ages.

Additional Species

Callicarpa bodinieri (bodinier beautyberry) is rarely seen by American growers but is grown in Europe. Native to China, plants are hardy in zones 5–7. 'Profusion' is a heavily fruited Dutch selection with 1/6" wide diameter violet fruit and large leaves. Abundant fruit occurs even on young plants. A white-fruited form also exists but is relatively unavailable to American growers.

C. dichotoma (purple beautyberry) is arguably more ornamental than *C. americana* but fruit is smaller (⅛″ wide) and does not encircle the nodes as in its American counterpart. The species is relatively fast-growing and multistemmed. Plants in Athens, GA, are 7 years old and bear over 30 marketable stems. Plants are more cold hardy than american beautyberry and grow well in zones 5–8. Postharvest tests at Georgia have been disappointing so far. The fruit falls off rapidly or dries to look like little purple raisins. Variety *albifructus* is a white-fruited form.

C. japonica (japanese beautyberry) is 4–8′ tall and mature plants are equal in width. They are not as heavily fruited as *C. americana* or *C. dichotoma* and some reports suggest the fruit is not as persistent. Plants have about the same hardiness as *C. dichotoma*. 'Leucocarpa' bears white fruit.

Pests and Diseases

Leaf spots (*Atractilina callicarpae*) occur as irregular, rustlike, scattered spots. Fungicide applications prior to fruit coloration may be necessary.

Black mold usually signifies an insect problem. Insects such as aphids secrete honeydew on which the mold grows. Controlling the insects generally controls the mold.

Reading

1. Dirr, M. A. 1990. *Manual of Woody Landscape Plants: Their Identification, Ornamental Characteristics, Culture, Propagation and Uses.* 4th ed. Stipes Publishing, Champaign, IL.

2. Vaughan, M. J. 1988. *The Complete Book of Cut Flower Care.* Timber Press, Portland, OR.

Cornus spp.   Dogwood

Approximately 40 species occur in the genus. Those used in the cut flower industry are grown either for the flowers (*C. florida, C. mas*) or for the brightly colored stems (*C. alba, C. sericea*).

Cornus alba	Tatarian Dogwood		8–10′/8′
Red stems	Asia	Cornaceae	Zones 2–6

Propagation

Cuttings: Softwood and hardwood cuttings root readily any time of year, but a 1000-ppm IBA dip should be used on cuttings taken in June and July (1). Hardwood cuttings (8–10″ long) are directly stuck into the field in late winter–early spring in some nurseries (1).

Seed: Seed should be stratified for 60–90 days at 41F (1).

Field Performance

Culture: For best stem color, plant in full sun and in areas where constant moisture may be maintained. Plants are normally found in the wild in wet, swampy areas. Neither *C. alba* nor *C. sericea* perform well in the South. Susceptibility to canker and poor stem coloration limit their usefulness south of zone 6.

Habit: Multistemmed shrubs with horizontal branches. The stems are relatively unbranched, making them particularly suitable for cutting. Plants spread readily by underground stems.

Transplanting: Growers may direct-stick long cuttings or transplant rooted cuttings in the spring or fall.

Spacing: Plants may be grown as large masses and spacing is only a concern to allow efficient harvesting. The stoloniferous growth eventually results in close spacing.

Fertilization: Reduce nitrogen fertilization in late summer. Excess fertilization, particularly nitrogen, results in soft growth, retards the development of stem coloration and retards leaf drop.

Harvesting: All stems should be cut close to the ground by late winter to allow new growth in the spring. The new stems have the most brilliant color in the spring and in the winter. The best color occurs in late winter on 1-year-old stems. Coloration is lost in the spring with leaf emergence.

Yield: A massed planting can become a thicket, particularly if mismanaged. Three-year-old plants should yield approximately 25 stems.

Stage of Harvest

The stems are best harvested after the foliage has fallen in the fall and can be harvested until foliage emerges in spring. If foliage is removed, the stems may be harvested whenever sufficient stem color has developed.

Postharvest

Storage: Stems may be stored in a humid area at 29F. Cold storage enhances stem color.

Cultivars

Many cultivars are available, but most differ only in their foliar characteristics. Few have more desirable stem color than the species. 'Kesselringii' produces purple stems, 'Sibirica' bears bright coral-red stems and 'Spaethii' has dark blood-red stems in winter.

A few cultivars also bear handsome leaves which may have potential as cut foliage. 'Argenteo-marginata' (also sold as 'Elegantissima') has gray-green leaves with irregular, creamy white margins. 'Spaethii' produces green foliage with strong yellow borders.

Pests and Diseases

Many fungi enjoy the delicacies of dogwood including those that cause canker, leaf blight, leaf spot, twig blight and mildews. Crown canker and twig blight can be particularly devastating to the species described here.

Crown canker is caused by *Phytophthora cactorum*. Leaves curl and shrivel, and later, twigs and even large branches die. Plants grown under stress (dry conditions, high temperatures) are more susceptible to canker. Plants may be treated in the early stages of infection, but once severely infected, plants eventually die. Cull badly affected plants. Plants must be rotated regularly to reduce the incidence of canker.

Twig blight is caused by a number of fungi; application of fungicides to the foliage and stems helps the problem.

Scale and bagworms also debilitate plants.

Cornus florida	Flowering Dogwood	15–30'/20'
White	Massachusetts to Florida	Cornaceae	Zones 5–9

Mainly used for forcing, few flowers are sold during the natural flowering time outdoors. Cut as a budded branch, stems are stored and then forced for winter bloom. The plant offers something in all seasons for the designer: in spring, lovely flowers; in summer, handsome foliage; in fall, red fruits and colored leaves; and in winter, unusual buds.

Propagation

Budding: Most cultivars are budded on seedling understock in July and August.

Cuttings: Collect softwood cuttings immediately after flowering. Treat with a quick dip of 1000 ppm IBA and root in peat/perlite medium under intermittent mist (1).

Seed: Seed requires 100–130 days at 41F for germination (1).

Field Performance

Culture: Plants tolerate partial shade, although full sun is acceptable. Normally found on the edges of woodlands in acidic soils. Even moisture and a cool root run are essential for maximum growth. Mulch is helpful and good drainage an absolute necessity.

Habit: Usually grown as a low-branched tree but occasionally shrubby in appearance.

Transplanting: Usually transplanted to the field as budded whips or 1- to 2-year-old seedlings.

Spacing: No data are available but a 5–7' spacing should allow for sufficient room as long as branches are annually pruned.

Harvesting: Harvest long branches back to a node but allow approximately ⅓ of the branch to remain.

Stage of Harvest

Forcing: Cut when buds are swollen. This may be accomplished 4–6 weeks prior to normal flowering time outdoors (2). Place stems in water at 65–70F. Use an acid preservative and change regularly. Flowers on stems cut in mid-March require 2–4 weeks to open (3).

Cut flowers: Harvest when the bracts are beginning to open but prior to pollen formation in the flower. Place the stems immediately in a floral preservative to reduce bacterial and fungal growth.

Postharvest

Fresh: Flowers persist 7–10 days if branches are split or crushed (2). Condition by immediately placing stems in hot (100F) water.

Cultivars

For cut stems, usually the species, grown from seed, is used. Pink-flowered forms are vegetatively propagated. However, many cultivars have been selected for the landscape trade and while they are more expensive, they may be useful in broadening the offerings of the niche grower. Some of the best for early flower bud set, large flowers and toughness include 'Barton', 'Cherokee Princess', and 'Cloud 9'. In Dr. Michael Dirr's book (see "Reading for *Cornus*"), he lists 68 taxa of flowering dogwood. Some are notable for their variegated foliage ('First Lady', 'Golden Nugget', 'Hohman's Gold', 'President Ford', 'Rainbow') or colorful foliage ('Purple Glory', 'Redleaf'), others for their large flowers ('Big Girl', 'Gigantea', 'Imperial White', 'Moon', 'Pluribracteata', 'White Giant'), double flowers ('Plena', 'Welch's Bay Beauty') or pink-to-red flowers ('American Red Beauty', 'Cherokee Chief', 'October Glory', 'Prosser Red', 'William's Red').

Pests and Diseases

Plants are susceptible to a number of pests and diseases such as borer, leaf and petal spots. The more stress a tree is under, the more likely damage will occur. Dogwood anthracnose, caused by *Discula* spp., has been a major concern for nursery growers in the North and Middle Atlantic states. The symptoms include irregular, purple-rimmed leaf spotting or tan blotches, infected leaves which stay on branches after normal leaf fall, die-back of twigs, water sprout formation and infection of bracts under rainy conditions (1). Trees are killed within 3 years of infection. By late 1991, the disease had been verified in 9 northeastern states and as far south as north Georgia (1).

Additional Species of *Cornus*

Cornus mas (cornelian cherry dogwood) is another species grown for its flowers. It grows 15–25' tall and 15–20' wide. Yellow flowers occur in small (¾" wide) inflorescences and appear naturally in late winter in the South and early spring in the North. The ½" wide fruit is bright cherry-red and formed during the summer. Possibly useful for winter forcing of flowers. Trees perform best in the North but are hardy in zones 5–7.

C. sericea (formerly *C. stolonifera*) is grown for its colorful stems. It is similar to *C. alba*, and some authorities believe it to be a subspecies of *C. alba*. Adaptable in zones 2–7, few differences in habit or culture exist between the 2 species. However, a number of cultivars of *C. sericea* are available which enhance the offerings of the grower. 'Cardinal' bears cherry-red stems. 'Flaviramea' is a marvelous form with bright yellow stems; if grown well, it is unbeatable for color. 'Silver and Gold' is a branch sport (chimera) of 'Flaviramea' and bears yellow stems. Potentially useful for its irregular, creamy-margined foliage as well.

Reading for *Cornus*

1. Dirr, M. A. 1990. *Manual of Woody Landscape Plants: Their Identification, Ornamental Characteristics, Culture, Propagation and Uses*. 4th ed. Stipes Publishing, Champaign, IL.

2. Kasperski, V. R. 1956. *How to Make Cut Flowers Last*. M. Barrows and Co., New York, NY.

3. Munroe, C. L. 1991. A winter extravaganza: forcing cut branches for indoor bloom. *Penn. Hort. Soc.* (January): 15–18.

Hydrangea quercifolia   Oakleaf Hydrangea   4–6'/6'
White   Southeastern United States   Saxifragaceae   Zones 5–9

Approximately 80 species occur and many have potential as cut flowers, either fresh or dried. Some species such as bigleaf hydrangea (*H. macrophylla*) and panicle hydrangea (*H. paniculata*) are well-known landscape plants throughout most of the country. *Hydrangea quercifolia* (oakleaf hydrangea) has undergone significant selection and cultivars with large double-flowered forms are becoming more available.

Propagation
Seed: Fresh seed germinates relatively easily.

Cuttings: Collect terminal cuttings in as early as April and as late as September. Early plants should be dipped in 3000 ppm KIBA, later cuttings in 5000 ppm KIBA. Place in 2:1 perlite/peat under intermittent mist (2). Cuttings root in approximately 4 weeks.

Field Performance
Habit: Oakleaf hydrangea is a stoloniferous shrub with few branches, particularly when young. However, after plants reach maturity, significant branching occurs. Flowers are formed in long terminal panicles on previous year's growth. The outer showy flowers are sterile, the inner ones fertile and non-ornamental. Cultivars are more useful for cut flowers than the species.

Transplanting: Transplant 2-year-old plants to the field from containers. Plants are commercially useful after 3–5 years in the field.

Spacing: Though no data are available, a spacing of 3–5' should be sufficient.

Yield: No data are available, but mature shrubs bear 15–20 stems, each stem producing 1 inflorescence.

Stage of Harvest

Stems should be harvested when ½ the flowers on the panicle are open. If panicles are dried, cut when sterile flowers (double flowers) turn crisp and papery (3).

Postharvest

Fresh: Flowers persist 4–9 days. Some authors state that stems should be split and either seared with flame or boiled for 30 seconds in acidic water (3). Condition stems overnight in cold water with pH 4.0 (3).

Dried: Wait until flowers are papery before harvesting. Strip leaves, bunch stems and hang in a warm, dark environment (1). Direct sunlight results in discoloration; dampness results in flowers turning brown. Two to three weeks are required for complete dryness (1).

Cultivars

'Alice' is a recent selection of Dr. Michael Dirr of the University of Georgia. Panicles are about 12" long and mainly bear large, sterile flowers that almost cover the fertile flowers. Plants are vigorous and grow 6–8' tall.

'Alison' is similar to 'Alice', but the panicles are a little smaller and held more upright. Plants are equally vigorous and can reach 8' in height. Also selected by Dr. Dirr.

'Snowflake' bears flowers with multiple bracts or sepals and look like double flowers. Panicles are 12–15" long and mainly sterile.

'Snow Queen' bears many more sterile flowers on the inflorescence than the species. Panicles are held more upright than those of 'Snowflake' and turn pink as they mature.

Additional Species

Hydrangea arborescens 'Annabelle' bears 10–12" wide, creamy white inflorescences (corymbs) in late June through September. Plants flower on current year's wood; therefore they may be cut to the ground in late winter. The resulting growth will produce sufficient flowers for cutting. A second flush of flowers is possible in southern climates in September if the first flush is removed by early July. The inflorescences are excellent for drying.

H. macrophylla (bigleaf hydrangea) has become an important crop, particularly for drying. The inflorescence consists of sterile outer flowers and some fertile inner flowers. The hortensias consist almost entirely of sterile flowers which form a rounded, heavy inflorescence. The lacecaps have a center of fertile flowers surrounded by an outer ring of sterile flwoers, producing a pinwheel effect. Many cultivars are available; the flower color may be strongly affected by the concentration of aluminum in the soil. The concentration of aluminum depends on the pH of the soil, being highest in acid soils and lowest in alkaline soils. Flowers are cut fully open. Hardy in zones 6–9.

H. paniculata 'Grandiflora' (peegee hydrangea) bears large panicles of white, sterile flowers in early to midsummer. The panicles are usually 6–8" long but can reach 12–18" in length if branches are selectively pruned. Such large inflorescences, however, may be too big for the cut flower market. 'Praecox' is similar to 'Grandiflora' but flowers approximately 2 weeks earlier. 'Tardiva' bears numerous sterile flowers on a 6" long inflorescence; its late-flowering habit (late September) makes it a useful option for extending the hydrangea market.

Pests and Diseases
Plants are essentially trouble-free.

Reading
1. Bullivant, E. 1989. *Dried Fresh Flowers From Your Garden.* Pelham Books/Stephen Greene Press, London, U.K.
2. Dirr, M. A. 1990. *Manual of Woody Landscape Plants: Their Identification, Ornamental Characteristics, Culture, Propagation and Uses.* 4th ed. Stipes Publishing, Champaign, IL.
3. Kasperski, V. R. 1956. *How to Make Cut Flowers Last.* M. Barrows and Co., New York, NY.

Ilex verticillata   Winterberry, Coralberry   6–10'/6'
Red fruit   North America   Aquifoliaceae   Zones 3–9

This species of *Ilex* (holly) is only one of the dozens of species and hundreds of cultivars of hollies available in the nursery trade. Some are useful for the evergreen foliage whereas others bear berrylike fruits (drupes) on deciduous shrubs which are harvested for the Christmas and Easter markets. Hollies are dioecious, meaning that plants are either male or female. Only the female plants bear fruit, but some males are necessary for pollination. Generally, any male holly can pollinate any female if flowering times overlap.

Propagation
Cuttings: Softwood cuttings root easily. Treat June or July cuttings with a quick-dip of 1000–3000 ppm IBA, stick in peat/perlite medium and place under intermittent mist. Ninety to one hundred percent rooting occurs in 6–8 weeks (1).
Seed: Seed exhibits a deep dormancy and patience is a must. Some seed may require up to 18 months. The mealy outside layers of the fruit should be removed from the hard seeds (nutlets) which are then sown in a suitable medium. Place at 70–75F in a humid area (1).

Growing-on
Plants are slow-growing and generally grown in containers. Acid condi-

tions (pH 4.5–6.5) and moderate fertility levels are recommended. They can be transplanted to the field as rooted cuttings in the spring, but fibrous roots dry out rapidly and significant losses may occur. One-gallon containerized plants reduce losses.

Field Performance

Habit: Plants are oval to rounded in shape and tend to form large multi-stemmed clumps. The foliage is deciduous but persists into late fall.

Spacing: Plants can grow 10–15' wide if left undisturbed; spacing of 20' × 20' has been used to facilitate mechanical harvesting. With selective cutting, denser spacing may be provided to produce mass plantings. Some growers space as densely as 4' apart and 10' between rows. Wider spacing allows more stems/plant but fewer stems/ft^2. With large plantings, spacing should be dictated by the equipment available for cultivating and harvesting.

Harvesting: Flower buds are set a year prior to flowering; severe harvesting therefore retards subsequent fruiting. If plants are cut back severely, approximately 3 years are necessary before plants can be reharvested (2). Mechanical mowing of 15–18" stems is also practiced (2).

Soils: Plants are native to swampy areas and can be grown with the entire root system submerged. Plants are also adaptable to "normal" field conditions. Drainage is not as important with this species as with other woody plants.

Stage of Harvest

Branches should be harvested before the fruit reaches maturity (2).

Postharvest

Abscission of foliage: While not necessary to remove the foliage from holly branches, some wholesalers believe the fruit is more ornamental when the branches are defoliated. A problem occurs when some, but not all, of the leaves and fruits abscise, resulting in an unattractive branch.

Storage of cut branches in high humidity chambers helps in the removal of foliage, whether foliage is removed mechanically or by hand.

Storage: Stems should be stored dry (2). Branches may be stored at 32F for 1–3 weeks in moisture-retentive boxes (3).

Cultivars

Numerous cultivars are available, most with red fruit but a few with yellow and orange-red fruit. A male form is needed to accompany the female cultivars listed. Approximately 1 male/20 females is sufficient.

'Cacapon' produces an abundance of truly red fruit on 6–8' tall plants.

'Christmas Gem', introduced by Jenkins Nursery in Maryland, bears dark red fruit.

'Chrysocarpa' bears yellow fruit but does not fruit as heavily as many of the red-fruited forms.

'Maryland Beauty' was also introduced by Jenkins and is a heavy producer.

'Shaver' has perhaps the largest fruit of all selections. The fruit is orange-red and produced on upright-growing plants.

'Sunset' bears bright red fruit which is slightly longer than that of 'Winter Red'.

'Tiasquam' produces excellent, persistent red fruit.

'Winter Gold', a branch sport of 'Winter Red', produces ¼" wide, pinkish orange fruit.

'Winter Red', introduced by Simpson Nursery, has performed exceptionally well in trials at the University of Georgia and many other sites. Bright red, ⅜" wide fruit is borne in great profusion and maintained through the winter.

Additional Species

Ilex decidua (possumhaw) is also a fall-fruiting, deciduous holly which is useful for the scarlet-red berries. Plants grow 7–15' tall and about 10' wide at maturity. Plants are hardy in zones 5–9, although differences among cultivars occur. Some useful cultivars include 'Council Fire' (orange fruit), 'Red Cascade' (red fruit), 'Sentry' (red fruit), 'Sundance' (orange-red fruit) and 'Warren Red' (red fruit). 'Red Escort' is a good male form.

I. serrata (finetooth holly) bears small (¼" wide) fruit and generally grows about 6–8' tall. The abundant fruit ripens early, and is showy. Unfortunately, the fruit on many selections does not hold well and fades on the side facing the sun. Cultivars include 'Leucocarpa' (white fruit) and 'Xanthocarpa' (yellow fruit).

I. verticillata × *I. serrata* crosses have resulted in some useful cultivars for the landscape; however, they are less suitable than *I. verticillata* forms for cut fruit. The fruit, in general, is slightly smaller than *I. verticillata* forms and usually less persistent. 'Autumn Glow' is 6–8' tall and produces red fruit which fades on the side facing the sun by Christmas. 'Bonfire' is a vigorous grower with red fruit. 'Sparkleberry' is one of the best cultivars bearing persistent, brilliant red fruit, often throughout the winter. Use 'Apollo' as the male form to accompany 'Sparkleberry'.

Pests and Diseases

Tar spot, caused by *Rhytisma concavum*, results in yellow spots on the foliage in spring which turn reddish brown in the summer and black in the fall. Treat with a fungicide in early spring.

Leaf spots are caused by numerous fungi and result in small, brown to black spots on the foliage. Increasing the vigor of the plants by reducing stress (keeping them well watered, etc.) reduces incidence of leaf spotting.

Powdery mildew is sometimes a problem, particularly in the South. Use of fungicides may be necessary.

Reading

1. Dirr, M. A. 1990. *Manual of Woody Landscape Plants: Their Identification, Ornamental Characteristics, Culture, Propagation and Uses.* 4th ed. Stipes Publishing, Champaign, IL.

2. Eisel, M. C. 1989. Deciduous woody plants for the florist trade. In *Proceedings of Commercial Field Production of Cut and Dried Flowers.* Univ. of Minnesota, The Center for Alternative Crops and Products, St. Paul, MN. 57–64.

3. Nowak, J., and R. M. Rudnicki. 1990. *Postharvest Handling and Storage of Cut Flowers, Florist Greens, and Potted Plants.* Timber Press, Portland, OR.

Salix spp.	Willow		6–20'/20'
Contorted/colorful stems	Worldwide	Salicaceae	Zones 3–8

Mainly grown for their colorful or contorted stems as well as their male catkins (pussy willows), willows are easy to propagate and fill an important niche in the cut branch market. Stems range from red to yellow, and a number of fast-growing species and cultivars with twisted stem shapes are also useful. These include those used for their contorted stems (*S. matsudana* 'Snake', 'Tortuosa'); flattened stems (*S. sachalinensis* 'Sekka'); stem color (*S. alba* 'Britzensis', 'Vitellina'); or a combination (*S. × erythroflexuosa* 'Golden Curls', 'Scarlet Curls').

Propagation
Cuttings: Easily propagated by soft and hardwood cuttings any time of year. Cut and stick.

Seed: Seed has no dormancy and germinates within 12–24 hours if provided with a moist environment (1).

Growing-on
After rooting, transplant into a 6″ or 1-gallon container until plants are large enough to transplant to the field.

Environmental Factors
Stems are most contorted and colored forms most colorful when young. Cool temperatures in late fall and winter and high light intensity result in more colorful stems.

Field Performance
All species grown for colored stems need to be cut back hard in late winter and early spring for best form and color in the fall and winter.

Stage of Harvest
Harvest leafless stems at peak of color.

Postharvest
When stems are cut, place immediately in water. Remove foliage. Stems may be stored dry at 29F.

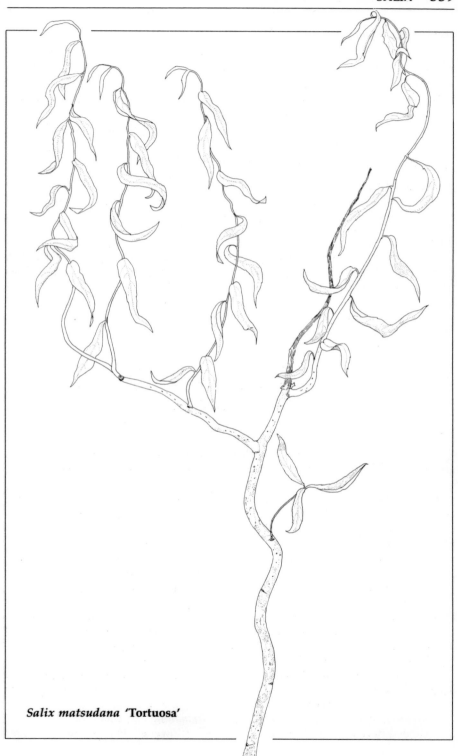

Salix matsudana 'Tortuosa'

Additional Species

Salix caprea (goat willow), *S. chaenomeloides* (japanese pussy willow), *S. discolor* (pussy willow), *S. gracilistyla* (rosegold pussy willow) and *S. melanostachys* (black pussy willow) are all grown for their handsome male catkins. The catkins of goat willow, a 15–25' tall tree, are 1–2" long and appear in March and early April. It is a better species for catkins than the true pussy willow, *S. discolor*, because of the latter species's susceptibility to canker. None are long-lasting in the field.

On harvesting, plunge the stems in water and store in a 35–40F cooler.

Pests and Diseases

All willows are fast-growing and short-lived. The wood is weak, and maintenance and upkeep are necessary to keep plants productive.

Reading

1. Dirr, M. A. 1990. *Manual of Woody Landscape Plants: Their Identification, Ornamental Characteristics, Culture, Propagation and Uses.* 4th ed. Stipes Publishing, Champaign, IL.

ADDITIONAL WOODY SPECIES SUITABLE FOR CUT FLOWER PRODUCTION

The species in the list which follows are useful not only for their flowers, but for their fragrance, fruit, foliage and colorful stems as well (1).

Amorpha canescens
(flowers/foliage) Purple and gray respectively.

Aronia arbutifolia
(fruit) Red and persistent.

Aucuba japonica
(foliage) Bold; variegated with gold.

Buxus spp.
(foliage) A lustrous dark green.

Calluna vulgaris
(flowers/foliage) Available in an unbelievable range of colors.

Calycanthus floridus
(flowers/foliage) Red-brown flowers; 'Athens' has yellowish, exceedingly fragrant flowers.

Camellia sasanqua
(flowers/foliage) Many colors available.

Celastrus orbiculatus
(fruit) Yellow-orange.

Celastrus scandens
(fruit) Yellow-orange; very popular.

Cercis canadensis 'Alba'
(flowers) A lovely white-flowered form.

Chimonanthus praecox
(flowers/fragrance) Waxy, yellow flowers with an outstanding fragrance.

Chionanthus retusus
(flowers/foliage) White flowers;

lustrous, leathery, dark green leaves.

Clethra alnifolia
(flowers/fragrance) Flowers in July; wonderful fragrance; var. *rosea* and 'Pink Spires' have good cut flower potential.

Corylopsis spp.
(flowers/fragrance) Soft yellow, fragrant blossoms in early spring.

Corylus avellana 'Contorta'
(stem shape) Twisted stems; handsome catkins.

Cotinus coggygria
(flowers) Smokey, pink-to-purple panicles in summer; gaining in popularity.

Cytisus spp.
(flowers/stem shape and color) Blooms ranging from white to yellow to garnet; green, angled stems.

Danae racemosa
(foliage) Rich evergreen "leaves."

Daphne × *burkwoodii*
(flowers/fragrance) Pinkish white, fragrant flowers; 'Carol Mackie' has added interest of foliage variegated with a creamy edge.

Daphne odora
(flowers/fragrance/foliage) Available in several forms, all exceedingly fragrant.

Erica spp.
(flowers/foliage) Winter-flowering; available in many colors.

Euonymus alatus
(stem shape) Corky and winged.

× *Fatshedera lizei*
(foliage) Rich, ivylike, evergreen.

Forsythia spp.
(flowers) Golden yellow; 10 new introductions have been made recently, 5 notable for their extreme flower bud hardiness (−25F).

Hamamelis × *intermedia*
(flowers/foliage) Worthy cultivars flower in copper ('Jelena'), bronze-red ('Diane' and 'Ruby Glow') and yellow ('Arnold Promise' and 'Pallida').

Itea virginica 'Henry's Garnet'
(flowers/fragrance/foliage)

Jasminum mesnyi
(flowers) Yellow, double-flowered.

Kerria japonica 'Picta'
(flowers/foliage) Yellow flowers; persistent cream-variegated foliage.

Koelreuteria bipinnata
(fruit) Pink-rose capsules in September.

Lonicera fragrantissima
(flowers/fragrance) Delightful scent.

Magnolia grandiflora
(flowers/foliage) Lovely flowers and lustrous, dark green leaves. Popular cultivars include 'Bracken's Brown Beauty', 'Little Gem' and 'Samuel Sommer'.

Michelia doltsopa
(flowers/fragrance/foliage) White blooms.

Michelia figo
(flowers/fragrance/foliage) Yellow flowers tinged with purple.

Morus australis 'Unryu'
(stem shape) Also known as 'Tortuosa'; poor man's contorted filbert.

Myrica cerifera
(fruit/foliage) Waxy, gray fruit; evergreen, scented foliage.

Myrica pensylvanica
(fruit/foliage) Waxy, gray fruit; scented foliage.

Nandina domestica
(flowers/fruit/foliage) 'Gulfstream' and 'Moyer's Red' have good cut foliage potential.

Oxydendrum arboreum
   (flowers/fragrance/fruit) Delicate, white "blueberry" flowers;
   interesting seed capsules.
Poncirus trifoliata
   (stem color) Bright green, thorny
   stems.
Prunus spp.
   (flowers) Branches of apricot,
   cherry, peach and plum are all
   easily forced.
Sarcococca hookerana
   (fragrance/foliage) Sweetly
   scented in early spring.
Skimmia japonica
   (flowers, fruit, foliage) Superb
   flowers; red fruit; evergreen
   foliage.
Skimmia reevesiana
   (fruit/foliage) Brilliant red fruit.
Spiraea × *bumalda*
   (flowers) Available in white, pink
   and carmine.
Spiraea japonica
   (flowers) Available in white, pink
   and rose.

Symphoricarpos albus
   (flowers/fruit) Rose-red and
   snowy white, respectively.
Syringa laciniata
   (flowers/fragrance) Heat-
   tolerant, lilac blooms.
Syringa vulgaris
   (flowers/fragrance) Available in
   a wide range of colors, both
   single- and double-flowered.
Ulmus alata
   (stem shape) Corky and winged.
Viburnum spp.
   (flowers/fragrance/foliage)
   Viburnum × *burkwoodii, V.* ×
   carlcephalum, V. carlesii and *V.* ×
   juddii are all fragrant semi-
   snowballs. *V. macrocephalum*
   produces large, white snowballs, 5–6" in diameter. *V.* ×
   pragense is useful for its
   lustrous, large, dark green
   leaves.

Reading

1. Dirr, M. A. 1989. "Woodies" with "cut" potential. In *Proceedings of 2nd National Conference on Specialty Cut Flowers*. Athens, GA. 168–171.

References

In writing this book, I always came back to the following books or articles for information. Many have been referenced in various crop reports for their particular usefulness to specialty cut flower growers, but all are important enough as general references to be included here. They are highly recommended.

Books

Armitage, A. M. 1989. *Herbaceous Perennial Plants: A Treatise on Their Identification, Culture, and Garden Attributes.* Varsity Press, Athens, GA.

A good, readable book on perennials. Morphological and taxonomic descriptions, uses and propagation of the common and not-so-common species are covered here. References are occasionally made to cut flower uses, but it is mainly a book for general perennial plant reference.

Bloom, Alan. 1956. *Hardy Perennials.* Faber and Faber, London, U.K.

The only reason for recommending this out-of-print book is the chapter on perennials for cutting (chapter 11). Mr. Bloom is best known for his nursery, Blooms of Bressingham, which specializes in garden perennials. He provides insightful comments on the use of perennials for cut flowers. His experiences in the early 1940s with selling market flowers provide much food for thought as to how far we have progressed, and yet how similar the problems which beset him are to the problems which face growers today. He experienced "the hazards and disappointments of market growing" and has "every sympathy for growers and understands their problems—including the need for variety."

Bullivant, Elizabeth. 1989. *Dried Fresh Flowers From Your Garden.* Pelham Books/Stephen Greene Press, London, U.K.

A delightful book written by one of the grande dames of English gardening and certainly a fountain of knowledge about drying flowers. Nothing is safe from her zeal for drying, and she includes a wealth of information on annuals, perennials, berries, foliage and even vegetables. Not written with the commercial, large-volume dryer in mind, this book nevertheless provides some excellent ideas and concepts. A great read.

De Hertogh, A. A. 1989. *Holland Bulb Forcer's Guide.* 4th ed. International Flower Bulb Center, Hillegom, The Netherlands.

The bible of bulb manuals, the guide has been expanded to include relevant information on cut flower crops for greenhouse and field production. While greenhouse forcing of tulips, daffodils and hyacinths still holds center stage, the sections on outdoor cut flowers, and diseases and pests of bulb species are particularly useful. A must for anyone even contemplating the growing of bulb crops.

Dirr, M. A. 1990. *Manual of Woody Landscape Plants.* 4th ed. Stipes Publishing Company, Champaign, IL.

If De Hertogh's manual is the bible for bulbs, this is the bible for woody plants. The manual's focus is the identification and use of woody species in the landscape, however, plant habit, propagation methods and the most up-to-date descriptions of cultivars of any publication are contained within. I refer to it constantly when working on woody plants. A truly enlightening book and an enjoyable read as well.

Nau, Jim. 1989. *Ball Culture Guide: The Encyclopedia of Seed Germination.* Ball Seed Co., West Chicago, IL.

An excellent guide to seed germination of many annual and perennial species. The number of seeds necessary to raise 1000 plants or the number of seeds for 1000 square feet of field production may be found with other tidbits about many cut flower species. Handy and informative.

Nowak, J., and R. M. Rudnicki. 1990. *Postharvest Handling and Storage of Cut Flowers, Florist Greens, and Potted Plants.* Timber Press, Portland, OR.

An in-depth reference on postharvest information on a wealth of cut flower crops. Written mainly for the scientist, the book brings together much of the literature on postharvest research from the early 1900s through the mid 1980s. A excellent resource for answering questions concerning stage of harvest, postharvest storage techniques and floral preservatives.

Pirone, P. P. 1989. *Diseases and Pests of Ornamental Plants.* 5th ed. Ronald Press, New York, NY.

All the diseases and pests you ever wanted to know about on most ornamental crops. General sections on common diseases caused by bacteria, fungi and viruses as well as common insect pests are covered. Genera are presented alphabetically and information concerning problems and their control for each genus and species are provided. A reference book of the highest caliber.

Sacalis, J. N. 1989. *Fresh (Cut) Flowers for Designs: Postproduction Guide* I. D. C. Kiplinger Chair in Floriculture, The Ohio State Univ., Columbus, OH.

   Dr. Sacalis has assembled much of the known literature in the post-harvest and handling of cut flowers. Each species is treated individually and completely. A useful guide for the major crops. It was republished in 1993 by Ball Publishing Co., Geneva, IL, as *Cut Flowers: Prolonging Freshness.*

Vaughan, Mary Jane. 1988. *The Complete Book of Cut Flower Care.* Timber Press, Portland, OR.

   A marvelous little book, specifically aimed at cut flower care for retailers and full of tips concerning vase life, storage when necessary, optimum stage of maturity and when flowers are usually available to the florist. A good section on flowers useful for drying is also included. Growers and wholesalers would do well to track down a copy of this book, now unfortunately out of print.

Book Set

The Handbook of Flowering (CRC Press, Boca Raton, FL) was edited by Dr. Abraham Halevy and consists of 4 volumes and 2 supplements published from 1985 through 1989. This set is by far the most comprehensive series of books dealing with the environmental and physiological aspects of flowering. Dr. Halevy has brought together dozens of scientists to provide up-to-date scientific data dealing with all aspects of flowering. Heavy reading, but excellent information for those who want to know more about the crops being produced. Available through university libraries.

Newsletters and Periodicals

The Cut Flower Quarterly, the newsletter of the Association of Specialty Cut Flower Growers (ASCFG), is an invaluable—and often the only—reference that provides a continuous flow of new information on the culture and marketing of specialty flowers. Published 4 times a year, it provides literature updates, regional synopses and articles of national interest by leading growers and researchers. Available through membership to ASCFG, MPO Box 268, Oberlin, OH 44074.

EuroFloratech and *FloraCulture* are international journals published for American growers by *Greenhouse Grower* and *GrowerTalks,* respectively. They concentrate on European floriculture and information on cut flowers is frequently provided.

Proceedings

Proceedings of Commercial Field Production of Cut and Dried Flowers. 1989. Univ. of Minnesota, The Center for Alternative Crops and Products, St. Paul, MN.
Proceedings from a conference held on 6–8 December 1988 in Minnesota. Many excellent talks were given and are provided in full.

Proceedings of 2nd National Conference on Specialty Cut Flowers. 1989. Univ. of Georgia, Athens, GA.
Unfortunately, the proceedings of the first national conference held in Athens in May 1987 were not published, but this one more than made up for it. The second conference was held 13–14 March 1989 and included talks on culture, marketing, dried flowers and much more.

Proceedings of 3rd National Conference on Specialty Cut Flowers. 1990. Ventura, CA.
The first conference conducted by the Association of Specialty Cut Flower Growers, it was held in September 1990 and consisted of concurrent seminars on labor laws, postharvest methods, cultural hints, new crops and research findings from various universities.

Proceedings of 4th National Conference on Specialty Cut Flowers. 1992. Cleveland, OH.
Another information-filled conference, this meeting, held in November 1991, featured many more discussions by growers ("Grower to Grower") on crop successes and failures. Marketing approaches, dried and fresh flower workshops and an excellent design seminar were presented.

Seed Guides

Many seed firms publish excellent catalogs including Ball Seed Co., Gloeckner Seed Co. and Park Seed Co. Kieft Bloemzaden, in Venhuizen, The Netherlands, also provides a grower guide to seed germination and special comments on culture and spacing. Although published with the European grower in mind, the information is relevant to the American grower as well. The manual is available through the ASCFG (see "Newsletters and

Periodicals" above). Cornelius Kieft, who passed away in 1991, was the first European representative of the Association of Specialty Cut Flower Growers. He is sorely missed.

Kieft, C. 1989. *Kieft's Growing Manual for Annual, Biennial and Perennial Cut Flowers and Ornamental Grasses Grown From Seed.* Kieft Bloemzaden, P.O. Box 63, 1606 ZH, Venhuizen, The Netherlands.

Specific References

Unfortunately, time and lack of expertise did not allow me to properly treat grains and grasses. This in no way makes them less important; in fact, many species and cultivars are without equal as dried flowers. Some good references include

Godwin, B. J. 1989. Grains for the florist trade. In *Proceedings of Commercial Field Production of Cut and Dried Flowers.* Univ. of Minnesota, The Center for Alternative Crops and Products, St. Paul, MN. 69–75.

Hockenberry-Meyer, M. 1989. Everlasting ornamental grasses. In *Proceedings of Commercial Field Production of Cut and Dried Flowers.* Univ. of Minnesota, The Center for Alternative Crops and Products, St. Paul, MN. 77–86.

Hurd, J. 1992. Grains and grasses. In *Proceedings of 4th National Conference on Specialty Cut Flowers.* Cleveland, OH. 45–57.

Stage of Harvest

The following list is a summary of recommendations for the optimal stage of harvest for specialty cut flowers to be used as fresh flowers. Additional details may be found under individual genera.

Achillea Flowers should not be harvested until pollen is visible on the inflorescence.

Acidanthera Harvest when 1–2 flowers are open.

Aconitum Inflorescences (racemes) should be harvested when 1–3 basal flowers are open.

Ageratum Harvest when flowers are just opening.

Agrostemma Stems should be harvested when 1–2 flowers are open on the inflorescence.

Allium Harvest most species when ½ the flowers are open. Flowers of *A. sphaerocephalon* may be harvested as early as when ¼ of the flowers are open.

Alstroemeria Pull stems when the first flowers are fully colored and the majority are showing color.

Amaranthus Cut when at least ¾ of the flowers on the inflorescence are open. If producing dried flowers, allow the flowers of all species to grow until seed has begun to set and the flowers feel firm to the touch.

Ammi Harvest when flower heads are approximately 80% open.

Anemone Harvest when the sepals have started to separate from the center but are not fully open.

349

Antirrhinum	Cut when ½ to ⅔ of the flowers are open. For long distance shipping, harvest when ⅓ of the flowers are open.
Asclepias	Harvest when ½ to ⅔ of the flowers are open, flowers do not open well once stems are cut.
Aster	Cut the stems when 2–4 flowers in the inflorescence have opened.
Astilbe	Inflorescences should be harvested when ½ to ¾ of the flowers are open. The uppermost buds should be swollen and showing color.
Astrantia	Harvest when the uppermost flowers are open.
Buddleia	Harvest when ½ the flowers on the inflorescence are open but before the open flowers have started to fade.
Callicarpa	Cut stems when the basal fruit clusters are fully colored and the terminal fruits are still green.
Callistephus	Harvest when outside ray florets begin to open.
Campanula	Harvest when 1–2 flowers of the inflorescence are open.
Carthamus	Cut stems when the majority of buds have begun to open and petals are clearly visible.
Caryopteris	Stems should be harvested when buds show color or when the first whorl of flowers is open.
Celosia	Flowers should be fully developed on crested forms and 90–100% developed in the plumose form.
Centaurea	For annuals, harvest when flowers are ¼ to ½ open. In the case of multiple flowered stems (i.e., sprays), the uppermost flower may be ¾ open. For *C. macrocephala*, harvest when flowers are ½ to ¾ open.
Centranthus	Harvest when the first flowers in the inflorescence are fully open.
Cirsium	Harvest when the flowers are open.
Consolida	Allow 2–5 basal flowers to open or up to ⅓ of the flowers on the stem.
Cornus	To harvest stems, cut after leaves have dropped and before new foliage appears. Harvest flowers when the bracts are beginning to open but prior to pollen formation in the flower.
Cosmos	Harvest when petals on first flower are just opening, but have not yet flattened out.
Crocosmia	The first few flower buds should be showing color but need not be open.

Dahlia	Harvest when the flowers are ¾ to fully open, but before the outer petals begin to decline.
Delphinium	Harvest when ⅓ to ¼ of the flowers on the stem are open.
Dianthus	Harvest when 10–20% of the flowers in the inflorescence are open.
Echinacea	Harvest when petals are expanding. If used as a disk flower only, allow additional time on the plant to color disk, then remove petals.
Echinops	Harvest flowers when ½ to ¾ of the globe has turned blue.
Emilia	Harvest stems when the first flower is fully open.
Eryngium	Flowers should be harvested when the entire flower head, including bracts, turns blue.
Euphorbia	Cut stems when bracts are fully colored but before the flowers are open.
Eustoma	Harvest when 1 flower in the inflorescence is fully colored.
Freesia	Harvest when the first flower is beginning to open and at least 2 additional flowers are showing color.
Gladiolus	Cut when 1–5 flowers on the spike are showing color.
Godetia	Harvest when the first flowers on the stem are open.
Gomphrena	Harvest when flowers are in color but before fully open.
Gypsophila	For the fresh flower market, stems should be cut with 60–70% of the flowers open. For drying, 80–90% of the flowers should be open.
Helianthus	Cut stems when the flowers are almost completely open.
Helichrysum	Cut flowers when bracts are unfolding and centers are visible. Always harvest before flowers are fully open.
Hydrangea	Stems should be harvested when ½ the flowers on the panicle are open.
Ilex	Branches should be harvested before the fruit reaches maturity.
Iris	Cut all dutch iris except 'Blue Ribbon' ('Prof Blaauw') when the flower has fully emerged from the sheath ("pencil" stage). 'Blue Ribbon' should be cut when the falls begin to open.
Lavatera	Cut when the flowers are uncurling or when they have just begun to open.

Liatris	Harvest when 3–4 flowers have opened.
Lilium	Cut when the first flower is fully colored, but not yet open.
Limonium	Harvest when approximately 80% of the flower head has opened.
Lunaria	Harvest when the pods are fully developed.
Lysimachia	Cut when flowers in the inflorescence are ⅓ to ½ open.
Matthiola	Stems should be harvested when ½ the flowers in the inflorescences are open.
Narcissus	Single, large flowers should be harvested when closed, but with color showing (goose-neck stage) and at a 90–120° angle from the stem. Harvest double-flowered cultivars when the flowers are just beginning to open.
Nerine	Harvest when the first flower is just about to open.
Nigella	Harvest when the pods are turning purple-bronze.
Ornithogalum	Harvest when the first flower is open if flowers are to be shipped long distances; approximately ¼ of the flowers may be open for local sales.
Oxypetalum	Harvest when approximately 6 cymes are present. The first 1 or 2 should be open, the last showing color.
Paeonia	As a general rule, flowers should be harvested when the first true color appears on top of the tight bud. Double-flowered types should be further developed than single forms and red cultivars should be more developed than whites.
Phlox	Harvest when ½ the flowers are open on the inflorescence.
Physalis	Harvest when the fruit is fully colored.
Physostegia	Flowers may be cut when the spikes are fully elongated but before individual flowers are open.
Platycodon	Harvest when 2–3 flowers are open on the flower stem.
Polianthes	Harvest when 2–4 flowers are open and others are showing color.
Ranunculus	Cut flowers when buds show color and are about to open.
Salix	Harvest leafless stems at peak of color.
Salvia	Flowers should be harvested when the white petals (corolla) emerge from the blue sepals (calyx) on the first 3–4 basal flowers.

Scabiosa	For the perennial *S. caucasica,* flowers may be harvested as soon as flower color is visible. The annual *S. atropurpurea* may be harvested when the flower is almost fully open.
Solidago	Harvest inflorescence when approximately ½ the flowers are open.
Solidaster	Harvest when ⅓ of the flowers are open.
Thalictrum	Flowers should be harvested when most of the flowers are open.
Trachelium	Harvest the stem when ¼ to ⅓ of the flowers are open.
Triteleia	Harvest when 4–6 flowers are open.
Tulipa	Harvest flowers when ½ to ¾ of the flower is colored.
Veronica	Cut when approximately ½ the flowers on the inflorescence are open.
Veronicastrum	Remove terminal flower and cut when the lateral flowers are approximately ⅓ open.
Zantedeschia	Flowers should be cut when the spathes unroll and are almost fully open.
Zinnia	Harvest when flowers are fully mature.

APPENDIX II:
Useful Conversions

CENTIMETERS / INCHES

Centimeters	Inches
16	
	6
15	
14	
13	
	5
12	
11	
	4
10	
9	
8	
	3
7	
6	
5	2
4	
3	
	1
2	
1	
0	0

CELSIUS / FAHRENHEIT

Celsius	Fahrenheit
30°	86°
29°	84.2°
28°	82.4°
27°	80.6°
26°	78.8°
25°	77°
24°	75.2°
23°	73.4°
22°	71.6°
21°	69.8°
20°	68°
19°	66.2°
18°	64.4°
17°	62.6°
16°	60.8°
15°	59°
14°	57.2°
13°	55.4°
12°	53.6°
11°	51.8°
10°	50°
9°	48.2°
8°	46.4°
7°	44.6°
6°	42.8°
5°	41°
4°	39.2°
3°	37.4°
2°	35.6°
1°	33.8°
0°	32°

GRAMS / OUNCES

	Grams	Ounces
	220	¾
		½
	210	
		¼
198	200	**7**
	190	¾
		½
	180	
		¼
170		**6**
		¾
	160	
		½
	150	¼
142		**5**
	140	
		¾
	130	
		½
	120	¼
113		**4**
	110	
		¾
	100	½
		¼
	90	
85		**3**
	80	¾
	70	½
		¼
	60	
57		**2**
	50	¾
		½
	40	
		¼
28	30	**1**
		¾
	20	
		½
	10	
		¼
	0	**0**

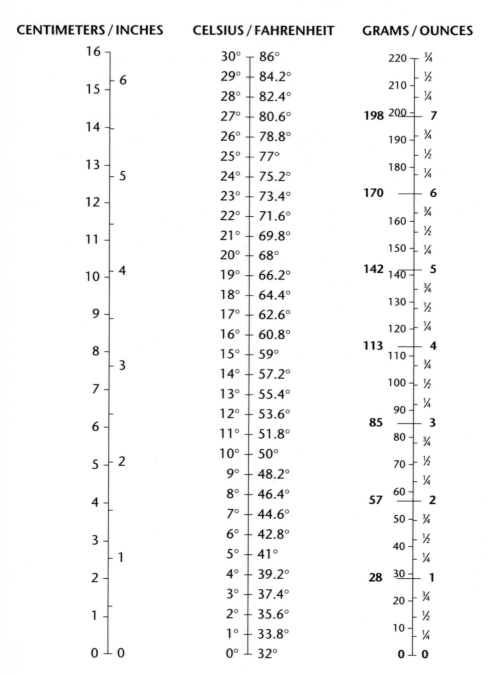

APPENDIX III:
Hardiness Map

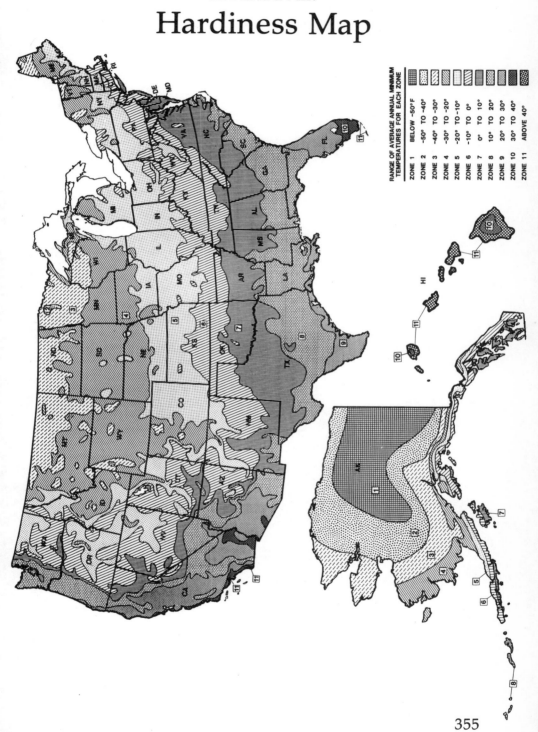

RANGE OF AVERAGE ANNUAL MINIMUM
TEMPERATURES FOR EACH ZONE

ZONE 1   BELOW -50°F
ZONE 2   -50° TO -40°
ZONE 3   -40° TO -30°
ZONE 4   -30° TO -20°
ZONE 5   -20° TO -10°
ZONE 6   -10° TO 0°
ZONE 7   0° TO 10°
ZONE 8   10° TO 20°
ZONE 9   20° TO 30°
ZONE 10   30° TO 40°
ZONE 11   ABOVE 40°

Index to Botanical Names

Numbers in italic refer to illustrations in the text, and the word *photo* refers to a color photograph of the plant in the section following page 272.

Index to Common Names

gayfeather
  kansas 284
  tall 287
gentian 248
giant sea pink 248
gladiolus 276
globe amaranth 33, 93
gloriosa daisy 142
golden amaranth 97
golden baby 102
golden drumstick 142
goldenrod 235
  canadian 235
  sweet 237
  wreath 237
goosefoot 142

heliopsis 248
holly 336
  finetooth 337
honesty 115
  perennial 117
hydrangea
  bigleaf 333, 334
  oakleaf 333
  panicle 333
  peegee 335

iceland poppy 142
immortelle 34, 142
iris
  dutch 281
  spuria 248
ixia 323

joseph's coat 43

larkspur 33, 72
lavender 34
leopard's bane 248
lily
  african 248
  arum 323
  asiatic 292
  easter 292
  formosa 292
  goldband 292
  guernsey 297
  hidden 323
  oriental 292
  peruvian 258
  resurrection 323
  scarborough 323
lily-of-the-valley 323

lisianthus 84
lobelia, giant blue 248
loosestrife
  gooseneck 214
  yellow 216
love-in-a-mist 33, 124
love-lies-bleeding 40

mallow flower 105
maltese cross 248
marigold, corn 142
masterwort 177
meadow-rue
  columbine 241
  yunnan 239
michaelmas daisy 168
migonette 142
money plant 34
monkshood
  azure 156
  common 156
  oriental 156
montbretia 266
mountain bluet 67, 185
mulberry, french 327
mullein 248

obedient plant 224
opium poppy 248
orache 142
ornamental corn 34, 142
ornamental kale 142
ornamental onion
  blue globe 257
  giant 254
  persian 257
ornamental pepper 142
oxalis 323

paper pumpkin seed 142
paperwhites 293
peony 217
peppergrass 34
phlox
  arend's 223
  spotted 223
  summer 221
  woodland 223
pincushion flower 134, 232
pinks
  cottage 196
  yellow 196
possumhaw 337
prairie gentian 84

primrose, cone 248
price of wales feather 63
prince's feather 43

queen anne's lace 33, 46

ranunculus 305
red cathedral 43
red hot poker 248
red valerian 185
rhodanthe 33, 142
rose campion 40
rose cockle 142
rose flower 34
rose of heaven 40

safflower 33, 57
sage
  anise-scented 134
  annual 134
  clary 134
  gentian 248
  meadow 134
  mealy-cup 133, 134
  mexican bush 131
  perennial hybrid 134, 248
  velvet 131
satin flower 88
scabious
  cream 234
  giant 248
  perennial 232
  shepherd's 142
scarlet plume 84
sea holly 34
  alpine 204
  flat 202
shasta daisy 248
shoo-fly 142
snapdragon 46
sneezewort 153
snow-on-the-mountain 83
solidaster 238
star-of-bethlehem 301
statice 209
  altaica 210
  annual 106
  caspia 213
  perez 212
  seafoam 212
  siberian 213
  sinuata 106
  rat tail 114
  russian 114